The Web of Hope

THE WEB OF HOPE

THE MEMOIRS OF GEORGE B. KOOSHIAN
HIS BIRTH AND EDUCATION IN TURKEY
HIS PASSAGE INTO EXILE AND GENOCIDE
HIS REBIRTH IN AMERICA

BY

GEORGE B. KOOSHIAN

EDITED BY GEORGE B. KOOSHIAN, JR.

THE IDEAL PRESS

ALTADENA, CALIFORNIA

2017

©2017 by George B. Kooshian, Jr. All rights reserved. No part of this document may be reproduced or transmitted in any form or by any means, electronic, mechanical, photocopying, recording, or otherwise, without prior written permission of George B. Kooshian, Jr.

Published by the The Ideal Press, 660 Figueroa Drive, Altadena, California 91001. For inquiries and for bulk orders please email to GEORGE.KOOSHIAN@THEIDEALPRESS.COM.

This edition of *The Web of Hope* by George B. Kooshian (1895-1984) (the Author) was edited and typeset from the Author's handwritten manuscript solely by George B. Kooshian, Jr., Ph.D. (the Editor). All aspects of book design and production by George B. Kooshian, Jr. Text set in Adobe Caslon Pro with headings in Linux Biolinum Capitals. Typesetting done with LyX, an open source document processor. The historical information and characterizations in this book are those of the Author based on his diaries, observations, recollections, and research. All numbered notes are the Author's unless indicated to be the Editor's. All commentary by the Editor is so marked. Place names reflect historical not modern usage. The reader may wish to consult a modern atlas for correspondences. Transliterations reflect Western Armenian pronunciation. All Turkish language references are to Ottoman Turkish. Modern Turkish orthography is anachronistic for this work and is deprecated. Foreign words are explained in the footnotes. Illustrations and Biblical epigraphs have been inserted by the Editor. The included article by Yepros Topalian was translated from the Armeno-Turkish by the Author from *Weekly Avedaper*, American Bible House, Constantinople, Vol. 53, No. 9, February 26, 1910; No. 10, March 5, 1910; No. 11, March 12, 1910.

Publisher's Cataloging- in -Publication Data
provided by Five Rainbows Cataloging Services

Names: Kooshian, George B. (George Barouyr), 1895-1984.
Title: The web of hope : the memoirs of George Kooshian, his birth and education in Turkey, his passage into exile and genocide, his rebirth in America / by George B. Kooshian.
Description: Altadena , CA : The Ideal Press , 2017.
Identifiers: LCCN 2017901634 | ISBN 978-0-9986679-1-1 (hardcover)
 | ISBN 978-0-9986679-0-4 (pbk.) | ISBN 978-0-9986679-2-8 (library binding)
Subjects: LCSH: Kooshian, George B. (George Barouyr), 1895-1984. | Armenians – Turkey – Biography. | Armenians – United States – Biography . | Armenian massacres, 1915-1923 . | Pasadena (Calif.) – Biography . | Emigration and immigration. | BISAC: BIOGRAPHY & AUTOBIOGRAPHY / Personal Memoirs. | SOCIAL SCIENCE / Emigration & Immigration. | HISTORY / Middle East / Turkey & Ottoman Empire.
Classification: LCC DR435.A7 K66 2017 (print) | DDC 973/.0491992/092 – dc23.

This is the digitally printed paperback edition (glued binding).

10 9 8 7 6

Dedicated to

Sarah Malian Kooshian

1869–1944

A NOBLE LADY OF HIGHLY EDUCATED HEART

BY HER AFFECTIONATE AND GRATEFUL SON

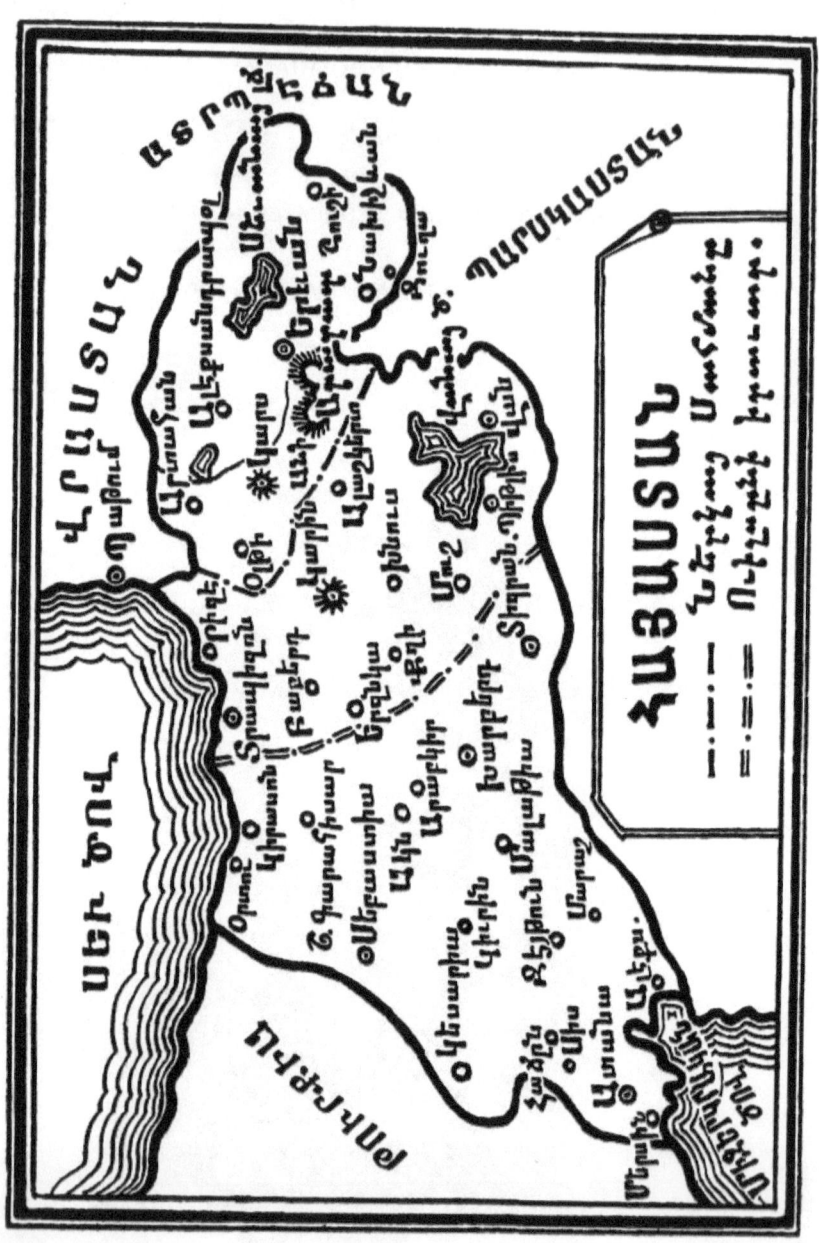

United Armenia

CONTENTS

List of Figures — ix
Foreword — xi
A Note to the Reader — xii
Preface — xv

Part I: Varjabed

1. My Birth — 3
2. My Native Country — 6
3. My Race — 8
4. My Father (1861–1902) — 11
5. My Paternal Grandfather (1820–1898) — 14
6. My Mother (1869–1944) — 16
7. Uncle Haroutune (1883–1944) — 18
8. Uncle Melidon (1867–1909) — 20
9. My Maternal Grandfather (1840–1917) — 29
10. We Return to Hadjin — 37
11. I Go to College — 45
12. To Fenesseh — 52
13. The Feast of the Transfiguration — 63
14. Aunt Gulenia and Her Infamous Husband — 67
15. Home Again — 75
16. Three Kittens — 79
17. The Shame of History — 83
18. Tahir Effendi — 91
19. Leave Every Hope Behind — 101
20. Bulgur Khan — 111

Part II: Youth, and a Gleam of Hope

21	Arrest in Aleppo	125
22	The March of Death	132
23	Mother Euphrates	143
24	In the Valley Which Was Full of Bones	147
25	Two Visitors	153
26	Where did you learn Armenian?	160
27	The Graves Recorder	171
28	Hafiz the Desert Judge	176
29	By the Rivers of Babylon	184
30	Ziyaret	195
31	The Caves	200
32	Meskeneh	208
33	Last Day on the Desert	218

Part III: To the Sun of My Hope

34	I Turn a New Page	225
35	The Preacher Tries to Betray Me	231
36	In Military Uniform	235
37	The Fall Of Aleppo	249
38	The Black List	255
39	Goodbye Aleppo	263
40	Good Morning Adana	267
41	The Web of Hope is Swept Away	273
42	Makroohi	279
43	A Bitter Memory	286
44	My Sister Mary Marries, and…	291
45	Farewell to Adana	296
46	Smyrna	307
47	Leah	313
48	Professor Gulbenkian	323
49	On the Aegean Sea	329

50 Marseilles   335
51 Last Day in Marseilles   341

Part IV: The Web of Hope

52 In the Land of the Free   353
53 Cousin Krikor   360
54 Cousin Sarkis Saves Me from Cousin Krikor   368
55 Peace Catches Up With Me   372
56 The Final Blow to Armenian Aspirations to Independence   385
57 Book Peddler   390
58 Pasadena, California   395
59 From Janitor to Tradesman   405
60 To Havana   412
61 Wedding Day   420
62 To Pasadena With a Bride (Or Two)   428
Editor's Epilogue   439
Appendix I: Anecdotes Relating to Father   441
Appendix II: Anecdotes Relating to Mother   446
Appendix III: Letters from Uncle Haroutune   452
Appendix IV: How I Survived Sai'-Getchit, by Yepros Topalian   463
Appendix V: Kooshian Ancestry   473
Biblical References   481
Notes   485
A Word of Thanks   494
Index   495
Illustration Credits   506
About the Author   507

The Web of Hope

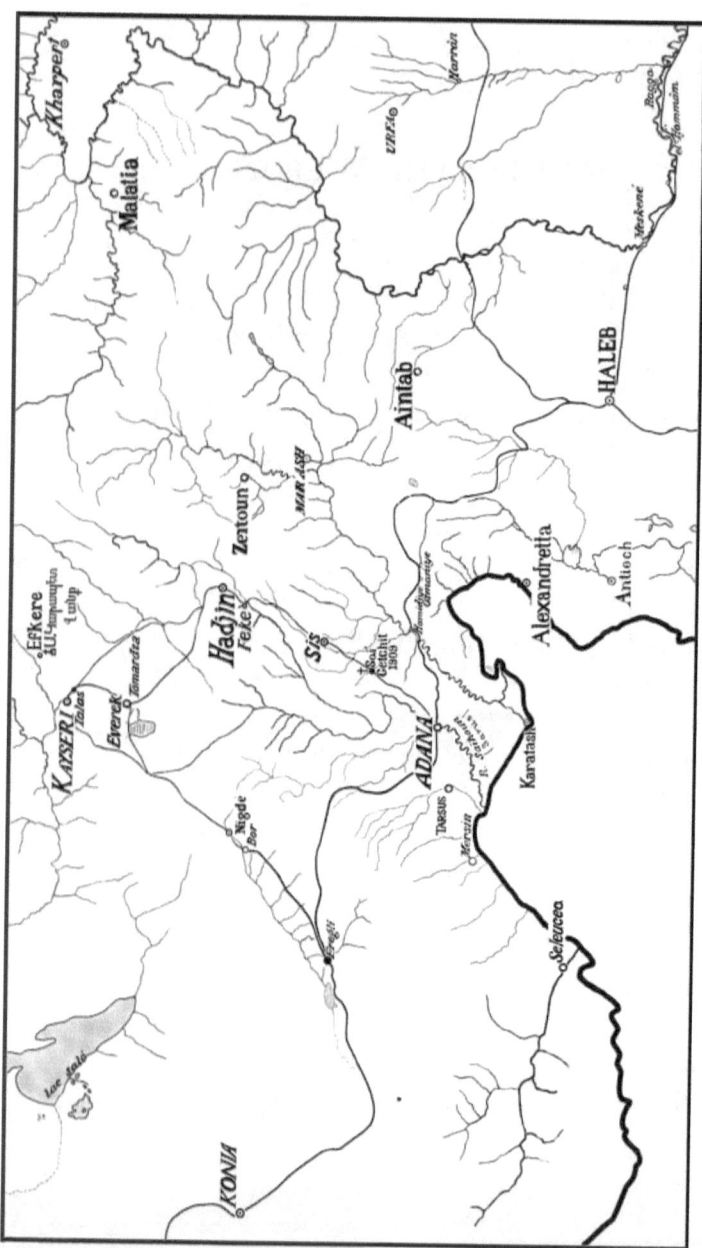

Southeast Asia Minor and northern Syria, extending from Cappadocia to Cilicia and Greater Armenia. The events of this book up until emigration to America took place in the area of this map.

LIST OF FIGURES

Maps

United Armenia	iv
Southeast Asia Minor and northern Syria	viii
The route of the first deportation	103
The route of the second deportation	199

Illustrations

Sarah Malian Kooshian	iii
George B. Kooshian, April 8, 1921, Binghamton, N.Y.	xiv
Hadjin, undated photograph	10
The fountain at Hadjin	12
The Reverend Melidon Effendi Malian	21
Missionaries in Hadjin, 1902	38
George Kooshian, David Gedigian (seated), Toros Pushian	41
The Reverend Dr. Haroutune Jenanian	47
Caesaraea, from an old book	73
Jenanian College Dormitory	80
The Reverend Dr. Armenag Haigazian	86
Annig Derghazarian	88
A cafe on the Seyhan River by the Stone Bridge	90
The Reverend Father Khachig Kahana Kroozian, 1935	112
Hokedoon alley, where George Kooshian was arrested	131

The Web of Hope

The Clock Tower at Bab al-Farouj, Aleppo	226
View of Aleppo from the Citadel, approximately 1900	247
Kooshian Family, before the deportations	248
George Kooshian, soda jerk	376
George Kooshian with his Model T Ford	408
George Kooshian in his press shop, December, 1929	410
The happy couple with attendants	423
The honeymooners at Moro Castle	424
Sanam, many years later	430
Sarah Malian Kooshian in Cyprus, 1941	447
Adana - Street in Christian Quarter, June '09	462
Adana - Minaret from which Turks Fired on Christians	462

FOREWORD

George B. Kooshian found himself thrust into the middle of the epic history of the early twentieth century in the Near East, Europe, and America. This day-by-day eyewitness account begins with the author's pre-World War I education in American schools in Turkey and continues to his arrest and exile into the merciless Syrian desert by the Ottoman government in 1915 and his harrowing escape from massacre between the legs of his executioner across the searing terrain to safety and ultimate emigration to the United States. He carried with him at all times his precious diary and pencil, and recorded everything he saw for posterity. Unforgettable saints and sinners populated his life: his beloved mother and his benefactor the Reverend Barker, the mysterious Tahir Effendi and his son Shukru, the monstrous Ahmed Chavoush and the elderly Hussein Effendi, the unfortunate Hampartzoum and Hafiz the desert judge, the rescuers Hripsime and Boghos Ouzunian, the deceitful Armenian minister and the just Turkish bey, and an unending procession of notable and not-so-notable characters. His memoirs, originally intended for his children and grandchildren, are an incredible testimony to the triumph of the human spirit in the face of the most extreme trials, sustained by "youth, and a gleam of hope."

My father wrote this manuscript in his later years in Pasadena, California before he passed away on March 15, 1984 at the age of 88, universally loved and respected by all who knew him as a gentleman of the highest order, a scholar and author, and a sterling example of Christian rectitude and honor. It has been my privilege to prepare this book for publication. Except for the epilogue and some explanatory material, I have added nothing except for the titles, chapter headings, organization, and formatting, and minor editing for consistency of spelling and usage.

    GBK Jr.
    Altadena, California
    March 15, 2005

A NOTE TO THE READER

George Kooshian was deeply familiar with the Bible as a part of his daily life. The many Biblical references and quotations in this book have been gathered together in an appendix for the convenience of the reader. Foreign words are explained in the footnotes.

The epigraph entitled "A Mohammedan Prayer" beginning Part II is from *Rev. Fredrick Greene, The Rule of the Turks and the Armenian Crisis* (New York and London: G. Putnam's Sons, 1897), p. 75, quoted in Boyajian, *Armenia: The Case for a Forgotten Genocide* (1972), p. 382. This was inserted by the author.

Sacra peregrinatio per sanctam crucis viam ad montem calvariae ("Holy pilgrimage by the way of the Holy Cross to Mount Calvary") is the title of a book of Good Friday devotions published in Kempten, Germany in 1761 by Andreas Stadler. This and the quotation from Luke 9:23–26 were inserted by the editor after the canonization by the Armenian Apostolic Church on April 23, 2015, of many persons mentioned in this book.

The well-known poem "The New Colossus" by Emma Lazarus is inscribed at the foot of the Statue of Liberty.

This Centenniel Edition follows a printing of 50 copies in 2005 for a class in the History of the Armenian Immigrants of California that I taught at UCLA. It is completely reformatted with additional notes, index, and editorial content as well as the inclusion of the first-person account by Yepros Topalian of the massacre at Saı'-Getchit.

    GBK Jr.
    January 1, 2017

Because he hath set his love upon me, therefore will I deliver him: I will set him on high, because he hath known my name.

He shall call upon me, and I will answer him: I will be with him in trouble; I will deliver him, and honour him.

With long life will I satisfy him, and shew him my salvation.

Psalm 91:14-16

George B. Kooshian, April 8, 1921, Binghamton, N.Y.

PREFACE

THE sole purpose in writing my life story is to acquaint my posterity, immediate or future, with the somewhat bizarre or colorful happenings I went through. In this account I must delve into the past as far back as my knowledge permits, despite the fact that no document or oral report of any sort has ever descended to me from my ancestry, recent or remote. Some facts bearing any relation to our narrative, however, will be utilized from other sources through research.

I believe that the life story of any one of my ancestors would have been read with more interest because of the richer and fuller nature of their romantic adventures. Also I am fully satisfied that it would have been a tragic negligence on my part if I did not attempt to prepare this record, because I happen to be the first Kooshian to emigrate to America.

Some questions have taxed my brain for a long time about my ancestors.

Who, and what, were they?

Where did they come from, and when did they settle in Armenia?

What was their social and political standing? Were they noblemen of high birth, warriors, or serfs?

These questions remain unanswered because of lack of records. The only reliable sources for answers to such questions were the church records, but the Turks ever deem it their religious, patriotic, and natural duty to destroy the Armenian churches, burn records and rare manuscripts, and massacre "the infidels."

The story of how long these forgotten ancestors of mine courageously sacrificed their dreams and aspirations for the preservation of their home, country and culture will remain an unsung and buried epic.

The Web of Hope

This book of facts, observations, recollections, and experiences should have been written long ago. "I have spent my days," once wrote Rabindranath Tagore, "stringing and restringing my instrument, while the song I came to sing remains unsung." Oliver Wendell Holmes expressed the same thought in a different way when he said: "Many people die with their music still in them."

So, this is my own "song."

Part I
Varjabed

CHAPTER I

MY BIRTH

SOME may reasonably doubt my birth. At times I have doubted it myself. There were no hospitals to be born in, in that far-off highland town of Hadjin, in that far-off legendary land of Cilicia I once called mine. No records were kept by any midwife or tax collector. There is no church register in existence to prove my birth or baptism. Furthermore, there is not now such a town as Hadjin on the face of the earth or on the map.

But my mother once said that I was really born, and her sacred word sufficed to dispel my doubts.

So, born I was.

I was made to accept that statement as an indisputable fact.

I was brought forth to breathe this mundane air and blink at solar brilliance on a certain day—on the 25th of September, in the blessed year of grace, 1895.

Blessed year? Now I am not very sure about its being "blessed."

I was given ample reason to believe that it was for the explicit purpose of weeding me out of existence (mistakenly thinking that I was the most dreaded person to be born) that a general massacre was ordered by the cruelest of all the Ottoman emperors, Sultan Abdul Hamid II, who reigned from 1876 to 1909, at which year he was deposed and imprisoned in Salonika.[1,2] This infamous decree was given one year prior to my birth to prevent me from being born. But I, being of a stubborn nature and fearless (?), scorned the satanic decree and decided to be born anyway. However, the diabolical plan was carried out with a growing impetus during the three years enveloping the events of my birth, 1894–1895–1896, but somehow it failed to touch me.

These massacres were repeated again on the "*giavour* Armenians"[3] in the whole province of my native land in 1909, wiping out 30,000 Armenians in ten days, just prior to the blood-thirsty tyrant's final downfall, but these measures also were to no avail, because no lethal hand touched me yet.

Then the "Committee of Union and Progress" (*Ittihad ve Terakki Jemiyeti*)4, the prototype of Germany's ignoble Nazi party of later years, membered by the blackest-hearted criminals, took hold of the helm of the Turkish Empire and in a few years plunged it into the First World War. This Party immediately applied itself in utmost secrecy, and with fanatical chauvinistic zeal, to the task of mapping up and carrying out a dastardly program of genocide, complete annihilation of the entire Armenian race. A few months after entering the War on the side of Kaiser Wilhelm's5 Germany, Turkey grabbed this opportunity (with the blessing of its ally) to execute its diabolical plan, first drafting the Armenian manpower into hard labor battalions, then terrorizing the remaining into giving up any and all sorts of firearms, even kitchen knives, pocket knives, books, and newspapers. Then came uprootings, deportings, robberies, rapings, enslavings, starving in far-off concentration camps in uninhabited desert places, literally butchering, crucifying, burning as torches, massacring in wholesale, and smashing of heads with rocks.

I was caught in the holocaust. They almost succeeded in getting rid of me this last time, but not quite. In spite of the unnumbered and endless outrages and enormities, miraculously I survived and returned five years later to my homeland, with head bloody yet unbowed. But my country, Cilicia the beautiful, although liberated by the victorious Allied forces and promised to be handed over to the Armenians as reward for their sacrificial and gallant fighting under British, French, and Russian commands, was, in a short span of time, treacherously sold out to the beaten, proven enemy, Turkey.

Again I was able to flee the Turk, the Turk who then conveniently shed his former regime of the vanquished and donned the new garb of the Kemalist. History's most baffling enigma is — how could the great representatives of the victorious powers, Britain, France, Italy, and the United States, after such an exhausting and devastating war, allow themselves to be bullied into accepting the incredible dictated terms of a conquered, inhuman enemy, Turkey? In the Lausanne Conference, the Allies shamefully capitulated to the Kemalists, equally murderous successors to the former infamous *Ittihad ve Terakki* regime.

My Birth

In the fall of 1920 I found myself in Smyrna, the city held by the occupying army of the Greeks. At that time, from the rubble of the hopelessly conquered Turkey, a hitherto-unknown army officer by the name of Mustafa Kemal emerged with a rebel army and marched forth leveling all obstacles in his way, chasing the occupying powers out of Turkey like a pack of cowardly rabbits and driving the Greek army into the sea at Smyrna. On capturing the city, they set it on fire, sent bullets and bayonet thrusts through every Christian inhabitant, Greek and Armenian alike, and razed the whole environs.

Seeing that I was not to be found among the dead, burned, maimed, or drowned, the unspeakable Turk kept the cauldron of terror and torture boiling up for a number of years in the vain hope of ensnaring, apprehending, and punishing me for the sin of remaining alive.

But when, at last, the Turks discovered that I was in America, the "Land of the Free," they sat down thinking what to do next, as I was out of their sticky grasp and destructive reach. What else could they do now but pretend to reform themselves by throwing away their religion (adopting nothing in its stead), their King and caliphate, their distinctive *fez* (hat), *shalvar* (balloon pants), and *charshaf* (woman's veil), and their borrowed or stolen Arabic alphabet in favor of the Latin, again borrowed or stolen.

Thus they hoped, and succeeded, in deceiving the world that they were vacating "the seat of the scornful" and abandoning "the way of the sinner" which history had assigned to them. Thus they managed to "sit" at the council table of the "just" and the "righteous."

CHAPTER 2

MY NATIVE COUNTRY

Near the north-eastern end of the Mediterranean Sea there is a bulge of land protruding into the sea towards the historic island of Cyprus. This bulge, multiplied several times with lands west, north, northeast, and east, comprises the province of Cilicia, the history of which gets lost in the haze of mythical antiquity.[6]

Xenophon (443–359 B.C.) describes Cilicia, this fertile place between Taurus and Amanus ranges, as "a large and beautiful plain, well watered, and full of sorts of trees and vines, abounding in sesame, panic, millet, wheat and barley," and "surrounded with a strong and high ridge of hills from sea to sea."

Strabo, the Greek geographer (63 B.C.–A.D. 21) says that Tarsus, the capital city of Cilicia, was build by Sardanapalus, the king of Assyria (?–626 B.C.), on the river Cydnus, about 6 miles from the sea. According to a legend Sardanapalus built Tarsus, the birthplace of Saint Paul, in one day.

The Cilicians worshiped the Assyrian god Baal, and in later centuries the Hercules of Greece. After the Assyrians, Cyrus the Younger of Persia (401 B.C.), who led the 10,000 Greeks against his brother Artaxerxes II, invaded the country. Then came Alexander the Great of Macedonia (356–323 B.C.), Tigranes of Armenia (89–36 B.C.), Pompey of Rome (106–48 B.C.), and many others. But the history shows that the most prosperous era in Cilician life was that of the Armenian domination in the Middle Ages. This kingdom, created by Roupen I, and brought to the climax of its glory by Leon the Great, lasted from 1080 to 1375, during which many valiant princes and kings aided the Crusaders with arms and supplies. For three centuries, Cilicia blocked the advance of Mohammedan hordes that were to swallow up the civilization of Europe.

But Europe, then, as now, fell prey to petty ambitions and dissensions among each other, and neglected her Christian and moral duty to aid Cilicia in her crucial moments to rid herself from the fangs of the ferocious Mohammedans. Thus faded the glory that once was Cilicia. Cilicia's immortal service in protecting Christendom from the all-sweeping Mohammedan tide, was repeatedly repaid by the Christian world with ingratitude and betrayal.

Cilicia's chief export was goat's hair, from which were made tents and floor coverings. King David and others wore hair shirts, and sat on hair carpets while mourning and repenting, which, most probably, were imported from Cilicia. Romans called these hair goods *cilicium*; the French derived from this Latin word the word *cilice*, and the English the words cilice, cilicious, cilician, and cilicium.

This country of Cilicia, since her occupation by the Mohammedans, became the vilayet of Adana, after the name of her capital city. The Arabic word *vilayet* corresponds to our "state."

The "strong and high ridge of hills" mentioned by Xenophon in the foregoing quotation is the Taurus Range, in a distant cozy lap of which a small town snuggled like an aerie. This was Hadjin, my birthplace.[7] It was founded by the Armenian warriors and refugees who, at the fall of their kingdom in 1375, retired to an inaccessible mountainhold in the Taurus Range and continued their fight for independence against the invading Egyptian Mamelukes and marauding Greeks. They built Hadjin around a mountain-sized fortress between two small rivers, the fortress dating from Assyrian or Roman eras. Research has revealed the ruins of a city of Hargan around the nearby spring of the river Kurdett, and the ruins of a Roman city, Badimon, a little eastward of Hadjin.[8]

My ancestors, most assuredly, came to Cilicia with Prince Roupen and helped build the Roupenian Dynasty there, after the Bagradoonian Kingdom in the Land of Ararat came to an end so treacherously by the hands of the Byzantines.

CHAPTER 3

MY RACE

Moses of Khoren of the fifth century A.D., the "Herodotus of Armenia," is the authority from whom we learn about the legendary beginnings of the Armenian race. He takes us back to the days of the Patriarch Noah. Noah's family, after leaving the ark resting on the "Mountains of Ararat" in the land of Armenia, journeyed from the east, and "dwelt in the land of Shinar," or Babylonia. Haik the son of Togarmah the son of Gomer the son of Japeth the son of Noah, was the first forefather of the Armenians, with whose name they have called themselves ever since. He left the plains of Shinar with 300 braves of his household during the building of the Tower of Babel in 2700 B.C., and went to live in the land of Ararat.

The legendary history of Armenia is a series of epic poems and stories.

But according to reliable evidence, drawn from recent archaeological discoveries, and reinforced by the physical characteristics of the Armenian of today, we know that, about 2000 years B.C., an Aryan people from the basin of the Caspian invaded the region of Van and gradually pushed its way towards the Euphrates, in the region of Harput. They called their country *Ar-Meni, Ar-Mina*, meaning Aryan land. Centuries later, perhaps between the tenth and twelfth centuries B.C., a new wave of invasion, proceeding from Thrace, by a kindred people of European origin, reached Ar-Meni, and became merged with its inhabitants. The Armenian race of today is a mixture of the two invading races and of the natives whom they assimilated, and is now recognized, like the Swiss, most French, South Germans, Austrians, and most Greeks, as a member of the Alpine branch of the European family.[9]

According to Herodotus (484–425 B.C.), the French archaeologist Jaques de Morgan (1857–1924), and many others, the Armenians, a race of the Indo-European stock, left their original home in Thrace in southeastern Europe approximately 1,000 B.C., and crossed the Bosphorus over into Bythinia. Thereupon they pushed east into Cappadocia and northern Cilicia, and about the seventh century B.C. reached the region of Mount Ararat, where they founded the state of Armenia.[10] In 600 B.C. King Herachia of Armenia was an ally of Nebuchadnezzar in the capture of Jerusalem. King Tigranes I (Dikran) became the ally of Cyrus the Great of Persia in the conquest of Babylonia and the consequent liberation of the Jews from seventy years of captivity in 538 B.C. Under Tigranes II the Great in the first century B.C., Armenia attained the height of her glory and power, extending from the Caspian to the Black Sea and to the Mediterranean, and from the Caucasus to the Mesopotamian plains, with an area exceeding 500,000 square miles and a population of 25,000,000 (Langlois; Lenormant).[11]

Dr. Harold H. Bender, Professor of Indo-Germanic Philology, Princeton University, writing about Armenian language and prehistory, says that it has been thoroughly established by the German philologist Heinrich Hübschmann, that Armenian is an Indo-European tongue and thus belongs to the same family of languages to which English belongs.

Besides Hübschmann, St. Martin, Villefroi and Doré recognize the Armenian as one of the Indo-European languages that has attained the highest degree of development, by a varied and ancient intellectual culture.

Armenia was an organized nation a thousand years before there was one in Europe, except Greece and Rome. Its last king, Leon VI, an exile from his own land, spent his last years in the effort to bring about an understanding between France and England, then in the struggle of the Hundred Years' War, and actually presided at a peace conference near Boulogne in 1386, which brought about the understanding that led to the end of that war. Armenia was evangelized by apostles St. Thaddeus and St. Bartholomew, fresh with the memory of our Lord, as early as A.D. 33, and as a nation adopted Christianity and founded a national church in 301 through the effort of St. Gregory the Illuminator and King Dirtad of Armenia. It was the same Dirtad (Tirdates), who, fired with a zeal for the Christian faith, led a crusade against Maximinus Daia, arch-foe of Christianity, winning a decisive victory over him. And this Christian Crusade was undertaken nearly 800 years before that of Godefroi de Bouillon (1099), the Latin sovereign of Jerusalem. In the fifth century the Armenian alphabet was invented by St. Mesrop the monk with the

Hadjin, undated photograph

collaboration of St. Sahak the Catholicos, and the translation of the Old Testament from the Septuagint was made into the vernacular by these scholars and their pupils. This Armenian Version is judged by some as the "Queen of all Versions." The New Testament was translated by the same scholars from its original Greek.

Then the golden age of Armenian literature came into being with original writings and translations of religious, philosophic, poetic, and scientific works from Latin, Greek, Syriac, and Arab masters.

CHAPTER 4

MY FATHER (1861–1902)

Alas, it was not given to me to know my father in person, the most important link in the chain that connects me with my ancestry. When I was seven years old, this link suddenly broke on the Sunday morning following the Easter of 1902, in Adana, the metropolis of Cilician Armenia.[12]

My father, Garabed Gejekooshian,[13] was the second eldest son of four children (the fourth being a daughter), and was born in 1861 in Hadjin, where his parents were also born. He died of pneumonia at the age of forty. Two weeks earlier he had gone to the outlying villages, had walked from hut to hut, the knapsack of cobbler's tools on his back, soliciting worn-out footwear to repair in order to earn a meager living for his family. But the denial of work, food, and shelter to a "giavour," the downpour of torrential rains and Turkish hostility over his head, compounded with the rising tide of fatigue, hunger, and despair, made his frail body an easy target for the darts of pneumonia. Dragging himself from the unfriendly country back to the loving arms of his wife in the city, he was put to bed that Easter day, and he closed his weary eyes a week later.

Dimly do I remember, and remember it with a piercing sorrow, that the bitter wailings of my mother, mingled with those of some sympathetic neighbors assembled there, woke me with a feeling of foreboding, of misfortune.

According to the social custom prevailing at the time, my father at the age of twenty-three married my mother at the age of thirteen, just after a year of engagement.

One day, five years earlier, my mother, a child of eight, was sent to the public fountain for water. On her way back, she espied a group of boys playing at marbles and, laying her jug of water aside, stood there to watch the game. The boys, noticing the unwelcome spectator, shooed her away. After some years a surprise visit was paid by the parents of

The Web of Hope

The fountain at Hadjin

one of those marble players to "ask the hand" of the girl from her parents. With the mutual agreement between the two pairs of parents, the two young persons were united in holy matrimony in 1884.

From 1884, the year he married, to 1902, the year he was buried, I doubt if he spent altogether five years with his bride. One month or two after their wedding, the poor bridegroom left his child-bride and parental home and went to *Séhél*,[14] the strange parts of the country, among strange people, in search of a living for his wife and his patriarchal family members.

What a crushing blow it must have been to this virile and wholesome young man's heart to be forced by economic drive to leave behind a thirteen-year-old child-bride, a sorely needed soul-mate, a rose-bud of

My Father (1861–1902)

rare beauty and fragrance, an exquisite bowl of intoxicating honey-wine, a river of happiness.

And who can fathom the depth of her anguish and disappointment? But they both saw and stout-heartedly accepted what grim fate had decreed for them.

His first *Séhél ishdole*, by a quirk of fate, lasted seven years, during which time seldom a word from him reached home. His homecoming after seven years lasted too short a time, because the payment of accumulated taxes of dubious authenticity quickly depleted his purse and he felt pressed by necessity to leave home again. After his second return I was born, their first son. At his third homecoming my sister was born.

On one of his "pilgrimages" to *Séhél*, my father had taken his younger brother Bedros with him. After seeing him married and settled there, he returned home to pack his family away from Hadjin to the city where Bedros was now residing. So on the 99th year of the 19th century he hired some pack-horses, placed his wife on the back of one, and from the sides of another he balanced two sturdy baskets in which he deposited his two young children, about four and two. Four days' journey brought us to Adana, and three days more brought us to Seleucia,[15] on the shores of the Mediterranean Sea. I remember nothing about our arrival there. The memories of Seleucia are deeply buried under the dense unconsciousness of tender childhood, but some incidents of those misty days bob out into the void of my memory as a silvery fish that sometimes jumps out of the water to sink back again.

I intend to relate some of these incidents a little later in this book.

Obviously my father did not find in Seleucia the ease and means of a modest living he was seeking. So, after some honest efforts of pecking at the hardwood tree of living, and finding himself unable to make a dent on it, a week or two before the Easter of 1902, he packed our belongings to take us back to Hadjin, this time with the addition of a new-born baby son. We stopped in Adana to find a new caravan going to Hadjin, and because the chances of finding one were so slim, Father went in search of work, but returned sick and died a few days later.

Providentially, a distant aunt of Mother's[16] living in Adana took us in until some months later we came to Hadjin through the assistance of Mother's eldest brother.

CHAPTER 5

MY PATERNAL GRANDFATHER (1820–1898)

I DO NOT HAVE the slightest recollection of this grand patriarch into whose household I was destined to be born just three years before his demise. Neither do I remember his wife. The old gentleman was born in Hadjin in the first or second decade of the nineteenth century and died a couple years before the dawn of the twentieth. He ruled over a household of three sons, one daughter, two daughters-in-law, and several granddaughters before my joining the clan. He and his worthy spouse must have felt elated with triumphant joy at my birth, for after three granddaughters from their eldest son Hampartzoum and one from the youngest son Bedros, I was the first male grandchild.

Grandfather's only daughter Hnazant ("Obedient"), having been married and gone into another household, also gave birth to a son around the time I was born.

I was told in later years that soon after their birth these two grandsons were presented to the patriarch at the same time. Taking both in each arm he pronounced his blessings on them. After returning his daughter's baby, he kept me in his feeble arms and after profusely praising my mother for honoring his wishes by giving birth to an heir to his name, he officially conferred his own name and title upon me — Hadji Kevork Agha Gejekooshian. "Hadji"[17] was a title. "Kevork" is equivalent to George, a common name. "Agha"[18] meant "master" or "sir." And Gejekooshian (as already explained in Chapter 4, Note 12) was the family name. (Because they were of no practical use to me, I eventually dropped from my long name "Hadji," "Agha," and "Geje.")

In his youthful days this gentleman had managed to make a long and hazardous pilgrimage to the Holy Lands, had visited all the sacred spots our Savior had lived and walked, and thus had received in Jerusalem the highly honored and coveted tattoos on his wrists and chest. All such pilgrims, after a considerable donation to the Temple, were privileged to

My Paternal Grandfather (1820–1898)

carry the title of Hadji, by which they were called and honored to the end of their natural lives.

I hope that the gentle spirit of the old gentleman has already forgiven me for the "ungrateful" act I committed by shedding away the meaningless titles with which he encumbered me. May his soul rest in peace.

It seems that this noble soul, after divesting himself from the dearly cherished titles that lent him prestige and dignity for a number of decades, found nothing more to do, so, he and his equally noble wife, soon folded their earthly tents and silently stole away with the rapidly dying century.

He had no gold or silver, neither a single copper to bequeath me, his heir. All the wealth he had was his dignity. He must have owned the house he lived in, which I do not recall. I came to learn in later years that he had left behind a vineyard on the hills, and a plot of garden on a flat above the rivulet of Chatakh, but none of these did my family any good, because a greedy neighbor, seeing in our family a forlorn young widow with three voiceless orphans, thought best to usurp them, in order to relieve us from their responsibility.

I did never care to learn who this "Alexander the coppersmith" (II Timothy 4:14) was, but I stand assured that "The Lord will reward him according to his works."

CHAPTER 6

MY MOTHER (1869–1944)

Were I not vitally related to her as her firstborn, I would still proclaim that my mother Sarah had all the needed prerequisites — beauty and grace, physical, spiritual, and intellectual — to be crowned a queen. She was born to be one, yet inexorable Fate ignored her.

She was the second eldest of twelve children born to Krikor and Mariam Malian, Hadjin, Cilicia, Turkey, in 1869. At my birth none but four of the twelve were living. Mariam, the mother of the dozen, had followed the departed eight in death.

A Child Bride

Mother was married at the tender age of thirteen, in 1889.

It grieves me to imagine the enormity of uncertainty and fear that might have been gnawing at the heart of this child-bride, for being snatched by thoughtless custom from the sheltered security of her parental home and cast amongst total strangers.

And strangers they really were to her, because she had, as the social custom of the era dictated, never met her husband-to-be, or known his family, until the day she was given to him in marriage. All matrimonial agreements, verbal or contractual, were made without the knowledge or consent of the bride-to-be, even against her refusal.

And this unfortunate child-bride was permitted to know nothing about the financial and social status of the new family. Neither did she know the number of the members in it, nor their habits, dispositions, and needs. Yet she was expected, by the force of convention and tradition, to serve every need, whim, or fancy; to wash the feet of everybody in the house and of every visitor; to be the last to retire at night and the first to rise at early hours to be ready to rush to serve every need; to go about her daily chores with inexhaustible patience and endurance, head and face

My Mother (1869–1944)

head heavily veiled; to kiss the hand of everyone who was not a child, and remain mute in the presence of in-laws, male or female, young or old. Infraction of any decree of tradition made any unfortunate bride immoral, a disgraced outcast, a target of poisonous darts of malicious gossip, which meant moral death.

Acute is my regret that while Mother was still alive I was not mentally awake enough to realize the value of information she could impart to me about her own early life, and also that of Father's. And now I feel the weight of my failure to avail myself of a rich goldmine, which is lost irretrievably.

Yet by the stroke of good luck, I am in possession of the next best. Uncle Haroutune, Mother's youngest brother, who died in 1944 one month earlier than Mother, sent me some valuable information in the year 1928 while living in Amiantos, Cyprus. This letter, reproduced later in this book together with some anecdotes of my memories from childhood with her, is the only window into the years of her tragically short married life, through the banishment of her brother and her father and stepmother, and the long periods of waiting for her husband to return from his long journeys in search of work.

In her thirty-third year she was left a widow with three helpless children. She never married again, but dedicated her life to service in orphanages in Hadjin, Adana, and in Aleppo during the years of her exile.

She shared the grim fate of her race, was deported with her children as marked victims of the Genocide, returned to Adana afflicted with acute rheumatism and other ailments to be deported again by Kemalist threat of a final massacre, and died after a stroke of two hours in her youngest son's home in Nicosia, Cyprus, on December 26, 1944.

CHAPTER 7

UNCLE HAROUTUNE (1883–1944)

IN A LETTER sent from Amiantos, Cyprus, and dated February 1930, my uncle Haroutune wrote extensively of himself. This letter is translated and reproduced in a section later in this book.

Uncle Haroutune was an expert tailor, a tailor's tailor, well known in Hadjin, and later on wherever he practiced his trade — Adana, Aleppo, Cyprus, and Beirut. During summer vacations I was allowed by the orphanage management to go to Uncle's shop and learn the tailor's trade. My duties in those early days were sweeping the inside and out of the store, bringing fresh water, watering down the street in front to prevent the rising dust from choking the Master and customers, or running errands. After these chores were done, the Master would push a tailor's thimble on the tip of my right middle finger and tie the thimble and finger in bent position. Then he would give me a threadless needle and direct me to push it through a piece of cloth using the side of the thimble. This was Lesson One. A tailor's thimble is another breed: open at the bottom, unlike a woman's. Hers is like a tiny cup with no handle. But the tailor's thimble, although like a cup with no handle, yet has no bottom. A seamstress pushes the needle through with the bottom of her thimble, while a tailor must push it through with the back of the thimble on bent finger. The temptation of a beginner is very strong to press the needle by the bare tip of the finger that wears the bottomless thimble, but only the prick cautions him. I often wondered why my uncle should torture me with such a senseless thimble.

I remember very well that when I was all alone in the shop I used to cut off the attractive round coin-shaped price tags from the balls of goods, and filling my pockets with them I would play, or distribute to friends in the orphanage. But, to my amazement, the Master discovered the losses one day, ordered me to stop cutting the tags. He made it plain to me that they were neither ornaments nor playthings, but they were attached to the goods for a useful purpose: to tell the price of a yard of each different

Uncle Haroutune (1883–1944)

material, and to know what to charge a customer when we make him a suit. Realizing what grave mistake I had committed, I promised never to do it again, and kept my word. We remained very good friends until his death.

He also was a self-taught guitarist and violinist. He could not read music but learned to play by ear. He did not acquire the academic education he craved for so much as a child, and attended an elementary class only one semester in his life, but it was amazing that he could read and write and was knowledgeable. All that knew him testify that he was an ardent worshiper of Bacchus and a pleasure-seeker, but in the last twenty years of his life he gave up all sorts of worldly pleasures and lived the life of a devout Christian and a respected deacon of the church.

Having moved from Cyprus to Beirut he passed away in 1944 after a stroke. His beloved sister Sarah, my mother, who "mothered" him in his childhood, passed away exactly one month later in Cyprus having suffered a stroke herself, December 26, 1944. Mother was not told of her only brother's death, but it is easy to imagine that she was happily surprised to see him waiting for her in heaven.

CHAPTER 8

UNCLE MELIDON (1867–1909)

All his life this gentleman, my mother's eldest brother, was known as Melidon Effendi.[19] I saw him very seldom, only when he came to Hadjin on rare occasions to see his family. Never did I see him after I was twelve years of age.

I remember him as an attractive man, tall and slender, intellectual and dignified, with an aura of a hero. He had a kindly face, soft voice, and friendly attitude towards everybody he met. The solidity of his mental, moral, and social character was such that countless lives were influenced by him wherever he taught, lectured, and preached or worked in any capacity. Those who had the privilege of knowing him sixty or more years ago have with tender recollections revered his memory to this day. A pupil of his of Hadjin days in 1902, who passed away late in the 1960s in Pasadena, testified that "Melidon Effendi was an exceptionally noble and able leader and teacher, an eloquent speaker and preacher."

He preceded my mother's birth by two years, being born in 1867, and preceded her death by 35 years, an untimely death by slaughter in 1909.

An article was published on "Preacher Melidon Malian" in a little book, *Pocket Almanac*, an Armenian annual publication of Brussa Orphanage for the year 1911. Two years later another article appeared about him in *Martyrs' Book of Remembrance* (G. and M. Keshishian Printing House, Constantinople, 1913). This book was ordered by the Evangelical Union of Churches of the Cilician District, and was written in the now obsolete and defunct Turkish language with the use of Armenian alphabet, instead of the Arabic, which was in vogue for several centuries.

One day in the fall of 1909, a few months after the massacre, Aunt Mutébéreh, my martyred uncle's widow, handed me a notebook containing Uncle's autobiography and asked me to pick out a few important data from it, set them down on paper, and mail it to a certain address at St. Paul's College in Tarsus.

Uncle Melidon (1867–1909)

The Reverend Melidon Effendi Malian. He was massacred in 1909 on his way to a church convention.

I was fourteen at the time, and knowing nothing about condensing a story, I began laboriously to copy the whole notebook verbatim, reasoning that my saintly uncle could write nothing that was of no importance. I mailed the thick copy I had prepared to its destination, and returned the original manuscript to my aunt. This valuable original eventually perished in fire when Hadjin and its inhabitants were destroyed in the fall of 1920.

Both the Armenian and the Turkish articles mentioned above were evidently based on the unabridged copy I had made and mailed. My conclusion is based on the fact that the author of both was the same person, a student of Tarsus College. (This gentleman, a man of Hadjin, Dr. Haig Bahadurian, lived in his later years in Pasadena until his death.)

In order that I may continue Uncle Melidon's adventuresome life story, I authorize myself, with no apologies to any one, to cull some pertinent information from those articles inasmuch as I was the first disseminator of them more than sixty years ago.

Melidon Effendi was born in Hadjin in 1867 of a well-to-do family. In early childhood he developed a fervent love towards the church as he invariably used to accompany his devout grandmother in the small hours of every morning, with a torch of resinous pine stick pointing out the dangers of the pitch dark on the way to the church. Gradually he became proficient in Grabar sharagans (classical liturgical songs), psalms, and the Bible readings. It gave him special pleasure to round up his playmates and, standing on a higher place, preach to them while still a child.

He received his early education in the parochial school. Later the desire to master the intricacies of the Osmanli language, Turkish, drove him to the service of the government. Up to the time of his death he was considered a specialist in that language, which was a conglomeration of a handful of barbaric Turkic words and a profusion of Arabic and Persian words and expressions.

At the age of sixteen he opened a peddler's shop, but the humdrum routine of a small businessman had no appeal or promise to his spiritually sensitive nature and intellectual idealism. Whenever he saw an opportunity to witness to someone about Christ, or to teach, to advise, to comfort or admonish, or to read a portion from the Bible and expound, he would not hesitate to close his shop for hours and rush "to the business of his heavenly Father." It didn't take too long to put an end to his venture in business.

About this time, 1886, he found himself as the leader of a movement, the purpose of which was spiritual enlightenment. He found about half a dozen colleagues to whose moral support he gave lectures every Sunday afternoon in one of the churches on mostly religious matters. He named the movement "Benevolent Society." The number of the members in a short time jumped to two hundred, and for the attendants four hundred. The intended enlightenment was tremendously successful. But, alas, a

Uncle Melidon (1867–1909)

malicious informer caused irreparable harm to this splendid movement, which ended in persecution, torture, imprisonment, and banishment.

About this movement and the subsequent events a correspondence appeared in the August issue of *Hunchag*, 1891, an Armenian monthly, London, England. (Reprinted in *Hadjin* Bimonthly, No. 19, 1940. Published in Pasadena, California. Editor George B. Kooshian.)

This correspondence states that some spiritual-minded soul in Hadjin had for some time past formed an "Association of Love," the aims and purposes of which were to revive the people to enlightenment, and to teach them that true peace, the peace inside and outside a person, was only possible through faith, hope, and charity; and charity that led one to brotherliness, harmony, and cooperation, and all this in moral and spiritual sense. The members of this unique Association employed their days in fasting, confessing of sins, praying, and praising. Their sole interest centered on spiritual meditation, reading the Bible, and listening to its reading. The Turkish government did not even bother to take notice of such a harmless ascetic practice. But the Devil has a legion of secret agents in his employ willing to do his dirty jobs. There arose among the people a traitorous character who presented malicious information to the naturally oppressive government about these innocent assemblies. The wicked accusations were that under the guise of innocent gatherings the leaders of this movement were plotting a political revolution and conspiring the overthrow of the government.

Suddenly, five of the leaders, Melidon Effendi being their chief, were arrested. He was cast into a dark and filthy jail for four months without trial, but because he contracted pneumonia there and his life was in danger he was sent home. After a short period of recuperation he was rearrested and tried at Sis, the all-Turk court deciding that they were all criminals. Melidon Effendi and his comrades were manacled and sent to Adana on July 29, 1889.

The article in *Hunchag* continues to inform that Mrs. Sarah Kutufian,[20] one of the arrested, a recent bride, gave birth to a daughter in Adana prison. These condemned leaders were dragged from one court to another in different cities, falsely accused, kept in different prisons, subjected to divers manners of torture month after month, and finally condemned to the dungeon of Akka.[21]

The *zindan* (dungeon), a number of repugnant underground cells inhabited by professional criminals of every sort, speaking a Babel of languages, became for refined and sensitive Melidon Effendi his home for about four years, and the filthy, stinking, foul-mouthed men became this spiritually far-removed gentleman's everyday companions. In this wretched atmosphere, foreign and openly antagonistic, he was *alone*, friendless, penniless, and hopeless. Those agonizing years of complete absence of needed things wrecked his physical health, but could not tarnish his spiritual health. A mighty Power within himself sustained him all the time, as it was with this power that Daniel of old was sustained in the lions' den, and St. Gregory for thirteen years in the snake-infested pit.

Thus the barbarity of the Turkish government was indelibly stamped on his sensitive soul through all his remaining sixteen years with recurring fevers, nervousness and insomnia contracted in the Akka dungeon. Although stubborn efforts were made to condemn him for life, he was set free at the end of four years.

Melidon Effendi and his fellow-leaders were sentenced, according to the article in Brussa Almanac, in 1889 and freed in 1893.

From the time of his arrest and during his years as a convict he had no news of home or of his world. And at his return to Adana he was told for the first time of the calamity of the persecution and banishment of his father and stepmother and the sealing of his parental home.

An immense grief and a crushing sense of futility invaded his heart, and in utter confusion he retired to Zilifkeh (Seleucia) to meditate and search out God's will for his life. The writer of the article in *Martyr's Book of Remembrance*, referring to his dark interim, states that Melidon Effendi, in his seclusion in Zilifkeh, "wrestled with God as Jacob, and bargained with Him," and as Gideon "tested Him," until he discovered that God was calling him to His service.

Acknowledging that he lacked formal education on a higher level in order to be efficient in his "Father's Business," he immediately sent an application to Dr. Christie, the newly appointed president of the College of Tarsus for admission. (This institution, founded in 1890 by the Reverend Dr. Haroutune Jenanian of Marash, was known as Jenanian College, but in 1895 the name was changed to Saint Paul's College. Dr. Jenanian sub-

Uncle Melidon (1867–1909)

sequently founded a new Jenanian College the same year in Konia.) In the fall of the same year, 1893, at the age of twenty-six, he entered the freshman class. After one year of study he was sent to teach school somewhere for the next year and return to college with the tuition. So, he studied one year and taught school the next until he graduated in 1901 at the age of thirty-four. His teaching and preaching engagements took him to Seleucia, Sis, Adana, Yerebakan, and Hadjin. After his graduation he taught a year in Hadjin, and it was at this time, 1902, that he became instrumental in bringing our orphaned and stranded family from Adana and placing my sister and me in the American Mennonite Orphanage. In this same year he reestablished the lecture system for Sunday afternoons in one of the local churches, which system continued until the destruction of Hadjin.

In the fall of the same year he entered the American Theological Seminary at Marash and graduated in 1905. Immediately after his graduation he was invited to appear before the Convention of the Evangelical Churches of Cilicia in Aintab, and, after examination, received a license to be a full preacher, although ordination was withheld as the custom of the day required. Many were licensed preachers who waited for years to be ordained. He spent the vacation months in between his Seminary years preaching in Yarpooz, Hadjin, or elsewhere.

Three months after graduation, he married Mutébéreh Munushian of Hadjin, who had graduated from the American Girls' College at Marash almost the same day he had from the Seminary. I dimly remember the wedding festivities, as I was ten.

Immediately afterward the newlyweds left for Sis to assume the pastorate of the church of Sis, on October 1, 1905.

Thus Melidon Effendi at long last found the fulfillment of his innermost yearnings — matrimonial bliss and felicity in the service of his Lord. In due time a baby son came to add to his well-deserved happiness. The past with its painful memories was behind him now, and the future was bright, with challenges of the wide field of service for which he was well prepared. There was left for him only one more desire to be fulfilled, and that was the anticipation of ordination.

He was not only loved and respected by his own congregation, but also by all the people of Sis. His knowledge, wisdom, courtesy, and eloquent fluency attracted the attention and respect of the reigning Catholicos of the day, His Holiness Sahag II Khabaian (b. 1849, reigned 1902–1939) and his retinue. (Sahag Catholicos, whose seat was Sis, was, incidentally, my wife Suzanne Kooshian's great uncle, whom I met once, in June of 1915, in Adana.)

The Council of the Evangelical Church Union of the District of Cilicia had scheduled its annual convention for 1909 in Adana. Pastors, deacons, delegates, and others, men and women from the churches all over the vilayet, prepared themselves weeks in advance to go to the convention, participate in the sessions, satiate their intellectual and spiritual hunger with varied fare, meet old friends and renowned personages, and bring to the home church fresh news hard to get.

Transportation in those days was primitive. Automobiles were never heard of. From one village to another, or to a city, one walked on foot, even if it took several days, except for one who could afford the fare to hire a horse or join a caravan. The journey was ever fraught with dangers — highway robbers or murderers. Therefore the convention-bound churchpeople from every direction made the first leg of the travel to a nearby central town, and they started from there in a larger group to insure safety. Their number grew at each central place.

Another group of convention people traveled from eastern churches of Cilicia converging on Adana, but stopped at Osmaniye the night before the opening of the convention.

The church at Sis also elected its delegates to accompany its beloved pastor, Melidon Effendi, whom the convention was to ordain in a solemn ceremony. The large group from northern Cilicia, joining the party at Sis, traveled towards Adana, but stopped at Saı'-Getchit, a Turkish village, just the night before the opening of the convention.[22] This group consisted of seventy-eight of the noblest people.

Unbeknownst to this group, unbeknownst to any group, and unbeknownst to any Armenian in any part of the wide country, sealed orders were issued by Sultan Abdul Hamid II (Abdul the Damned as he was called in Europe), to the vali, mutasarif, kaimakam, and mudir of every town and hamlet to massacre mercilessly every Armenian they could find. In this particular day, the 2nd of April, the royal seals were broken, the

Uncle Melidon (1867–1909)

diabolical decree read in the mosques, the savage blood-thirsty instinct of the Turk inflamed and fanned by the imam, the priest of the Moslem Allah, with the Mohommedan promise of a huri — a gorgeous virgin — for each giavour killed. The voluptuous, the vulgarly sensual Turk needs no other incentive to kill except, of course, to pillage, to plunder, to expropriate.

So, on this particular night, at the signal given by Mudir Hadji Bey, the Turkish mob of professional cut-throats attacked the unsuspecting company of pastors and church leaders in Saı'-Getchit and slaughtered every one of them with axes and butcher knives. Among the seventy-eight victims Melidon Effendi also was butchered by a ferocious Turk. This fiend was later seen with Melidon Effendi's pocket watch bearing his initials, but what Armenian could dare to bring a Moslem to the court of justice?

Meanwhile the convention-bound party in Osmaniye was set on fire in the Armenian church, where they had fled the murderous mob. Hundreds of towns and villages were burned, millions of dollars worth of Armenian possessions were carried away, and more than 30,000 innocent Armenians were massacred in the Province of Adana, leaving unnumbered widows and orphans.

My widowed young aunt Mutébéreh returned to Hadjin soon after the brutal killing of her husband and made her home with her own parents. Eking out a living for herself and her baby, Barkev (Gift), was impossible in Hadjin at that time, so she applied to the Mennonite missionaries, who gave her a position in Evérék-Fénésséh to teach Turkish to the missionaries and English in their high school. When the World War broke out and the missionary establishments were closed out, she was compelled to return to Hadjin again with her child. Somehow she remained in her parental home all through the war years while Hadjin people were deported and decimated in exile.

At the termination of the war a small remnant of the survivors of the Genocide returned to Hadjin, and a few American missionaries had the courage to come back to pick up the broken pieces of their former educational and philanthropic programs. Soon Aunt Mutébéreh was called upon to help with the care of young girls who had lost their parents victim to the recent holocaust.

Short months after the fierce hordes of Mustafa Kemal succeeded in throwing the victorious Allied Occupational Forces out of Turkey, they besieged Hadjin also in the spring of 1920 and leveled it to the ground on October 16.

The night before the last day of the beleaguered city a company of Kemalist brutes descended upon the girls' school, kicked the doors open, and, brandishing their blood-dripping scimitars, demanded ten of the loveliest girls to ravage.

— None can you have while I breathe, roared my aunt, throwing herself forward and pushing the scoundrels aside.

But, alas! the raised scimitar of one of the sensually crazed villains fell on her neck and severed her lovely head from the body which housed her heroic spirit.

The foregoing story reached me through my mother and brother, who were told it years later by one of the girls who survived the ensuing panic, rape, and slaughter.

My mind staggers when I try to find a plausible reason why the Turk should torture, for a trumped-up crime, a boy of seventeen or eighteen who never dreamed of committing an unlawful act against the government, then to sentence him to spend years in a dark and dank dungeon in a land and language foreign to him and subject him to ill-health for the rest of his life; and then years later, at the peak of his usefulness as a man of God and teacher of goodness, the Turk should cut his head off; and a decade later the Turk should sever the head of his hapless widow and her twelve-year-old only son.

Why, why, why the Turk should find pleasure in massacring the children, the women, and the men of another race?

Victor Hugo, the great French poet, wrote:

> The murder of a man in Europe is a crime and is punished by the capital punishment of the murderer; whereas the massacre of thousands of Christians by Turks in the East is only an "event" and none of the murderers is punished in any way.[23]

CHAPTER 9

MY MATERNAL GRANDFATHER (1840-1917)

NOTHING IS KNOWN at this late date about Krikor (Gregory) Agha Malian's birth, childhood, schooling, youth, environment, and marriage, except the fact that (inasmuch as he became my grandfather), he must have been born some years before the second half of the 19th century, he grew up into an industrious and respected businessman and someday in his twenties he married a girl of his native town of Hadjin. By and by twelve babies were born to him, but most of them died either at birth or in early childhood. Only four of them grew into adulthood—Uncle Melidon, next my mother Sarah, then Aunt Gulie, and fourth Uncle Haroutune.

(Melidon, 1867–1909, Saí-Getchit)
(Sarah, 1869–1944, Cyprus)
(Gulie, 1875–1964, Boston)
(Haroutune, 1883–1944, Beirut)

Grandfather had one brother, Hovanness (John), and two sisters, Anaguz and Mariam, all married and the parents of a number of children. But all of them perished in the 1915–1920 genocide the Turks committed on the Armenians.

Malians were numerous in Hadjin, having branched out of an ancient stock. At present many descendants of Malians of wiped-out Hadjin can be found wherever Armenians are scattered.

In my eyes my grandfather was a colorful man, although I knew nothing about him. He was an old man, bent, slow of walk and reluctant of much talk. I have no recollection of any conversation with him. I always had the impression, and in fact thought, that he was an unlettered, unschooled, and uneducated man. The majority of the people of Hadjin didn't have the opportunity to acquire even a rudimentary education. And my grandfather couldn't have been different. There was not a single book in his house, no paper, no pencil or ink, and no desk of any sort.

Seldom I had occasion to visit him. But one summer evening in 1910, on a rare visit to his home, I was dumbfounded to notice that grandfather took out of a hidden pocket in his bosom a small notebook and a worn-out stub of a pencil, and began to scribble something.

"What are you writing, Grandfather?" I asked.

"Greek," he answered, plunging me into deeper astonishment.

"Where did you learn to write and read Greek?" I asked. "Not in Hadjin?"

"No, not in Hadjin, but in Athens, Greece," he condescended to satisfy my curiosity.

At once my grandfather grew out of proportion, and became a mysterious, awe-inspiring giant.

My curiosity had no bounds. But to my further questions of "When?" and "How?" he would stop short by saying that it was too painful a story to tell.

I could get nothing more from him.

But it was only many years later, when the real actors of the tragedy were gone forever, and I had come to the United States to reside, that I learned some fragments of the chain of tragic events my grandfather was destined to go through, and all these before I was born.

A number of calamities had visited him on the heels of one another. Two thirds of his children — eight out of twelve — had died; his eldest son, Melidon, the pride and the pillar of his hopes and anticipations, was forcibly snatched from him and banished to unknown darkness; his wife, the brave little lady who had the strength and dutifulness to give birth to a dozen babies, had at last succumbed and left him alone with a six-year-old boy; he had remarried, and misfortune and misery had dogged this blessing with unforeseen grief.

These series of events precipitated in the more or less placid life of Hadjin extensive arrests, persecution, torture, imprisonment, and banishment.

Shortly after the death of his wife he married again, in 1889, to a maiden who, unwittingly, became the spark to the political, social, and religious conflagration of the particular period.

My Maternal Grandfather (1840-1917)

The Reverend Sarkis H. Devirian (February 3, 1850–September 22, 1946) was the pastor of the First Protestant Church in Hadjin, Turkey, for almost twenty years, beginning in 1877. This venerable old gentleman and I happened to be members of a church committee in Pasadena during the 1920s. One day he loaned me a book he had written in 1897, *Our Troubles in Asia*, published in Binghamton, New York. I am sure that he did not know that the reading of it would give me a pleasant surprise, although he knew that I was a native of Hadjin.

I found in this book the bizarre story of my grandfather, which he had found "too painful to talk about," when I asked him on a summer evening in 1910 to relate it to me.

The account follows, as told by Devirian:

The Koran says of Moslem women:

"They are not lawful for the unbelievers to have in marriage, neither are the unbelievers lawful for them." Sura 60

Now about twenty years ago, a female child, the daughter of a Kurd in one of the villages near Harput, became an orphan when little more than an infant. Her nearest relation was an uncle living in the city of Adana, and to him the child was sent. She was brought up in his family, and for some years was well-cared for. While yet a little child, allowed to play freely in the streets, she made the acquaintance of a Christian grape-seller, who had a habit of gathering the neighborhood children about him as he sat among his fruits, and telling them stories. These stories were always from the New Testament, the teachings and the deeds of Christ and his twelve Fishers-of-men.

When she was about fourteen the uncle also died. She then lived with kindred in a neighboring village, but could have no real home until she was married. The grape-seller's stories had never been forgotten, and pondering upon them she concluded that she would be a Christian.

Going to Catholicos at Adana, she declared her belief in Christ, and asked to be baptized and taken in to communion with the Church. That good man listened and advised her not to be hasty, saying:

"My daughter, I am very glad that you believe in Christ, but I will send you to the convent at Hadjin, where you may be under the bishop's teaching concerning the doctrines of the Church. If after six months you are still of the same desire, I will gladly baptize you."

This was done, and at the end of the time she was baptized, and became a Christian in all belief and custom. The convent became her home, as her change of faith had severed all ties with the old life.

She had grown up very beautiful, going with unveiled faith according to Christian custom. Her beauty, and also her consistent Christian character, attracted the regard of a young Armenian named Gregory Mallian. Loving her, and being in good circumstances, he appealed to the convent for permission to marry her, it was granted, and they were married and lived very happily together for about two years.

Then in some manner, it came into the recollection of Mohammedans who knew her that she was a Kurd by birth. It reached the ear of the authorities. She was arrested, being taken from her husband's house during his absence, and brought before them for question.

I was present in the government office during this inquisition, and I well remember the woman's anguish. She avowed her Christian faith, but declared with tears that she was blameless; that she had left her Kurdish village when a little child, and learning of Christ, could not help following him.

She was asked: "Who baptized you? and who married you, a Kurdish woman to an Armenian man?" She gave the names; and the priest, bishop, and archbishop were immediately arrested. But the priest who had married them was a very old man, and extreme old age is one of the few things held in respect by the Turk. Moreover, he was able to show the written order of his superior, whom he might not disobey, directing him to "marry Miram to this young man." He also declared that he had not known that she was a Kurd, when he performed the ceremony. So he was released. But the archbishop who had given him permission to marry them, was sent to Aleppo on foot, tried, and condemned to imprisonment in a Circassian village near Aleppo, where no one knew his language. Here he was scourged an starved, and he suffered other indignities because of his part in this affair. The bishop who had baptized her was exiled to a Syrian fortress, and I have heard since I left Armenia that he is still there.

The wife was taken to prison for a few days before her removal to Adana, and while there, was abused and outraged by the officers in such a way that all Christians who had loved and honored her might know of the indignities she suffered. Such provocation is often given with the direct intention of rousing the Christians into such agonized resentment that they will attack their brutal masters and attempt a rescue. And such attacks are always fiercely punished; lives are forfeited and property confiscated. In this case the people held still in despair.

Bound on horseback, surrounded by Turkish soldiers, the poor woman started for Adana. In the dusk of the first evening they met what seemed a company, from the sound of trampling. Fearing that some Christians had banded together for the release of this woman, the soldiers halted and challenged. But the answer came back, "It is only I, Gregory Mallian, with my sheep"; for the husband was a butcher by occupation, and had been out in the country collecting a flock for the needs of his business, and knew nothing of the calamity that had come upon his household in his absence. Joyfully taking him into custody, they continued on their way. At Adana they were separated, and he never saw his wife again. No one knows what has become of her.

He himself was condemned for life to an island fortress in the Mediterranean. Going thither while the ship lay in a Greek port taking cargo, he attracted the sympathy of some Greek sailors, as he lay in chains on the deck. "Roll yourself off into the sea," commanded they, "Do not fear the weight of the chains, we will save you." They succeeded in making his rescue thus, and when the Turkish zaptiahs made their demand of the Greeks for their prisoner, they answered, "Not so; we have rescued a man from the sea, and is it not written, 'Whatsoever thou takest from the sea thou mayest keep'? We will not surrender him." The law they had quoted was very old, and it is seldom broken. The Turks were obliged to yield and the man was saved.

Two Armenian merchants were traveling on the same steamer. They had no connection or knowledge of Mallian, being from the city of Marash, and were going to Constantinople to buy goods. Of course they had with them, for such a purpose, a considerable sum of money. The zapitahs, on arriving at the harbor of Smyrna, notified the authorities that they lost their prisoner, and stated the manner of it: but accused the merchants of advising and conniving his escape. They were taken into custody and kept in prison until they gave up all their money as a bribe to the officials, when they were released.

Mallian's rescuers conveyed him to Athens, where he was safe. But knowing nothing of the language, and having landed in utter destitution, he found subsistence very difficult, and by and by the homesick longing for the sound of his own language and the sight of his own country brought him secretly back. He was discovered, and as before, thrown into prison where, if living, he yet remains, for no one can help him.

My Maternal Grandfather (1840-1917)

Now what was the fault of this wife and husband, that such awful suffering should be visited upon them? The one had married a Kurdish woman who had been converted to Christianity; the other, born a Moslem had married a Christian. Both of these crimes (they call it so) are counted worthy of death by Koranic law.

Is it any wonder that, in Turkey, one almost never hears of a Mohammedan being converted to Christianity? Nor can any Christian who has made confession of faith in the Prophet, for his safety's sake, ever dare to recant. He would be treated worse than if he had always remained a Christian.

Devirian is, no doubt, a reliable source, inasmuch as he was an invited audience as the leader of the Protestant community of Hadjin at the unfortunate Mrs. Mallian's initial trial. It is evident that he must have left the country for America while Krikor Mallian was again dragged to prison after his covert return from exile. So he ends his story with a dismal finality: "...if living...no one can help him."

But help came Providentially.

In the *General History of Hadjin* (H. Boghosian, 1942), a page is given to the same story of my grandfather (p. 542). Although the name of the person who supplied the story is not given, yet it is evident that it was Dr. John S. Martin, missionary and founder of Hadjin Boys' Academy (1860–1939; in Hadjin 1892–1906).

This story is, in essence, the same, with some supplementary information. The Christian "grape seller" of the Devirian version is here a Christian "peddler." The Kurdish-born girl, young, buxom, and singularly beautiful, is arrested. The officers in authority bestially wreak havoc upon her body. The priest, Hagop Baba Kirkyasharian, who performed the wedding ceremony, gets exonerated because of extreme old age. Parsegh Vartabed Mangurian gets exiled to Akka and thrown into the dungeon. Archbishop Hovanness Kazanjian, the Primate, is exiled on foot to a village near Aleppo, inhabited by hostile Circassians whose language is completely foreign to him.

According to the story, Malian secretly returns home after ten years of misery in Athens and gets apprehended, chained, and under heavy guard forced-marches to exile. At some distance from the town, near Sazak, the party meets a foreigner, Dr. Martin, the British-subject missionary, who questions the zapitahs about the nature of the crimes of the beaten, worn-out prisoner staggering under chains. Once in Hadjin, he continues his inquiry, and, after comparing what the zapitahs had told him with what facts he learns from the local people, he immediately dispatches a detailed report of the gross injustice to Sir Philip Curry, the British Ambassador in Constantinople. Sometime later the Ambassador obtains from the Sultan the release of the Vartabed from Akka, of the Archbishop from Syria, and that of Krikor Malian from Adana.

The Kurdish girl?

From the outset of the tragic drama she vanished, leaving no trace behind her.

Grandfather Krikor Agha, free at last, came home, and learned that his son Melidon also was back from exile and studying in Tarsus The younger son he had left behind when arrested many years before had left home in search of a trade. He felt utterly lonely, and the house he was forced to leave desolate these many years needed the presence and care of a wife. So he married again, an Armenian lady of Hadjin. When I reached the age of awareness, knowing nothing of the past, I accepted the fact that, besides having a *babig*, I had a loving *mamig* and a little aunt, Siroon, a few years younger than I.

Grandfather passed away in 1917, in Hadjin. Grandmother and her daughter perished in 1920 when Hadjin was ravaged to rise no more.

CHAPTER 10

WE RETURN TO HADJIN

M Y FATHER having died in 1902 of pneumonia in Adana as we were about to return to Hadjin, Mother was left in utter destitution, and in sole charge of me, seven, sister Mary, five, and an infant brother, two months old.

It was only through the financial help and management of Uncle Melidon that we could leave Adana for Hadjin.

Uncle was, at the time, a schoolmaster in Hadjin. He immediately arranged with the management of the American Mennonite Orphanage for the admission of us two older children. He took Mother and her baby under his care. We two remained in the orphanage more than ten years, until World War I put an end to it.

This home of mercy was opened in 1898 by two American young ladies, Miss Maria Guerber and Miss Rose Lambert, for orphans of the 1896 massacres. It had two separate homes, one for boys, and another for girls. This institution became a veritable source of blessing in many ways not only to the inmates, but to the town and the surrounding region also.

Miss Guerber died in Pasadena in 1917 and was buried in the local cemetery. Miss Lambert, the guardian angel in the 1909 massacre, left Hadjin the following year, wrote a book in the U.S.A. with the title *Hadjin*,[24] and became Mrs. Musselman. She visited Pasadena with her youngest son, John, in 1946 and was honored with grateful affection by the Armenian colony of Hadjin people and others. She lived in Texas and corresponded with me until her death in 1975.

I received my religious and moral training at the hands of the saintly missionaries of the orphanage, and early schooling in the American Academy for Boys in the city. Sister received hers in the same manner

Missionaries in Hadjin, 1902. From left, The Reverend and Mrs. Tomford Barker, Mr. J. Fidler, The Reverend Henry Maurer, Miss Rose Lambert Miss Elizabeth Hank, Maurer's wife-to-be. The unnamed individuals are Turkish escorts. Maurer was massacred in Adana in 1909.

in the Home School for Girls.

For the summers and the interim between June 1909 to September 1910, the management of the orphanage assigned me to work in its textile factory, where, sitting front of a spinning wheel, I would wind wet and sticky yarn on thin spools of reed for the master weavers' shuttles.

And now, reminiscing on this rare opportunity, I realize what a great fool I was for not finding the experience pleasant and enriching, instead of continuous moroseness, grumbling, and complaining for the supposed injustice, the loss of schooling.

We Return to Hadjin

Orphanage Moves Away

In the fall of 1910, one year after the massacre of Adana and its environs, at which time more than 30,000 Armenians were killed, the Orphanage for Boys was transferred from Hadjin to Evérék-Fénésséh, a city on the eastern plains of Mount Erjias (Argeus, 12,848 feet), in the Province of Kayseri (Caesarea on Cappadocia).

More than one hundred orphans, several missionaries, and twenty-five or thirty teachers and helpers left Hadjin. But the president of the orphanage decided to leave behind the students of the higher classes to continue their studies in the Hadjin Academy. The reason for this action was the lack of accommodations in the living quarters and shortage of competent teachers for the higher classes. The combined cities of Fénésséh and Evérék had never had an Evangelical or American high school in their history. Beside, the administration of the orphanage had no need throughout its twelve-year existence to venture into the field of education as long as the Academy for Boys (also, the Home School for Girls) filled the need of the orphans and outsiders.

Left Behind

So, I was in the group of thirty left behind. With some others of this group I was to finish my sophomore year in Hadjin.

Arrangements were made for us to be housed in the upper floor of the textile factory which short time before had been closed out. A superintendent was appointed over us, Bedros Sharian, a former fellow-orphan, a college graduate at that time (Reverend Sharian now lives in Decatur, Illinois). To supply our provisions we had the services of the old agent. For our cook the president left behind my mother, Sarah, who had been the cook of the orphanage since 1906.

The school year ended in June, 1911.

That summer for a few weeks I was permitted to take a vacation in Goksum (Cucusus, where St. John Chrysostom was exiled in A.D. 404) and visit a cousin, Esther, and her consumptive husband. She and her children were massacred later, as well as her sisters and their families. At the end of September I joined the orphanage in Fénésséh.

Mother goes to Adana

But there was no place for Mother in the new schedule. She was left to shift on her own.

When an opportunity presented itself, Mother took her youngest child, leaving her daughter Mary in the Girls' Orphanage, and went to Adana to accept the position of chief cook in the Ottoman Orphanage, established a short time before for the orphans of the 1909 massacre.

I Go to Evérék-Fénésséh

When the school was opened in Fénésséh in October 1911, I was one of three students to form the junior class in the new high school. The school did not have a senior class, and had only four teachers. One of them was Mr. Levon Tourian (now living in Teaneck, New Jersey), to this day a very dear friend, who, with his wife, visits us each summer when they spend their vacation in Pasadena.

I Graduate from High School

In 1913 I graduated from this high school in Fénésséh as one of the three students of the first graduating class.

For the first commencement exercises ever held in the township of Evérék-Fénésséh, the local government dignitaries and the representatives of the local intellectual community were invited. All three of us graduates delivered our carefully prepared speeches. Mine was in Armenian. I fail at this late hour to recall the subject matter of my speech, but I do remember with some pride that I received two prizes, one from the Faculty, a volume of world history in the Turkish language with Arabic characters, and a very welcome book, a French to Armenian dictionary, the gift of the well-known apothecary of Fénésséh, Mr. Sarkis Kellejian.

I received also for this momentous occasion a pocket watch with chain from Mother in Adana, and a pocket knife from sister Mary in Hadjin.

All through my school years three teachers stand out as unforgettable and the most influential in my life. The first of these was Mr. Kaloust Aijian (1910–1911 in Hadjin); the second one was Mr. Levon Tourian (1911–1912 in Fénésséh); and the third was Mr. Mardiros Sarkisian (1912–1913, in Fénésséh, in my senior year). They remain warm friends to this day.

My classmates were David Gedigian, whom I never saw or heard from again after our graduation, and Toros Pushian, who, at this writing, lives alone in Palm Springs, California, having lost his wife some years ago.

George Kooshian, David Gedigian (seated), Toros Pushian

Plans Are Made for Me

A day or two after graduation the Reverend Tomford Barker, the Principal of the whole Mennonite establishment of both Hadjin and Fénésséh, called me to his office to tell me that my days in the orphanage had come to an end. I was free now to go anywhere and do anything I pleased. But, he said, there was one little matter that I had to straighten out with the orphanage that had sheltered, fed, clothed, and educated me. It was a matter of five liras, about twenty-five dollars. I owed this sum not for anything else but for the beautiful blue serge suit the tailor had made for my graduation.

For the gentle way he presented this delicate matter tears welled in my eyes and I said, "I came to realize how heavily I am indebted to you, which I can never repay in full. But, Badveli (a term of affection and respect, meaning Revered One), how can I pay you this sum of money when I do not possess a penny?"

"Don't worry about that," he said. "I have some plans already made for you. You will serve as a teacher in our school here, your board and lodging will be provided, and at the end of the school year you will have paid in full and be free to move on."

I was more than glad to agree.

"But," he continued, "I have further plans for you. I will send you to college in the fall, and at the fall of the next year you will begin to teach."

The interview was over.

At the end of the interview I was advised to apply for labor work at the construction that was going to start next morning.

Construction Laborer

At this time construction of a new building was begun on a nearby land donated to the orphanage by the people of Fénésséh. I considered myself very fortunate when I was accepted to work on this construction. I was going to earn my keep for the first time in my life of seventeen years. I was a man now, honest, responsible, and dependable. I would earn money with my own sweat, enough money that might pay part of my debt.

Knowing next to nothing about the art of physical labor I applied myself from the first moment to the tasks pointed to me with alacrity, enthusiasm, and idealism. On that hot June morning I rolled my shirt sleeves way up, dug ditches, hodded heavy loads of rock and dirt, and was all ears to catch orders flying around. In my "all-knowing" ignorance I thought that the job demanded of me this kind of service. But before midday lunch hour arrived I was a complete wreck, bare arms severely sunburned, legs on strike to move, head screaming to burst open, and badly roasting in the "Three Hebrew Children's Furnace." After several days of intensive care I was discharged to spend the summer days in Hadjin to recuperate.

This was the beginning and the end of my labor at construction.

Last Visit to Hadjin

I came to Hadjin to recuperate from the disastrous effects of my labor in the construction job. My mother and younger brother had returned from Adana to visit my sister, who was still in the Girls' Orphanage.

This was the year we had our last family photograph taken. There was only one photographer in Hadjin, Murad Khoja, a teacher of many years in the Boys' Academy and a friend or ours.

It was a rare privilege to spend the hot month of August with Aunt Satchian and her large family in their summer camp on one of their grain-fields on the beautiful highland beyond the northeastern Taurus Mountains. The Satchians were wealthy in grain-fields, cattle, and herds. They were shepherds by profession.

That same month of August, forever the last, provided me with a wealth of pleasurable moments which have haunted me all these years with nostalgic, poignant longing.

There, on the spacious Valley of Sarunj, in the month of August, Haiganoush had a pastoral, idyllic wedding that could only be described by Shakespeare. Haiganoush (meaning, goddess descended from Haig, the mythical forefather of the Armenians) was Aunt Satchian's elder daughter, 16, and extremely beautiful. The wedding took place under a giant spreading oak tree; a wedding simple yet elaborate, rustic yet regal; a ceremony profoundly reverent and exuberant to which a great number of priests, choral children, and guests were invited from Hadjin and the neighboring fields. The festivities and dinners, horse races and different games continued for seven days and seven nights.

One day, after the wedding, I was offered the rarest of all opportunities, to accompany the shepherd of the Satchian herd of goats and his flock to Canyon of the Daggers, famous and equally infamous. Famous because of its breath-taking awesome splendor, and infamous because of the mammoth gorge where, at one point, a shaky wooden bridge over the swift Gök Sü River connects one densely wooded mountain to another perpendicular one, which are the favorite haunts of merciless Turkish desperadoes, bandits, and murderers.

Even one single day spent with a shepherd and his herd in the heart of the virgin nature would be equivalent to a term in college.

The noble Satchian family perished less than three years later at the hands of the Turks in the great Genocide in the Syrian deserts.

More will be told in another chapter about Satchians.

Enough to add that Asadoor, the eldest son, survived several massacres, remarried, and leaving his second homeland France went in 1947 to Soviet Armenia, where he died in 1968.

In the fall of 1968, a friend returning from a tour of Armenia brought me a letter with a small gift from a schoolteacher in Erevan, capital of Soviet Armenia. She wrote that her name was Haiganoush Satchian, daughter of Asadoor, and she was greatly excited when she read in *Nor Hadjin* monthly, published in Buenos Aires, Argentina, my article "One Month with Satchians in 1913." She informed me that she was named after her aunt, the original Haiganoush about whom I had written so glowingly. She also wrote that her newly-dead father had often talked about us and his life of old tragic days. She said in her letter that she was one of five Satchian children, and without ever seeing us knew about us, and wanted to know more. Her requests were gladly complied with. In a subsequent letter she let me know that she was married to Dr. Aharon Kurkyasharian, the son of a cousin and student of mine from the 1919–1920 period, Dr. Haigazoon Kurkyasharian.

The month on the Valley of Sarunj with Satchians swiftly marched on, Mother with my younger brother left for Adana, and I for Fénésséh.

I never saw Hadjin again.

The Turks wiped it off the face of the globe seven years later.

CHAPTER II

I GO TO COLLEGE

ONCE in Fénésséh, Badveli Barker, having ordered whatever was necessary for a college student, put me on my way in a hired two-horse-driven covered wagon. At the end of the second day I paid off the wagon driver and boarded the train at Eregli. Next evening arriving at Konia I lugged along my belongings, carrying some on my back, some under my arms and some others dragging behind me, and at last made it to the campus of Jenanian College.

It was a pleasant surprise in this far-off province to find about a dozen people of Hadjin as students and teachers. Even the president of the college was a man of Hadjin, the Reverend Dr. Armenag Haigazian, educated in America. The minister of the campus church, the only Evangelical one in town, was of Hadjin. He was the Reverend Samuel Rejebian, my professor in English, a distant relative of Mother's, who later pastored many churches, including Cilicia Congregational Church in Pasadena, and is now buried in this city. It was my privilege to speak at his funeral, as it also was at Dr. Haigazian's widow's funeral two years ago.

We students of Hadjin often came together and conversed in our dialect. Sometimes we were invited by our professors for a social hour.

The language used in the campus was English. It was compulsory, so strict, that any one overheard using a foreign word in his English conversation was compelled to pay two pennies for each such word. At the end of the school year, the account I kept showed that I had paid six precious pennies, although, in truth, I merited a heavier penalty, because I was not caught. Naturally, we spoke Armenian, French, or Turkish in those classes.

During the two years in the Fénésséh High School the compulsory language was Armenian, and those who used Turkish or dialectal words or sentences were handed a booby doll by some one who deservedly had received it from another alert victim. At the assembly in the auditorium after the recess was over, all the dolls were collected, and the unlucky student holding the ridiculous doll was made abashed. The humiliation of holding a doll was punishment enough for many a sensitive student. It happened to me a few times when I was not sufficiently on my guard, and after having been handed the doll I failed to find another victim to pass it on to.

It was on November 25, 1913, that I saw for the first time, in fact the whole city saw, an aeroplane manned by two Frenchmen, Dancourt and Rou. They landed their craft on a field outside the city, where the whole population, including all the schools, rushed there to see this marvelous mechanical bird.

On December 20 the city and I witnessed a second aeroplane land, and, to our horror, fall down on its take-off and smash its wings.

On the night before Christmas, at the entrance of the dormitory, while scraping my shoes on the blade of the scraper, I discovered to my dismay that the sticky mud of the street had robbed me of one of my sorely needed rubber shoes. Long search in the deeply-mired streets the same night by candle light with the help of sympathetic friends uncovered no trace of the precious shoe. I could ill afford to buy another pair but that was exactly what I was forced to do. As fickle fate would have it, the elusive shoe turned up a few days later, making me unnecessarily the richest person in college with two pairs of overshoes.

Jenanian College, also known as The Apostolic Institute, was located in Konia, the city made famous by St. Paul's missionary visits.

The Reverend Dr. Haroutune Jenanian of Marash, educated in the U.S.A., founded St. Paul's College in Tarsus, the birthplace of the great Apostle, in the 1880s, but having been forced out of his institution, he founded the Apostolic Institute in 1893, which was named after him. He also founded the city of Yettem, California, in 1900. (Yettem is an Armenian word, meaning The Garden of Eden.) He died in 1907.

The president of the college, the successor of the founder, was Dr. Haigazian, who, at the hand of the Turks, was killed at the end of several weeks-long march of death in 1921.[25]

I Go to College

The Reverend Dr. Haroutune Jenanian, founder of Jenanian College

KONIA (ICONIUM)

Konia is an ancient city mentioned by Xenophon (434–355 B.C.), the Greek general and historian, in his *Anabasis*. Saints Paul and Barnabas visited it on their missionary journey, mentioned in Acts 13:51; 14:1–6; 14:21. A church synod was held there in A.D. 235. In about 1074 it fell into the hands of the Seljuk Turks, who five years later made it their capital. The town played a prominent part in the Crusades, being occupied by Godfrey of Bouillon and Fredrick Barbarossa in 1190. Here Ibrahim Pasha of Egypt defeated the Turks in 1832. From the capture of Nicaea by the Crusaders down to the time of Genghis Khan, the Mongol conqueror of Central Asia (1167–1227), it remained the capital of the Seljuk sultans.

Konia as a city is in the province of the same name, 143 miles south of Ankara, the capital of modern Turkey, with an altitude of 3320 feet.

The population in my day was over 60,000, with thousands of Armenians, Greeks, and Jews.

One of the many beautiful mosques contains the tomb reputed to be that of the founder of the famed whirling dervishes. Other noteworthy buildings are an ancient Byzantine church, massive government Konabs (office buildings), and the remains of the palace of Sultan Ala-ed-Din, who reigned from 1219 to 1236.

Armenians and Greeks had their own churches on the hill of Ala-ed-Din alongside the Mohammedan mosque. On Sundays the students of the college were permitted to attend those Orthodox churches. No Christian churches exist there now, having been destroyed by the Turks.

The Whirling Dervishes

On one occasion, April 24, 1914, in company of several schoolmates, I visited the Mosque of the Mevlavies, the Whirling Dervishes, who were locally called Dédés. Squeezing through the dense Moslem throng all over the grounds, we found ourselves on the balcony overlooking the sanctuary, in the middle of which dervishes of all ages, young and old, were whirling like spinning tops. The performers were whirling on their heels, silently, arms horizontally stretched, to the mournful music of a rustic flute made of reed, a tambourine, and a primitive violin, played by other dervishes in the fraternity.

They were clad in brown robes reaching down to their ankles. They shed these outer robes as the whirl gathered speed, and white or yellow robes underneath came to view. Those who fell into a trance after half an hour or so retired and others came forward to resume the spinning, which they call *zikr*. They believe that by whirling and falling into a trance after exhaustion they establish a supernatural communion. Their sanctuary is named by them Séma-Hané, House of Heaven.

This sect of Islam was founded by Jélal-ed-Din-er-Roumi-Mavlana, who died in Konia in 1273. The chief of the Mevlavies was privileged to gird the sword of sovereignty on each Sultan-Khalif of Turkey.

This sect symbolized the mystery of human ways of worship as the prayer-wheel-spinning of Tibet, the great stone faces on Easter Island, the overpowering ruins of Angkor Wat, and the ritual pillars of Stonehenge.

The beginning of the end of this strange sect came when their monasteries were closed in 1925 in a government reprisal against an abortive dervish-led uprising in Turkey.

THE REVEREND TOMFORD F. BARKER IN KONIA

A letter received from Fénésséh Orphanage had already informed me that Badveli Barker was on his way to the United States to place his eldest daughter Ruth in college, and would stop at Konia to see me. On the morning of May 8 he made a tour of the college, having Dr. Samuel Jamgotchian (Jamentz), the vice president, as his guide. (Dr. Jamentz was married to Dr. Jenanian's sister. He was a native of Marash, grew up in Hadjin, attended the Academy, studied medicine in the U.S.A., taught in Hadjin Academy and Jenanian College, and after World War I dwelt in Pasadena, where he is buried.)

Meeting me in the auditorium Badveli Barker indicated that I should see him in his room in the American hospital where he was lodging. In order that they might express their affection and respect to the beloved benefactor of the orphans of Hadjin all the nine students and two teachers, natives of Hadjin, gathered together after school and went to see the Badveli. He received us graciously and gave fresh news from Hadjin and Fénésséh. As the visitors were about to leave he motioned for me to linger.

Once alone with him, he embraced and kissed me. He made me sit by him. He told me that he was pleased with my credits and deportment as a college freshman, and he had need of me as a teacher next fall in the orphanage high school.

I listened with pleased interest.

Then he laid before me his terms.

1. For the six month period I would be employed as a teacher I would receive thirty liras in all.

2. From this sum five liras would be deducted for my graduation debt of the previous year.

3. From this sum six liras would be deducted for my meals and lodging.

4. From this sum half of my college tuition and book expenses and my travel fares would be deducted.

5. I would have no other responsibilities in the orphanage except teaching in the classrooms.

6. For the summer months the orphanage management would not be responsible for me.

I had no penny in the world that I could call mine.

But there was nothing in the world I could say but to agree to the terms.

Badveli Barker left for America the next day. He left his wife and children in Fénésséh with the orphanage in the hope that he would return shortly, but the specter of World War I loomed up in less than two months and turned the whole world upside down. I never saw him again.

My Health

Because the ten liras paid the school by Mr. Barker was, evidently, less than the required tuition, I was assigned the duty of a waiter in the student dining room. This job deprived me of the pleasure of joining the choral group that I wanted so much. So, after two months, I was glad to exchange this "high" position of a waiter with the "higher" rank of a noonday dishwasher with another helper. This service I continued to perform to the end of the school year.

I learned and practiced to keep a detailed account of every penny I spent. My first year's expense in college, including tuition, books, travel, and incidentals, came to a staggering total of seventeen liras (about eighty-five dollars).

Physically I never was robust. My weight never went beyond 110 lbs. All through childhood and young manhood I was afflicted with an annoying disease — taeniasis — ill health due to tapeworms. To the eternal credit of my beloved "Badveli," I must record here that several personal efforts were made by him both in Hadjin and Fénésséh to relieve me from the destructive domination of this detestable disease, but to no avail. This disgusting condition came to an abrupt and undramatic end three years after my marriage, when, early one morning in Mulkigian vineyard in Fresno, I happened to eat an enormous amount of apricots, picking them from the tree. The invincible army of the lowly apricots charged to demolish the thirty-six-year-old fortress of the tapeworms and forced them to abandon their perch and vacate their abode once and for all.

During this college year I often suffered from fever, chills, fatigue, susceptibility to colds. Bad eyesight and nearsightedness, obviously inherited from my father, were with me from early childhood, and in 1912 Badveli sent me with two other students from Fénésséh to Talas (near Kayseri) to be fitted with eyeglasses at the American Hospital. And this year, my Algebra and Bacteriology professor, Dr. Samuel Jamgotchian, fitted me with new glasses.

June 28, 1914

A very dull and ordinary day.

But I had no knowledge, and I don't suppose anybody else had, that this drab day was destined to be inscribed in world history as the beginning of a world-shaking havoc. A horrendous crime was committed in an obscure town Sarajevo in an obscure country in the Balkans, Bosnia. An insane university student assassinated Archduke Franz Ferdinand, the heir-apparent to the throne of Austria-Hungary, and his wife. I did not know, and no one else did, that this crime would immediately unleash World War I, into which would be sucked all the "civilized" governments of the world. Turkey would take advantage of the situation to plan and execute history's first genocide on the Armenians living in Turkey.

CHAPTER 12

TO FENESSEH

Thus my first year in college came to its end.
I had no guarantee that I would have any more years of college.
The students and the faculty left for their homes in the neighboring or distant cities.

On July 15, 1914, in the company of five others, I boarded the train in Konia to Eregli to continue my travel from there in a horse-driven covered wagon to Fénésséh. I was heading towards the orphanage, because it was the only home I had known since 1902 as a child of seven.

My five traveling companions were Haigazoon Parseghian of Eregli, Giragos Gurunlian of Bor, Toros Barabian of Gurune, Gilbert Topalian of Hadjin, and a young lady whose name escapes me.

It was after midnight when we alighted from the train in Eregli. Haigazoon found his mother and sister waiting for him and left with them for home. Giragos also met his brother and traveled with him to Bor. The remaining four of us went to an inn to rest for the night, and in the morrow hire a wagon to take us the rest of our journey.

Early next morning Haigazoon came to assist us in the search for a conveyance, but nothing was to be found. To console us in our dismay he took us to his home to introduce us to his folks. After some entertainment he took us around the town, to the Armenian church, to the local school, and at about 4 P.M. to our inn. To our great joy the innkeeper told us that he had located an *araba* (covered wagon) that would take us to Evérék-Fénésséh. Immediately we hired it, and agreed to leave at 4 A.M. the next morning.

Haigazoon, the classmate of Gilbert and mine, was on hand to bid us goodbye. This farewell was the last, for I saw him no more.

Early afternoon our carriage, entering a beautiful highway lined on both sides with green trees, made its stop at the city of Bor. Classmates Mamas Haroutunian and Arshag Bedrosian, and schoolmates Haroutune Koyoumjian and Hmayag Markarian were waiting for us. Instead of acceding to their persistent pleadings to spend the night in their homes, we persuaded them to keep company with us in our inn as late as they cared to. Then we all took a stroll in their lovely city enjoying the sights, and then we went to their homes to pay our respect to their families. In the evening they, in company of more friends, came to the inn with gifts.

The ensuing conversation evolved around what means to employ to improve the educational and cultural life of the Armenian community. The need of a public library like the one in the college we had just left behind was emphasized. It was evident, and we were pleased to observe, that the burden of responsibility in respect to educating the youth, and elevating the standard of the community, was weighing heavily on our young friends. They were dedicated idealists, ready and willing to sacrifice themselves at the altar of service to their beloved home folk.

They were all on hand next morning at 4:00 when we started our journey. They accompanied us for a mile or two, reluctant to part with us. At last we boarded the carriage and they returned to their homes.

Two hours of journey took us to Nigdeh, but, before entering the city, we saw a man traveling on foot from Eregli to Evérék. This man, a Turk from Erzerum, a couple days before in Eregli had begged us to allow him to ride with us in our carriage and we had refused to grant his request, not because he said that he could not share the fare, but because we were uncomfortably overcrowded with our luggage and the four of us, including the young lady. But now, seeing him trudging on, bent under his back-pack and dragging his tired feet, we relented and invited him in, after making a hurried place for him in our narrow vehicle.

The late afternoon made us alight from our uncomfortable carriage in the courtyard of the infamous Arabli Inn, just a day's distance from our destination, Evérék-Fénésséh. The memory of the night I spent there the previous September came to torment me. But there was no escape. We had to stay there overnight to give the horses the rest they needed.

We were assigned to the only "guest room" available, on the ground floor. It did not have a door, but only a small opening for a window. The window had never seen a shutter, nor had seen glass. It is probable that the innkeeper did not even know what glass was. The earth floor was damp with the dung and urine of animals. The stench was sharp and cutting. The inn-keeper, a devout Moslem who seven times a day faithfully performed his ritual of *namaz* (prayer), considered it an insult to his religion to clean up the place for those who were not of his faith.

As soon as we laid our bed rolls on the dirt floor and stretched out for the night's rest, an army of innumerable tiny insects — flies, mosquitoes, fleas, lice, mice, and bedbugs — swarmed on us as if to welcome or initiate us into a secret "fraternity." Through the main opening, which served as an entrance, three large dogs skulked in and started to explore our food. (Dogs usually do not have any masters in Turkey. They multiply unhindered and are allowed to roam at will.) Then through the window, on floor level, a number of hens, ducks, another dog, and a cat made their way inside to make our acquaintance and to peck at or lick our hands, faces, and other bare spots on our bodies. The cat succeeded in tearing apart the cloth bag of madzoon and applied itself to enjoying it.

These animals were so fearless and shameless that no amount, no force of chase or kick would persuade them to leave. They would slink and hide in the dark for a while, and then boldly show up again to resume their exploration for food.

Oh, the bites and stings of the swarms of bugs — would ache painfully and swell up as high as peanuts.

At last we lost the war. The invaders forced us to flee the torture room and find refuge in two vacant carriages whose owners were Armenians.

As I, with my traveling companions, climbed into the carriage in the early dawn, the comforting expectation that the day's allotment of revolutions of the wheels would bring me to the end of my journey by evening made me promptly forget all the unpleasantness of the night at Arabli Khan.

The morning spent itself in monotone. Leaving Develoo Karahisar behind, the horses gaily trotted on, until at about midday we reached the vast Tchorak Valley and discovered that the entire valley had been inundated by torrential rains. The hitherto easy roll of the wheels gradually became arduous, and at a certain juncture the horses, veterans of many an unfortunate situation, found themselves powerless to pull the wheels out of the sticky mire that had sucked them up to their axles.

The driver, after weighing the seriousness of the situation, decided then and there to let his beasts have a little rest, and in order to coax and cajole them he offered them their feedbags. When he deemed that the period of "coffee break" for his horses had been long enough, he asked us to get out of our perch and give an assist to them by pushing and lifting the carriage as they began their strenuous toiling. With our concerted help and encouragement the valiant horses succeeded at last in extricating themselves and the carriage. Our clothes were soiled and our shoes weighted with "tons" of thick, sticky, gluey mud that resisted scraping and made it difficult to walk. The carriage bogged down in the morass repeatedly and each time we were forced to toil to free it.

At long last, happily leaving the sea of mud behind, we made it to Soysali, a village in the valley of Evérék-Fénésséh, where we washed ourselves and cleaned our clothes as best we could. At 5:00 P.M. the carriage made its final stop at the Khan in Fénésséh. Friends were waiting to greet us.

Leaving my traveling companions at the Khan, I wended my way to the orphanage. But before leaving, I assisted Gilbert Topalian in finding two beasts for him and the girl to continue their travel to Hadjin next morning. But for Toros Barakian to travel to Gurune no vehicle or beast was available. Two days later he went to Caesarea (Kayseri) in the same carriage.

Fénésséh in 1914

As mentioned before, I was one of the three students of the first graduating class of the American High School in Fénésséh. On my return there after a year in college, I was privileged to witness the second (and forever the last) graduation exercises of my beloved high school, in which I was scheduled to teach in the fall.

The elite of the Armenian community, the faculty of the schools of the town, and high government officials came to the school to listen to the oral examinations of the graduating class in different studies, and were impelled to commend the high caliber of teaching. After several days of public examinations the long-awaited commencement exercises were held in the local church, where, in the presence of special guests, each of the three graduating students delivered a speech of his own in three different languages.

One couldn't but be proud and happy.

One day in 1966 a letter mailed from Leninakan, Soviet Armenia, reached my hand. The writer, whose name at first did not ring a bell in my memory, said that he had learned of my whereabouts from Boyajian's *General History of Hadjin* and *Nor Hadjin* monthly, and had obtained my address from a mutual friend now living in Chasse, France (Boghos Abrazian of Hadjin, to whose first-born son I had become godfather in 1920, in Adana, Cilicia).

My correspondent reminded me that he, Manoog Sermayehsizian, was one of the 1914 graduates from the Fénésséh High School, and that I had helped him in preparing his commencement oration. He recalled this "help" with "gratitude," and with "nostalgia" those carefree days of our young manhood in Évérék-Fénésséh, one of hundreds of towns and villages sprawled on the luxuriant and fertile outskirts of the snow-clad Mount Erjias (12,848 feet). He further mentioned that our paths again crossed after our miraculous return from the Genocide to Adana in 1920, when, as he claimed, I found him a sorely needed job.

Excursion to Saint Garabed

Miss Nora Lambert[26] was the acting president at this time because of the absence of "Badveli," the Reverend T. F. Barker, who was on a speaking tour in England and the United States. Miss Lambert assigned me some duties until the opening of school in October. I should tutor the Reverend and Mrs. Storms[27], a young couple who had recently arrived at the mission, copy hymns translated into Armenian along with the music for Mrs. Storms's use, and act as their companion and interpreter on official visits to and from government officials.

On overhearing on a hot July day the discussion between a couple of retiring former teachers about going on a short excursion to Saint Garabed in a day or two, I expressed my wish to join them. They readily agreed to have me. The occasion was the Feast of Vartavar (Transfiguration), which fell on Sunday, July 26 that year, when pilgrims from provinces far and near in caravan after caravan would gather at the monastery, famed for the generosity of its patron saint in granting their voiced and unvoiced wishes. Burdened with the weight of vows, and laden with modest or rich gifts to the saint, men and women undertook these pilgrimages to make thank-offerings and sacrifices of animals, or to petition the saint to grant healing to the diseased, a lover to the homely and overlooked, a son to the barren, prosperity to the destitute, etc.

The purpose of my joining the trip was, beside grabbing the opportunity to see this great traditional festival of the Armenian Church for the first time in my life, to pay a visit to my aunt Gulenia Alajajian in Kayseri. In a former correspondence I had learned that she had lost her husband a few months earlier.

In the pitch darkness of the early Friday morning Haroutune Kalfaian woke me up. Soon the other two companions were at the gate, already on their mounts. Immediately all four of us, the two former teachers H. Kalfaian and Roupen Esayian, and Roupen Markarian the minister, started on the road towards Erjias, and after skirting it to continue to Zinji – Dereh – Talas – Kayseri – Efkereh – Sourp Garabed.

This road was not altogether unknown to me as I had been on it twice before. In the fall of 1911 for the first time I had trudged on foot to Zinji Dereh, Talas, and Kayseri and returned the next day, with seven other companions from the orphanage. The occasion was one of unprecedented rebellion against a small, tyrannical teacher-overseer. The second trip on this road was made in October of the following year, in a carriage. All three students of the senior class, Toros Pushian, David Gedigian, and I, went to the American Hospital in Talas to have eyeglasses fitted.

In the afternoon, while driving our mounts through the streets of Talas I spied a lad from Hadjin, from whom I learned that about 150 families had made the pilgrimage from Hadjin and were camping in the church square. Immediately we headed for the church and found many old friends and acquaintances.

Talas

My colleagues Kalfaian and Esayian were both graduates of Tarsus College, and knew a friend who had just graduated from their Alma Mater. So, Mr. Setrak Evkhanian became our gracious host for the time we chose to stay in the town. After dinner he had four more beds prepared for us on the rooftop of his house, from which we could watch the fireworks and hear the music of the festivities the government was providing in celebration of the declaration of the constitutional government in 1908.

After breakfast next morning we made the tour of the "city built on twin hills," visited the churches, the girls' and boys' schools, and the hospital. We climbed the belfry of the Church of St. Toros to see the great well donated by the Talas-born Armenians living in the United States. The road to the boys' school was hedged with beautiful gardens and green, cluster-laden vineyards. The imposing school reigned over the panorama from a height as if it were a castle. No wonder Sultan Hamid coveted this commanding parcel of land and the buildings on it, and by direct orders or devious machinations connived to confiscate it, but the Absolute Monarch was defeated in his nefarious scheme by the adamant rebuff of the fearless director, the American missionary Mr. William Wingate. This was long years ago, before the Red Sultan was deposed in 1909.

Mr. Levon Giridlian of Pasadena told me that during the massacres of 1895 he, as a child, witnessed that thousands of terrified Armenians found shelter in the Kayseri American Mission Compound. When blood-thirsty Turks, with chilling shouts invoking the rewards of their Allah and his "only" prophet Mohammed, charged towards the mission, intent on invading the buildings to plunder, rape, kill, and burn, Mr. Wingate, young, tall, and lanky, calmly walked out to the mob, holding an American flag in his left hand and a revolver in his right, and challenged any one to come near him. None dared, and thousands of lives were saved by his heroic stand.

And now, this same Mr. Wingate graciously volunteered to guide us through the buildings and the grounds, explaining, describing, reminiscing.

Mrs. Jane Smith Wingate, like her famous husband, and also like her illustrious father, Dr. Eli Smith, linguist and one of the group of translators of the Bible into modern Armenian, and president of the college at Marsovan, was well versed in both modern and classical Armenian language and literature. She was born in Marsovan and went to local school with Armenian students. She fell in love with the Armenian classics, and translated into metered English St. Nerses Shnorhali's (1101–1173) *Hisus Vordi* (Jesus, Son), a book of metered prayer. Mrs. Wingate published this translation in New York in 1947.

Talas was the vacationer's paradise, with its pleasant and healthful weather, pure and cool water, beautiful scenery, and historic spots.

In the afternoon, the Reverend Mibar Muncherian, the minister of the local Evangelical church (in former years, minister of the Fénésséh church), came to the house to pay us a courtesy visit, along with many other visitors. He quickly channeled the conversation to religion, and continually talked about a book he had just published, *The Existence of God*, and the second volume he had planned to write soon. The arguments he advanced did not impress me much, because the year before I had a course in college on the same specific subject, using a textbook, *Is there a God?*

After the evening meal we were invited to attend a debate in the Cultural Club. Muncherian was the chairman. The debate was on "Who bears the heavier burden of mankind, the man or the woman?" The team defending the feminine side included our host, Mr. Evkhanian, and the proprietor of Mazhak publishing house. The defenders of the masculine side were two young men newly graduated from St. Garabed Seminary.

Although the team defending the feminine viewpoint won the debate, the dispute continued. A young lady stood up to add that because of the pangs of childbearing and rearing, the woman is the bearer of heavier loads in life. Immediately a young man from the St. Garbed faction jumped on his feet to refute Miss Nelly's contention. "If," said he, "the woman is the bearer of heavier loads in life, why is it that Our Savior Jesus Christ, who bore the weight of all human sins, was not born a woman?"

This sudden burst of unique inventiveness evoked a general merriment.

Next morning, after bidding our host adieu, we mounted a hired carountza (a two-horse carriage), the taxi of the era, and in an hour arrived at Kayseri. Temporarily leaving my companions to rest a while in an apothecary's, I followed a guide to find my aunt's residence. Entering a large courtyard, I was directed to her apartment. She was seated next to her young son in front of an enormous loom weaving a gorgeous Oriental rug. Her daughter, Rachael, fourteen, was engaged in the same kind of work in front of a smaller loom. A girl of three, Azniv, was playing on the earthen floor nearby, and baby boy, not quite a year old, was in the cradle. This was the whole family now that her husband had died a couple months earlier and her eldest son, Krikor, a year or so older than I, had left for the U.S.A. several months before his father's death.

Seeing a stranger enter the open door, all three jumped up from their toil to welcome the visitor. When my aunt recognized me, she fell on my neck and welcomed me with tearful kisses. In order not to let her go out of her way to detain and entertain me in her customary lavish way, I told her that I had only a few short minutes to visit her, as I was on my way to Sourp Garabed in company of three others, and that, on my return from the pilgrimage, I could spend a day or two with her before returning to Evérék. Thereupon Aunt and her son Stephen (a year or two younger than I) persuaded me to detach myself from my mates and go to Sourp Garabed later that day with Stephen.

Finding my companions at the Apothecary's Stephen and I informed them of our plan. They immediately left for Sourp Garabed, leaving us to return home.

My unexpected stepping into their life made the drab day one of festival. The urgency of the looms was unheeded. They were abandoned. At once Aunt plunged into preparing various kinds of pastries and dishes at which the women of Kayseri were unequaled. And Rachael, the embodiment of shyness, gentleness, and sweetness, busied herself in the impossible task of ridding the paneless and screenless apartment of swarms of insurgent flies, savage mosquitoes, and stubborn insects.

Without losing a moment, Stephen took pride in getting possession of me. On the same morning he took me through his city for sight seeing.

Caesarea, the historic Cappadocian metropolis, is about one hundred miles southeast of Ankara, the modern capital of Turkey. It had, at this time, a population of between 60,000 and 72,000, of which only 20,000 were Armenians. There were thousands of Greeks, but no Jews. The Jews could not secure a toe-hold, because, as it was said, in business the Armenians of Kayseri were more clever than the Jews. The present population must be far more than the 1960s census, 102,795. According to the legendary History of Armenia, written by the 5th century historian Moses of Khoren, Aram, a valiant prince of the Haigazian dynasty, invaded and conquered Cappadocia. He stationed an army in the city of Mazaca, the city his lieutenant Mazhak (Mushag) had built. Mazaca in the course of centuries was given the names of Eusebes by the Greeks, Caesarea

To Fenesseh

Mazaca or Caesarea Cappadus by the Romans (because of repairs made to it by Julius Caesar) and Kayseri by the Turks.

During its occupation by Dikran the Great thousands of Armenians were settled in Caesarea and the neighboring regions.

Sourp Krikor, the immortal illuminator of the Armenian state in the faith of Christ, was brought to this city as an infant and brought up into manhood. It was here that his two sons Aristages and Virtanes were born. It was here, in Caesarea, that he was ordained and consecrated to be our first Catholicos, and, in later years, his two sons were consecrated for the same office as his successors.

And now, as Cousin Stephen was taking me around business and residential sections, government post office telegraph centers, and the public park with its shade trees, benches, flowers, wells, and water wheels, I could not but muse: Were these Turkish-speaking Armenians the remnant from the days of Aram? or Dikran? or Gagik? or of the later Roupinian dispersion? And immediately I assured myself that no one had the right to blame them for replacing their "Adam and Eve Spoken Armenian Language" with the unloved Turkish, because the Janissaries, in the centuries of their unbridled outlawry, found pleasure in cutting out the tongue that spoke any other language.

At 3 o'clock on the same afternoon, Stephen and I hired a carountza for Sourp Garabed. It did not occur to us to be displeased when we discovered that there were already three other young pilgrims in it bound for the same destination. A journey of three hours brought us to Efkereli, and shortly after, the trotting horses halted at the main gate of the monastery, having ploughed through a dense crowd occupying the vast courtyard. Unnumbered families of men, women, children, donkeys, sheep, goats, and chickens were milling around in search of an empty space to camp. Outside the courtyard the outlying orchards, fields, slopes, and valleys were swarming with happy, boisterous people. It was evening mealtime. Some were cooking. The aroma of rich pilaf and shish kebab, with skewered onions, green peppers, tomatoes, and tender eggplants filled the air. Some others were occupied with slaughtering sacrificial animals. Yet others were drinking and making merry, telling stories, playing rustic reed flutes, striking with their palms and fingertips at rim-jingled tambourines, singing, dancing, and quarreling. All of a sudden Stephen and I found ourselves all alone in this Babylon. We needed a place to sleep, and finding accommodations was next to impossible, because we knew no one there.

But a happy thought flashed through my mind: to head towards the sector designated for the people of Hadjin, with the dim hope that an old acquaintance would be found to help us. Lady Fortune smiled at us in the person of our Aunt Satchian, grandfather's sister. (I have already made mention of her, relating the idyllic experience I had with her flock of goats one August night on a desolate mountain.)

With a gush of affection at the sight of the two sons of her two nieces she rushed to embrace us. After receiving satisfactory news of our mothers and the casual purpose of our presence she insisted and "persuaded" us to come back at each meal time and join her table. We thought it was an insult to her hospitality to resist the "persuasion." She was here, she said, with her younger son, Haji Bob, two young daughters, Haiganoush and Zabel, and her daughter-in-law, Mariam. "Neneh" Satchian confided in us the reason for this pilgrimage: to fulfill a vow she had made for her eldest son Asadoor's safe return form the Balkan War, but also for her daughter Peprooni's restoration to health after a critical sickness.

In our roamings in the Hadjin camp, I was surprised to find all three of the recent graduates of the high school who were still in Fénésséh when I left. Now they joined our wanderings to see the grounds and to study the people of different ways of life, although they were all Armenians come from different regions.

After bidding good night to our companions we stumbled upon our three companions with whom we had traveled in the afternoon from Kayseri. These friends invited us to their room and offered us beds to sleep on.

CHAPTER 13

THE FEAST OF THE TRANSFIGURATION

Sunday, July 26, 1914

Early in the morning we entered the cathedral through the widely-known elaborately ornate door which was, in a by-gone age, inlaid with exquisite nacre (mother-of-pearl) by an unknown Armenian artist. (This priceless door, with many other objects of museum value, was stolen by the Germans during World War I and sent to Germany. And the ancient, irreplaceable manuscripts, volumes, and scrolls of the Monastery's very rich collection of centuries were all robbed by the barbarous Turks, and used as wrapping papers in their shops and homes.)

We found the church tightly packed with pilgrims heavily weighted with vows, entreaties, and anguished hearts. Many worshipers were tear-drenched as the smoke of the burning candles and incense filled the vast interior with a thick odorous cloud, and the Divine Liturgy was plucking heart-strings. Unable to find any room to stand, we regretfully left the Sanctuary.

This was the historic Church of St. Garabed, the Forerunner of Christ, John the Baptist, the Son of the Barren, the burial place of the "greatest prophet." The French Orientalist Jean d'Arget and many church dignitaries and monks had their tombstones around the grounds.

Tradition persists that this monastery was built on the Mount of the Holy Cross by none other than the Apostle Thaddeus, the first evangel of the Armenians, and later rebuilt by St. Gregory the Illuminator. This walled enclave of culture and magnificence of architecture, miniature, illumination, manuscripts, spacious orchards and cattle was always the object of the Turks' envy and covetousness, and was too often subjected to Turkish attacks, destruction, pillage, and looting.

After leaving the devout pilgrims in their worship, Stephen and I, joined by some Fénésséh students, took a walk to nearby Efkereh, a tiny village sprawled on the face of a hill and lording it over a vast valley luxuriant with deep green orchards. In this Garden of Eden we refreshed ourselves with water which we drew out of a well with the overhead wheel (locally called *dolab*) and pail, and after roaming about for a while, we returned to the monastery. Our steps did not stop until we were in our beneficent Neneh's room, where she fed us with food and blessings.

Then we walked around in the orchard of the monastery. The people, after leaving the church service, had resorted to the cool shade of the trees to escape the searing heat of a July day. I found a walnut tree in a secluded spot and, sitting in its shade, jotted down a few notes in my diary. All at once a violent quarrel broke out between some drunks and gendarmes, but luckily it got settled through the intervention of a monk and peace returned.

At 5:00 o'clock the next morning, the second day of the popular Feast of Vartavar, I awakened my companions. After a light breakfast we all headed towards Sourp Taniel Vank (Monastery of St. Daniel), a distance of twenty minutes from Sourp Garabed. No pilgrimage would ever satisfy St. Garabed, we were told by unimpeachable authorities, if with a visit the nearby St. Daniel were not venerated.

We enjoyed a guided tour inside the beautiful little monastery. We learned that this Vank also was founded by St. Thaddeus, and repaired by St. Gregory, although an inscription above the door to the Sanctuary tells that Prince Osheen, an Armenian king, built it in the eleventh century. The grounds around contain the tombs of princes and other celebrities. The Vank was, once, very opulent, but vandals in frequent forays emptied it.

Then we followed our guide, on hands and knees, through an opening into a subterranean cave. The wearisome crawl ended at a room, dimly lit by an olive-oil lamp suspended from the ceiling. Here the guide, pointing to a spot, told us that the bones and relics of the patron saint were buried. The ground was holy, he assured his pilgrim audience, and he advised that a handful of the sacred soil would heal any disease and protect from any sickness. Some in the group were eager to get a pinch or two for themselves and their dear ones. I? At eighteen I had no fear of sickness, and I did not feel that I needed St. Daniel's protection.

The guide then led us to a well outside the cave, and drawing out some water he offered each one of us a drink, extolling its miraculous property to keep us in perfect health all through our lives. (At this writing I am more than seventy-nine years old. Who knows? Maybe I owe my health to that drink.) We all gave gifts to the Saint before we left the grounds.

St. Daniel and John the Baptist on this festive occasion received enough gifts to last them decades, but the ever-hungry Turk, having no respect for any saint, robbed them shortly after once and for all. After a lunch in Efkereh, we returned to the camp, and saw that the innumerable mass of pilgrims was astir packing to leave for their homes. One could easily conclude that these grounds, bustling with activity and festivity for the last several days, would be desolate in the morrow but for monks with a handy-man or two busy cleaning the debris left behind. So we hurried to bid a fond and grateful farewell to our beloved Neneh for all her kindnesses before she left with her family. Never forgotten are the tears she shed when she showered us with her last kisses.

The following year, the year of the infamous genocide conceived and executed by the Turkish government and people, Neneh Satchian and her family joined the Hadjin caravan to deportation. Her beautiful daughters and daughters-in-law were snatched from her protective arms. Her youngest son Haji Bob was drowned in the Euphrates. The male members of her family were separated from her and shot. Left all alone, bereft and broken, this gentle soul joined the about two million Armenian victims of the Genocide.

Neneh's husband, eldest son, and the two girls, however, survived the long years of living death, found each other, and returned to Hadjin to build a new life for themselves. But that too was denied them. The brigands of Mustafa Kemal Pasha (later the first president of Turkey) after besieging Hadjin and subjecting it for eight months to starvation, exhaustion, and defenselessness, stormed, pillaged, burned, and massacred it. Thus the survivors of this great family perished in the holocaust, except Asadoor, the eldest son who had lost his wife and children in the Genocide. Asadoor somehow managed a miraculous escape from the carnage that permanently put an end to historic Hadjin, founded in the fourteenth century.

Asadoor eventually remarried in Adana. At the evacuation of Cilicia he established his home in Chasse, France, and in 1947 he emigrated with his wife Sarah and five children to Soviet Armenia. He passed away in Erevan in 1968. His children — now doctor, writer, teacher, in responsible positions, have kept in touch with me occasionally, as he used to do from France.

Under the circumstances the only thing for us was to look for our own transportation. Stephen and I, luckily, spotted the same carriage that had brought us from Kayseri, and hired it for five passengers, including my three colleagues from Fénésséh.

This pilgrimage was the first and last I made to Saint Garabed.

We arrived at Stephen's home at 6:00 P.M. Aunt Gulenia spread a feast before her unexpected guests and invited them to stay for the night. After dinner, Stephen took us all for sightseeing around Kayseri. Early next morning the travelers left for Fénésséh, expressing thanks to the generous-hearted hostess and her son and the hope to see me in the fall at the opening of school.

CHAPTER 14

AUNT GULENIA AND HER INFAMOUS HUSBAND

Aunt Gulie, as she was known to us, was made to marry at the tender age of 13 like her only living sister before her — my mother. She was a young lady of gentle and docile nature, graceful of build, light of hair and complexion and blue of eyes. She married an attractive and promising young weaver of cloth, originally born in Marash, but at that time engaged in his trade in Hadjin. His name was Toros Alajajian. The name Alajajian indicates that his father and forefathers may have been weavers themselves.

Aunt Gulenia and Uncle Toros soon after their marriage moved to Marash, and in the course of time had five children. Their eldest son, Krikor, to escape forced military service in the Balkan War, left for the United States in 1913, where he changed his name to George Elgin. Uncle Toros passed away a year later, in the spring of 1914, leaving behind his widow and four other children — Stephen, Rachael, Azniv, and a baby.

Uncle Toros was the embodiment of courtesy, kindness, and good manners with everybody he met. At his own table, in the presence of company, or at business he was gracious, generous, solicitous, and impeccable. No one could be found in Hadjin, Marash, Kayseri, or anywhere else who did not like Master Weaver Toros Alajajian. But at home…he was altogether a different person, a Mr. Hyde, a malicious, vicious, spiteful, mean person, a devil, a Turk.

He was a master in the art of weaving, a skillful artist in creating designs of exquisite taste. In later years, applying his technic in another field of weaving, he became one of the widely recognized and sought-after masters in the designing, weaving, repairing, and dying of Oriental rugs of any type, size, pattern, and value. Kayseri was famed as a center of high-class rug weaving (as well as producing the most excellent basturma in the world).

Here in Kayseri, where Toros and his family had resided for more than a decade, he had erected in his house looms of different sizes on which he produced rugs faster than any weaver in the town. He set up a loom for each: the wife, the son and daughter, and even a small loom for the four-year-old girl. Constantly grumpy at home, he used to grumble about the baby in the crib for not being able to tie a knot a day at least, and instead, demanded attention and care, when all attention and care should be given to the looms. The nursing and cleaning of the child he invariably begrudged.

At no fault or sin of his, this unfortunate child was born an albino. Albinism is defined as a lack of pigmentation in certain cells of the skin, hair, and eyes, giving the victim a very white or pale appearance. And Toros, the father of this abnormal white bundle of life, otherwise perfect in all respects, vociferously rejected the poor child, accusing his wife in the meantime of having gotten him from someone else.

> Now as Jesus passed by, He saw a man who was blind from birth. And His disciples asked Him, saying, "Rabbi, who sinned, this man or his parents, that he was born blind?"
> Jesus answered, "Neither this man nor his parents sinned, but that the works of God should be revealed in him."

And I ask, why was this child born an albino? Was it the result of Toros's sins? Maybe so.

The decrees of this autocrat were as unalterable as those of the ancient kings of the Medes and the Persians. His "slaves" — the family members — were to rise in the morning as the darkness gave way to the timid light of the approaching dawn, and sit in front of their accursed looms to tie an exorbitant number of woolen or silken knots in a given period of time in order to earn the right to a morsel of food. He turned deaf ears and steel heart to their entreaties for food, drink, recess, or nature's call. He refused to unlock the food-cupboard, keeping the key in a deep fold of his waist-wrapper until the prescribed number of knots had been completed. Only then would he grudgingly allot them a miserly portion of bread, cheese, onion, and drink.

I have a sneaking suspicion (although I have no documents to prove it) that Toros was a scion of Monsieur Grandet, the notoriously miserly father of Eugenie Grandet, the tenderhearted heroine of Honore de Balzac's well-known novel. Grandet, as Balzac depicts him, carefully weighed, measured, and supervised bread, sugar, milk, and everything else that was consumed in his house.

Toros "Grandet" would bring out of the padlocked closet choice portions of cheese, basturma, eggs, and other delicacies to devour in front of the hungry and contemptuous side-glances of his "slaves." But they, at the end of their scanty repast, would resume their knottings as fast as the intensity of their half-hidden hatred would spur them.

He was aware of their anger and contempt, and he did not care.

He beat, cursed, and abused them trifling reasons. He punished them with the severest measures, even forcing them to stand in bare feet on ice or snow outside the locked door.

One winter day he ordered his wife to spend the night standing on the ice in front of the door. Some compassionate neighbors, to keep my shivering aunt from freezing, secretly gave her a shawl to cover herself with and a mat to stand on, and then came to her brother with the horrible news. Immediately my uncle Haroutune and his cousin Uncle Mugurdich rushed to the villain's house and at gunpoint threatened to kill him if he did not cease such atrocities.

Thereupon this unprincipled scoundrel rushed to the open window overlooking the Turkish sector and began shouting, "Moslems, come to the aid of another Moslem! The accursed giavours are killing me!"

The terror-stricken defenders had to vanish before the coming of the blood-thirsty Turks to the aid of the rogue who was not a Moslem at all.

In the latter months of 1913, Toros the Tyrant fell ill. His belly and limbs began to swell. Finally, he was forced to confine himself to his bed, from which he could not get up. But still he continued to issue orders about the number of knots. He still guarded the precious food-key under his belt.

At last exasperated and infuriated, Stephen, the eldest, left his seat in front of the loom and defiantly walked to his father's bed. Boldly he began to probe for the Key of Life. The sick devil was in no condition to shower fire upon such insolence.

Finding the mysterious key, Stephen opened the storehouse and generously distributed portions of food to his starving mother and sisters. They all ate to their hearts' content, paying no attention to the tyrant's impotent threats and curses.

The key was not returned.

Stephen declared a general strike against the looms.

The "tyrant," unable to bear such an open rebellion against his authority by his "slaves," instead of relenting and repenting, decided to die the same day.

The glad news of his death rapidly spread far and near. Neighbors, acquaintances, and friends came to Aunt Gulenia to celebrate the downfall of tyranny and the birth of liberty.

All these things and more were told me in the first few days of my stay in my aunt's house, some by neighbors, and some by Stephen. The second night Mariam, a garrulous and uncouth middle-aged widow living next door came in to see and chat with her neighbor's guest. She told me many things about her "hated" neighbor, and confessed that she felt a singular pleasure in running her needle deep into the dead man's flesh while she was sewing his shroud, to make sure that he was really dead and not faking.

Another night, Mariam deliberately attempted to engage me in a religious argument. Neither my aunt nor my cousin Stephen was interested in her harangue. They merely tolerated her. She was, it became clear, brought up in the faith of the Armenian Apostolic Church. And having been told that I was a product of Protestant education—evidently she hated the Protestants—with no appropriate introduction to her tirade, and with an exaggerated sense of superiority or show of sophistry, she abruptly began to accuse the Protestants of adulterating the essentials of the Christian faith.

"How?" I asked. "What have the Protestants done?"

She sternly scolded me—as if I was the culprit who originated Protestantism—for denying that the Virgin Mary was the Mother of God.

"You, as a *Porod*" (leper, a derogatory term used for a Protestant), she said, pointing a menacing finger at me, "are a sinner going directly to hell. How can you be so ungrateful that you accept and enjoy Jesus Christ, the Heavenly Food, God's Son (she made the Sign of the Cross upon mentioning the holy name of the Savior), and at the same time reject and

Aunt Gulenia and Her Infamous Husband

scorn the golden receptacle, the platter of the Heavenly Treasure, Mary, the eternally virgin Mother of God?"

Stephen, as the new head of the family since the death of his tyrannical father, had tasted the sweetness of freedom and independence. He loved making plans for my enjoyment for as long as I stayed in his house. The dreaded looms, the symbol of "slavery," were all dismantled, except the largest one on which a silk rug of exquisite artistry was in the stage of completion, and at which the whole family loved to work at will and whim, with no despot overhead to drive them.

Stephen would take me wherever his fancy would lead, to friends, weavers, stores, churches, schools, parks, and historic spots. We both were as carefree as birds, because Aunt Gulenia was the personification of indulgence. We had a world of our own to enjoy, and remained uninformed of what was going on in the world outside. All my conscious life, a dozen years, had been spent in an orphanage where I was known only by a number, and now here, at my aunt's, I was being treated as an important person. Why should any event outside this rare period of worthiness and notice matter to me? So we were constantly out, making the rounds of the city, hopping from branch to branch like a couple of sparrows free of trouble or anxiety.

On one of such carefree days (August 3, 1914) I decided to hire a donkey to travel to Fénésséh. When we came to the market place for this purpose, we saw a group of five fine donkeys with an attendant nearby. I asked the man if he would hire out one of them to take me to Evérék-Fénésséh in a day or two. But before the owner opened his mouth, these donkeys, all five of them, raised their heads, opened their mouths, and let out a chorus of measured brays and stopped at the same moment, as if an orchestra conductor was giving the cue. Who was the stupid one who called these elegant creatures stupid?

The owner of the donkeys, with a forced laugh, said that the donkeys had already given their answer. Then he continued in a melancholy note that a short time ago, on the same day, the crier had broadcast that from now on all means of transportation in the whole country, including donkeys, were promptly appropriated by the government, and those violating this law should be severely punished.

"And I don't understand what all this means," he added, shaking his head.

Leaving the donkeys with their master to mull over their mutual woes, we shouldered our own woes and hurried away to Stephen's godfather in the Covered Market to seek information concerning the political situation. All of a sudden the gaudy bubble of my private world burst, when Sahag Agha confirmed the town crier's announcement about the confiscation of all kinds of animals and the abrogation of the right to travel. He further informed us that a war had started between Austro-Hungary and Serbia, and the Turkish government had decided to take drastic measures for the country's safety by calling up all the male population between the ages of eighteen and sixty for military service.

Fear with a sudden force seized me. I was almost eighteen, neatly dressed, bespectacled, in the prime of youth. Any of many unscrupulous and mean officials would love to seize and drag me to a filthy concentration center before sending me to service.

Sahag Agha advised us both to stay out of sight, and meanwhile, he said, I should try by any means to get back home to Fénésséh. Stephen and I mustered a little courage and decided to make the rounds of all the khans he knew to hire a carriage for my travel immediately. But none could be had at any price. We learned that carriages, vehicles of any sort, horses, camels, cattle, and water buffalo were impounded indefinitely under the threat of imprisonment or death for both the driver and traveler in case of violation.

Returning home, I explained the unusual situation to Aunt Gulenia, and she assured me that as long as I chose or was compelled to stay, she would treat me as one of her children.

The next day Hagop Agha, the elder of the sector where our house was, came to see me. He told me that the shops, stores, and all sorts of business places in the city were closed, men were being apprehended and pressed into service after spending undetermined length of time in jails and concentration camps, and, he also said, that there would be a great scarcity of goods, foodstuffs, and communication. He strongly warned us, Stephen and me, not to step out of hiding, and promising that he would watch over us he left.

Aunt Gulenia and Her Infamous Husband

Caesaraea, from an old book

The elder came again the next day with more disturbing news. The market place was empty: the donkeys were being seized from under the rider with no regard to age or position and men were destined for jail. The crier was continually "inviting" men, young and old, to surrender themselves to the government. Men and women of the neighborhood came to sympathize with me with words of comfort and advice.

In spite of the affection I was surrounded with in my aunt's family, still gloom was steadily drizzling over my uncertain condition each passing day. On one of these days Hagop Agha sent his son to escort me to his khan. On my arrival he introduced me to a sturdy old peasant, Omar Agha, who, after sizing me up with a piercing look, gave his consent to Hagop Agha to take me safely to Evérék. The innkeeper told me to pay the man a certain amount of money, and to trust him whatever happened or however long it took.

After a tearful farewell, I left Aunt Gulenia and her family to board Omar Agha's cart, pulled by two giant water buffaloes. Omar Agha made me lie down in the cart and covered me. When we started at 6:00 o'clock in the evening the squeak, for which carts of this sort were famous, was penetrating the atmosphere from every direction, making detection and arrest very easy.

After a while, the chirping of crickets and croaking of toads and frogs, intermingling with the music of the squeaking and creaking of the cart wheels, formed an unusual concert that had the soothing effect of a lullaby which put me to sleep, to sleep away all my fears and anxieties.

Omar Agha woke me up before the dawn. He had already unyoked the buffaloes and led them to their stalls. We were in front of a hut in a village called Asarjik. Once inside, he introduced me to his wife and ordered food. The inside was bare of any kind of furniture. Mrs. Omar Agha set on the bare earthen floor a pot of soup in which there was a generous quantity of boiled water, with pieces of squash floating on the surface and some wheat kernels resting at the bottom. We both sat on the floor around the soup. The gracious hostess handed me the only remaining broken spoon. We topped this sumptuous meal with dampened lavash (sheet bread).

After the meal Omar Agha spread himself on the floor and went to sleep, which was punctuated with various types of snores. Before he went to sleep he told me that all the day I was his house guest, and warned me not to step out of the door at all. Time weighed heavily on my hands. But I knew pretty well that a giavour does not engage in conversation with a Moslem woman. So I kept myself busy writing lines in my diary resting it on my knee, and reading a book I had in my pocket.

In the evening, after refreshing ourselves with the same feast we had in the morning, we began our journey, this time on a donkey. After an uneventful night we arrived before dawn at the American Mission in Fénésséh.

Omar Agha was as good as his promise.

CHAPTER 15

HOME AGAIN

I WAS GLAD at last to be back "home" in the orphanage from the perils of uncertainty away from home. I had not known and I did not have any home except the American Orphanage. But now, I was no longer considered one of its "children." I could expect safety only as a schoolmaster for the school year, if the menacing clouds cleared up in the political sky of the country.

The August days in Evérék and Fénésséh were as ominous and oppressing as those in Kayseri and all over the country. Tranquility, as we knew it, had vanished, not to return anymore. Men of all levels of life, living anywhere, city, town or village, men between the ages of eighteen and sixty, were ordered by criers to come to the seat of government in Evérék, and get registered.

And they hastened in fear of punishment, in the hope of getting done with the evil of forced registration and returning to their usual tasks until further notification. But the matter of registration was a farce. These unfortunate people were cruelly abandoned to their fate in the streets of the whole combined cities of Fénésséh and Evérék. They did not receive any show of welcome, care, or shelter, nor food, clothing, or medicine. They came from the outlying countryside, peasants bearded and bare foot, camping wherever they could, awaiting registration that did not take place.

The notes of my diary of those dismal days say:

They simply threw themselves down anywhere, under walls, trees, gardens, open fields, hugging their despair, poverty, hunger, fatigue, and lice. Under the burning sun of the day and the chilling wind and soaking rain of the night, the acrid waves of their fuming ire and curses against the irresponsible authorities responsible for their misery constantly pierced our ears in the Mission Buildings. And it pained the handful of woman missionaries that they could do nothing with their limited means to alleviate their misery.

Caravan after caravan these unfortunates were being marched to Kayseri, yet the streets and the church and mosque ground were teeming with new thousands.

The goods in the market place suddenly grew scarce and more costly. Imports from abroad stopped altogether. Banks closed their doors to business. The Mission unexpectedly found itself unable to cash checks. The banks refused to honor credit. Under these dire circumstances, the director of the mission decided to wire the vacationing "children" of the orphanage to stay where they were and not to return to Fénésséh until further notice.

On the afternoon of August 23, Friday, after returning to my room from a Turkish language class with the Reverend and Mrs. Storms, I noticed a gradual darkening of the brightness all around me. It suddenly dawned on me that this might be an eclipse of the sun. And so it was. I ran out, an immediately I rounded up some of the "children" and asked them to hold pieces of glass over the smoke of burning matches. We all watched through these soot-covered glasses while the moon hid the sun behind it. This was a unique experience for us.

Usually the people of Turkey, anywhere in the whole country, would fire shots at the evil Jinni to scare it away from vanquishing the life-sustaining sun. But no shots were fired this time. A legion of jinn had overtaken the world, and no amount of shots could drive them out.

After some time the sun emerged from behind the moon, victorious, not even a particle of its glory missing.

Sixty years later, at the writing of this chronicle, I reflect that this eclipse was a portent of what was in store for us Armenians of Turkey in the immediate years of the global upheaval: The Armenian race would go through the most barbaric genocide at the bloody hands of the Turk, but at the end, what little is left alive as a surviving remnant will emerge and grow brighter as the sun itself.

A few days later, before the ominous month of August was spent, the grim hand of the militarized government snatched my colleagues H. Kalfaian and R. Esayian, and dispatched them to the officers' school in Istanbul.

Home Again

Armenian merchants, tradesmen and field workers, teachers, heads of families of four or more, rich and poor, robust or sickly, brothers, fathers and sons, all waited, day in and day out, in front of the government office to be processed and sent away to unknown destinations.

A baker, the proprietor of three bakeries, was ordered to bake for the use of the military arm of the country, using his own stock and workers, all at his own expense, as his patriotic duty.

I knew a man who built a new house for his family of several children, and diligently stored his family's winter ration. The government confiscated what he had garnered, seized his workhorse, the only means of his living, and called him to service. I saw him that day, a sack with his belongings on his back, standing in the crowd waiting in front of the processing center.

In the motley rabble it was painful to see men with one arm, with one leg, blind in one eye, men with gaping sores, all ordered to leave their homes and loiter on and on.

"If this inhuman barbarity of the Turkish government were told in America, the people would feel entertained by hearing a funny story, a novel, a myth. They cannot understand or imagine that such acts could happen," said Mr. Storms to me at the time of his lesson. (A baby was born to Mr. and Mrs. Storms one of those days, and they named him Evérék.)

At that time I was totally ignorant of what all the turmoil was all about, and thought, as everybody else did, that very soon normalcy would return.

I did not know that the major world powers had been taking sides to wage a cataclysmic war: Great Britain, France and Russia as Triple Entente on one side, and Germany, Austria-Hungary, and Italy as Triple Alliance on the other.

I was not aware then that a couple of months earlier, on June 28, Archduke Franz Ferdinand, heir to the throne of Austria-Hungary, had been shot dead, his wife also with him, by a student at Sarajevo, in the Austrian district of Bosnia. This district was inhabited largely by Slavs who were not content under Austrian rule, and Austrians declared that

Serbia had fanned the unrest in Bosnia. They claimed that Serbia's anti-Austrian policy was responsible for the Sarajevo murders.

Later I learned also that the Austrian government had decided that Serbia's acceptance of eight demands and refusal of the other two in the ten-point ultimatum was unsatisfactory, and so, on July 28, she declared war on that country.

Germany declared war on Russia on July 31, and two days later on France.

On August 4 Great Britain declared war on Germany.

On August 23 Japan declared war on Germany.

Turkey joined the war in October on the side of Germany.

Italy, having changed sides, declared war on Austria on May 25, 1915, and on Turkey on August 21.

The United States joined the war on April 6, 1917.

CHAPTER 16

THREE KITTENS

Abruption and abrogation of whatever civil, social, educational, and religious rights one was supposed to have in a country like Turkey, which was founded and continued for centuries on the principles of absolutism, multiplied day after day. The prospect of opening the Mission High School grew dimmer as funds from America and England stopped. The orphans, cared for and educated by the mission since 1898, were placed in local homes or sent to relatives in the hope that they would be gathered again as the political clouds dissipated.

Mrs. Ada Barker, the wife of the president of the mission, advised me not to stay in Fénésséh anymore, but to go back to college for my sophomore year. Immediately my application for registration was wired to Jenanian College at Konia in case it was scheduled to open for the 1914–1915 school year. In response to Mrs. Barker's wire Dr. Haigazian, the president, wired back that the college would be opened on October 1, and the tuition for each semester would be ten liras (about fifty dollars) a semester.

A few days later a pitiful letter came to me from Toros Pushian in Hadjin, moaning that "all" his former colleagues would be leaving in three days' time for Fénésséh on their way to Jenanian College, and that only he would be left behind for lack of funds. He was frightened by the prevailing political uncertainty, and begged me to intercede with Mrs. Barker for a loan of college tuition. The good-hearted wife of our "father" Barker readily agreed that I should wire to him to come to Fénésséh with the others.

On the morning of September 24, 1914, a happy group of five "children" of the orphanage—Toros Pushian, Michael Vazejian, Michael Narinian, Antranig Balian, and myself—squeezed inside a carriage to start our travel to Konia. Four days later we arrived at the college, where we found my classmates of last year Arsham Loosinian, Yeran Sarvoni,

Apraham Ateshian, and Avak Mehagian of the senior class — all of Hadjin.

The inscription in George Kooshian's handwriting: Jenanian College Dormitory My bed was top corner, between left and right windows. 1913-1914

Turkey entered the war in October, declaring war on giants. A succession of gradually darkening days hung over the country, and no one could foresee or foretell the enormity of the destruction, bloodshed, barbarity, and genocide the Turkish government was planning to visit upon the Armenians.

Around the end of November a letter from my sister informed me that the Hadjin Girls' Orphanage had been closed and the orphans scattered, as the missionaries had already left for America. She wrote that our uncle Haroutune was going to take her to our mother in Adana.

Three Kittens

Another letter from Fénésséh shattered my hopes when I read that the American Ambassador in Constantinople had ordered all American institutions immediately closed or abandoned, all American citizens to leave for home. Fénésséh Mission was closed, the teachers had been forced into military service, the missionaries already gone, and the orphans dispersed. Fear in a sudden gush overwhelmed me. My school tuition for the second semester was not paid. Dr. Haigazian, the president of the college, informed me between Christmas and New Year that if I did not pay the tuition I must leave the campus on the first of February. Where was I going to get ten liras, the equivalent of fifty dollars? In my eighteen years I had never owned even one dollar. Konia was to me as a foreign land, with no friends except a few students as poor as I. The winters were severe in these parts of the country, with cold, rain, mud, snow, and ice. Outside the sheltering walls of the college was war, terror, hunger, and a fiercely cruel world. I had no one to turn to.

After leaving the president's office I immediately wrote a letter to my mother in Adana, explaining the situation and asking for a lira as travel fare from Konia to Adana. Mother was, at that time, working in the Ottoman Orphanage as its dietitian. This orphanage had been built by the governor, Jemal Pasha, shortly after the massacres in the vilayet of Adana, for the Armenian orphans the Turk had created.

As soon as she received my letter of despair, Mother took it to the director, Vahagn Effendi,[28] to have him read it to her. When they both became aware of my predicament, he, who held my mother in high regard and until then had not known that she had a son in college, suggested that they send me ten liras to continue my education and at the end of the school year I should come to Adana to teach in the orphanage.

Before the end of January, Mother's ten liras in my hand, I went to the president's office to turn over the sum to him, but he surprised me when he said that he had already received my tuition from Mrs. Barker in Italy. A few days later a note confirmed the good news that on her way to the United States Mrs. Barker had decided to pay my second tuition. This letter from Naples, Italy, restored the peace of my mind. (But I did not waste my mother's ten liras. I returned them to her when I went to Adana. This meager sum worked wonders in insuring the survival of our family of four in the years of exile. On one frantic occasion in the Syrian

Desert, a quarter lira, about $1.25, offered to the Turkish gendarme as a bribe, was large enough a sum to let the officer untie my wrists and to allow me to escape from death.)

After the two weeks Christmas vacation the classes were scheduled to open, but an order from the government forbade the opening until notified, on the pretext of an epidemic of typhus in the city. The school remained closed for two months. The day students and teachers were not permitted to come to the campus, and the boarding students were bored for lack of classes, amusement, or activity. During those two months of compulsory vacation there were few social or educational programs. On one occasion I was privileged to read a paper on the subject, "What did we gain at Avarair?" a battle fought by the Armenians and Persians in A.D. 451. On another occasion a debate was scheduled on the subject, "Art or Thought?" I teamed up with a student, the poet-laureate of the college, in defense of "Thought," while a classmate of mine, a poet himself, joined another in defense of "Art." The jury adjudged "Thought" the winner. I recall that another debate took place on "Is war really necessary?" To think that this dangerous debate was undertaken while despotic Turkey was desperately engaged in a universal war! At last on the first of March permission was granted for the reopening of the school, and the day students attended their classes. This period lasted only a month, because then Easter vacation started.

On one of these days I spied three newborn kittens in a corner of the kitchen. "O Mother Osannah," I said to the cook, "look, their eyes are not open yet."

"My Son," she said with the air of a wise counselor, "don't ever look at a newborn kitten that has not opened its eyes yet. If you do, you will never see happiness in your life."

"What will happen now that I have looked on them?" I asked half amused, half perturbed.

"This being your first offense," she laughed, "you will be deprived of happiness for a few years."

What a prophecy! Happiness truly eluded me for long years.

CHAPTER 17

THE SHAME OF HISTORY

ITTIHAD VE TERAKKI, the notorious political party that had held the helm of the Ottoman Empire since 1908, grabbed the opportunity presented by the coming of the war to rid the country of all foreign and alien elements and influences. The double murder at Sarajevo provided the occasion, with unhindered, irresponsible, unlimited excesses in ruthlessness, to launch a system of plunder and robbery. The expropriation and confiscation of properties, institutions, homes, shops, goods, foodstuffs, and livestock were directed towards everybody but the Turk.

Our Boys' Orphanage in Fénésséh, and that of the Girls' in Hadjin, along with scores of other orphanages and schools and thousands of humanitarian institutions all over the country, were ordered closed and the unfortunate inmates and workers thrown to the insensate winds. Foreigners were driven out of the country or incarcerated. Armenian men, young and old, were, by the tens of thousands, pressed into military labor battalions with no pay, no rations, and no accommodations for any physical need.

Under these nefarious circumstances it was a miracle that the withering breath of the government had yet not reached Jenanian College when it opened its academic year in the fall, as it had done every year since 1893. Students came as usual from far and near: Armenian, Greek, Serb, Bulgar, Syrian, Egyptian, and Turk.

Among the students there were only two Turks, sons of highly situated officials. I never learned which class they attended, what course they took, or how many years they were in the school, nor do I remember ever talking to them. They did not associate with each other, either. One of them kept himself always aloof, distant, repelling; while the other one was friendly, affable. This second young man would regularly attend church services on Sundays, sit for the school's opening prayer period every morning, and gustily join in the singing of all the hymns the students sang. I remember watching him with an askant look while he sang with us a favorite hymn:

> Somebody did a golden deed,
> Proving himself a friend in need.
> Somebody sang a cheerful song,
> Brightening the sky the whole day long.
> Somebody fought a valiant fight,
> Bravely he lived to shield the right.
> Was that somebody you?

Half a century later I learned from a reliable source that both of these young Turks had been planted amongst us as spies, and they subsequently brought great harm to the college and the Armenian population of Konia.

The school year continued to spend itself away in seeming tranquility. Nobody was prophet enough to foresee what poisonous draught was brewing for the Armenians to drink. The rulers of Turkey were ruminating sinister schemes in the dark: the wholesale murder of an ancient nation whose homeland the Turk had invaded and appropriated five centuries before.

One day in early April an incredible bit of news was afloat among the students that a number of men of Zeitoon, an Armenian city in the Taurus Mountains of Cilicia, had been brought to far-off Konia and dumped in a Turkish khan not far from the college. In the company of a couple of my fellow-Cilicians I went to see them and learn the reason why they had been brought there.

The spectacle was heart-rending.

Once proud and independence-loving men of Zeitoon who had won the admiration of Napoleon by their dauntless spirit and victorious stand against the onslaught of Turkish armies bent on subjugating them were now crushed, broken, dispirited, and dumped like rubbish all over the filthy place. They were denied food, drink, toilet facilities, or the right to step out of the filthy premises, which were infested with lice, fleas, cockroaches, and rats.

"What has happened to the men of Zeitoon, the pride of all Armenians, the invincible Zeitoon? Why are you here in this miserable state and not in your formidable mountain-holds?" I brought myself to ask in agonizing accents.

"We are here in this condition," answered one of them painfully, "because we are fools and dupes, and not the 'Valiant Men of Zeitoon' you used to sing about for years. We believed a lie, unlike our fathers and forefathers, and surrendered our firearms. And that is the reason we are here."

"How did that happen?" I asked, and he answered:

"In the past we would never believe the word of the Turk, no matter how flattering and full of promises. Their oaths were lies to us. So we never bowed to them, gave no quarter, and asked none from them. That way we enjoyed our independence. But when our Catholicos (head of the Church in the See of Cilicia) came to us in our fastness and begged us tearfully to give in to the government's demand and disarm to insure the political safety of millions of Armenians within the country, we obeyed him despite our deep-rooted suspicion of the wily Turk. The beloved Catholicos offered us the unrestrained lavish promises of complete clemency on the part of the government, which the government had no intention of honoring. As soon as we disarmed and turned over our weapons to the government, our men were separated from their families, divided into small groups, and exiled to different parts of the country."

At the Sunday morning breakfast, May 16, 1915, Dr. Jamgotchian, the vice president, announced the shocking, unbelievable news that Dr. Haigazian, the president, had been arrested at midnight and immediately exiled in company of all the leading Armenians of the community. He exhorted the student body to remain calm and continue as if nothing had changed. But four days later, on the 20th, a harsh order from the government demanded that the institution immediately disperse the students and turn over the whole property to the government to be used as a military hospital. Meanwhile Dr. Jamgotchian, the professors, and the senior students were conscripted into service.

I left Konia the next day and joined my mother, sister, and brother in Adana. It was May 28, 1915.

Mother, as a young widow with an infant in her arms, after placing her two tender-aged children in the orphanages, had been offered the opportunity to work in the same institution now as a laundress, then seam-

The Reverend Dr. Armenag Haigazian. He was arrested and marched into the desert, where he died in 1921.

stress, ironer, and nurse. Later, in 1906, she was appointed cook, which position she filled faithfully until the autumn of 1911. It was at this time that the Boys' Orphanage was transferred from Hadjin to Fénésséh. I was one of the last to leave Hadjin, having finished my sophomore year.

Mother, being out of a job, was glad to accept a call from Adana to become the head cook in the Ottoman Orphanage, where Armenian orphans were being cared for under an Armenian director, Mr. Vahagn Datevian, and an Armenian staff. She took her youngest son, Setrak, now nine years old, with her. In the summer of 1913 she and her child returned to Hadjin for a brief vacation, at which time I joined her after having graduated from the new high school of the American Orphanage in Evérék-Fénésséh. In September she returned to Adana to resume her position, and I to Fénésséh and from there to college.

And now that the threat of political upheaval had interrupted my education and forced me to come to Adana, I thought I would find peace and safety and an opportunity to teach in the Ottoman Orphanage, where my mother was safe with my sister and brother sheltered under her protective wings. Instead of that hope, a rude awakening was in store for me. I did not know that the Terror that had gripped the country had also infected Adana.

In the train from Konia to Bozanti, in the coaches from Bozanti to Tarsus, during our stay of three days in Tarsus College as Dr. Christie's guests, and finally in the short train ride from Tarsus to Adana, several of my schoolmates were traveling with me, some bound for Hadjin, and a few for Adana. Of these, Toros Pushian and Michael Vayejian expressed their wish to see their "Mother Sarah" of orphanage days in Hadjin and offer her their respects before going on to their relatives. So I invited them to ride with me in the same coach I had hired to take us to the well-known Ottoman Orphanage.

It was 3 o'clock in the afternoon when we three settled in the carriage. Before the coachman had time to crack his whip to make the horses start a young man of about twenty approached us, and said:

"Excuse my boldness, Sir, but may I ask where you are coming from?"

"From Konia," I answered. "From Jenanian College."

"Your name, please," he asked again.

"Kevork Barouyr," I answered.

"Where is your coach going now?" he persisted.

"To the Ottoman Orphanage," I said, "because my mother is the cook there."

The young man jumped into the coach, shook hand with me, and ordered the coachman to disregard my order for the Ottoman Orphanage and drive to the Tuz Bagh sector in Adana. Before I could collect my senses, this young man said that his name was Aram Dirtadian, the son of Mother Dirouhi, the second cook at the orphanage, and that his mother and mine had both left their posts the day before and were now living together in a rented house in Tuz Bagh. To verify what he was saying, he produced a card I had mailed to Mother eight days earlier to announce my coming to her. He said that my card had reached Mother that very noon, and she had sent him to the station to find out when the train would arrive. And now, he said, when he saw several young men leaving the train and hiring coaches, he became curious, and when he heard me

Annig Derghazarian

giving orders to the coachman to take us to the Ottoman Orphanage he became convinced that I was the young man he was looking for.

We arrived at the house where these two mothers, Aram's and mine, were expecting information about the train schedule. But they were delighted, instead, to see a carriage stop in front of the house, and Aram bring with him three young men.

My mother ran towards me and in a shower of tears and kisses embraced me. Then recognizing the other two as her "Hadjin orphanage sons" she welcomed them. At that moment my sister and brother Setrak rushed towards me.

As we three students were made comfortable on cushions laid side by side in the parlor Mother introduced us to some of her visitors who had left the orphanage the day before, when most of the working staff had been discharged. Among those introduced was a small, delicate girl of twelve or thirteen years. "This is Annig Derghazarian," she said. "You can consider her your second sister." Annig was also one of those turned out of the orphanage. This girl was destined to be my wife fifteen years later in the United States and by and by the mother of our four sons. She often recalled with a mischievous relish our first providential meeting, and would tell me that when she saw at that memorable hour three young college students sitting together in that little parlor of the Tuz Bagh sector of Adana she pestered her "Sarah Mairig" (Mother Sarah) to point out her "brother." And Mother handed her the tray of three demitasses of Turkish coffee, and introduced her to us as she served us.

Annig, my "new sister," found time to visit us every now and then throughout the three months of our stay in Adana before we were forced to join the uprooted and exiled Armenian populace. I knew nothing about her because of lack of interest on my part. I learned later, when she became my wife, that she had no father or mother, having lost them in the 1909 massacre in Adana. She, as a child of five, and a younger only brother were found in the streets together and taken into the orphanage. When she left the orphanage, at the time she was visiting us, she was taken in by foster parents, Yervant and Ripsimeh Kalpakjian. This family had no children for thirteen years, but a year later they had a son, and then a daughter also. The man was an engineer in the employ of the Germans, who were feverishly building a railway to tie Berlin with Baghdad, the oil-rich Middle East.

As the new member of the Kalpakjian family she was taken to Constantinople and placed in a school.

She never experienced the tortures of deportations from one place to another, as my family did. After graduating from her school she worked as a registered nurse in Greece from 1922 to 1928. In 1930 I went to Havana, Cuba, where she had come two years earlier, married her, and brought her to Pasadena on May 1, 1930.

A cafe on the Seyhan River by the Stone Bridge, from a book published in 1879.

CHAPTER 18

TAHIR EFFENDI

DURING THE NEXT FEW DAYS after my arrival in Adana, I came to learn why the wholesale expulsion of the Armenians from the Ottoman Orphanage had taken place. A few weeks earlier a number of police officers had invaded the orphanage, seized Vahagn Effendi, the director, led him to prison, and confiscated all his effects — clothes, records, books, everything. Then a Turkish director was brought in, who immediately began a systematic purge by expelling all the teachers, the cooks, the helpers, and the older orphans, and replacing them with Turks.

On several occasions in the months before my exile I paid a visit to the prison either to bring Vahagn Bey fresh laundry, or food, or news. He was treated by his keepers as a prince because of his high standing with his bosom-friend Governor Jemal Pasha, one of the then three all-powerful dictators of Turkey (Enver — Talaat — Jemal). But in the fall, after Adana had been completely vacated of its Armenian populace, he was hanged at the order of his political colleague of long years and intimate friend, the Governor, Jemal Pasha.

The owners of the house Mother and her friend had rented and in which we had lived for about a month returned from exile through a false reprieve and wanted their house back. We had to move out, and we knew not where. But we were fortunate that on June 10 we were able to move to the house of the Abuna[29] of the Chaldean church, who was planning to go on a vacation for the hot summer month and was looking for a reliable family to occupy it free until he returned in September. Aunt Naomi Malian, Mother's cousin's wife, let us know about this opportunity. She lived across the street from the Chaldean church and was a friend of the good priest, the Abuna. So she made the arrangements with him and let us meet him, after which the Abuna left on his vacation. The next morning we moved in. The compound had walled-in living quarters and a large courtyard with a well of fresh water. We lived in this house in the Kara Soku sector from June 10 to September 6, when we were deported.

My constant search for a job was as futile as finding bread in the heart of a stone. Jobs or positions were not to be had at any price. A job for a member of an outcast race that was condemned to annihilation would be as genuine a miracle as Peter's fishing a coin out of the belly of a fish.

But on a lucky morning the miracle happened.

On the last day of July of this portentous period Uncle Hampartzoum Malian took me to a Turkish restaurant on the banks of the Seyhan River, in the exclusive Turkish section of the city. Leaving me at the door of the hostile environment he boldly walked in, and after a few minutes returned to usher me in. I found myself facing a middle-aged Turk, short in stature, stout in build, and with a kind of composure and serenity that is seldom found in a Turk.

"Mehmed Tahir Effendi," said Uncle to the Turk, "this is the young man I told you about. His name is Kevork."

The Effendi silently sized me up from his seated position with a sweeping gaze, and then nodded his approval of me, after which Uncle left with a "Thank you."

"I am Mehmed Tahir Effendi, as you heard from your uncle," said he in a gentle voice. "I am the proprietor of 'Turan Locantasi' (restaurant). I must tell you right now that Turan's dining clientele consists of civil and military officers of the government. I am employing you to serve at the tables. You will eat here and will be paid a small amount of wages at the end of the month."

A pleasant sense of amazement and astonishment replaced my initial apprehension of the hostile Turkish environment when my new master led me to a corner, set some food before me, and then showed me the duties he expected of me.

In those days the Turks used the Arabic alphabet.

I was greatly surprised when I found tucked inside my diary a piece of paper which must have been a letterhead.

Under the Turkish emblem of the crescent and star it reads:

Turan (over the scratched word *Afiyet*) *Locantasi*
Seyhan nehri sahitinde

Tahir Effendi

hususi yemek salonu dur
Mudiri Mehmed Tahir

Translated,

    Turan Restaurant,
    on the bank of River Seyhan
    Special food salon
    Director Mehmed Tahir

At night when I told Mother about my miraculous employment and kind treatment at the hand of a Turk whom we had never seen before, she too wondered.

And I went to work day after day, fearing that each one would be my last. Because, far from being an expert in this line of service, in such an overcharged atmosphere, I would, sometimes, clumsily drop one of those exquisite pieces of gold-plated glass and china ware, or serve a mixed-up order. Yet, wonder of wonders, nobody ever scolded me, no one jumped at my throat. Not even Tahir Effendi, whom all the Turk waiters feared, would frown at me. From day to day I plunged into the depths of wonderment about this extraordinary tolerance, when tolerance of a person like me was considered a crime worthy of hanging.

A few days later Tahir Effendi introduced me to his son Shukru, a boy slightly younger than I, thin, spirited, and warm. He was the Effendi's only son, and, for that reason, pampered. He immediately attached himself to me, impelled by a mysterious tie. He came to the Turan Locanta almost every day after he met me, would not let me go about my duties, but would rather insist that we sit together on a bench facing the placidity or the turbulence of the river flowing before us and discus such academic subjects as religions, languages, literature, history, and foreign countries. He was thoroughly and fanatically a Turk, imbued with an intense hatred of the Armenian race whom he honestly believed to be subversive, traitorous enemies of his beloved fatherland. His conclusions, after each discussion, would invariably be that Moslem civilization, in all its facets, was far superior to any other. And who was I to dare to disagree with him? Did Daniel try to argue any point with the lions? What would be my fate if I ventured to tell him "the fatherland" he was boasting of was the fatherland of the Greeks and Armenians long before the existence of the Turk was ever known?

No day passed in this fateful August of 1915 that an endless stream of uprooted Armenians from all the western and northern Anatolian towns did not drag on tired, swollen, faltering steps across the stone bridge spanning the Seyhan. They were marching long distances, over mountains and canyons, exhausted, haggard, beggared, bedraggled. With bleeding heart I could recognize in this crushed and devastated mass of humanity the hollow, sallow faces of my erstwhile fellow orphans and classmates, a professor, a clergyman, a priest, even a nun.

My heart melted at the sight of these awful, woeful deportations to unknown destinations, but it never occurred to me that less than a month later the same grievous fate was waiting for my family, too.

It was on June 14, a little over two weeks after my arrival at Adana, that I was strolling around the train station, in the company of my classmate Toros, in the hope of earning a few elusive pennies. As the Constantinople train arrived, we both rushed towards it to help carry baggage. We noticed that from a wagon a group of distinguished-looking men stepped, down, followed by a couple of Turkish guards with their bayoneted rifles ready to be discharged at the least instigation Yervant. It was not hard for me to recognize three or four of them from their widely-known pictures in my school books. The leading personage was the princely Krikor Zohrab, a beloved author, editor, international lawyer, and one of the foremost members of the Ottoman Parliament. Another one of the group was Roupen Zartarian, teacher, editor, author, leader. Agnouni was the third one, orator, writer, political worker. The others were, as some one nearby pointed out, Vartkes, Khazhag, Minassian, Jangulian, all intellectuals of high standing. They had been apprehended in the middle of the night, snatched from their beds, and now were on their way to exile. Zohrab's brilliant intellect was forever extinguished in the following few days on the way to Ourfa by a fiend named Ahmed. This beast boasted with sordid delight that he had crushed Zohrab's head between two rocks. The others were promptly done away with, too.

Tahir Effendi

One cheerless day of the augured month of August Shukru caught me casting an agonized glance at the unending caravan of the wretched wrecks, trudging over the bridge a few steps away from the table where we were sitting in the open-air part of "Turan Locantasi." He, the Armenophobe Turk, good-heartedly admonished me to "at once accept the faith of Islam" by just confessing "*La ilahe ill Allah, Mohammed el ressul Allah*" (there is no God but Allah, and Mohammed is his prophet), and thus save myself from the fatal destiny of those "treacherous traitors." He rebuked me that such a good man as I "with so much knowledge about everything" would stubbornly cling to a "false religion that teaches to worship three gods" (the Trinity) and "honor *stavros* (the Cross) on which Isa (Jesus) was crucified for some wrongdoing of his." He accused me also for putting a divine value on a book of history written by and for "Yahoudies" (Jews).

I was touched by his concern for my welfare, thanked him, and said nothing more.

In Turan Restaurant, the hotbed of racial and religious hatred and violent detestation, my Armenian sensitivity constantly kept me on the alert to discern the intent and content of each political pronouncement freely made.

"Turan Locantasi" was, in effect, the Den of Turanism.

My continued exposure to their inner sanctum conversations made me convinced that these high-placed Turks were the most rapacious, plunder-loving people, extremely obsessed by the evil genius of xenophobia, hating and distrusting of strangers and foreigners. They would gladly welcome and embrace their own Shaitan — Satan — rather than an Armenian.

On the morning of August 19 suddenly an enemy airplane appeared over the city circling quietly, but when from minaret tops Turks began firing at it, it dropped a small bomb on a mosque, killing four innocent persons. And the wicked "politicians" of the Turan Restaurant vindictively gave their verdict that the "giavour Armenians," already on their death march, were responsible for this unpardonable act.

Two days later an unusual phenomenon occurred. Suddenly the sky grew darker. This condition continued the whole day. Slowly it became evident that an endless army of locusts was emigrating from somewhere to somewhere, but God only knew where. These voracious, ravenous winged insects made up their minds to settle on the vast fertile valley of Adana for a while and feast on its rich golden grain and lush vegetation. A school of them wished to camp all around the "Turan" grounds, devouring and defiling everything they touched.

Engaged in a heated discussion of this natural occurrence, several uniformed army officers, supposedly sensible, educated, important leaders, arrived at the conclusion that "the traitorous, treacherous, treasonous Armenians" must have released these insects to devastate the fields, gardens, vineyards, farms, and orchards of the "innocent Turks." One of these discussants, directly inspired by Shaitan whom he and his ilk serve faithfully, turning to Tahir Effendi solemnly said:

"Let Allah send us all kinds of locusts, grasshoppers, and rats. We will willingly endure them. But let him take away the Armenians from the face of the earth. The Armenians are far more dangerous and destructive than all the insects and vermin of the world."

Another disciple of Shaitan then asserted:

"Yes, Armenians are contemptible, ignoble, and ignominious. They deserve worse fate than exile and death. They have revolted in the Province of Van against the government's order to leave their homes and go where the government sends them as all their people all over the country have done. How dare they kill Turks? I care not the least if all Armenians are, infant and aged, put to torture and death. I will be happy if our plan is successfully carried through."

On another occasion I heard a female Turk swear:

"Let me be an Armenian if I am lying."

It seemed strange to me that none of these fiends suspected except Tahir Effendi to be sure that a terrified Armenian lad was listening at an ear-shot away.

Seyhan, the old river, keeps on flowing in front of the Turan Restaurant. Ever since its birth on a misty prehistoric day it has faithfully kept its rendezvous with the blue waters of the Great Sea. At times its waters are muddy and murky, and at other times translucent and gay. But in recent months the river seems to have slowed down in its pace to sing a mournful dirge, to murmur fragments of heart-rending tales of atrocities and release snatches of the sighs of half-slaughtered, half-dead human beings. Seyhan is endeavoring now and then to expose to view a head, a leg, an arm, a torso, pieces of clothing, but it is careful to hide the torrents of blood it has diluted in its unstable waters.

Faithful Seyhan performed its same sorry mission time and time again in immemorial days, in 1375, in 1895, in 1909, from 1915 to 1922.

Once in a while Tahir Effendi would hand me a tray of food to take home, and convey to Mother his greetings.

Mother and I often oscillated from one wonderment to another about Tahir Effendi's enigmatic "friendship." One day, when he sent word with me that the next evening he would pay a visit to her, our amazement soared to its zenith.

Mother, like the magnanimous and pure-hearted lady that she was, nevertheless put her surprise aside, and tidied the house to welcome her mysterious caller. Next evening my patron, Tahir Effendi, accompanied me to our home. Mother, tall, slender, and attractive, graciously admitted the honored guest into the room after I had introduced him to her as my employer and benefactor.

Once the preliminary exchange of polite greetings was over, Mother expressed her gratitude to him for his goodness at such a time when no Turk would employ an Armenian, when all Armenians were being persecuted.

Naturally the conversation was being conducted in the language of the Turk, but after Mother's touching little speech, my hitherto grave, correct, and dignified Master suddenly seized her hand and kissed it. Meanwhile changing his language from Turkish to the dialect of Hadjin, he said:

"Sister Sarah, after these many decades of eventful years, the Voice of the Blood has brought me to your feet."

"Voice of the Blood? What Blood?" I wondered.

But Mother, at this strange declaration, silently scrutinized for a moment or two the plain countenance of the alien man facing her, and softly, full of compassion and affection answered him, reverting to the Armenian dialect he had used.

"Haji Hagop, my dear brother of by-gone years of childhood days, how happy I am to see you now. May Allah continue to prosper and bless you. You are still the same noble person that I knew when we played in together in front of our house in Hadjin in those days of happy innocence that will return no more."

"I wish," Tahir Effendi wistfully moaned, "I was the same poor barefoot Armenian boy again that happily played with you and your brother Melidon, cousin Hampartzoum and the other children forty or more years ago. I wish I could go with you and those of my Blood to exile and ultimate death, than be a Turk and share the crime committed against my real race."

"But," he continued weighted with agony, "it is too late to alter the situation. Fate has decreed that I remain a Turk, and take a chance to ask my good friend Adil Bey, the all-powerful chief of police who directs the deportations, to spare your family. In a few days I hope I will be able to bring you the good news."

He stood up, returned the empty cup of the Turkish coffee he had sipped to the tray my sister was holding at a respectful distance, gave her a silver mejidiyeh (worth one dollar at the time), and silently walked out of the door onto the street.

Two days passed, and Saturday September 4 dawned as any other day. I went to work as usual. Still Shukru appropriated my time and myself. Still the endless line of deportees trekked over the stone bridge build by Queen Helena, the saintly mother of Constantine the Great, the founder of the Byzantine Empire.

On this day a sinister drama was taking place at the street door of our residence, of which I was to learn at noon when Mother sent for me.

Soon after I had left for work, Aram's six-year-old brother Dirtad knocked at our outer door, shouting:

"Open the door, Sarah Mairig, I brought you a friend of your son's. He didn't know where you lived, but I told him. I told your friend everything he asked me about you."

Mother opened the door to the courtyard with mixed feelings, and found Dirtad with a neatly dressed and smugly smiling stranger.

"Sarah Hanum," began he addressing her, "I am your son Kevork's friend. I had many good times with him in England. I just returned from there and learned from this child that Kevork Effendi is here living with you and your other children. I would like to see him."

Dirtad, Mother's friend's innocent child, seemingly seeking recognition of the good deed he had performed, repeated:

"Ya, Sarah Mairig, this Effendi didn't know where you lived, and I told him where. When he asked me who else lives with you, I told him that your eldest son lived with you after he came from England."

A sudden attack of cold shivers seized her, seeing the diabolical scheme of the pretender, but without losing her presence of mind she answered courteously:

"Effendi, you are mistaken. My son was never in England. He came home from Konia when his school was over about three months ago."

The dreaded Turkish policeman in civilian clothes at once cast off his pretense of friendship, and reverting to his natural vulgarity, barked at her:

"You bitch, show me your son now, or else I will break your bones."

"Bey Effendi," answered Mother in complete control of her rising anger, contempt, and fear, "my son Kevork, of whom this child had given you wrong information, is at work in Tahir Effendi's Turan Restaurant. If you want to see him, I can send for him."

Dirtad attempted once more to gain his "Mother Sarah's" approving commendation for his unique "good deed."

"Ya, Sarah Mairig, your friend didn't know where you lived, and I brought him to you."

Then the evil agent who pretended to be my friend in a fictitious sojourn in England thundered down the fires of Hell on my mother's head, declaring:

"Send for your son right now, and tell him to come to the headquarters to register. Day after tomorrow, Monday afternoon, your whole family will be deported with the rest of the giavours remaining in Adana. This is the order of Adil Bey for you."

Then he stomped out of the door, dragging Dirtad with him to go to his house, so that this agent of evil could bring hell-fire on Dirouhi Mairig's head, Dirtad's mother. But lovable Dirtad managed to stick his little head inside the door and gleefully say for the last time:

"Ya, Sarah Mairig, it was I who brought your friend to you. He didn't know where you were."

And Mother, forgetting her devastating terror for a moment, answered him with a smile:

"Thank you, Dirtad, for bringing *our friend* to us."

When I came home with my twelve year old brother in response to Mother's urgent call and was told the terrible news, immediately I rushed to the police headquarters and registered all four of us in the family. The same formal sentence was given again: Deportation in two days.

"Where?" I asked.

"Don't ask questions, giavour," the officer threatened me. "This is Adil Bey's order." (*Adil* in Arabic means "Just." This "Just" man was sending tens of thousands of the Armenian population of Adana and the vicinity to death.)

In the evening I went back to Turan Locantasi to inform my boss, Tahir Effendi, about the exile order we had received. The good man shook his head from left to right, murmuring some unintelligible sounds. Then he paid me five silver mejidiyehs (about five dollars) as wages for my five weeks' service, bidding us Allah's protection.

And Allah honored Mehmed Tahir Effendi's farewell prayer by protecting us through the darkest and cruelest years of our ordeal and allowing us to return after five years. A few days after our return, on behalf of Mother I went to call on him to extend our greetings, but was disappointed to find the elite restaurant in the hands of a stranger. In answer to my inquiry he told me that Tahir Effendi had died a few years earlier in a mysterious way, and that he knew nothing about Shukru's whereabouts.

CHAPTER 19

LEAVE EVERY HOPE BEHIND

THUMBING THROUGH the scanty pages of my diary of the period, I read that the day following the decree for exile handed down to us was Sunday, the day of the Almighty, the day of rest and peace and worship. But it was none of these. It was a black, bleak, and cheerless day. The sky had fallen down. Not a Christian church was open. There was no shepherd, no flock, no fold. Only wolves everywhere. From childhood I used to sing in church choirs, find spiritual sustenance and delight in the spoken and written Word, and participate in prayer and praise. But, today, when I needed them most, none was to be had.

Mother, in grim tones, told us two boys to take to the bazaar everything we had and convert it into cash. The "benevolent" Turkish government, by criers and posters all over the country, had strictly forbidden the deportees to take with them any provision for more than three days. Mother, a devout person all her life, murmured a prayer to the effect that this non-spiritual act to which she was ordering us on this Lord's Day might be accepted by him as a form of worship.

I am sure that God, whom Mother and her children loved, understood her heart.

My brother Setrak and I found the marketplace buzzing.

We found the marketplace buzzing with swarms of buzzards — Turks and mostly non-Christians — who unashamedly cursed and insulted us as they threw at us insignificant coins as charity while grabbing a mattress, a blanket, priceless pieces of jewelry, needlework, clothing, shoes, household goods, and furniture.

The same fatiguing, hustling, and fruitless pursuit again on Monday forenoon. And for all our wearing labor, the cash obtained from the sale amounted to a pitiful pittance of three dollars. With tears in our eyes, jeers in our ears, lumps in our throats, and tons of iron in our hearts we went home to pack a few small allowable bundles to take with us.

Annig, the little orphan girl who was destined to be my wife fifteen years later, happened to pass through the bazaar that morning, and having been told that we were on our way to exile, came to pay her last respects to her "Orphanage Mother." She stayed with us all through the packing until the carriage we had hired came to take us to the train station.

At the moment of parting we could not control the streams of tears coursing down our cheeks. Mother took Annig in her arms, kissed her and prophetically admonished and exhorted her to keep herself pure and chaste, endeavor to grow in wisdom and grace and make her her "daughter" again.

Mother and Annig never saw each other again, but Mother, in absentia, blessed her daughter-in-law Annig profusely for giving her four grandsons in the United States of America.

The open space around the station was transformed into a sea of humanity surrounded with their belongings, waiting for the train which arrived in the late hours of the cold, chilly night. Men, women, and children, not knowing where they were going, elbowing and pushing each other, scrambled to board dark wagons designated for them. These scant wagons, infiltrated with the pungent stench and acrid droppings of cattle and beasts, were packed as inhumanely as the Turk can devise. The sudden onrush of the unbearable, foul stench staggered Mother and me, but our momentary hesitation to board was quickened by the bayonet and the obscenities of the gendarme behind us. Once inside the densely packed wagon, we found no room to sit or stand comfortably, no space to drop our bundles, no possibility to sleep, no fresh air to breathe. My mind went back several months, when in college I was reading Dante's Divine Comedy. A pointed statement had arrested my attention at the time. *All you who enter here leave every hope behind* was the inscription above the entrance to Inferno, as the poet had said. And now that we had been shoved into this sealed inferno, the poet's graphic depiction recurred to my mind with increasing vehemence and significance: Leave every hope of survival behind.

It was a wonder that we survived the suffocating incarceration of the wagon, but when, hours later, the train dumped us, its unwanted load, on the plains of Osmaniye, the chilly, fresh air animated us. The great plain was a larger, fouler, stinkier "sea" of humanity this time. Human

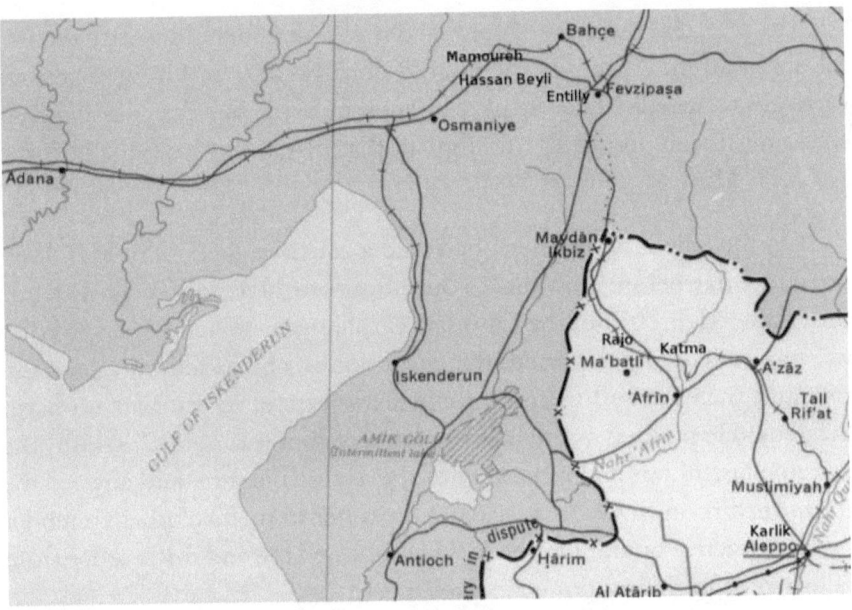

The deportation route approximately followed the line of the railroad from Adana to Aleppo, which was then under construction beyond Osmaniyeh. Some place names mentioned in the text have been added to this modern map.

filth covered the surface of the field whichever way one could go. We managed to tidy up a parcel of pollution to make room for us to camp and rest.

As the sun rose and our chills and cramps thawed out, we two boys found a donkey, hired it, put our mother on it, and traveled towards the town, but guards directed us to the camp of Adana people, outside the town.

The Turks and their allied Moslem savages of Osmaniye region were notorious for having massacring thousands of Armenians in 1909. During that massacre they burned the Armenian church sheltering terror-stricken men, women, and children inside, among them a number of college professors and ministers on their way to the annual church conference. My eldest paternal uncle's two daughters, Haiganoush and Rebecca, and their husbands, children, and relations also perished in the same fire.

The record of my diary of our first day in exile concludes with a sorrowful observation. "The wealthy in gold don't hesitate in hiring expensive carriages to speedily take them to Aleppo in Syria, but the poor like ourselves must wait and trudge on foot all that distance. Our hope is in the Lord. In Him do we trust."

On the advice of Mother I had paid a courtesy visit on Sunday afternoon, the day before our exile, to our imprisoned friend Vahagn Effendi, the cashiered director of the Ottoman Orphanage. When he learned that we, too, were being deported, this great lion in chains fell into deep sorrow and then advised us to be particularly careful to see that no harm befell us. He pointed out to me (the conversation was not in Turkish) the extreme lustfulness and sensuality of the Turkish nature, and advised me to smear dirt on my sister's face and dress her in men's clothes to render her unattractive on our long trek. He cautioned me and my brother from falling prey to their sodomistic tendencies.

And now that we were really exposed to the whims and unbridled passions of detestable savages marauding camps and roadsides, the wise warnings of our friend flashed in our minds. We disguised Mary, who was at this time a very attractive buxom young lady of seventeen, a jewel of a girl, with boy's clothes and dirt and a deep cap.

We met here, in Adana Camp, some of our friends, among them Toros Pushian, my Hadjin, Evérék, Konia, and Adana chum; Aram, Dirtad's brother; Garabed Keshishian of Hadjin and Konia professor, and many other friends.

After two days of camping in this miserable place, with no shelter or essential accommodations, we received orders to move on. From nowhere a lad, younger than I, Athanas Kulahjian, whose mother was a cousin to my mother, found us and attached himself to us.

Surely God fashioned Mother's heart of nobler stuff and abundance of goodness and charitableness. She never refused to lend a generous hand to the needy. Athanas remained with us as another member of the family and traveled with us.

God must have loved us, the little Kooshian family. We could have been driven by the cracking of whips from Adana to Osmaniye on foot, as tens of thousands were, but, in retrospect, I must admit that the train ride was a disguised blessing, although it was not meant to be. The long and tortuous march would have depleted our meager cash and provisions and wear us out into wrecks.

Our long and endless caravan began to march from the camp, leaving it filthier than we had found it. The following caravans, driven from all points of the country, would add more pollution to the camp grounds and fall away rapidly through lice, germs, viruses, dysentery, and divers diseases.

The trudge was long and arduous, mile after mile, with no rest breaks. For the gendarmes, a liberal number of them, were on horseback, head and neck covered, whip in hand, bayoneted rifle on shoulder, a pouch of bread, cheese, and onion and a canteen of water hanging from the saddle of their mounts, having no other concern at all. At the urge of the mood, they would sing in a monotone, or start to use all the invectives and obscenities in their catalogue, or drive their animals into the lines and whip those too tired or foot-swollen to walk faster.

The length of the road from Osmaniye on was overcrowded for hundreds of miles with one direction of traffic of the Damned and the Doomed. Traffic was of all sorts, on foot and in conveyances: the affluent in expensive carriages; others trudging on bearing on their backs their children or their sick, feeble, or aged dear ones; still others carrying bundles, necessities, or even unneeded, cumbersome furniture. The roadside was strewn with abandoned household goods, personal belongings, baby stuff, broken-down vehicles, and the most heart-rending, with those who at the end of human endurance had fallen down to rise no more.

The dreary, weary days drifted along, dragging us from one stopping place to another, places with ominous names, Mamoureh, Kanli-Dereh (Bloody Valley), Hassan Beyli, Entilly.

On the road or at a campsite we met long-lost or forgotten friends and acquaintances, or distant relatives from whom we had never heard before. One evening, when we were ordered to camp in the gorge called Bloody Valley, Mother found "Uncle Boghos," a relative whom she knew from 1898 when Father had taken us to Seleucia.

Uncle Boghos came to our camp to look for his own family, who had been exiled from Seleucia, and Mother recognized him. He had been conscripted into the Turkish Army a year or two earlier and had been forced into a labor battalion. While he sat with us around the cooking fire we had lighted, this unfortunate man confided in us that as soon as he located his family he planned to throw his pick and shovel in the face of his Turkish taskmaster and join the March of Death. Late that night he left us to dream what we could dream in a bloody valley and went back to his army hovel to repeat his nightly search for his dear ones.

Day after day we were forced to march over mountains, valleys, and canyons, as wounded, footsore, thirsty, and hungry as we were. In all these regions, camps and settlements were provided for the thousands of Armenian engineers and those of allied skills along with laborers in free employ of the Germans, who were feverishly engaged in the construction of tunnels and roads for the Berlin to Baghdad Railway. In a mountainous area called Entilly, when our caravan was commanded to rest a while, surprise of surprises, Mardiros Sarkisian spotted us. In my Hadjin orphanage days Mardiros, one of the older orphans, was one of Mother's favored boys. He was a graduate of St. Paul's College in Tarsus, and became my teacher at Evérék-Fénésséh. His younger brother Eranos was my classmate in college. Mardiros was in the employ of the Germans as an interpreter between his employer and the British war captives who were working as laborers.

He brought us food, fruits, and drink, and cheered and comforted our hearts.

(At the writing of these recollections—January 1975—Mardiros, a man of letters, an editor, a retired octogenarian celibate, has moved from New York to Palm Springs, California. He called us on the phone to pay him a visit. We have planned to visit him on Tuesday, February 4, taking with us Mr. and Mrs. Levon Tourian of Teaneck, New Jersey. Levon, eighty-five like Mardiros, was in the Hadjin orphanage and became my teacher in Fénésséh the year before Mardiros was my teacher.)

It was now ten days since we had started from Osmaniye. The drudgery of the days and the nights, and the uncertainty of the next hour on this seemingly endless road tortuously winding high and low at last begin to take their toll on Mother, our guardian angel, strengthener, and comforter. At the next stopping-place, Islahiyeh, the drinking water was so badly polluted that nobody could drink it. Here Mother contracted dysentery and high fever.

Frantic, we went about looking for a cart to lay Mother on. We succeeded in finding a kindly-looking Turk who consented to take Mother and us to Aleppo if we would pay him in advance. I gladly paid his princely price and hired his dirty, two-wheeled, creaky, one-horse open cart. He would not permit any of us children to ride in it. Mother would lie in it all day unattended, with no drink or food or medicine. Milk was impossible to dream of, let alone find. We could only talk to her and assure her that we were strong enough to walk. She lay on the cart under the searing sun by day and the shivering fog of morn and eve. She repeatedly assured us that she was in communion with her Lord and that she was not lonely at all. We never heard any word of complaint or any request from her.

At the next station she grew worse. Hope fled us. Tears flowed down our cheeks. With each weary step by the side of the cart we continually prayed.

At Rajio, another station, I managed to buy a little water to moisten Mother's parched lips and cool her fevered forehead. We children could feel the ghastly form of Death lurking by. Many had fallen by the wayside and not one of us was permitted to linger to shed a tear or to lisp a parting prayer, let alone to bury them.

A couple of days later, late in the night, our good cartman silently drove away, leaving us in the lurch. Luckily, the next stop was not too far. Mother felt a little better and walked the rest of the way with us.

On the 21st day of September, after fourteen days of forced march, we arrived at Katma, where a measureless expanse of humanity had been dumped. This concentration camp was the last before Aleppo, a metropolis of Syria.

We were told that Katma was our camp until further order to move on. How we thanked God for putting a temporary end to our march and providing a respite for Mother to rest. Immediately we bought an old, tattered tent from one of our company, put it up, and made Mother as comfortable as we could. Next we went a mile away to fetch water from a well guarded by a Turkish gendarme, paid him for the privilege, and rushed to our tent with the precious liquid. Immediately Sister boiled some water and made a soup out of a few handfuls of flour, fit for the palate of royalty, although we had no bread to go with it. Mother enjoyed it very much. It was a wonder to see that Mother, a dauntless spirit, had latent resources of physical and moral strength to recover from her shattering illness. And God, whom she loved, rewarded her.

In thanking God for Mother's miraculous restoration to health against tremendous odds, my mind went back about ten years earlier when the stone wall of the orphanage came crashing down the split second after she had stepped out of the way.

A day or two after we had camped in Katma, Sister and we boys washed our first laundry since we left Adana. The guard at the well felt it his patriotic duty to bombard us with a volley of curses, insults, and abuses.

Athanas, our cousin, left us there as randomly as he had found us in Osmaniye. (He, his wife, and his two sons found us in Pasadena in 1963 and stayed with us about a week. He passed away in Hollywood in 1974.)

September came to its end, and our stay in Katma also came to its end. Orders were barked at us to be on the move again. Someone bitterly suggested that the "benevolent," "merciful" Ottoman government had prepared lavish accommodations for our comfort in Aleppo.

Early in the morning we started marching, a queue of thousands of once healthy, dignified, useful men and women with their children. All along the roadside Turks, Kurds, Arabs, and other Moslems of neighboring villages and hamlets lined up, like famished jackals, waiting for a chance to snatch a child, a mother, a young lady or girl, and to steal, to rob, to grab. The successful culprit, his booty in hand, fled swiftly, disregarding the agonized wailing of the distraught mother. Nothing is sacred, nothing is moral, nothing is unlawful for these people.

Our little family, thank God, was spared thus far. Sister was still "unattractive" to any evil-minded abductor in her dirty trousers and dirtier face.

Although occasionally I had noticed abandoned dead, or half-dead, stripped of their clothing, yet the lifeless body of a budding young lady, who knows whose pride and joy she once was, drew out tears from my eyes and planted a fig in my throat. But for the mercies of God this hapless girl might have been my own sister Mary walking beside me on the path to lurking death.

The terrifying scenes and sly dangers were the same on the following day. Mother would advise us repeatedly to multiply our caution not to attract attention, but to keep praying for our own safety and that of our party.

Late in the moonless night, still on the march, we spied the flickering lights of Aleppo from afar, as Moses had viewed the Land of Canaan from Mount Pisgah but was not permitted to enter it. We, too, were not permitted to enter Aleppo; instead, we were herded into the concentration camp of Jemiliyeh.

Scores of caravans before us had left their accumulated debris for us to camp on. We found a spot, brushed the dirt aside, and settled down to eat a meal of almost nothing. We prayerfully waited for the morning to steal away into Aleppo. Mother told me to enter the city alone, and to be sure to locate her brother, Uncle Haroutune Malian, who was a master tailor in the Tailor's Division of the Turkish Army, and to inform him of our arrival at Jemiliyeh. If I did not act fast and successfully, our family, with the rest of the great caravan, would be moving on to the Syrian deserts, the immense graveyard of the unfortunate Armenian people.

Early in the morning I succeeded in evading the guards and slipped into the city. At the Armenian church I was directed to the house where Uncle Haroutune lived. The venture was crowned with success. Mother later told me that she had prayed for the Divine Hand that had restored her health to her to guide my steps away from the evil police to the right people.

My uncle was sad that we, too, had been deported. But he was glad that he was in Aleppo at such a time to save us from being sent to destruction. After feeding me he sent me back to Mother to assure her that everything would be well.

After a couple of hours Uncle, armed with a military permit for us, "his family," came to the camp and took us out of the hands of the officers. He took us directly to his quarters, where Sima Baji[30], a good friend of Uncle's, took care of us while he went to his military duties. For the first time, after an anxious period of want on our trek, we began to enjoy better meals, comfortable beds, and comparative safety. Sima Baji was a native of Aleppo and spoke Arabic as well as Armenian and Turkish. She warned us not to appear freely in the streets.

The Web of Hope

Syria, like Lebanon, was a part of Turkey at that time. And Aleppo, as the doorstep to the Syrian deserts on which the Armenian race was condemned to extermination by the secret councils of the Turkish government, was encircled by several distribution camps. No Armenians were permitted to enter the city, although there were thousands of Armenians in hiding. The houses in Aleppo were built with one mother-door, leading into a paved courtyard, around which were a number of separate apartments with their separate entrances and occupants. These houses were one, two, or three storied castle-like buildings. The city at that time had a population of 200,000, of which 90,000 were Arabs of Moslem faith, and the rest Assyrians, Chaldeans, Orthodox and Roman Catholic Greeks, Maronites, and Armenians.

For some inexplicable reason the native Armenians of Aleppo were left untouched by the decree of genocide. These people spoke Arabic and appeared no different from other natives, except that they were Orthodox Christians with their own churches, schools, and community properties, and had a bishop as their primate along with a number of priests. The church had an ample communal hostel or inn, called Hokedoon (House of the Soul) for the free stay of pilgrims to and from Jerusalem.

The schools were closed on account of the extraordinary times and the influx of refugees occupying the courtyards and all the available space in the church, the school, Hokedoon, and other communal properties.

The refugees, the daring ones who had found ways of escaping the general or special massacres, were easily recognized by the keen and malicious eye of any terror-inspiring gendarmes, uniformed or civil police, or the commissioner, whose most soul-satisfying duty was to arrest them and send them to centers of slaughter. No Armenian was ever safe, no one could afford to be off guard, even if he had official papers or permits with the signature of the highest official of the War Department.

CHAPTER 20

BULGUR KHAN

VERY SOON, with the help of Uncle Haroutune, we rented an apartment in the same courtyard. Cautiously we ventured out for small shopping, or we went to church. On one such day Mother chanced to meet Mrs. Armenouhi, the former matron of the Ottoman Orphanage of Adana, who told her that she needed her as a cook in Bulgur Khan,[31] a center for refugees in the city.

The project of Bulgur Khan was under a German missionary, Miss Beatrice Rohner (1876–1947), and through her powerful influence with the war government she could easily get immunity and permits for her workers.

Mother was happy to accept the Matron's offer for its promise of service, security, and something to eat. Wages or salary were impossible to think of at such a time. Besides, they did not exist. The only concern was to stay alive. Mother used to come home at night with some bread for us. Two weeks later, Mother told me that Mr. Khachadoor Kroozian, the Principal of Bulgur Khan, wanted me to be the overseer of the center.

Mr. Kroozian was a native of Van, Armenia, an educator, a man of letters, and before the war, for some years, the director of the Monastery Orphanage in Hadjin. In his later years he was ordained a priest and served in that capacity at St. John Armenian Apostolic Church in San Francisco until the day of his death in 1941.[32]

Bulgur Khan was a massive mausoleum, a gloomy structure three stories high with balconies and many chambers. The courtyard, stairways, porches, and rooms were all paved with marble slabs, cold and slippery. The whole building was completely bare of the least trace of furnishings, and devoid of any semblance of a door, window pane, or shutter.

The ration sent to this "house" was, in reality, a farce. By the time the provision-loaded wagon reached the "house" the load had dwindled to its minimal measure and almost useless stage. On its short way from the warehouse to Bulgur Khan the wagon made some dubious stops to

The Web of Hope

Khachadoor Kroozian as the Reverend Father Khachig Kahana Kroozian, San Francisco, California, 1935

unload bags and kegs, and then proceed to dump the left-overs on the "house."

Honesty had, like a flock of scared swallows, taken to flight, and crows with black hearts descended to stay.

The leftovers were sacks of head-onions, of which a room was already bulging, and radishes, turnips, and leeks, ready to rot. The sacks were filled with bulgur, beans, lentils, and worms, bugs, and baby mice.

The two-year-old child of my aunt Gulie died of eating onions, finding nothing else to eat.

Meat was never had, and the bread, the size of a saucer, was part flour, part ashes.

The government had not an ounce of compassion for the wretched plight of the Armenians, yet it had consented to turn over this stately edifice to the German missionary to house and care for as many unfortunates as the center would hold. Miss Rohner even succeeded in having the government donate some rations to her house of mercy.

When I came to Bulgur Khan as overseer I found the building extremely overcrowded with men and women of all ages. Typhus and dysentery were on the rampage. Lice covered the body of every one sheltered there. No one made an effort to control them because efforts were futile. No one cared, no one. Human filth and waste covered the floors, the steps, and the courtyard so badly that there was not one clean spot to step on. Dirt and disease were carried wherever one walked or touched. Sickness was rife, delirium and screams were uncontrolled, scrofula, leg ulcers, abscesses, gangrene, and eye diseases were preponderant. Concepts of discipline, self-control, and the sense of self-preservation had vanished from these once cultured and refined people. Drained of vitality and sanity, they simply laid down in their filth and died like poisoned flies. And every day the government would send a huge wagon or two to cart off all the dead and half-dead, and dump them unceremoniously into a pit. No one to weep over them, no one to murmur the Lord's Prayer. The dogs of the city and the jackals of the field were grateful to the Turkish government for providing them with such a banquet.

Around the end of October, the day I first joined the Bulgur Khan staff, it was rumored that the deported caravan from Kayseri was at Sebill, one of the camps outside the city. On hearing this rumor and hoping that her sister, my aunt Gulie, might be among the group, Mother sent me to find Uncle Haroutune and tell him the rumor. Uncle immediately secured a permit, rushed to Sebill, found his sister and her children and brought them to our apartment in Sima Baji's courtyard.

The next day Mother took her sister to Bulgur Khan and Mr. Kroozian appointed her to be my mother's helper. The children — Stephen, Rachael, Azniv, and the two-year-old Carnig, whom I last saw in Kayseri — stayed with us until Mother found a suitable room for all of us on the third floor of Bulgur Khan.

Meanwhile I wrote a letter to the Reverend and Mrs. T. F. Barker in the United States. I explained in the letter what was taking place in the country, and asked if he could do anything to help. I mailed it through the American consulate.

All American citizens and their families caught in the maelstrom of the war received protection and financial aid from the consulate. Several times I applied to the consulate for help as a former student of an American institution, but I was not eligible for any kind of assistance. Had recent experiences on the tortuous road slowly been draining my strength and fortitude without my knowing? It was evidently so. The shock of the hellish conditions prevailing in this cesspool of human misery was too much for me to stand. It did not take much more than a fortnight to shatter my health. No amount of caution could prevent the overseer from contact. To open one's mouth was to inhale pollution and swallow virus.

On my first day at Bulgur Khan lice found in me a new and fresh body to exploit. They were of various classes: biting, sucking and boring; internal and external; of the head and of the body; visible and invisible; young and old; soft and hardy; indestructible, inexhaustible like the sand of the desert.

My younger brother fell sick first, and then on November 9, 1915 I followed him.

We were both stricken with typhus, an acute, contagious disease caused by a microorganism and marked by high fever, with eruptions of red spots, cerebral disorders, and extreme prostration. No doubt the culprit was the louse, one of the many trillions feasting in Bulgur Khan, on the dead and the quick. Sister Mary kept vigil on us both and attended to our needs, while Mother attended to her cooking for the increasing residents of the compound.

During my constant rounds of inspection, before I fell sick, I had come to the conclusion that no one could exert his authority or enforce any semblance of order in this chaos. As mentioned already, a score or more dead were found daily, and to make room for others, they were dragged into a dark room on the ground floor and thrown one over the other helter-skelter until the arrival of the horse-drawn rubbish wagons. I could never venture to cast a glance inside this realm of the dead, from which I could sometimes hear a moan, a plea, a faint cough. My protests on such occasions fell on deaf ears, on the grounds that the half-dead would be all-dead in a few hours anyway.

A number of days after, when we two brothers were still in delirium, four huge tough women whose assignment was the removal of the dead, invaded our room on the third floor and began to drag the two unconscious bodies over the marble floor to throw on the heap of the dead. Sister's frantic cries and pleadings did not have any effect on their hardened souls. These good women were intent on performing their duty. In such circumstances they could not afford to be respecters of persons, no matter who that person might be. So they pushed Sister aside, threw our coverings inside the room, and dragged us by the limbs to the top of the stairs.

All of a sudden, Mother appeared at the head of the stairs and, like an infuriated lioness, lunged and plunged at the insensitive Amazons, scattering them helter-skelter and taking possessions of her cubs.

That night was the most critical for us, the sick, and the most agonizing for Mother. We were already given up by everybody as doomed. Hope for our recovery was abandoned by the director, the women's overseer, Aunt Gulenia, and the other staff members. Mother was the sole person who did not lose her hope and faith. Mother and Sister kept vigil, sitting on the bare cold marble floor all that winter night long, as if in penance like Job of old, and adding their own coverings to ours in order to ward off the chill of death from claiming us. The details of a magnificent sacrifice made that same night were told me by the same Sister in 1966, two years before her death, here, in Pasadena. She told me that Mother gathered my two almost frozen feet and kept them warm until morning between her two chaste breasts. So did Sister with her younger brother's feet. Meanwhile these two women, mother and daughter, following the example of Mary of the Gospel, continued to wash the invisible feet of the Savior with their nard-like tears and bombard the throne of their Heavenly Father with salvos of fiery prayers.

The dawn was never so late in coming. And when it did come at last, Mrs. Armenouhi, Aunt Gulie, Mr. Kroozian, and others came to the paneless, shutterless window to express their deep sympathy for losing her two sons at the same time, but were amazed to learn that we had successfully passed the crisis.

Mother praised God for the miracle.

Return to consciousness was not coming to us fast and easy. The deadening environment, lack of proper nourishment and the nonexistence of a doctor, medicine, or nurse were not conducive to our quick recuperation. The place was, besides being a domain of the rapidly dying and the dead, also a domain of the incurably diseased, the few recovering at the speed of a tortoise, and the walking skeletons. Those of the sick who showed a ray of hope of recovery were laid side by side in a larger chamber and cared for by their relatives, if they had any. My brother and I were placed there under our sister's vigilant care. We were still seriously sick, unable to leave our beds.

December had come. Christmas, the season for joy and activity, was at hand. But no one had the spirit to care. Joy had vanished from the earth along with Peace and Good Will. Anguish and misery were everywhere; Death was stalking around brazenly, reaping lives impudently.

Such was the prevailing circumstance when, late in the night of December 22, a group of gendarmes raided Bulgur Khan, the "house of mercy" under the "protection" of the German missionary Fraulein Rohner, whom the governor of Syria and commander of Aleppo affectionately called "My Sister." These gendarmes fiercely barked orders all around the huge place for every one to pack up and wait in the courtyard for carts to transport them to Der-ez-Zor, a town beyond the vast desert, on the left bank of the River Euphrates.

(Years later, in the United States, from documents I learned that Zeki Bey, the governor of Der-ez-Zor, had been sending urgent wires to the deportation authorities in Aleppo to speed up the dispatching of large caravans of Armenians, so that he could perform his patriotic duty by completing their annihilation. The document concludes that this ogre, with blacker heart than Shaitan whose favorite emissary he was, subsequently massacred more than 200,000 Armenians.)

After dragging every one out of their hiding places, these ruffians entered the sick room where a score or more of us were dangling between life and death, and began to spread terror by kicking and trampling over us, cursing us to stand up and line up in the yard. Try as I did, I could not muster strength even to sit up, let alone stand.

As I began to plead for mercy in the name of Allah, the despicable creature stomped on both of us, and deeming in his hate-filled black heart that tromping was not enough punishment for a criminal like me he began to lay ruthless lashes on my skeletal back. These villains, self-appointed overlords of our lives, always sported a whip in their hands, both to inflate their worthless egos and to instill fear in those whom they persecuted.

Seeing our plight with alarm, Mother and Sister rushed to wrap us up in blankets, shawls, and coats, and carefully led us down the slippery marble steps to the already crowded courtyard. The cold was biting as we sat on our bundles in shivers waiting for the carts to come.

About ten carts arrived at midnight and lined up outside the main entrance. Those of the crowd who were fast enough to board were driven away. One or two members of some families climbed into the wagons thinking that the rest of their families had also boarded. Thus they became separated forever.

The yard was half empty by now. And, because we could not move fast enough and secure sitting room in the carts for ourselves, we were sad and disappointed, murmuring and complaining about our bad luck. It is a human frailty, an intellectual blindness, not to recognize a blessing in the guise of disappointment.

The gendarme guarding us harshly told us to wait for the arrival of the next batch of carts. We sat the whole night through, storing up its cold in our bodies, but arrive they did not.

In the morning the frustrated guard left us with his threats and curses, and we retired to our quarters to get some much needed rest before the arrival of the "promised" carts. All day long apprehension did not leave us.

Those who went away in those carts that dismal night went directly to their death, for none returned to their family after the war.

Brother and I, after the experience of the hellish night, fell back into our former unconscious sickness. Meanwhile, as we learned later, changes were taking place in our situation.

The Web of Hope

On the last day of December 1915 Bulgur Khan was vacated, and what remained of its residents were removed to the British Gardens. This enclave became officially known as the German Orphanage, under the firmer control of Miss Rohner. The surroundings were clean, pleasant, and sanitary, food and care better, and shelter more comfortable. Brother and I slowly regained our health.

Mother and Aunt Gulie, with their daughters, were sent to Shekeriyeh, another "center," where the two sisters were to cook for both the Boys' and Girls' Orphanages.

While yet in Bulgur Khan, before I was smitten with typhus, I had met Miss Rohner only once, presumably the only time she paid a reluctant visit to that infernal death-trap. Not knowing who she was, and being astonished to find a foreign gentle lady in this defilement, I had addressed her in French and she had responded in English. (I was afraid to speak English first, because the British were considered the arch-enemy of Turkey.)

As I recovered completely from recurring sickness and finding that I was too old to be considered an "orphan" among children, I left the orphanage in the beginning of March 1916. Mother suggested that I stay at Sima Baji's, and keep myself in hiding.

A few days later I learned that Mr. Kroozian of Bulgur Khan days was now the superintendent of the Armenian Orphanage, housed in the school grounds adjoining the Church of the Forty Children. With the knowledge of Sima Baji, my protectress, I paid a cautious visit to my old friend, who was very glad to see me out of the deadly clutches of typhus and offered me the shaky and dubious position of overseer and teacher in his orphanage. The church, through the contributions of food and money by the native Armenians of Aleppo, was responsible for this clandestine orphanage, unauthorized, unrecognized, and unprotected by the government.

Although Mr. Kroozian warned me of the risks of being picked up, I was glad to accept his kindly offer for its promise of enough food, shelter, relative safety, and opportunity to be useful. I moved in immediately, on March 10, 1916.

During my stay of five months in this place, I, as an Armenian young man of some schooling, had absolutely no right to be living when all were dying and being arrested all over the country and killed wholesale. I had no status whatsoever in the sight of the Turkish policy. It was impossible for me to obtain a permit, a license, or identification card to be free to live, to be let alone, not to fear arrest as a fugitive from death.

So, on alarms relayed from mouth to mouth of raids into our sanctuary, everyone would disappear. On such terrifying occasions I used to climb up on the flat roofs of the adjoining buildings and hide for hours behind chimney stacks, attempting to write poetry or read a book to while away the heavy hours.

Every evening, invariably, an old priest — Mesrob Vartabed — came to the school hall, and in the presence of all the inmates — women, girls, boys, and a few men — led the evening prayer. The hour of prayer was emotion-packed, heart rending, and, at the same time, comforting. There was not one among us the broken-hearted and the crushed who had not lost a number of dear ones and whose heart was not aflame with sorrow and grief. Besides, we all knew that our own lives were suspended by a hair.

The prayer poured out was usually that magnificent supplication on folded knees, "Believing I confess and prostrate beseech Thee, Father, Son, and Holy Ghost," composed by Saint Nerses the Graceful in the eleventh century, and offered by millions of Armenian hearts for 800 years. Tears rolled down cheeks as all the twenty-five stanzas were repeated in unison, each stanza ending in a heart-piercing refrain, "Have mercy upon Thy creatures and me, the greatest of sinners."

On other occasions, one of the most vibrant and throbbing liturgical petitions, "Der voghormia," (Lord have mercy — Kyrie Eleison) was sung so dolefully, mournfully, sobbingly. We all believed in the power of prayer, we all fully believed that God the merciful Father heard our heart-sent petitions, and we also believed that the Turk was immensely more wicked than God was good; that the Turk was the negation of good, the nullity of God, the perSINification and the excesSINation of Shaitan.

This until recently operative parish school, with its only entrance through a door opening from the church courtyard, was endowed with a rich library, a veritable Garden of Eden for a scholar and a bibliophile. The shelves of this unique library contained volumes both in classical and modern Armenian. Fortunately Grabar, the ancient Armenian with its enchanting intricacies, was not unintelligible to me, as I had spent four years in its study. Translations from internationally known ancient and modern masters were there. A great number of old and new magazines with different titles and contents, bound into volumes, were stacked row on row. But there was no one to care for them. They, too, being Armenian, were abandoned as widows and orphans. Probably some of them already met the same fateful destiny of loss, never to return to life again.

But I had a field day with them as long as I stayed there. I read day and night, took copious notes, committed beauteous passages into memory, forgetting meanwhile that education and erudition were never able to stop the Turk's mailed club, rifle butt, bayonet, or ax from falling on the Armenian neck. Although outside these walls the fires of hell were raging, I had the peace and joy of the Garden of Eden inside. I can still recite by memory, sixty years later, in classical Armenian the opening paragraph of Fenelon's Telemachus:

"Calypso [the nymph] was in inconsolable grief because of Odysseus' departure [from her island of Ogygia where he had been shipwrecked seven years earlier] and her own immortality seemed to her unfortunate because of the intensity of her grief."

Part II
Youth, and a Gleam of Hope

Sacra peregrinatio per sanctam crucis viam ad montem Calvariae

And he said to them all, If any man will come after me, let him deny himself, and take up his cross daily, and follow me.

For whosoever will save his life shall lose it: but whosoever will lose his life for my sake, the same shall save it.

For what is a man advantaged, if he gain the whole world, and lose himself, or be cast away?

For whosoever shall be ashamed of me and of my words, of him shall the Son of man be ashamed, when he shall come in his own glory, and in his Father's, and of the holy angels.

Luke 9:23–26

Eighty-one days on the desert, massacre on the sixty-ninth night

Sunday, August 13: Arrest in Aleppo
Tuesday, August 15: March of death (1st day on the desert)
Sunday, August 20: Arrived at Meskeneh (6th day on the desert)
Tuesday, August 22: Arrived at Abu Harrar (8th day on the desert)
Sunday, August 27: Abu Harrar (13th day on the desert)
Sunday September 3: Abu Harrar (20th day on the desert)
Sunday, September 10: Abu Harrar (27th day on the desert)
Sunday, September 17: Abu Harrar (34th day on the desert)
Sunday, September 24: Abu Harrar (41st day on the desert)
Sunday, October 1: Abu Harrar (48th day on the desert)
Sunday, October 8: Abu Harrar (55th day on the desert)
Sunday, October 15: Abu Harrar (62nd day on the desert)
Friday, October 20: Left Abu Harrar (67th day on the desert)
Sunday, October 22: Arrived at Hamam massacre (69th day on the desert)
Sunday, October 29: Hamam (76th day on the desert)
Friday, November 3: Aleppo (81st day on the desert)

A Mohammedan Prayer

I seek refuge with Allah from Satan, the accursed.

In the name of Allah the Compassionate, the Merciful!

O Lord of all creatures! O Allah! Destroy the infidels and polytheists, thine enemies, the enemies of the religion!

O Allah! Make their children orphans, and defile their abodes!

Cause their feet to slip; give them and their families, their households and their women, their children and relations by marriage, their brothers and their friends, their possessions and their race, their wealth and their lands, as booty to the Moslem, O Lord of all Creatures!

CHAPTER 21

ARREST IN ALEPPO

Sunday, August 13, 1916

Sunday dawned on the 13th of August, a day not so dissimilar to former Sundays. Of course the day was pregnant, but I had no particular inkling of it. As usual I gathered my flock of pupils together and led them to the church next door to attend the morning Mass. During the worship hour I felt that the age-old mysticism of the holy atmosphere, enhanced by the pervasive aroma of the burning incense, and the delightful melodies of ancient hymns, chants, and prayers, did elevate my mind, spirit, and soul to Heaven, the felicific abode of the phalanges of light-robed angels. The vibrating, thrilling, throbbing, living descants of sharagans were, after contacting the sacred dome above, falling in myriad particles on my heart like manna.

My mind left the holy place for a moment and strayed away to the tortuous months of misery and agony of the recent past; then it went to the deserts and slaughter-places where tens of thousands were perishing daily; and then my mind came back to the few fortunate pitiable survivors who had somehow managed to filter back to the courtyard outside, more than half naked, sore, emaciated, ill, and haunted by gruesome tales. I did recall walking among them once in a while, handing out a covering, a dish of food, or a piece of bread to some sprawled on the cold marble pavement. Oblivious of everything sacred around me, my tortured mind strayed to dwell on those still in the desert vastness, writhing under the searing sun and chilling night winds covering their starved ghost-like bodies, not to rise again in the morrow. Do they have a priest to sustain them with a prayer or a word of spiritual comfort?

At this point the congregation's lusty participation in the Nicene Creed

The Web of Hope

> We believe in one God, the Father almighty, Maker of
> heaven and earth, of things visible and invisible…

roused me out of my reverie. Without joining in the "I believe…" I let a fervent prayer stream out of my grateful heart, praising Him for keeping our little family intact and unharmed thus far, while worthier ones were perishing the same hour in countless numbers.

"Oh Father," I added, "please put an end to this holocaust visited on Thy people. Make the light of Thy face to shine upon us in our darkest days, and let us go back to our own churches to worship Thee in peace…"

The worship hour had ended, and our burdened hearts comforted.

I led my "children" back inside the school compound to get ready for dinner.

I was surprised to see my younger brother Setrak waiting for me in my room.

"Do you have anything special to tell me?" I asked uneasily.

"Mother is sick and wants to see you," he said.

"Is it serious?" I inquired.

"I don't know," he answered.

I wasted no time. Keeping Mr. Kroozian, the superintendent, informed of the situation, I accompanied my brother to Hokedoon, a distance not more than five minute's walk, through a narrow street which was rendered into a tunnel by the houses built over it. The walk was safe. We encountered no danger.

The separate buildings of Shekeriyeh and Hokedoon faced onto the same narrow dead street, and were annexed to each other, but with separate entrances of their own. The workers in Shekeriyeh, Mother and Aunt Gulenia as cooks, and sister Mary as teacher, were assigned to rooms in Hokedoon. Fraulein Rohner, the German missionary, who was permitted by the masters of the Ottoman government to keep her orphanage, had secured official permits for her workers and teaching staff. So Aunt, Mother, and Sister had their permits, but I could by no means get one. Even Mr. Kroozian did not have one.

When I entered Mother's room on the second floor I found her in bed. The room was altogether bare and I had to sit on the floor on one edge of her spread. No sooner than a few words had been exchanged, the dread form of a gendarme appeared at the threshold.

"*Vessica?*" he bellowed.

Instantly I felt the whole sky fall on me. I knew I was doomed, a candidate for the desert's slow death or for one of the many slaughter spots. How could I produce a *vessica*, a permit?

"I have none," I muttered.

He pushed me out of my terrified mother's door and down the stairs.

Mother forthwith jumped out of her bed leaving behind the fever and aches tormenting her minutes before, and rushed with her sister and my sister after us crying, begging, hugging the contemptible creature's feet, but to no avail. One might as well try to move a rock to pity.

Mother's physical exhaustion and sickness now gave way to sickness of her innermost consciousness, torture of the real self: mind, soul, and spirit, a torture worse than death itself. Mother's agony was too much for me to bear, so I, too, broke down to bitter tears. The more disgust these fiends engendered in their victims, the more pleasure they derived from it.

Round-up of this God-forsaken people for the slaughter centers with terrifying names—the deserts, the banks of the Euphrates, Ras-ul-Ain, Der-ez-Zor—had lately slackened somewhat. The reason for this laxness was due to the observing of the holy month of Ramadan, the month Moslems spend in fasting from sunrise to sunset. But now that Ramadan and its torpor of fasting were over, they were too eager to take up the hounding they had been reluctant to relax. They were wolves, hungry for Armenian flesh, thirsty for Armenian blood, covetous of whatever the Armenian may have had left.

Strictest orders from masters in the capital poured down through the wires for intensified raids into houses, hiding holes, caves, and wherever an Armenian could be found.

I had been preaching caution to my charges. And now I had been caught having thrown caution aside.

As my arrester led me outside the main gate, I was horrified to see a chain-gang waiting. There were about forty unfortunate men, young and old, who had been hunted out and seized. They were fastened two by two to a long and sturdy chain. Two gendarmes were guarding them.

The Web of Hope

My arrester fastened me to the chain at the rear of the gang in front of my mother's tear-flooded eyes.

When five more searches came out of Hokedoon having found no other prey than me, we were ordered to move on. The eight happy patriots, with their bayonets mounted on rifles pointed at us, "the traitors of the Ottoman fatherland," and paraded us through the streets of Aleppo, augmenting our number at each step until the chain ran out of links. After hours of wearisome trek we were taken to different police stations and divided up as their "honored guests."

In the guard-house in Jideideh I was "honored" into a cell. The small dark cell could not afford another inch of standing room for a newcomer. But the dutiful guard squeezed me somehow among the twenty-five other condemned already inside. The dirt floor could not be any dirtier than it already was. The stench of sweat, the struggle for breath, the impossible urge to turn around, and now, lice, fleas, and nameless creeping things made my unbearable life more unbearable. I was dressed in my blue serge Sunday suit, white shirt with detachable starched collar and a tie, tight fitting polished shoes, and gold-rimmed pince-nez eyeglasses, fitted in college in a previous year by Dr. Jamgotchian, the vice president and my Algebra professor. It did not occur at all to these Turkish officers arresting me to think that the outfit I was wearing was fit only for church, and not for jail.

After some time we all were taken out and joined to a group of several hundred others. Under heavy guard we were then ordered to march out of the city to Karluk, the notorious *Sevkiyet Merkezi* or Dispatching Center.

During the months of my relative safety in the seclusion of the Armenian Orphanage, I used to hear hair-raising tales of this fearsome place, but never expected to be incarcerated there myself. In my studied estimation Hell could be more endurable than Karluk, because Hell was supposed to have been devised by a just God to punish sin and wickedness; while the Turk created Karluk (and many other Karluks) to punish innocent children, harmless old men and women, guileless young men, and gentle young ladies.

This was the place for which Dante could have said, as he said for Inferno, those who enter here throw your hopes away.

Arrest in Aleppo

Our group was turned over to the custody of Hussein Effendi, the chief officer in charge of the center. We were now inside the enclosure, fenced with heavy chains and posted on four sides by countless guards with cocked guns and unsheathed swords.

What a waste of sorely needed manpower, I thought. If all these scores of thousands of officers and petty guards with their firearms were sent to the front to fight the enemy, most probably the country could win the war.

But the Turk is as foolish as he is wicked.

About evening another large group was brought to the center, among which were the two doorkeepers of the church and the school. But the most devastating of all was to see ten of the tender young girls, aged fourteen to seventeen, of "my orphanage," all in tears. The same hounds that seized me this morning had, later, raided the church and school grounds, and picked up these flowers, deeming them worthy to be trampled on and crushed. Were they gifts to somebody? Oh, nothing is sacred for the Turk, absolutely nothing.

Their eyes were limpid pools of tears. And through the rainbow of their tears seeing me sadly gazing at them, these lovely girls showed shock and commiseration with an imperceptible flicker of smile; tear washed smile that, although powerless to hearten me, seemed to me as the smile of the dew-washed rosebud at the morning sun.

It is night now. *Sevkiyet Merkezi* is at the edge of the desert. The cold desert wind is whistling and throwing sifted sand into eyes, ears, nose, and mouth. Since the night breakfast of the early morning I have eaten nothing and drunk nothing. No comfort, no money, no cover for the night. Left alone with my memories, dreams, ideals, loves all turned to dust, ashes, desert sand.

I take off my coat, turn it inside out, hide my glasses in a pocket, unfasten the collar and tie, and spreading the coat on the pebbly ground spread my weary body on it. Rest and sleep evade me.

"*Gha-ra-beet Ogh-loo Kee-fo-o-ork!*"

What? Am I dreaming?

The call repeats for the second time.

I jump up and walk towards the voice, careful not to step on lying bodies.

The Web of Hope

On the other side of the chain fence I saw the most welcome figure of Uncle Haroutune, smartly dressed in his chic military uniform and black goatskin cap which he designed and tailored.

"This Bey Effendi has come to see you," said the guard respectful of Uncle's officer's uniform.

Uncle Haroutune handed me an ample bundle of food and a heavy blanket. He encouraged me not to give up hope with promises of applying to proper authorities for my release and bringing Mother in the morning.

After Uncle left I felt the contents of the bag and the blanket to make sure that all this was not a dream.

Instead of the coat this time I spread the blanket for my bed, for a pillow looked around for a suitable rock, then laid me down covering myself tightly to ward off the bite of the raging wind. I clutched to my bosom my priceless bag of food as a miser clutches his gold. But sleep was far from me. The pieces of rocks under the blanket forced me to change location several times that night.

The thought of escape occurred once, but before I could mull over it much, Hussein Effendi bellowed for every one of us to witness the punishment of an unfortunate who had tried to break away and was caught.

The poor fellow had been captured at night, and was badly beaten up already. In the morning he was brought out. A couple of guards tightly twisted straps of hide around his ankles and inserted a rifle between the tied legs to hold them up for another to apply the lashes. Flogging took some time to make it more impressive. The beaten man was left in front of us half dead with blood streaming from his feet.

The lesson the Chief wanted to impress made me completely abandon the entertainment of any notion to escape. I knew for sure that I could not outlive such flagellation.

The alley leading to Hokedoon, where George Kooshian was arrested

CHAPTER 22

THE MARCH OF DEATH

Tuesday, August 15, 1916: First day on the desert

ON THE THIRD DAY of our incarceration in this infamous *Merkez* (Center) an order arrived for the release of the ten virgins from "my orphanage." Despite my desperate state I found a reason to thank God for the sake of these innocent girls. At the happy moment of their parting they could do nothing but to express their heart-felt sympathies and promise to pray for me.

The bitter-sweet and undefined feeling lingering in my heart at the freedom and departure of the girls soon gave way to the solid joy of seeing Mother and her brother, my beloved uncle Haroutune, at the outer side of the fence. Both did their best to cheer me up, exhorting me not to give up hope, something might happen soon for my release.

But, "just for precaution," Mother had brought a bag full of underclothes and necessities one might need on a long journey.[33] She had prepared and brought another bag also full of dried foods.

I sensed the hopelessness of their appeals to the authorities. Suddenly I began to feel the surge of an ocean of love and pity within me for Mother. Her intense agony in the form of tears poured down in rivulets through the furrows of her tortured cheeks. And now as she gently deposited a parting kiss on my brow in the chill of that morning I felt the intensity of the fire burning in her heart.

Then she left silently, in a queenly gait, Uncle following her.

It is midday now.

Hussein Effendi rounds up his "herd of cattle." Loudly calls up the roll. Hands out a small loaf of bread to each one, with the "apology" for the necessity of sending us "eastward," for our good.

A few minutes before the order to march is issued, three of my youngest students come to give me the love and sympathy of the inmates of the orphanage and hand me some food sent by them. Remembering that, where I am about to go, I will have no use for my eyeglasses, collar, studs, tie, and sundry items, I beg the boys to take them to my mother.

As soon as the children have left, the order to march is given to our band of five hundred captured "criminals." A feeling of thirst at this moment makes me approach a guard with a canteen to beg for a drop of water. The man in whom I thought I detected a spark of human decency gives me two strokes of his inseparable whip before I can slink away dragging with me my "guilt" of daring to ask for a drink. This man of the highest rank in the Turkish scheme of affairs feels his civic, religious, and patriotic duty to deny any favor to one of the "cattle" he was driving to the slaughter.

My two most precious bundles and the blanket are too bulky and heavy for me to carry alone. Hampartzoum Krajian volunteers to carry one. Hampartzoum was a schoolmate of mine through all the years of my Hadjin and Fénésséh life. The Catholic family betrayed their house servant to the Armenian-catchers, and the poor boy arrived at the Center late last night. When I discovered him this morning, he was shivering, hungry, and in tears. Yesterday when he was picked up, his master wouldn't even let him have a hat, a coat, shoes, food, or money. He was dressed only in a thin muslin robe, and nothing, absolutely nothing more.

Astonished to find each other in this dreadful place we fell on each other's arms in mutual realization of our desperation, and forged an unspoken pact to stick together through thick and thin.

We are marching now for hours on the desert sand. An old man too sick to walk sinks down. A couple of our ten mounted escorts dismount, raise the feet of the man up, and beat him so severely that, when they are convinced that he will never walk again, let us continue on the march.

How expert these Turks are in instilling terror and submission in their captives!

The Web of Hope

It was dark when we were ordered to stop to camp. My feet, and those of Hampartzoum, were swollen and burning with pain. I was so pleased, and blessed my mother, for packing some salt in the bundles. Immediately I made a salt solution and rubbed our feet with it. Then, eating something, we wrapped ourselves in the blanket and went to sleep. We were too tired to stay awake and mourn over our misery.

But, miseries were in store.

A violent kick given to Hampartzoum woke us up. At once he sat up. I did not. It was Ahmed Chavoush[34], *Sevkiyet Memouri*, the sergeant in charge, who had done the kicking. He was walking among the sleeping crowd like a ghoul, an evil spirit, bent on preying on corpses and robbing graves.

The reason why this revolting creature was walking amongst us, thus stealthily, in the pitch dark when everyone was sleeping after a toilsome march, did not occur to either one of us at the moment. But when the contemptible beast ordered the boy to go to the edge of the camp with him, and the unsuspecting boy did as he was told, I suddenly recalled the warning Vahagn Effendi, the great Armenian patriot, gave me on my last visit to him in Adana prison, shortly before he was hanged: "On you way to exile beware of falling into the hands of homosexuals. The Turks are especially notorious in sodomy, the most loathsome, the most repugnant of sexual practices."

A few minutes later I heard poor Hampartzoum pleading in tearful sobs to have pity on him, leave him alone, to stop beating, biting, and pinching, "for the sake of Allah, for the sake of the Prophet."

But the crazed ravager of former caravans, resorting to a false pretext, loudly threatened to kill his prey for refusing to "go to the village nearby and fetch barley for his horse." And the boy vainly protested that he would gladly go, if he was let alone, anywhere to get feed for his horse.

The beatings and the fearsome cries continued for a while, and then muffled sobs followed.

The boy returned to me shortly after. He was trembling like a leaf, drowned in sobs and tears, and cold as a piece of ice as he found shelter under my blanket. Thrusting his chilled hands in mine he sought comfort, sympathy, and strength from me for his ravaged body and spirit. Choked with welling emotions, and a vengeful anger that could find no outer expression, I prayed for this despoiled boy, then for myself, next for others, and then for the punishment of this Ahmed the Demon, then repeated the whole process of entreaty until morning, Hampartzoum's hands still in mine.

And the Sodomite, as the sex-crazed maniac that he was, kept on searching for other victims, kicking one, stomping on another, cursing, beating, ravaging.

Wednesday, August 16, 1916: Second day on the desert

At Sunrise we lined up to resume our march towards the east. The sand extended on to all points of the circular horizon, filling our hearts with pervasive despair. Hampartzoum was walking on my side, an extra shirt on his back and a kerchief on his head to ward off the burning darts of the desert sun, marching in bare feet and carrying one of my two bags.

At the head of the line, one of the guards had spread a red bandanna on the sand, and was compelling each one as he passed to drop on it an amount of two kurushes (two one-hundredths of a gold lira) for Ahmed Chavoush, in appreciation of his benevolent protection in the night against Arab marauders.

Oh, what a comedy of life! Contributions of love for the despicable Ghoul of last night!

I have urged my companion to walk with me in the front of the caravan to evade the evil notice of the guards and thus escape receiving eventual lashings and rifle-barrel or -butt blows at the hand of the monsters on horseback for lagging feet. We had occasion to witness already poor unfortunates stumble under horses' feet. I saw two women give up their last breath under blows for not keeping up the pace. While the sun from above and sand from below were roasting us, we were forced to keep up with the horses. Neither was there escape from wing-raked sand lodging in our eyes and nostrils, blinding, choking, hungering, thirsting.

The small loaf of bread that, as "a token of good-heartedness" was distributed to us by Hussein Effendi yesterday noon at roll-call, has already been devoured, and the planned process of starvation started. Money, if any one has hidden on his body, has no value for him at all. Nothing he could buy with it, not even his freedom. Freedom was not for sale at this juncture, because because his life and his possessions were at the mercy of these paltry riff-raff guards.

I have a feeling that I am one of a few who have some money and a supply of food, dry bread, onion, cheese, beans, lentils, and bulgur; matches, and a small pan and cup. A good spirit must have guided Mother's hands as she was preparing my "traveling bags." Despite her inconsolable anguish for losing her first son to the deserts, Mother must have had a prophetic instinct to know within her God-loving heart that one day he would safely return to her arms. With that unfaltering conviction the Prophetess must have dropped in one of the bags a pencil and an ample pad of paper on which I kept my daily record during the subsequent months.

As we approached a well we were ordered to take a rest. Every step these Turks took, every act they performed, were calculated. The well had no wheel, no rope, no pail. Most of us were already tortured by thirst. Beside my thirst, I wanted badly to bathe my feet in salt solution, because my swollen feet refused to keep my position in the front ranks. Waist wraps, small pieces of rope and bandannas tied together formed a rope long enough to reach the bottom of the well and draw out the precious liquid in a utensil attached to it. We found to our dismay that the water was polluted, foul, stinking. But we fell on it, drank, washed, and filled our cups. I filled up a small canteen I had discovered at the bottom of my bag, and thanked God again for the thousandth time for a mother so fore-knowing, so intuitive, so sagacious.

Meanwhile three daring souls foolishly took advantage of the fabricated confusion at the well and made an attempt to run away for freedom. But the wily creatures of the deceptive distraction swiftly rounded them up and brought them before us for a spectacle. The tortures so ruthlessly inflicted on them reminded me of the 400-year long period of the Spanish Inquisition, and the persecutions initiated by the Roman emperors in early centuries. I could not help but conclude that either Nero was a Turk, or the Turks are descendants of inhuman Nero. Where else could the present day Neros study the barbaric details of the gory art of torture and persecution?

The three disabled men then were ordered under the watch of the guards to drag their miserable bodies after the marching caravan on their dislocated ankles and blood-streaming inflated feet.

A little further on our company walked over an old woman, left behind from a former caravan of deportees. She had lost all semblance of the image God created after His own. She was as naked at the point of her approaching death as she was many years ago at her birth. She was nearer to death than to life, wasted in hunger, thirst, and exhaustion. Her eyes were now half shut, then half open. Her parched dark lips were moving in wordless, voiceless speech — most probably in prayer and blessing for her dear ones. Grief over her overwhelmed us, and we gently moved her from under feet to the edge of the road where others like her were also abandoned.

Barbarism began to take another shape as we marched deeper into the desert on this hot August afternoon. The guards on their horses suddenly felt festive. They, all ten of them, were in the mood for sport. Their animal nature sought a new channel of pleasure. Now they began to race their horses on the helpless crowd, striking right and left, laughing as hyenas when some one falls under hooves. I saw men and women trampled, crushed, cracked open.

The diary I kept throughout those horrible months, after recording all these events in some detail, adds an anguished and angry outburst which verbatim transcribed is as follows:

"Yes, I saw it all. I am an eye-witness to all these happenings. I will testify anytime, anywhere about these crimes to those who have ears to hear and willingness to render justice."

About evening time our decimated party arrived at a stopping place called Nardip Khan. Fortunately the water was sweet and plentiful. Those who managed to survive the "innocent game" of wanton massacre were allowed to find rest and sleep on warm rubbish and dung heaps piled up inside the courtyard of the khan.

This night, my second on the forbidding desert, the nightmarish horror and agony Hampar and I went through last night were to repeat again. To receive the hated kick was my turn this time. When I saw the ghoulish form of Ahmed Chavoush towering over me, shaking with terror, I implored within me for the dung heap to swallow me in, but as it dawned on me that Ahmed and the dung were the same stuff, I turned my heart to God in prayer:

"Oh God, please save me out of the claws of this venomous reptile."

"Where have you been hiding during the daytime that I never saw you?" asked the sadistic Sodomite.

"Bey Effendi," I said, although he was neither a bey, nor effendi. He was just an inflated big zero. Yet I had to address him as to my superior, because at that time I was, in worth, less than a zero.

"Bey Effendi, during the daytime I march at the head of the line."

The horrid hyena barked at me the same sharp and abrupt order that he had barked last night at poor Hampartzoum: "Go to the edge of the camp and sleep there."

"Honorable Sir," I dared to answer back, although he had no honor at all and could never be a sir. And I said,

"Honorable Sir, I cannot leave my three other companions and go away from them. We stay together."

"Where are your friends?" he asked.

I pointed to the three others lying next to me on the mound of rubbish. "Here they are," I said.

With a kick he compelled each one to sit up.

"Where are you from?" he asked me first.

"Adana," I answered.

"Hadjin," said Hampartzoum.

"Ada Bazar," muttered Garbis.

"Kayseri," replied Hagop.

"*Khunuzurlar*," (swine) roared the Chavoush. "How can you be friends when you are not even from the same town? *Yatun* (lie down), *geberesijeler* (you who are worthy to die)!" he ordered us and went on his ghoulish hunt elsewhere.

"Oh, thank you, God, thank you for your mercy," I said and went to sleep.

Thursday, August 17, 1916: Third day on the desert

Our notorious demon jackal Ahmed Chavoush was beside himself this morning. Very early in the morning he began raining down on us a stream of accusations, curses, profanities, and denunciations. And then he began to praise himself, standing on the second floor balcony of the khan. Part of his speech, as transcribed from diary of the day, is the following:

"You giavours, listen to me carefully. I want you to know that I have the honor of personally killing on this road a full dozen of your cursed race. Four of them I killed with the bayonet, the second four died with bullets and the last four I murdered by blows of this rifle-butt. I have a *firman* (a special decree, license) from the Grand Vezir to slaughter you all right here. There is no one in the whole country to hold me accountable for massacring you. Right now I am your Allah. You do not have one. If you had, he would save you from my hands. Do you realize that you are our property, captives, servants, dogs, our dung…"

Then he came down from the balcony, and with his helpers he began to collect a fee for his speech. After this collection another of his aides suggested that another collection should be taken for the permission to sleep on the warm dung-pile.

As Ahmed noticed me dropping my contribution, he called me to him and gave me a severe beating for the disappointment of the night before.

The March of Death

The vast expanses of the Syrian Desert lie before us.

On foot, thousands and thousands of us, in separate caravans, every day.

Whipped, flogged, trampled, cursed at.

Struck down with the rifle-butt at the hand of a Turk.

At night a prey to his sodomistic lust, or a victim to his violent passions.

If ever the silence of the sleeping desert sang, it was an unending dirge:

March on to your death, at the blood-dripping hand of the Turk, the heartless Turk, the murderous Turk.

> It was a Turk that cut a new-born baby into halves, and with a diabolical laughter joked to the writhing mother—
>
> Here, you have twin babies instead of one. Be happy.
>
> Was the sand white or golden?
>
> Was the sky blue? Copper? Leaden?
>
> I don't know, I don't know, I don't know, although I spent several miserable months on the desert.
>
> Did I ever hear a bird sing?
>
> See a flower smile at me?
>
> No, No, No!
>
> Poetry was already murdered, sensitivities blunted.
>
> I had no eye to see beauty, but only the deviltry of the Turk.
>
> Death, and the Turk.
>
> Devil, and the Turk.
>
> Turk, Devil, and Death were partners in the desert, and on the face of the whole country.

Despite the big threat of the really small Ahmed, we are allowed to resume the march to another rendezvous with death.

Two more enfeebled women fall exhausted. Guards make sure that they are dead before leaving them behind.

I thank God for my pouch of food and canteen of water. I feel an urge to share my blessings with some of my comrades. We are all a family of sufferers. We respect each other. The good suit on my back and shoes on my feet must have commended their esteem as a teacher and a man of education.

I tell them stories from "Arabian Nights" which I have read just a few weeks ago. I encourage them with examples and passages from the Bible.

An entry in the diary of this particular day reads as follows:

"The prayers and blessings I receive daily from these fellow sufferers will combine with the prayer, tears and good deeds of my mother and save me out of this desperate state, when the proper time arrives."

The March of Death

It was about noon when we arrived at Der-Havr, our camp for the night. Water, the most precious thing needed on the desert, was plentiful here. A number of Arab men and women sprang up around us to sell vegetables, tomatoes, cucumbers, and grapes. Those of us who could bought and shared with others.

Here, too, the guards captured a fugitive. With a blow they sent him reeling down. Then raising his feet up, they broke two sticks on his blood-spurting feet.

The warning given after each such object lesson was the same: "Don't ever try to escape as this fool did. Your punishment will be worse."

A rumor went around that this was the night when our caravan would be turned over to another corps of guards.

About 4 o'clock in the afternoon, the guards suddenly began to separate the young and healthy looking ones in the caravan and them drive them all a little distance away from the camp. At a spot they ordered us to halt. The guards began to tie each captive's hands on his back, and then tie couples together back-to-back.

With bent head, in dark contemplation over this turn of events, I was watching for my fate, when my arch foe, Ahmed, spotted me, and said with a jeer:

"Why are you so sad as a new bride about to leave her mother's home?"

Then letting loose a volley of curses directed at me and the race I represent, he dealt me such a blow in the back that I sank to my knees in excruciating pain. He called a guard and turned me over to him, ordering him to take care of Hampartzoum and me together. After Ahmed left, this fellow, in a friendly tone asked my name, and then father's and mother's family names. I told him.

Then he became more eager to know the name of my native town. I said,

"Hadjin."

"Are you both from Hadjin?" he asked, stopping his tying for a second.

"Yes," I answered.

This subordinate of heartless Ahmed, told me in a lowered voice that he was from Hadjin also, from a nearby village, and he knew that Malians and Gejekooshians were good, respectable people. He said his name was Haji Hanefee Chavoush.

"It is out of my hands to help you, but I can do a very small favor to you both. I will tie you loosely and separately to the oxcart nearby, so that you can sit down, stand up, and move around when you get tired."

He did as he said. He made us as comfortable as his position would permit.

"I cannot predict what fate is in wait for you, but I wish you good luck," he said, and joined his corps.

What was the "fate" waiting for us two, for all of us bound, for all in the caravan? The anticipation of terror was tearing my heart apart. What was it doing to the other unfortunates?

The night was advancing. The winds blew, the sands churned and the desert chill penetrated into our marrows. And we waited, Hampartzoum and I, leaning our tired and aching backs on the cartwheel. Waited for the "fate" that was long in coming.

Sometime after midnight some new officers sought us out and relieved us from our bonds, with the usual warning not to try to escape.

Ahmed Chavoush had departed with his gang of murderers for Aleppo, to escort from *Sevkiyet Merkezi* a new caravan of captured victims, armed with absolute license granted him by a firman from the country's highest lords, Talaat Pasha and Enver Pasha, pile havoc after havoc on the unfortunates, and satiate his insane lusts.

The new corps of guards permitted us to return to the camp and enjoy an unmolested sleep till morning.

CHAPTER 23

MOTHER EUPHRATES

Friday, August 18, 1916: Fourth day on the desert

A NEW ERA has dawned for us with this morning. We are marching merrily on, although in the "Shadow of Death," happily in the fact that this shadow is no more that of Ahmed Chavoush, the sadistic sodomite, the shameless extortionist, the ruthless murderer and...

Still in the front of the marchers, I continue to tell the sequence of a broken tale begun on the previous day, or begin a new yarn. The act of telling and listening of these unreal myths in the "Shadow of Death" has a beneficent effect on each one in lightening the heaviness of our hearts, in brightening the face of the "Shadow" and sweetening the grim look of "Death."

All of a sudden, the specter of an unannounced anguish begins to show its ugly head. Hampartzoum begins lagging behind, falling back, unable to keep up the pace with us. He admits that he is ill. This admission fills me with alarm. He is the only brother here that ties my past and present together.

In his talks with me he let me know that he never could understand, nor forgive, the treachery of his master and mistress in letting him to be captured and then refusing to let him have his clothes, some food, and some money.

His nearly bare body, unshod feet, and hatless head could withstand no more the severe heat and cold, wind and sand, hunger, thirst, and fatigue of the open desert land.

Last night's nightmarish rendezvous with "fate," and the physical and moral ruination he went through at the hands of Ahmed, the homosexual devil, so badly damaged his fragile spirit that his will to live slowly began to deteriorate, until he saw no longer any sense in continuing the struggle for survival.

Friends joined me in encouraging him to try hard to keep on marching, so that he would not be flogged, or trampled under feet and hoofs. My anguish about him increased when I noticed that he was burning with fever as he leaned on me for help. I lent him the support he needed to walk. I carried him on my back, while others willingly carried my bags. I let him have all the drink he wanted until not a drop was left in the canteen. Others also helped him in any way they could. I was told by those who knew that no water could be found from Der-Havr to Meskeneh. These comrades told me that this march was not the first for them. They had been sent to the desert several times, and each time they had run away when they found the opportunity to do so. They assured me that even I would attempt to run away.

On this leg of the march, Hampartzoum's weight, worry, and weariness began to burden me heavily. But the prime of youth and instinct for survival urged me on. Streams of sweat and growing thirst made the going a drudgery. My endurance was wearing away with the day. The last rays of the dying sun began to play tricks on my perturbed mind, making my eyes see a mirage of a river of water, winding its serpentine body through the sand dunes.

"It is the river, it is Euphrates!" someone shouted.

I don't know from where I drew a fresh supply of vim and vigor to enable me to run towards the mirage, dragging Hampar with me. Stopping at the bank of the great river I laid Hampar gently on the sandbank, bathed his face and limbs, and cooled his lips. Then I took care of my needs.

As the crowd reached the edge of the water they threw themselves at it as a child throws itself on the rich breast of its mother.

A prayer of thanks could be heard from many mouths. Mother Euphrates was merciful. She met the needs of every child. She dispensed drink and comfort to those who sought them, and eternal peace to a number of desperate women who threw themselves into her arms, and she lovingly swept them away from the outrages of the Turks.

Hampartzoum was able to eat a little with me.

The night slowly spread its black canopy over our fatigued bodies as we camped on the west bank of the River. And she kept on singing sweet lullaby while all the caravan went to sleep.

Mother Euphrates

Saturday, August 19, 1916: Fifth day on the desert

On an uncertain hour of the night a loud commotion put an end to our much needed sleep. And it was revealed that an old man had been captured as he was leaving the sleeping camp, instead of sleeping along with the rest. What right had he to head for freedom when all his breed was condemned to extermination camp somewhere deep in the desert? The man had to take his due punishment.

The guards laid him on his back, tied his legs with straps, and flogged him until he was unconscious. Then after pouring pails of water on his head, the guards buried him in the sand. In the morning the same guards unearthed the body and shoved him into the river.

I never boasted that I was a prophet to foretell what would happen any time. And nobody told me that the old man's misadventure would cost me dearly.

To witness the spectacle of his gruesome execution and the ensuing burial, the whole caravan was forced to attend. While I was in attendance, a "brother" in the caravan, evidently less than a "brother," had broken into my bag and stolen all the food I had and left the torn bag on the sand.

My anguish at losing the most precious things at such a time and place was nothing compared to poor and ill Hampartzoum's loss to the same thief of his borrowed thin footwear and a piece of bread given him by a comrade.

Quite a number from our camp had successfully made their escape in the night to nearby Meskeneh.

About a mile away from where we camped there was a considerable settlement of Armenian families living in tents around the slope of a hill. These were men of means who, somehow, had secured special permits to live there unmolested and protected against fugitives and undesirables. All fugitives are undesirable here, although tolerated by the Armenians, but not by the Turkish guards. These fugitives who find shelter in Meskeneh either find their way to Aleppo, or are picked up again. It is probable that our thief needed our supply of food and Hampar's stocking-like foot-cover for his escape.

Despondency and hopelessness are more prevalent among women than among men. A desperate woman slowly walked into the River and ducked her head in. Her body sank down with her head. Another woman followed her example and did the same. Some of us pulled the bodies out, but life and misery had already left their bodies. We handed them back to the River.

Oh, how fortunate we are! Our keepers are this evening are this evening distributing to each one of us a loaf of bread. But who cares if the loaf is half the size of your palm and mixed with sand, soot, and ashes? It is a picnic, a feast.

People started bartering, exchanging their bread for jackets, trousers, shoes, and other items.

We were told several times before that we would be given bread at the next station, but they all proved false. What happened that we should be thus objects of mercy, we could not understand.

The day went by snatching sighs and tears, prayers and complaints, resignation and fumes of anger.

On one of the quiet hours I pulled out my pad and pencil and jotted down, as I did in the days past, the happenings of the day as I witnessed them.

We camped on the sandbank of the great river for the second night, and slept listening again to the sing-song whistle of the wind and the lullaby of the eddying and moving water.

CHAPTER 24

IN THE VALLEY WHICH WAS FULL OF BONES

Sunday, August 20, 1916: Sixth day on the desert

This is the sixth day on the unfriendly desert, and the eighth from the Sunday I was seized as a criminal escaped from Turkish justice and condemned to live out a dark fate in the searing heart of the desert. Last night was too turbulent for me.

The wind, with the velocity of a gale, in terrifying rage, was churning the sand and shoving in spadefuls into my mouth, eyes, ears, and nose, making it impossible to sleep, when sleep was the most priceless thing I wanted next to freedom.

In snatches of sleep a good fairy carried me back to Hadjin. Grandfather and Grandmother were sitting up in their beds spread on the roof of a relation's house that served as our front yard. We grandchildren surrounded them and begged for a story. After that Mother began to tell them all the suffering, sickness, want, and heartache we went through on the road to exile. And then there were relatives and friends all around, games, things to eat and drink. Happiness had spread her peaceful wings over us as a canopy to shield against harm and hurt. The music of laughter was ringing in my ears…when a fierce gale pierced my side with a jab, screaming, "All are lies, all are lies!"

And lies they were. The stark truth was the present reality, with its sand, the roaring river, the raging gale and the specter of march of death. The vanishing of the dream of happiness drew a stream of bitter, bitter tears from my eyes, wetting a little more my already wet blanket spread on the wet sand.

When, in the morning everyone had to rise, some did not rise. They were buried alive. We unearthed some, but they were either dead already, or in their last gasp.

The Web of Hope

A group of two hundred newly captured fugitives was brought from the settlement of Meskeneh and mingled with us to be pushed further back in the desert whence they had run away.

Before the start of the march, a couple of Armenian residents of Meskeneh brought a wagonful of bread and distributed it to us.

The wild west wind, blowing from our back, pushed and shoved us forward. We almost flew on wings. Even the wind conspired against us hurrying us to our "fate."

Our course wound around huge dunes and sparse rocks. And Euphrates played a game of hide-and-seek with us. Now she appeared to be a few steps away, and then she disappeared behind hills and sand dunes. But at no time were we allowed to step out of our line to get a drink, lest our insatiable thirst run her dry. A river that has from immemorial beginnings been flowing down her 1,800 mile course from the highlands of historic Armenia to the Persian Gulf, with her width of from 300 to 1200 yards and a depth of ten to thirty feet, at no time fordable.

The wretched marchers were suffering with sore eyes, sore and swollen and bare feet, parched lips and throats, dysentery; half naked and sore in spirit.

At sunset we arrived at a stopping place, called Dibse, with a khan. Although in the past it was an important station, necessarily with some accommodations for merchant caravans and legions bent on conquest between East and West, now Thapsacus (Dibse) was a deserted, forlorn spot in the great Syrian desert. Yet it was only to expedite the wholesale extermination of the Armenian race that a number of guards were kept and supplied in the Khan.

Under this gruesome shadow of death the cultivated traits of taste, reason, and sensitivity were oozing out of our mutilated character. But still it was impossible not to wonder how and from where could these swarms of husky and well-fed dogs congregate here, in this no man's land, a desert spot with no villages or settlements for miles.

But a ghastly sight was waiting for us to behold.

When on the urge of natural need some of us retired behind the khan to a distance of a few hundred feet, we discovered to our horror that the whole surface of the desert, as far as eye could see, was covered with all sizes of human skulls, limbs, spinal columns, vertebrae, and a million of other bones, all stripped clean of their flesh by these packs of specially imported immigrant dogs turned wild.

Skulls by the thousands from all directions stared at us in ghastly gaze through empty cavities that once held eyes. Were these stares in pity for us, or in entreaty for ultimate justice?

And the dogs at the sight of us, smelling fresh blood and flesh, began to lick their chops in anticipation of a new banquet. We could stand it no longer; we ran back to the camp in terror.

One of our guard was stationed at the bank of the eternal river to charge a price for the privilege of a drink. He searched my pockets and finding a piece of a broken mirror, he appropriated it with a juicy curse and turned me back. (I had wrapped my rapidly dwindling supply of cash around my leg, below the left knee, the trouser leg covering it from his evil eyes.)

We were let to drop our miserable bodies on the cobbles, pebbles, rocks, and sand drenched with the innocent blood of the myriad slaughtered martyrs, our sisters and brothers. Would their loving spirits hover over us as we slept?

Monday, August 21, 1916: Seventh day on the desert

Euphrates, God's blessing, with her immense quantity of water was rolling down next to the road we were drudging on, singing and laughing, roaring and calling, but for two days our escorts had not allowed us to drink a drop. Hampartzoum's condition was worsening and the support I was lending him was weakening. I wrapped his sore, bare feet in the remnants of the bag a "brother" had broken into two or three days before to relieve me of my supply of food. But in a short time the rags turned into tatters and the kerchief on his head could not soften the stabs of the sun's arrows. His constant need was a drink and I bought it for him from comrades who had some.

Two women and their sons were caught running away from the caravan of death. What right did they have to run away from death? They received their "due" punishment, severe flogging.

The guards — Turk, Arab, Kurd, or Circassian — were always on the alert to discover what we had that they wanted. He commands you to hand it over to him. He gets it anyway. Either you give it to him willingly or he gets it after you are tortured. This happened all the time.

Himfish, the Arab guard on his saddleless horse, approached one of the men, Hovhannes of Arapkir, and commanded him to hand over the coat he was carrying on his shoulders. The man hesitated to part with the coat that served him as a cover against the cold and wind. Himfish dealt him a blow with his rifle butt and got the coat.

Having been warned of such eventualities, I was always careful to hide my things. The silver pocket watch with its chain that Mother had sent me from Adana as a graduation gift from high school in Fénésséh was hidden somewhere deep on my body. The hat I was wearing had lost its shape and look. My good, thick, warm coat was turned inside out and purposely soiled, and on the trousers I was wearing I had inflicted cuts and tears. Himfish and his like could find on me nothing to covet.

Ten thousand steps taken in the desert give you the illusion of walking in a circle, or retracing your steps. The only diverting phenomenon is the sun with its rising and setting. The scenery is always the same. The sand of our acre here is no different from the sand of an acre a thousand miles away, unless there is a khan, or water, or ruins, or a settlement.

At noon we arrived at a place called Abu Harrar, a spot marked with a khan and a guard house. The sole mission of these guards in this dreary, desolate furnace by day and ice-box by night was to capture fugitives and prescribe the manner of their punishment. The commanding site of the khan and guardhouse on a small hill overlooking the whole expanse of the desert afforded these fiends the ability to smell out any moving creature and rush to extirpate it.

Behind the hill Euphrates was rolling on her turbulent course witnessing all this.

Here, too, extended another "valley which was full of bones," and these guards, paid and supported by the government, presided over it, in company with the pack of dogs. The Prophet Ezekiel's vision[35] was of only one valley, but the "valleys" and "hills" of Armenian bones were countless, and "the voice of the Lord" heard by the Prophet concerning the bones of slain Hebrews was never heard about Armenian bones. The Turk had silenced God's voice.

The first thing we the army of the desperate did was to run into the arms of the River, the only friend we had in the "shadow of death," in the "valley of bones," to quench our days-old thirst and seek for our hurts cooling, soothing balms.

Two women, in full resignation, sank their bodies, head and all, into the welcome lap of the waters, but the guards pulled them out and threw them on the beach with profuse curses. The Turks evidently can't do anything without a curse.

After cooling myself somewhat, "the hand of the Lord...carried me" towards the khan on the hill, knowing not why. Ordinarily I should not go there, the lair of jackals, but an inner force urged me on. At the door of the guardhouse a young man was standing, gazing at the new arrivals. As soon as our eyes met, we threw ourselves into each other's arms and wept for joy and for sorrow. He was Samuel Toursarkisian, one of my Hadjin and Evérék orphanage intimates.

Samuel was, for the time being, engaged in cooking and serving the Abu Harrar guards. He asked for news about his younger brothers. Having seen and talked with both of them in recent weeks, I gave him satisfactory news.

As we walked together in the deserted khan, he told me how miserably Vartivar Yapoojian had expired a few yards away. Vartivar was an inmate of the Hadjin orphanage, as were we. Then, as a graduate from Tarsus College, he became our beloved teacher in Evérék. He was a genius in many fields of education, a gymnast and an athlete and a musician. This specimen of health and virility wasted away into a slender reed, unable to stand on his legs, and died while his old mother was beseeching him to eat the sand-hopper, a bug she was offering him.

With Vartivar, he said, he had run away from Bab several times, and each time at the edge of the city or the at the gate of the Aleppo church they were picked up, tortured, and sent back. They both came to Abu Harrar some months ago, Vartivar and his mother perished, and Samuel became cook and servant at the guardhouse.

While I was still talking with my friend, I saw a comrade run towards me with my knapsack in his hand.

"Here, take it," he said, handing my bag to me. "Hampartzoum threw himself into the river. He won't need this bread anymore." He bit a mouthful from a chunk of bread belonging to Hampartzoum.

My friend and I ran down the hill to the riverbank and saw a gendarme pull his limp body out of the water. Fortunately the boy did not have enough time to drown. He was wet and shivering with sickness, despondency, cold, and disappointment.

At once I was let to take charge of him. With Samuel's help I pulled his wet robe off, rubbed his body dry, dressed him in extra underwear from my knapsack, and wrapped him in my blanket.

Samuel ran back to his kitchen in the guardhouse and a few minutes later returned to us with a large sheet-bread wrapped around some pilaf and chunks of meat. We made the sick boy eat first, then I enjoyed the rest.

It was surprising to see so many strange Arabs, true sons of the sand, crop up from nowhere and leisurely stroll among us. A man, one of our number, was carrying a shovel on his shoulder, presumably to dig a hole in the sand to sleep in. The slowly-following Arab, all of a sudden, snatched the shovel and after hitting the poor man on the ear with the surface of it, ran and disappeared like an evil spirit.

CHAPTER 25

TWO VISITORS

Tuesday, August 22, 1916: Eighth day on the desert

There were many "successful" escapes in the night. The control over us has relaxed. The escorts have gone back, leaving us in the custody of the old, slightly limping Turkish gentleman, Hussein Effendi, and Himfish the Arab.

It is evident that Abu Harrar, this death valley of bleached and blanched bones, will be our home, far away from civilization. Cities and human settlement are too far for our "successful" runaways, who will eventually be robbed by waylaying nondescript desert rats, be killed, or get arrested and sent back until the Ottoman Plan of Extermination is achieved.

Those among us who had been here before told us that there were a few Arab villages some distance away, whose fields were not too far from us. Himfish caught two women and three boys stealing corn from these Arab fields. Himfish himself administered their due punishment.

Today I feel deeply dejected. I am suffering from the pangs of hunger. The cash wrapped around my knee cannot cheer me, because it cannot buy food that does not exist. Everybody is hungry. Mothers and children, men and women, wail away their day in tears and prayers. My diary records an unwitting sacrilege from my own Christian heart:

"I do not know if these heart-rending, agonized moans and griefs will ever touch God's heart."

Starvation had its start today.

We are strictly forbidden, under penalty of death, to stray away to Arab tents to beg or buy.

On this forbidding face of the desert there is not a single tree, not a single shade, not a single shelter from heat and cold, not a single...

A rumble of carriages rolling on the road between the river and the guardhouse roused me out of my melancholy depression and directed my steps towards them. The two carriages made their stop near the river's edge for a short rest.

The carriage masters were Armenians, coming from Aleppo and delivering government goods to Hamam, the next station from here. I knew none of these men, and they did not know me either. I asked them news from Hokedoon. One of the two men asked who I was. I told him. Then he told me that he, too, was from Hadjin, and his name, Boghos Ouzounian. He said that his wife was a classmate of my sister's in the Hadjin orphanage, and that he had seen my mother and sister in Hokedoon a few nights earlier and they had begged him to look for me in the desert. He comforted me, encouraged me, and promised that by all means he would let them know soon that he had seen me. Then digging into his pouch he gave me an onion and a chunk of bread. Again my diary records my feeling: "I will never forget this noble man's generosity."

Mr. Ouzounian then explained the location of his tent in Hamam, inviting me to find shelter there if and when I happened to be there.

This man was a prophet, but neither one of us knew that at the time.

He drove away, after cheering me up with hope and providing my evening feast.

Hussein Effendi, a humane exception among Turk officials, permitted us to find shelter in the khan.

Wednesday, August 23, 1916: Ninth day on the desert

Today Arabs of the desert villages came to our camp to sell their produce.

One of our men exchanged his dollar's worth fez for a watermelon. Someone gave his jacket for a melon. Another one bought a cucumber with his trousers.

There are thefts every day and every night. In the morning pitiful cries are heard from many who have lost their bread, foot-wear, hats, or other items of clothes.

Today I bought barley cakes, each one as thick as the paper I am writing on and as big as half my open palm, each for a kurush. One could eat a hundred of them and not be filled.

Arab women are very smart and cunning. They know how to rob you. They give you a very small quantity of what they sell, and pull out of you a pound of flesh.

Thursday, August 24, 1916: Tenth day on the desert

The pitiful cries of captured and tortured runaways are so common now that they serve only to disturb your sleep at night or to become a diversion.

Again the severity of the heat in the daytime and the cold of the night is taking its toll. Several of our number were found dead in the morning. Hussein Effendi ordered some of us to drag the corpses away and bury them in the sand. The pack of dogs is expert at digging them out to devour.

This is desert. Where can we find something to make fire with? Some fortunate souls have found cakes of human and animal dung to kindle fire on which I saw them roast a handful of barley or corn they had either stolen or bought.

It is so heart-rending to see women and men of refinement and well-breeding fight over a piece of wilted melon, watermelon, or cucumber rind.

You cannot take a bite of anything without someone watching you with pleading eyes and gaping mouth.

News from runaways come to warn us against the robbing, torturing, and killing done by the waylaying Arabs, denizens of the desert. A woman began to tell of a frightful experience. During one of her escapes towards Aleppo she was assailed by an Arab, who robbed her of her tattered coverings and then began a search for gold coins in her mouth, ears, and around her breasts. Not finding anything there, he probed into her two cavities front and back. Others told similar experiences. Someone else told of a horrendous sight she had witnessed: the robber, disappointed at not finding the gold he was looking for, slashed open the poor victim's belly and searched for the accursed metal in her bowels.

After listening to these hideous accounts I lost the last vestiges of any desire I might have had to run away. Lethargy of complete resignation and unresisting submission to my fate took possession of me.

I strolled with a friend to the river bank, sat down on the sand, and began reminiscing about our former days.

All of a sudden my attention was drawn by an unmatched war between a small company of ants and a giant bug the size of a walnut. The company surrounded the enemy, but were scattered away with the blow of a powerful leg. Soon an army of ants reached the battlefield and quickly laid the bug defenseless. The piercing and sucking stings of so many attackers were too much for the giant. The ants tore its carcass into particles and carried them off into their stores.

"Thank God," I said, encouraged with the object-lesson I had just witnessed. "Germany and Turkey will eventually fall like this giant." Then I resolved within me not to resign myself to the blind "fate," but to wait patiently for God's leading.

Today a Circassian came from Aleppo and said that he had been sent as the governor of our camp. In order to quiet down the growing resentment of the desperate and starving people, this wily fellow started a rumor that a lot of flour sacks were on the way for us. Then he began to enlist prospective laborers and carpenters to rebuild the khan. Most enlisted in the hope that they would stay alive by working for the government, but I did not. I had a premonition that the fellow was lying.

Friday, August 25, 1916: Eleventh day on the desert

We are dumped here to rot.

The starving people can find nothing to eat. The desert where we are produces nothing. The river bank on our side does not have one single tree, one single blade of grass, one single river bug. Some of our ingenious ones, envious of the guards' horses, have dared to steal grains of barley from their nose-bags or scratch apart their droppings to separate undigested grains.

A woman today sold her little girl to an Arab woman for two small cakes of barley bread. Wise woman?

Samuel, the guards' servant, once in a while sneaks out to me some bread or pilaf, and mostly through this blessing, Hampartzoum is slowly gaining back the health of his body, mind, and spirit, which makes both Samuel and me glad.

Two Visitors

Saturday, August 26, 1916: Twelfth day on the desert

A carriage stopped at the river bank this morning. With the loneliness of a Robinson Crusoe I ran towards it. The man seemed to be a foreigner, probably a European. The driver wouldn't say who he was. I asked the gentleman on what benevolent mission he was making this hazardous trip to the desert camps of the Armenian refugees. I repeated my question in both English and French, but he betrayed no sign of understanding me. But, through the driver, the stranger handed the Circassian ten paper liras (about ten dollars) to be distributed among the more than two hundred of us.

Then the driven and the foreigner drove away.

The Circassian left for Meskeneh in the evening with the promise that with this money he would buy some flour and distribute it among us, so that when the stranger stopped again on his return trip, we could tell him what an honest man he — the Circassian — was.

I consider myself lucky to be able to buy barley cakes. Barley, the feed of animals and asses. We, any of us human derelicts, would eat it with great relish, if only we could get it. Asses are more fortunate, more honored.

Misery and sickness, filth and lice, and extreme hunger and derangement claimed two more lives in front of my eyes.

All night long and all day long, moans and sighs and tears and prayers.

My diary has the following passage:

"It is not too difficult for me to understand the heard-heartedness of Pharaoh to listen to Israel's cries of anguish, but it is harder for me to understand why the merciful Lord God remains deaf to these cries of sorrow."

Nakedness is an accepted order of things. Ladies, daughters of Eve, walk around on unsteady legs, carrying heroically their emaciated skeletons and bloated stomachs, their once beautiful but now matted hair a nest for a million lice.

There is a ferment of rebellion brewing in every aching heart, but none of us has the stomach to stand bare-handed against rifle, bayonet, ax, and club, all in the hands of the Turk, the Arab, the Circassian, and the Kurd.

We fume in silence.

Sunday, August 27, 1916: Thirteenth day on the desert

Today a father sold his five-year-old son to an Arab for two kurushes (two pennies).

I couldn't find one single family intact. Either the father was missing, or the mother, or parents, or children.

Most of these bereft mothers or fathers are ready and willing to sell their children, but can't find a buyer. How I wish I could buy them. If I had food enough…for me…for them.

Monday, August 28, 1916: Fourteenth day on the desert

It has become a habit with me to dream about my dear ones, always surrounded by their love and care. But at once the grim reality comes to rob me of my happy dreams and move me to sobs.

In the night a sudden jab of a pain in my right middle finger forced me to wake up. Those who knew of such things told me it was *dolama*, an infectious boil.

The cold had been torturing me all night long, even in my clothes, better than anyone's in the camp, and the blanket with the possession of which I was blessed.

Today dysentery started to make me suffer. As if I had nothing else to worry about. To find a doctor in this God-forsaken heart of the desert wasteland, the Extermination Camp for the Armenians, was equivalent to finding a drop of mercy in the heart of a Turk.

Tuesday, August 29, 1916: Fifteenth day on the desert

The Circassian brought with him ten sacks of flour from Meskeneh where he had gone three days earlier with the ten liras the stranger had donated for distribution among the exiled. He kept eight sacks for himself and his aide for their services to us, and distributed the contents of the other two by a handful to each one, as long as it lasted. That the mood of despondency bordering on rebellion could depend on so little as a few ounces of flour to change it to contentment was an amazing phenomenon in human nature.

I combined my share with that of Hampartzoum's and kneaded it to make a couple of flat cakes. We saved a portion to boil a German soup with it. This was the first hot stuff going into our bellies since our arrest two weeks before. How delicious it tasted — just water and flour.

The Circassian brought back with him a young girl who had escaped to Meskeneh some days ago. An old man was asking the girl some questions about conditions in general, in the presence of others.

A guard using this situation as a pretext accused the man of flirting, and, with the help of other guards, flogged him in beastly fury. After the lashes he spat on the old man's face, cut one of his moustaches with his sword, and took the bewildered girl into his "protective custody."

CHAPTER 26

WHERE DID YOU LEARN ARMENIAN?

Wednesday, August 30, 1916: Sixteenth day on the desert

The August heat is too heavy to bear. My heart is "the valley of death" for all my fading and wilting hopes. My heart is depressed so low today that I would willingly welcome the End. If in my eternal sleep the Turk will continue to exile me to places and conditions like this, I would neither want to die, nor to live. O God, what shall I do?

I wonder who has stopped the Arab women from coming to our camp to sell food. For several days they have not showed up. Starvation is stalking amongst us with threatening claims en masse. We are craving for the unchewable Arab cakes made of straw and barley which we cannot find, while our guards are stuffing themselves with plenty, glutting in front of us.

O you women of refinement, talent, and sensitivity, how can I gaze at your nakedness without conceiving and invoking unuttered curses to fall on the children of the devil responsible for your present plight? What sort of punishment should I mete them, if authority were granted me to do so, for robbing you of your refinement, talent, and sensitivity and reducing you to search for something to eat in animal filth?

I didn't know we had a fortune-teller among us until a friend brought her to me. She tried to convince me that happiness was in store for me in a short time.

Happiness, what kind? That of the grave? But there are no graves in the desert, only dogs that strip your bones of flesh and leave them for the sun to bleach and the elements to disintegrate.

Is this the kind of happiness you are prophesying for me? And what about your own fortune, my dear unfortunate fortune-telling sister?

For some time new caravans of exiles did not arrive to add to our number. Rumor reached us that a new caravan of 150 arrested "criminals guilty of being born Armenian" had arrived at Meskeneh. Every one began to conjecture that on their arrival we all would be driven further to fall into the bloody hands of fiercer executioners.

Thursday, August 31, 1916: Seventeenth day on the desert

Thoughts of running away from this hell of privation and planned starvation visit my mind every once in a while, but the horror of Arab robbing and ax and club blows quickly push these thoughts out.

I forgot to mention before (says my diary for today) that every morning one of our guards collects from each one of us a "protection fee" on the grounds that what we have is already theirs, and we are "enjoying luxuries" they have "mercifully allowed" us to have. Besides this, they compel us with beatings to go, under guard, to the Arab settlements and get by force straw, barley, and corn for the use of our "masters" and bring it to them on our backs to their quarters. Every once in a while they whip us to do some other slave jobs as walking all directions on the sand looking for kindling wood for them. They are on horseback, water canteens full, whip, rifle, and bayonet ready for use. And all these are done by us without a drop of drink or a bite to eat.

Almost everybody is a walking skeleton. Death has been reaping a rich harvest. Today ten.

Friday, September 1, 1916: Eighteenth day on the desert

Today the Arab women came to sell. But these female devils drive a devilish bargain. They ask for and get your pants, jacket, or shirt in exchange for a small cucumber, an unripe melon or watermelon, or a thin cake of bread one would not eat at home.

For the last three days I had nothing to eat, so I managed to buy a small quantity of bread. The Arab women are so filthy that their already black bread becomes more black and soiled by their constant handling before it falls into your hand.

My pal Hampartzoum ran away from the camp last night.[36] Saner and more heroic act than suicide. All young and daring souls have taken advantage of the relatively relaxed situation and the darkness of the night to seek their freedom. Only cowards and the old and sick are left behind. But I am not very sure that most of the runaways will escape the tearing claws of Arabs in ambush.

I lament the waste of my days without a page to read, without holding a Bible in my hand. All I have is a pencil and a pad of paper my mother had the foresight to drop in the pouch she brought to me in the concentration camp in Karluk.

An ominous silence and loneliness envelops the desert vastness on which we are dumped. The pervasive silence is broken only by the roll and roar of the Euphrates at the spot we are dumped; by the cries of hunger and agony and floggings; and by the twisting and rotating columns of desert hurricanes, spreading depression of spirit, soreness of eyes, and sweep of the scant possessions you have.

Agoraphobia (fear of open spaces)? Necrophobia (fear of dead bodies)? Not at all. Only Turkophobia, fear and hatred of the smell of a Turk.

Saturday, September 2, 1916: Nineteenth day on the desert

Last night a sudden attack of fever began to roast me, despite the chilling cold outside my flimsy cover. Sleep had already denied me its rest because of the increasing throb of the excruciating pain in my finger since last Sunday.

My blanket has also lost its ability to protect me. I have nothing to spread on the damp sand.

I was astonished today to find a rare commodity in a small number of women. These naked and dirt-covered angels showed me sympathy because of my youth (21 years), "difference" from the others, and because of the unbearable pain plus the fever I was suffering with. Their good-hearted advice and good wishes cheered and buoyed my sinking heart. God bless their souls.

These people, ordinarily decent and God-fearing in their former days, have turned out to be like mindless animals with no feelings of respect, consideration, or reverence. Profane curses against God and outright denials of His existence are proclaimed loudly. "If He is the God we worshiped in our churches for centuries, and if He exists, why does He permit the Turks to do all these evil things unpunished?"

To such questions I could find no answer but to scratch the nest of lice in my bushy hair.

There was an attorney from Evérék, the only learned man among us, who immediately recognized me as the one student who successfully passed his examination in *Mejelleh* (Turkish Law) three years before in the American High School in his home town. We both sought each other's company from the day we met on our death march.

This gentleman was a professed atheist. He constantly railed against God whenever we were together, as if I was His representative. Our conversations usually verged on matters above and beyond our knowledge and understanding: God's existence, the beginning of life, the creation or formation of the universe, why evil exists, why the Turk was created...

I was not a match to this master of logic and law. The arguments I quoted from Wallace Cook's *Is There a God?* a course I had taken in college a couple of years earlier, and points from other sources, could not budge my friend from his negative convictions. He was a confirmed apostle of pessimism and hopelessness.

Sunday, September 3, 1916: Twentieth day on the desert

Necrophobia? Terror of death? No more. Just pity and sorrow.

All night long the skeletal body of a child was lying by me. His moans made me talk to him in gentle tones, touch him on the forehead, hands, and freezing feet. The child died. My condition was not much better than his, and death was a welcome friend, as common as breathing.

So I greeted the rising sun with animation and anticipation of something good to happen, My fever had left and gone with the night. A sort of cheerfulness came over me for no obvious reason. The round of the guards to collect the usual "protection tribute" and the consequent laying of thongs did not dampen my cheerful mood until the child's mother came along, and without a sign of grief, without a drop of tear, pulled off the tatters from the dead body and sold it to an Arab for a cake of bread. Someone dragged the child's body a little distance away and left it on the field of bones for the waiting dogs to devour.

That afternoon I spotted the Stranger's carriage stop at the riverbank on his return from Hamam. As I rushed to meet him he asked to know how his gift of ten banknotes had been used. I told him about the flour distributed, purchased with his generous donation. Then he gave two loaves of bread to each who was around him, and drove away towards Meskeneh and Aleppo. I could never learn who this good man was.

That afternoon a new group of runaways was brought to our camp. These all were barefoot, ill-clad, ill-fed, ill-treated Armenian men and women of staunch heroic souls who had escaped from our camp or another death center, enduring the pangs of hunger and thirst, defying the cold of the desert night and the heat of the day, and dodging the fatal ambush of ruthless cutthroats. And now in the relative safety of Meskeneh they were picked up and sent back. Back to starvation and death.

By the addition of this large group to ours the space in the ruins of the khan became too small to accommodate all of us; therefore we were ordered to move out into the open and camp on a designated plot. The guards pitched — no, we did — their large tent on the western end of the camp ground so that they could have a stricter watch on any movement of their prisoners.

Today was no exception for the Turks guarding us to give their prisoners their daily ration of curses and whips. How these villains love to lay blows with rifle-butts on our faces and heads.

Monday, September 4, 1916: Twenty-first day on the desert

Again, and always, the cold has been penetrating deep into my bones. Sleep rarely visits me.

A medley of pitiful cries is rising now, early in the morning, from every torn heart towards heaven, but no higher than a few feet. Streams of prayerful tears are drenching the sand, but not for a flower to bloom.

Hunger, hunger in every body, nakedness, bones covered only with taut skin, and distended bellies. Not only lack of cover at night, but lack of a shirt, lack of shorts, lack, lack...Everything sold for a bite to eat.

A little study of my condition convinced me beyond a doubt that the day by day deterioration of my health was due mainly to the filthy black cakes of bread I so eagerly bought from the female Arab devils. And I decided that from now on I would buy only pure wheat bread. A futile dream of heaven in hell.

Our guards, dividing into two opposing factions, had been feuding with each other for sole custody of the camp. Today the Arab faction, getting the upper hand in the controversy, ordered all the inmates of the camp to move to a new location on the river bank fifteen minutes further back to the west. This move brought us fifteen minutes nearer Aleppo out of a four or five day long unhindered journey on foot.

This unexpected turn of events filled every desolate heart with unfounded hope. It was just like one in the middle of the Euphrates holding onto a straw to save his life from drowning. This move might be, conjectured many "drowning straw-holders," the beginning of an order to return home. Maybe a royal amnesty had been issued by the Sultan and our guards were benignly holding it back to save us from going crazy with a sudden outburst of happiness.

This self-deception rapidly grew into "reality" in deranged minds, so that they began to congratulate each other with good wishes, grateful prayers for the Sultan, Talaat, Enver, and all those arch-murderers who planned and executed the genocide of a race.

TUESDAY, SEPTEMBER 5, 1916; TWENTY-SECOND DAY ON THE DESERT

Today our Arab guardians distributed flour, about half a pound to each. I divided it into two portions. With one I baked bread, just flour and a little water. With the other portion I prepared soup, just plenty of water and a little flour. What a delicious soup it was. I doubt if the Sultan of Turkey ever tasted such an invention. Europe and America have not have not seen the likes of my soup. I think that my evening meal, the invention of a genius like me — cucumber boiled in water — should be recognized by the Ottoman Empire, and the Sultan should grant me a patent, a monopoly.

There is an activity going on in our new camp. People are engaged in devising for themselves shelters or shades. Some have managed to erect tents, open on all sides. No shelter or tent is pitched just for the sake of privacy. No one has a thought or reason for privacy. The circumstance of each one is exactly the same.

Although I have considered myself probably the luckiest in this company of deserted and impoverished, yet I did not have anything in the shape of a prop to shore up a shade for myself. But, lucky as I was, a group of ladies offered me a sitting space in their flimsy "tent"—an elegant palace in my estimation—and laid down a "mat" for me to sit on. The goodness of these "angels from heaven" in their extreme destitution brought tears to my eyes as I stammered my gratitude.

WEDNESDAY, SEPTEMBER 6, 1916: TWENTY-THIRD DAY ON THE DESERT

Nothing unusual.

THURSDAY, SEPTEMBER 7, 1916: TWENTY-FOURTH DAY ON THE DESERT

Nothing unusual.

FRIDAY, SEPTEMBER 8, 1916: TWENTY-FIFTH DAY ON THE DESERT

We were ordered to break camp again and move fifteen minutes' walk back to our former position near the khan. Most probably this order to move back was the result of the tug of war going on for some time between the two factions of our guards. But, no matter what the motive behind our moving back might have been, it was not intended for our good.

Moving back and forth from one spot on the desert to another similar spot was meant to create more hardship on the already exhausted skeletons.

We were treated by these masters of life and death as pack animals. Not only did we have to carry our bodies on weakened legs and our scant belongings on our backs, but we also had to carry our hated masters' tent and other stuff.

Our "belongings"? They were more essential, more vital to us than gold and silver and diamonds. Most of these people, like myself, were carrying with them carefully guarded and highly valued animal dung used as fuel; rusty and shapeless pieces of metal found on the desert among the bleached bones and shaped into a cup or a pan; anything a vanished caravan had discarded or left behind; shreds of rags and strings dug out of the sand.

My own belongings were my priceless pencil and pad, the relatively good clothes on my body, shoes on my feet, a watch and chain in hiding, my blanket, and almost empty knapsack that held a cup, a pan, a spoon, and a little carefully-saved bread.

There were among us people too sick to walk. They had to lean on friends, take a few steps, and then collapse.

The Arabs sold us meat today. I didn't know, and even didn't care to know, from what animal it was. Dog? Cat? Dead horse or donkey? I bought some, boiled it and ate it, the first meat dinner since my arrest.

This evening again flour was distributed, no more than a handful, lest the "ungrateful" prisoners get fat and saucy against authority.

Until now I was utterly ignorant about the art of eating flour. But today I noticed that there are several ways of eating it.

I knew only two ways: baking bread and making soup. But now I saw that some ate the flour as it was. Some ate it in wet lumps. Some melted it in water, as if it was sugar, and drank it. (O sugar, from where did you happen to fall on my desert mind at this time?) Others made it a dough, warmed it on fire, and ate it unbaked. (Who can wait until it is baked?) Some exchange their portion of flour for bread, money, anything.

On the day—rare day—flour is distributed, many have a blinding smoke in front of them, burning rags or dung that refuses to burn.

The two sisters who befriended me by offering a space under their shade and dressed my still-aching right middle finger, washed my underclothes. This was my first laundry since I left Mother. Of course, the sisters did not have soap or warm water. They took their own clothes and mine to the brink of Euphrates, shook the million lice into her lap, and with their hands rubbed and rubbed the soaked clothes until they were free of lice and soil.

I don't know if these angels in rags, from Dubne village of Tigranocerta, had any sins that needed washing as their ragged coverings did.

Saturday, September 9, 1916: Twenty-fifth day on the desert

There was a shrewd man among us who bought an ox, butchered it, and sold every bit of it.

It was not horrid anymore to see some men and women rush to the slaughtered animal with cupped palms to collect a bit of warm blood and lap it off.

I bought a little fresh meat, cooked it, and ate with great appetite. The voice of frugality stopped me from eating up the whole thing at one time and made me save some for the morrow. As the days go with us here, who knows, tomorrow might be a day of hunger for me, so it would be wise of me to save. But immediately the stronger voice of still unsatisfied appetite, combined with that of fear of losing the precious portion to a thief, silenced the voice of frugality. "Let the unborn tomorrow take care of itself," I heard the "voice" whisper. Thereupon I finished the rest of my meat at once, thus depriving the poor hungry thief of enjoying a free feast.

Sunday, September 10, 1916: Twenty-seventh day on the desert

I had been brought up with a healthy outlook on life, and superstition had never found in me a fertile soil for its seeds to grow. Dreams also had no special significance for me, not being an Egyptian Pharaoh or a Babylonian monarch. Yet the terrible dreams of the last night shook me violently. What had happened to my adored Mother who was seriously ill at the time I was arrested and added to the chain-gang? Sister? and Brother?

The intensity of worry and longing for them made the desperation of my condition, caused by constant hunger, slow exhaustion, unending cold, and legions of self-propagating lice, so insignificant.

Monday, September 11, 1916: Twenty-eighth day on the desert

I made a new friend today who invited me to eat with him. A rare case of hospitality in such a dire circumstance warmed my heart much more than his soup warmed my bowels.

It was about 10:00 o'clock in the morning, while I was talking with my new friend, that a gendarme tapped me on the shoulder with the barrel of his rifle and announced, *"Angaria"* (forced service). Half a dozen of us were selected for this honor of rendering "service of love" to our executioners. He led us to a horse cart, made us climb into it, and drove far into the desert villages for straw. In each village this devil knew exactly where the Arabs kept their straw. Without obtaining the consent of the villagers, he would order us to dig. And we were expected to dig the hardened earth and sand covering the pit to get to the straw with nothing, because the devil had not even bothered to think of shovels or picks. Neither had he any sack for straw, which we carried to the cart in our coats or shirts, while he was aiming his bayonet at us.

Despite my efforts not to make my ineptitude so obvious, the gendarme noticed my awkward movements at digging with my fingers, and began to ridicule me before dealing his customary blows.

"Look at this *yessir* (slave)," he jeered. "He is pretending inexperience to deceive me, as if he was a *mu-allim* (a man of learning)."

"Yes, agha," dared to answer one of our number. "He is a muallim. He has never done such menial labor before."

Then the fierce Turk surprised us when he addressed me in Armenian. *"Kheghj Varjabed* (poor teacher), forget what you were before and remember that you are now a *keri* in our hands, and not a varjabed anymore. Here we do not give you friendly advice nor scold you in gentle tones. Our duty is to give you kicks, blows, floggings, and death. You, too, Varjabed, are compelled to obey our every wish and order as any one else is. Don't expect from any Turk, from any Arab, sympathy and respect."

"Hayeren oor sorvetsar?" (Where did you learn Armenian?) I asked, and he replied,

"In Ourfa (Edessa), from my Armenian friends."

Another caravan of arrested Armenians also was brought this evening and added to our camp of condemned.

Tuesday, September 12, 1916: Twenty-ninth day on the desert

None could stand the severity of the cold all night long. No one could sleep lengthwise. All were rolled into a porcupine ball, except those who did not get up with the rising sun. Burying our dead was out of the question. The pack of hungry dogs would not permit it. We had no priest, no minister, no Bible. The dead did not have a tear or a whisper of "Our Father which art in heaven." They just went into the bellies of Turkish dogs, and their bones to cover the face of the desert.

For the seventh time in twenty days we were ordered to move to another location in the same vicinity of Abu Harrar, not too far from the Euphrates.

Wednesday, September 13, 1916: Thirtieth day on the desert

Today only two deaths occurred. Seldom a day goes by without claiming some lives, valuable for us, but valueless to the Turk.

CHAPTER 27

THE GRAVES RECORDER

Thursday, September 14, 1916: Thirty-first day on the desert

Last night a few desperate skeletons on their last legs managed to catch one of those imported dogs that were allowed to fatten themselves on Armenian flesh and blood and butchered it.

I saw an ironic justice in this not too unexpected act. The Armenian ate the dog that ate the Armenian.

This morning Hussein Effendi sent for me.

As I entered his tent, the old man asked me to sit on a rug. Then he began to tell me that he had been told I was a teacher, and he presumed that I must be acquainted with *Osmanlija*, the Turkish script in Arabic alif-ba. When he received my affirmative answer, he continued,

"Muallim Effendi, I have received from the War and Interior Ministries orders to send them reports about how effectively the program of annihilation is progressing. I am appointing you as my recorder to prepare a daily list of the dead, with their names, sex, age, and date of death. I will also give you four grave-diggers from your own people to help you."

Two groups of picked-up unfortunates arrived this afternoon two hours apart from each other. Our number is increasing by new additions like this, but as long as love of life and liberty is inherent in every Armenian heart, they keep on running away every night, no matter how many times they get arrested and sent back to extermination camps like ours.

Today my new-found friend and I contracted on our word of honor to form a company to sell any available article that a deprived community like ours might need. Mr. and Mrs. Levon Somoonjian were nothing less than sweetness, courtesy, and refinement. I considered it an honor for me to be associated with them.

Levon had no money. At least, that is what he told me. So I provided the capital. To have a couple liras would make you a millionaire in our present "civilization" in Abu-Harrar. There may have been some "billionaires" (with a hoard of ten liras), but no one would dare to let anybody know he was a "millionaire."

My partner and his good wife took me under their wing by offering me shelter in their fine tent. I hadn't seen the like of such a tent in all my life of almost two months spent on the desert.

Friday, September 15, 1916: Thirty-second day on the desert

Today I prepared my first list of the day's dead. There were a number of them about whom no one could supply the needed details. I had to invent them before turning the list over to Hussein Effendi.

Saturday, September 16, 1916: Thirty-third day on the desert

We opened our shop today to do business. Our shop is in front of the tent. We have nothing much to sell and no customers. Who has money among the living dead? And what would they want to do with any wares and objects when what they need is food, food only, nothing else.

Sunday, September 17, 1916: Thirty-fourth day on the desert

We closed the shop. The president dissolved the company. He resigned from the presidency and I resigned from the vice-presidency.

Monday, September 18, 1916: Thirty-fifth day on the desert

Another moving was ordered today. We never complain about where we stay. Besides, the sand on this spot is not softer or harder than the sand of another spot. Starvation and deprivation are the same, the cold and cyclone are equally ferocious both here and there and everywhere in the desert. Please, Lord, stop the Turks from doing this senseless thing.

Today I found five dead. Two were found before we had to move. One died on the road while we were marching, too sick to walk. The other two died in the new camp, after a heroic march which drained their last ounce of vigor.

Tuesday, September 19, 1916: Thirty-sixth day on the desert

When I went as usual to the Euphrates this morning to wash my face, neck, and arms, and to shake out the nest of the disgusting "Turk inhabitants" in the tangles of my hair, I discovered a body stretched out lying face down on the beach. Ordinarily such a sight would not have attracted my attention, because death had no more horror for me. Yet I took notice of it now, because of my new appointment to the position of "Obituary Recorder" for the benefit of the Great Ottoman Empire, the Country to which I owed implicit loyalty for raping and wiping out an "undesirable" race.

Was it the body of a desperate inmate of our local camp, or that of an unfortunate washed down the river from another massacre center? I could not decide which of these suppositions was true, neither had I the heart to determine its sex. So I invented all the vital information and entered it in my report. I am sure that the heads of both the War and Interior Ministries in Istanbul will be happy to know that their program of extermination is progressing so rapidly.

Immediately I rounded up my grave-diggers and had them bury the unknown body in the sand deep enough to discourage the Armenian-eating Turkish dogs from unearthing it. It was one of the rare bodies that was buried with the Lord's Prayer. I could perform this very small reverential service now because of the official authority invested in me by the supreme order of the Extermination Camp Superintendent, His Excellency Hussein Effendi in Abu Harrar.

As soon as we returned to the camp someone rushed to me with the sad information that a young man who had thrown himself into the river just a few minutes ago was lying on the shore. His lifeless body was buried next to his comrade in fate.

Wednesday, September 20, 1916: Thirty-seventh day on the desert

After the rude disappointment in my partner's honesty, and the stunning debacle of our one-day long venture into business, I decided to start a business of my own. This time I wanted to be the whole company myself—president, vice president, secretary, treasurer, and salesman. I decided that the greatest need of the starving inmates of the Camp was bread, and that I should start baking and selling it.

But I knew nothing about baking bread as bakers in Hadjin, Adana, and Aleppo baked. But I trusted my simple talent. I would mix flour and water together, and drop a soggy batch on a salvaged piece of tin that I had flattened out into a sheet and warmed over a smoldering, smoking fire of dung.

My store of cash was dealt a severe blow through my unwise trust in my "trusty" new friend and partner, to whom I had handed sixty kurushes on the day of our famous "dinner" of flour soup at his tent, in his wife's presence. What cash was left to me was hardly enough to tide me over another month in this Starvation Camp.

So I made a survey of what I had in my knapsack, and discovered to my delight several unused shirts and shorts, handkerchiefs, and woolen stockings, neatly packed by the hands of my mother. It was a miracle that would-be thieves among us respected this little "pillow" of mine and never came near it.

And when the Arab villagers came to sell their things to us, I showed my supply to an Arab who was fascinated with them. I offered to exchange them for flour, and he consented, but did not have any with him.

So we both walked to Hussein Effendi's tent, explained the situation to him, and asked him if he would permit me to go with the Arab to his village and get my flour.

"Muallim," the old gentleman said, "I trust you that you will be back. I permit you to go. But don't trust these Arabs too much."

Then he called a guard to let me out of the camp limits.

I had never been alone with an *Enegeh*, desert Arab, before. Yet, strangely, I had no fear of him. He could have clubbed, robbed, even killed me, if he wished, but he did none of these. Whether it was because I appealed to his sacred honor to protect me when I said, *"Da khil ek"* (I am in your hands now as Allah's loan), I do not know. He walked on the hot sand in bare feet as fast as a camel, and I could not keep up with him even running.

Once in his tent this child of the desert treated me as Allah's *amanat* (loan) and made a fair exchange with me.

With the precious bag of flour on my back, I returned in due time to the camp, and immediately reported to the Superintendent. He was surprised to see me back, as he was half-expecting that I would take advantage of the chance and run away.

Thursday, September 21, 1916: Thirty-eighth day on the desert

The cold of the night claimed its share of the dead, and the heat of the daytime its own, keeping me busy with burial and recording the list. I did not have time to bake bread and sell.

Friday, September 22, 1916: Thirty-ninth day on the desert

Today officially the fall came to the desert to stay.

I cannot predict what is in store for us when the nights get colder, and the number of dead keeps on increasing.

Saturday, September 23, 1916: Fortieth day on the desert

Today there were ten dead, men, women, and children. They had nothing to live on, nothing to live for. Will someone answer for these someday?

CHAPTER 28

HAFIZ THE DESERT JUDGE

Sunday, September 24, 1916: Forty-first day on the desert

One of the caravans of the seized that have been frequently arriving here in Abu Harrar brought with it some weeks ago a totally sightless man, with whom my frequent visits developed into friendship. This elderly gentleman was called *Hafiz*,[37] out of respect for his blindness, age, and ability to recite poetry. His memory was very bright and he could recall the minutest details, and he was wise and bold in expressing what was right or wrong according to his judgment. Once when I remarked that why didn't he stop to think that some people might be embarrassed by his outspokenness, he answered in a cryptic phrase, "My eyes do not see, therefore my cheeks do not blush."

Today I paid him a customary visit, just for the pleasure of talking to him. He asked me how I was faring. Reluctantly I told him that my heart was aching because of the treachery a trusted friend had played on me. "But the fault was mine. I shouldn't have played the fool," I added.

"What happened, Varjabed, tell me," he asked, suddenly becoming interested.

I told him, in order to get it off my chest, that about ten days previously a man named Levon Somoonjian, seemingly warm-hearted, sincere, and respectable, had invited me to his tent to have "dinner" with him and his wife. Then he proposed a business partnership, using his tent as our shop, to sell clothes, shoes, blankets, and food stuff. He convinced me that he had private means to get all the stuff we needed, as he was a merchant in his home town. He knew, he said, that there were people among us who had money and were waiting to buy what we would sell them. The only set-back to this plan, he confided, was a small capital, just two liras.

He said that he would be the president and treasurer of our "company" as an experienced businessman, and I would be vice president and secretary. And he offered me the shelter of his tent as a partner.

I told him that I was glad to be a partner with him, but I did not have two liras, (which in truth I did not), but I could give him sixty kurushes only. He was disappointed at such a paltry sum with which he could not get much stuff. "It isn't enough," my new partner said, "but under the circumstances that will do."

I handed him the sixty kurushes I had promised.

After a few days my partner told me that our partnership was dissolved, because he had lost the capital I had given him.

"And now," I concluded my account of the fraud, "he refuses to pay me back."

"Right now," said my sightless friend, after hearing my story, "go and tell the attorney from Evérék that I would like to see him on an important matter."

When the attorney from Evérék greeted the blind poet, Hafiz briefed him about the matter hurriedly, and asked him to fetch Mr. and Mrs. Somoonjian to him. Meanwhile he sent me to locate and bring to him the Catholic Varjabed, a respected inmate of the camp.

The field of sand on which we, about five or six of us, were scattered, each, as an individual or a group, had made a "home" for himself as best he could. So it didn't take more than a few minutes to locate Pasqual Varjabed and walk with him to our mutual friend, the camp's "Homer."

When all were gathered around him and sat down, the blind philosopher took the role of a stern judge and began to say that he had called them to help solve a critical case. He called our attention to the cold fact that we, brothers and sisters of the same blood, were brought to this desert condemned to slow death, and in such a situation none of us had the right to cheat or defraud any other brother-in-suffering.

Then turning towards me, he asked, "Varjabed, did you have any business dealings with anyone sitting in this group?"

I started to recount the story I had told him before: forming a partnership with Mr. Somoonjian to open a shop; my handing over to him more than half a lira; his failure to provide the merchandise; his "losing" of all the money I had given him; and his abrupt cancellation of the three-day-old partnership.

"Did you sign any contract, do you hold a receipt for what money you gave him, or do you have any witnesses?" the "judge" asked.

"No, Sir," I replied, "all the transactions were made orally, on trust in each other's integrity. Mrs. Somoonjian was the only witness to both the partnership talks and transfer of money from my hand to his."

"Do you swear that what you stated are all true?"

"No, Sir," I said. "I do not believe in taking an oath. My Yes is yes, and my No is no."

Then Hafiz asked Mr. Somoonjian what he had to say about this accusation.

Mr. Somoonjian did not hesitate to make an outright denial of ever forming a partnership or receiving money from me.

"Do you swear to the truth of your denial?" asked Hafiz.

"Of course I do," brazenly declared the man.

My heart sank as my money had sunk.

Then Hafiz the judge, nailing his sightless stare at the direction from where Mrs. Somoonjian had greeted him, asked, "Mrs. Somoonjian, will you put your right hand on your heart?" The woman did so at once, unthinking.

"Will you repeat the words I am now going to say: I, Mariam Somoonjian, never saw…"

The woman repeated all these words.

"…never saw Varjabed Kevork pay sixty kurushes to my husband…"

The woman at this point hesitated for a moment, and then suddenly broke down into sobs, looking at her husband's face plaintively, reproachfully.

The husband, seeing her shame and agony on his account in front of these highly honored men, admitted that he had indeed received the stated sum from me.

"Where is that money now?" asked the attorney from Evérék.

"I cannot tell where it is gone, but it cannot be retrieved and returned to Varjabed anymore," said the confessed defendant with a note of despair.

"Do you know," intervened Varjabed Pasqual, "that Varjabed Kevork is now the official Obituary Recorder for the Interior Ministry, appointed to this position by Hussein Effendi, the Supervisor? If this case gets reported to him, you may be sure that you will be at the mercy of either the hungry pack of dogs waiting out there, or the swift currents of the Euphrates down there."

Thus the poor man was forced to confess that he had paid all that money to the guards to let him and his wife escape, but the treacherous Turks had beaten him after taking his money.

"You are a criminal worse that a Turk for this heinous act, against a brother who is as badly in need of freedom as you and any of us," said Hafiz with contempt, acting as the Justice of the Law. Without losing his dignity the blind man of high standard of morality and justice then passed a judgment against the defendant.

"You, Levon and Mariam, will immediately vacate your tent and turn it over to the man whose trust you did not deserve and whose money you swindled."

Sarkis Effendi, the lawyer from Evérék and Pasqual Effendi, the Catholic man of learning, walked with us to the tent to supervise the transfer from the Somoonjians to me.

From that day on I do not recall seeing that poor couple in the camp.

Monday, September 25, 1916: Forty-second Day On The Desert

I am twenty-one years old today. (September 25, 1895)

In the monotonic drag of similar days in this death-trap sometimes unforeseen circumstances arise with their incidental happenings of stealing, deception, heart-ache, and acts of justice and recompense. Such an unexpected chain of events made me the possessor of a real tent that would protect me from now on for an uncertain length of time against the onrush of autumn in the desert and the onslaught of winter.

I moved my newly-acquired tent to a different location, placed my belongings in it, and started to engage in the business for which I had bought flour from the Enezeh tribesman.

I hired three helpers to start my business.

Tuesday, September 26, 1916: Forty-third day on the desert

I buried ten dead today. No day passes by that starvation, lice, dysentery, and other diseases do not claim their share of precious lives.

"Precious lives," in the sight of God, as I was taught to believe by the infallible authority of the Word of God. "Worthless lives," "rubbish," "chattel," and "dung" by the estimation of the Turk.

Which view is right?

Wednesday, September 27, 1916: Forty-fourth day on the desert

Today six people were found dead, two men and four women.

Fountains of tears and sorrow are dry in every heart. There was not a drop shed for any of these unfortunates, while there was cheer among the Turks.

Thursday, September 28, 1916: Forty-fifth day on the desert

I bought a large copper pot today, and with the help of my assistants started to cook *keshkek*—a porridge prepared with shredded meat mixed with broken wheat and water. Adequate seasoning made the food very appealing to those who could afford to buy and eat.

With the use of citric acid crystals I managed to develop yeast for bread dough. My bread was so successful that it surprised me.

Yesterday morning, with Hussein Effendi's permission, I accompanied some Arabs to their village and bought from them a quantity of tobacco. My helpers rolled the tobacco with writing paper (of which I had plenty, thanks to my position as Recorder), and I sold three or four cigarettes for a penny.

My tent turned out to be a department store where meal, bread, and cigarettes could be bought.

Friday, September 29, 1916: Forty-sixth day on the desert

My business venture showed signs of progress. If it continues to be as good as it was yesterday, I will be better fed than before, and others will be fed too.

I owed a great debt of gratitude to inimitable Hafiz, whose unflinching sense of justice and moral and intellectual rectitude restored my confidence in the inherent nobleness of my brothers and sisters in suffering. It was a pity that Mr. and Mrs. Somoonjian, ordinarily a charming couple, should be victimized themselves soon after victimizing me. Even their tent, in which they lived their joys and sorrows together, having been offended at their swindle of me, changed sides and came to be mine.

Today eight deaths occurred in the camp. They were all buried with a prayer.

Saturday, September 30, 1916: Forty-seventh day on the desert

Today I washed my clothes and took a bath on a far-off bank of Euphrates.

Sunday, October 1, 1916: Forty-eighth day on the desert

Today is Sunday again, the eighth I have spent in the desert with all my captive brothers and sisters. Sundays have nothing here in this Extermination Center that should make them holier than any other day. No one has a trace of religious feeling left in him. No manifestation of it has been evident. The Turk has so effectively succeeded in uprooting that fundamental feeling of attachment to God, to His Son, to His Word, to His Spirit.

I haven't seen one single copy of the Holy Bible, nor a Prayer Book. No hymns or sharagans were heard, no warble of a bird or a child.

"Faith, hope, and charity," the trinity of Christian virtues, were left behind when we were arrested, chained together, and driven away just because we were Christian Armenians with faith, hope, and charity.

No, there is no Sunday in Hell.

Today is Sunday, the day dedicated to worship and holy meditation, to the Gospel and to sacred music. Today is *Kyriake*, the Lord's Day, the day in which the Savior of the world rose from the dead. But unnumbered and unnamed myriads, followers of the Divine Savior, are falling dead all the length and breadth of the forbidding desert.

If the exile of Israel and Judah was for their idolatry, hypocrisy, and arrogance at the hands of Sennacherib of Assyria and Nebuchadnezzar of Babylon, on what ground was this terrible judgment passed on the God-fearing, Christ-worshiping, and faithful church-building, non-political Armenians at the hands of the Turks, the cruelest of all the cruels of history?

Happy exiles of Babylon, happy sons and daughters of Zion!

"The rivers of Babylon" offered you the cool shade of their green willows on whose swaying boughs to hand your harps. But Euphrates had not even one shrub on her bank to afford us a misery shade, not even a single willow to hang our dead hopes on.

Monday, October 2, 1916: Forty-ninth day on the desert

Who started this bit of news, I don't know, but a rumor is going around that *Kyrban Bayrami*, the great Turkish feast, is approaching. (*Corban*, an offering to God among the Jews of olden days.)

In the first week of October *el hejira*, Mohammed's flight from Mecca to Medina in A.D. 622, will usher in the 1355th year of the Moslem calendar. Therefore, insisted the rumor, a royal amnesty will soon be granted to all Armenian captives to enable us to return to our abandoned homes and resume our former peaceful pursuits.

Poor, wretched dupes.

The frenzy of expectation of the impossible was, by degrees, whipping up their hopes beyond proportion.

Where they found it was a mystery to me, but they did really find a large Armenian Bible and brought it to me to read to an assembled large group the 137th Psalm and other portions from Jeremiah and Ezekiel. They demanded, in particular, the reading and expounding of Daniel's prophecies about times and numbers.

I began to read in the 12th chapter of Daniel that Michael, the prime of angels, was appointed to stand guard over "your" nation; the warning that greater anguish than than previous sufferings in history will come over you; the promise that the people of God shall shine brightly as the sun's brilliance; and the heart-wringing question of "How long will it be until all these terrors end?"

When I came to the 12th verse, "And blessed are those who wait and remain until the 1335th day!" they began to weep for joy, because, as they were convinced, Daniel's prophecy of the mystic figure of 1335 surely meant the Moslem year of 1335, just four days later, on October 7.

I didn't have the heart to quench their misguided hope by telling them that these two figures did not mean the same thing, and that there was a period of almost a thousand years between Daniel's prophecy and the beginning of the Mohammedan era.

Even my friend the atheist condescended "as a favor to me" to believe in God and the infallibility of the Bible "if the first day of 1335 brings us freedom."

Tuesday, October 3, 1916: Fiftieth day on the desert

Most of the young, men and women, starved or not, those in whom still glittered a spark for life and freedom, against all odds, are running away. Thus the inhabitants of the camp are growing smaller in number with continued deaths.

Today Hussein Effendi disclosed to me that shortly he would be leaving for Aleppo on the occasion of the coming Bayram, and that I should find two other companions in the camp that could pay him one lira each to accompany him.

Wednesday, October 4, 1916: Fifty-first day on the desert

Last night a strange meteorological phenomenon attracted everybody's attention which had no logical explanation. For about fifteen minutes an object appeared near the moon in the shape of balances, and then disappeared. As it happens with desperate people like us, there were a variety of explanations and interpretations in favor of freedom from this hell very soon.

I was the most ignorant person among so many wise people. I could venture no explanation.

CHAPTER 29

BY THE RIVERS OF BABYLON

Thursday, October 5, 1916: Fifty-second Day on the Desert

For a long time now no flour has been distributed to the rapidly dying through hunger and exposure. Sporadic distributions of a handful or two of impure, adulterated flour have injected in the condemned people the false hope that the "Most benevolent Sultan of the Invincible Ottoman Empire" cares for the welfare of his loyal subjects in distress.

Starvation has been reaping a rich harvest today, twenty dead.

We have no contact with the outer world. We do not even care if there is an outer world engaged in a life and death struggle with each other.

The feeling of interest is dead in all of us.

But not quite so.

A group of about a dozen fellow prisoners came to my tent this afternoon to discuss with me "a very serious matter," a matter "of life and death," they said.

One of them spoke for the rest.

"Varjabed, we have talked it over with each other, and decided to ask your opinion on this vital matter.

"We know that we are persecuted and being massacred all because we are Christians. We have gained nothing for being Christians all these centuries. We believe that if we renounce our Christian faith and embrace the faith of Islam we will be allowed to return to our homes and occupations. After the world affairs get settled, we will return to our former Christian faith. What would be your advice about this matter?"

"My brothers," I began, "You are all older and wiser than I am. You are free to do anything that will give you freedom from death. But I will not join you if you renounce your two-thousand-year-old faith for an inferior faith that creates murderous devils like the Turks. If you turn to be Turks, I would be afraid of you because you would be called to do to me and your Armenian brothers and sisters just the same crimes that these criminals are doing. I cannot take my Christianity and Armenianness off like a jacket for a while and then pick it up another time. Katch (brave) Vartan had a Vassag[38], and the Savior had a Judas. Do you wish to be traitors to the sacred memory of all these poor innocent people we are burying every day and all the tens of thousands whose flesh the dogs and the fish ate?

"You are asking my advice. You can go to Hussein Effendi and lie to him with *La ila ill Allah, Muhammed el resoul Allah*." And I concluded, "I would rather die than pronounce that false confession."

The spokesman scrutinized the humiliation on the faces of his comrades and replied, "We knew you wouldn't approve, and we wouldn't be traitors either." Then they got up and left.

FRIDAY, OCTOBER 6, 1916: FIFTY-THIRD DAY ON THE DESERT

I have a group of four funeral helpers who inform me first when they find a dead body so that I can prepare my record for the Superintendent, and then they take the body to a spot on the field of bones and dig a trench for it. We all join in the Lord's Prayer and bury the innocent victim of Turkish genocide.

Each one of my grave-diggers deserve describing. I do not intend to offend their gentle spirits after these sixty years, but humbly ask them to forgive me when I reproduce their description out of my diary of this day in 1916.

At the outset I am compelled to state that my corpse would be terrified to be manhandled, carried, and buried by them.

My first grave-digger was a giant sparingly dressed in tattered rags, cast-offs by the poorest. His two bare feet were swollen out of proportion, and he was a one-eyed ogre with sallow and sunken cheeks. He was a skilled undresser and robber of the corpse.

The Web of Hope

The second grave-digger would remind one of Robinson Crusoe in dress, with a far-off and ghastly, ghostly gaze, short in stature, and with a raw sore nose.

The third one had an extraordinarily fat and large mouth, as if ready to devour anything he could lay his enormous paws on, even you, if you should meet him in the dark.

And the fourth looked like a feared monster, heavily lame in one leg, a creature who would not let any other creature or a dog come near a dying person until it was hopelessly dead and he alone could appropriate what the poor corpse had left behind.

My diary notes that these four "ghosts" often came into my dreams to molest my corpse, and my corpse would wake up in a shudder. Fortunately day-to-day contact with them dulled my abhorrence, and developed sympathy for them.

Today Hussein Effendi, the outwardly mild-tempered gentleman, asked me an outlandish, devilish, and most detestable question that only a Turk could ask.

"Muallim, when will this damnable people die off and come to its end so that you and I can return home?"

This was a wish only a Turk is capable of making, not a human being. The death of a nation was a fun, a joke, a job for him.

It is not surprising that Victor Hugo could read with a keen mind the Turk's black heart long years ago.

Louis Adolphe Thiers (1797–1877), the well-known statesman and historian and one-time president of France, once said of Turkey:

"The Sick Man will die soon, but its corpse will stink up all Europe for fifty years to come."

"The Sick Man" died morally and spiritually when it initiated the first genocide of history by killing about two million Armenians, and its corpse has continued to foul up not only Europe, but also the whole world, and not only fifty years to come, but for all time.

About a month ago the count of the inmates would reach four hundred, but today one hundred of them are buried. Skeletons in Adamic nakedness are roaming, like apparitions from the Nether World, in futile search of a bird's feed, and none is able to help the other without hurting himself. Sanity of mind, sensitivity of heart, and devoutness of soul and spirit are vanishing in rapid degrees.

O Lord, show us Your mercy, You who have eyes to hear the heart-rending sighs and cries of a people condemned to death; You who have a sensitive nose to smell the rivers of blood shed by innocent children; You who have a compassionate heart to feel the injustice and torment perpetrated on this most defenseless people.

To whom can we turn now but to You? You are our last hope and refuge.

Please Lord, listen, and save.

Saturday, October 7, 1916: Fifty-fourth day on the desert

Today is the beginning of the Turkish *Bayram*, one of two great feasts, on which occasion almost everybody in the Extermination Camp had been expecting a general pardon, which never came.

Pardon, for what? What crime is there in being born an Armenian, or a Greek, or an Assyrian, that he, with all his race, should be condemned to genocide?

Yet the naive, good-hearted, long-suffering and God-fearing captives expected goodness from their rulers, who never knew what fear of God was.

Neither did Hussein Effendi's promised carriage arrive to take him to Aleppo to let him celebrate his feast of *Corban*. He, too, was deceived by his superiors, probably as a punishment because he did not succeed in annihilating his share of captives.

A wonderful thing happened to me this afternoon.

I was at the river-bank when a carriage came from the Aleppo road and made a stop. The driver called me to ask if I knew anybody by the name of Kevork Gejekooshian. Excited, I said,

"I am Kevork."

"Do you have a mother?"

"Yes," I said, "she is in Hokedoon."

Then the man asked what my mother's name was. I answered,

"Sarah."

The man said that he had been looking for me everywhere on the desert, in Meskeneh, Dipse, and all along.

Then he reached inside the carriage, pulled out a large bundle, and gave it to me, saying that my mother and sister had prepared it for me.

"I never expected to find you so easily," he said, "because who can locate one person in a million who are sent to the desert to starve and die. But I couldn't stand against your mother's tears for you, and against hope I took the package to return it back to her later."

And now, he said, he was so happy that he had succeeded in his hopeless mission.

The package contained a heavy blanket, shirts, undergarments, a pair of new shoes, and imperishable items of food. My joy is great. Every item I touch makes me feel that I am communing with my dear ones.

SUNDAY, OCTOBER 8, 1916: FIFTY-FIFTH DAY ON THE DESERT

These barbarians have reverence neither for their own *Juma'a*, nor for the Christian's *Bazar* (Sunday).

On this holy day several gendarmes walked through the prisoners and began whipping right and left, calling, "*Angaria*, forced labor for your masters!" They rounded up a large task force, compelling them to ford the formidable and unfordable Euphrates to a distant island, whether a man could swim or not, to cut fire-wood for the Center in Meskeneh.

A gendarme, unknown to me, laid several lashes on my head, face, and back to make me join the labor force. I told him that I didn't know how to swim, but he wouldn't listen. Then another gendarme who knew me stopped my tormentor, telling him of my position as Recorder, responsible to Hussein Effendi.

What magic quality my worthless position as Recorder had, was a pleasant surprise to me.

Those prisoners who were too sick or otherwise unable to do that kind of labor were set free after paying a tribute.

Another unbearable situation was created by Armenian night-guards, recruited and appointed by the Turk gendarmes from among us. These contemptible creatures were invested with the right to extract tribute from us, their fellow-sufferers, for their services to the Turks. These degenerates would not hesitate to resort to violence by extortion, beating, and even killing. I witnessed all these cruelties heaped upon our heads by these detestable traitors.

Monday, October 9, 1916: Fifty-sixth day on the desert

Very strange. Unbelievable!

The Arab, with whom I had gone to his village two weeks ago and bought flour from him in exchange for my unused undergarments, came to the camp this morning with his camel, to help me escape to Aleppo. His kindness was so touching, I gave him a gift, thanked him, and declined his offer.

Tuesday, October 10, 1916: Fifty-seventh day on the desert

There is nothing, absolutely nothing, that would cheer you up when you are surrounded by so many lifeless, dead, and dead on wobbly legs walking towards their last breath.

And the desert hurricane, creating itself from nowhere, takes an ominous shape, plunges its hungry trunk into the sand, lifts an enormous quantity of it, twists itself in swift revolutions, and sweeps away from one horizon to another.

And melancholy is pressing on my heart today with its heavy paw, to crush all the remaining emotions, to numb all aspirations for freedom and beauty.

In such a mood I sat down on the sand-bank of mighty Euphrates and composed a sonnet addressed to my mother.

The substance of the poem was the following:

> Your son, Mother, is passing away like a comet gliding away
> into the depths of the sky, and like the fading of the
> sun's last ray behind the blue arc of heaven.

> Dismal Fate's blows have effected an end to his hopes. He came like the wind, and blew away like a whisper.

> Don't be grieved over the sward of grass that whithers at the setting of the sun.

And then my depressed mood suddenly took a turn towards hope, hope that can never die — the last object still remaining at the bottom of Pandora's Chest — and concluded with a brighter note:

> Halt your mournful tears, Sweet Mother. The spring will come with green on its trail, and you will bloom again with the spring.

Wednesday, October 11, 1916: Fifty-eighth day on the desert

Himfish, the wily Arab gendarme, having returned from Meskeneh, woke us all up in the middle of the night pretending that something good was in store for us. He immediately began to record each one's trade, occupation, and profession. He was too sly to "reveal" the purpose of his out-of-season trickery. Almost everybody enthusiastically and hopefully entered into Himfish's list.

My diary is specific in noting that I did not enlist "because I am certain that this is a Turkish bluff intended to deceive us." Besides, I had no trade, neither occupation, nor profession. I had no room in Himfish's scheme.

In contrast to the extensive misery and excessive starvation in the camp, there are among us some really wealthy prisoners who remain aloof from the rest of us, and manage to get their own way with the guards.

These people occasionally slaughter a sheep or an ox or a camel. And after keeping the choice portions for their use they sell the rest to those of us who can afford to pay their price.

It is a heart-tearing scene to see the impoverished madly stampede each other to catch some of the animal's blood in their palms, pans, or cups. I saw some lapping and licking the soaked sands as a dog would;

some drinking the warm liquid while it was spurting from the severed jugular veins; some boiling the stuff to the hardness of a piece of liver.

I witnessed bitter and fierce fights between men and women over the spilt blood or cast-off refuse. These unfortunates habitually steal each others' last crumb, thus filling the air with the din of constant quarrels.

It is probable that a revolution will break out if the guards continue to withhold the distribution of flour stacked in scores of sacks in the guard house.

Thursday, October 12, 1916: Fifty-ninth day on the desert

The expected revolution of the desperate finally started this morning. But it was misplaced, misdirected. The revolting mob was duped. Instead of directing the revolution against the oppressor, the Turk, the gendarme, and the guard, the mob turned on the Arab women who had come to sell food to us.

Beside Hussein Effendi, the Superintendent of the camp, there were about fifteen gendarmes, all armed, well-fed, and trained in the art of ruthlessness and extortion, and about two dozens of guards — Turkish and turn-coat prisoners — equally oppressive.

But the mob, at the instigation of the gendarmes and the guards — the real culprits — attacked the vendors of food, upsetting their merchandise, scattering, trampling, plundering, devouring.

The terrified black daughters of the desert looked for a way to escape, but were forced to remain and fight. Some women of the mob went underfoot and were left unconscious. There was destruction, uproar, and bloodshed.

Still at the spur of the hated gendarmes, the women of the camp gave a different direction to their insurrection. All the women shouldered their rags and rusty pans this noon, and began to march towards Meskeneh. And adding farce to the comedy, the whole force of gendarmes joined the women to go to Meskeneh. To protect them? Of course not. To molest them.

The poor, aged, and lame Hussein Effendi was left powerless to stop them. He appealed to the corps of guards, and they succeeded in quelling the "Womens' Revolution" and turned the revolutionaries back to the relative safety of the camp.

Hussein Effendi publicly announced that a high government official would soon pay us an investigative visit.

Friday, October 13, 1916: Sixtieth day on the desert

Last night another caravan of exiles came and without stopping continued their way deep into the desert. There were about fifty carriages tightly packed with unfortunate captives. This was ominous. No captives had been brought before in carriages to our part of the desert. These people in carriages, it occurred to me, must be destined to immediate liquidation, and soon the turn will be ours. The name of Der Zor struck every Armenian heart with terror because of eye-witness accounts of massacres and drownings in wholesale.

After the caravan of carriages disappeared into the desert night, two carriages with bread arrived from Meskeneh. Two loaves were distributed to each prisoner. No cries of hunger were heard all night long.

At noon today a rich-looking carriage arrived. Out of it came down an angry-looking Turkish officer. He was Haccu Bey, the high official we were told to expect. He was one of the notorious architects and formulators of the present genocide. He was virtually the master of our lives, having forcibly usurped that right from the hand of God. Being one of the chiefs of devils, he created a new hell wherever he stepped.

As soon as he stepped down from his comfortable carriage and surveyed the fields dotted with so many tents and people sprawled around, his Turkish rage was roused at Hussein Effendi and his corps of gendarmes for their dereliction of duty in putting a swift end to these *"mundar zitil"* (accursed rubbish).

He ordered an immediate *sevkiyet*, march, to Ziyaret, a misnamed slaughter point. (*Ziyaret* means visit. He was ordering us to visit Death.)

Haccu Bey then went around to investigate everything. When he was examining the ruins of the khan and the adjoining gendarmery on the hill he discovered the two Armenian boys in the service of the gendarmes. He curtly ordered them to join the *sevkiyet* being formed down in the camp. The boys came to my tent. One of them was Samuel, my friend who had been occasionally sneaking food to me, and the other boy was Hovsep, his younger brother, whom I had found in a caravan two weeks earlier and sent to Samuel. We all three were "brothers" from the Hadjin and Fénésséh orphanages, and sitting together in my tent, were discussing our situation when Haccu Bey happened to pass. Recognizing the boys, he ordered us to tear down the tent and immediately get into the line of marchers.

I had already heard him give an order to Hussein Effendi to keep the tent-owners there until he sent carriages for them from Ziyaret. Leaving my tent, my friends and I hid in someone else's tent until the executioner Haccu Bey had gone, driving his victims before him under heavy guard. Then we returned to my tent, and suddenly I felt the beginning of a sickness in my body.

Saturday, October 14, 1916: Sixty-first day on the desert

Haccu Bey sent bread for us from Hamam. Hussein Effendi told us, as he distributed it, that Haccu Bey would sent carriages from Ziyaret to accommodate our travel.

Sunday, October 15, 1916: Sixty-second day on the desert

I am not well at all.

There are others who are not well.

There is a young girl next to my tent, in company with her father.

This girl has a painful boil under her right arm. She is moaning, begging, beseeching her father to help break its head and squeeze out the pus. The father continues to be deaf to her entreaties until the poor girl promises to give him her small loaf of bread that evening.

This evening the girl gave him her bread. The father, after receiving the bread, broke the boil and relieved the girl. Then he made a fire, boiled on it some sort of concoction, turned his back to the daughter, and devoured his bread, her bread, and the soup, all by himself.

The starved, half-naked and shivering girl, in order to warm herself, crouched over the fire her father had made for his soup, and dozed off. In the middle of the night a deafening shriek revealed that she was on fire.

Monday, October 16, 1916: Sixty-third day on the desert

Right at the time the tragic burning was taking place, two small one-horse wagons arrived, sent by Haccu Bey.

This morning everybody was ordered to strike his tent and load it in the carriages. Everyone was hurrying back to throw their bundles in. But the carriages could hardly hold half the load. So those of us who were too slow to pack and find room for our belongings had to stay behind and wait for extra carts to arrive.

I pitched my tent back again, and exhausted because of my sickness, lay wrapped in my blankets.

CHAPTER 30

ZIYARET

Friday, October 20, 1916: Sixty-seventh day on the desert

When I opened my eyes this morning, "Thank God!" said Samuel, who, with his brother Hovsep, was hovering over me, as if I had been sick for several days.

"Good that you regained your consciousness in time so that you can go with us in the *sevkiyet* today," they said. "Last night two wagons arrived for the rest of us in Abu Harrar to move on to Ziyaret."

"You would have been dumped into the river if you hadn't awakened," they added.

The order to move on had already been given, the tents were being pulled down, and everybody was busy making his bundle.

My pals, after feeding me some quickly-prepared hot soup, wrapped me in my blanket and placed me, with the consent of my chief Hussein Effendi, in one of the carts, all my belongings by my side.

Thus I left Abu Harrar where I had spent more than two months of my twenty-one years in direst misery — misery experienced through sight and hearing; misery experienced physically, mentally, and spiritually; a misery whose indelible imprint will remain on my soul as long as I am permitted to live.

And this poor innocent horse was pulling me to a rendezvous with an uncertain, sinister Fate.

All day long we traveled on the endless desert, now seeing Euphrates, then losing sight of her. I was in the cart, and my friends were marching with the rest of the company towards an unknown destiny. The sun was good to me today. Its light and warmth served my aching body as elixir.

When we arrived at Hamam late in the afternoon, the first station on the way to Ziyaret, our caravan of more that fifty men and women with tents and possessions, was ordered to camp about ten minutes' distance from the officially permitted settlement.

My two "brothers" helped me down from the cart and tried to make me as comfortable as they could. And because the six-day long sickness had exhausted my resistance, they put me back into my heavy quilt and coaxed me to go to sleep.

"Sleep well until midnight," Samuel said into my ear, "because at midnight we three are going to escape into the Armenian settlement."

Knowing that Samuel was a veteran of several previous escapes with his ability to speak Arabic, I went to sleep with dreams of a successful escape.

But the quality of my dreams changed from pleasant to unpleasant. A band of cutthroats had descended upon us, I continued to dream, and were shooting, looting, axing, slashing, clubbing. And a couple of these ugly monsters, with their axes poised high and aimed at my head, were standing over me.

Terrified by my dream, I opened my eyes, and to my multiplied horror, I saw that my dream was not a dream at all, but real. The cutthroats were really in action with their slaughtering and looting. And, worst of all, the two dreadful ax-wielding devils were really poised over my head.

In a twinkling of an eye, before either one of the two axes came down, as fast as a butterfly leaving its cocoon, I slipped out of my blanket, crept through the arched legs and kept on creeping in the pitch dark, not knowing where I was heading. I dared not stand up and run on foot for fear of being detected, but kept creeping on and on. The sounds of shooting and the cries of the poor victims urged me on, unmindful that I was a sick man.

I could not tell how long my creep took. It must have been a very long hour. At long last my unseeing head bumped into a goats' hair tent in the middle of nowhere. Immediately I pushed my tortured body inside, no matter whose tent it was, a cutthroat foe's or a "friend's."

But surprisingly it was vacant. It had neither owner, not a shred of furniture.

I sat down in the middle of it, on the cold sand, shivering, and meanwhile thanking God for returning my consciousness in time to see the murderous axes over my head; for the split-second decision and extraordinary liveliness to escape; for guiding me in the dark straight to this shelter, and for its vacantness.

"Dear Lord," I continued, "forgive me my foolish complaints in Abu Harrar. Now that You saved me from the massacre, I am confident that You will lead me by Your own hand to freedom and to my mother. Thank you, Lord."

Saturday, October 21, 1916: Sixty-eighth day on the desert

The morning sun brought its warmth to the desert outside and quickly it penetrated the tent. Hunger had been with me for several days while I was deliriously sick, and now thirst and the growing heat of the tent came to torment me. Still I did not dare to peek out for fear of being picked up as one who had cheated the massacre.

At last, late in the afternoon, a strange onrush of courage pushed me out of the over-heated and unaccommodating tent.

What a heart-warming discovery was waiting for me!

I discovered that it was definitely God's Hand that had directed my blind creeping in the bleak night to this particular tent. This vacant tent was the last one on the outer edge of the Armenian settlement.

As I proceeded cautiously and aimlessly through the maze of the tents the sweetest female voice caressed my ears.

"Brother Kevork. Brother Kevork!"

Automatically I turned my head towards the tent the voice was coming from.

A youngish woman ran to me and holding my hand led me to her tent.

"Who are you?" I asked perplexed.

"I am Hripsimeh, your sister Mary's classmate in Hadjin. I could recognize you anywhere."

Immediately Hripsimeh brought in front of me several balls of kufteh and a pitcher of tahn.[39]

While I was still eating, her husband walked in and, surprised at seeing me in his tent, asked his wife, "Hripsimeh, how did you find Kevork?"

He was Boghos Effendi Ouzounian of Hadjin, who, unknown to either of us, had comforted me with a substantial chunk of bread and an onion on the riverbank in Abu Harrar several weeks earlier. The instant I saw him I recalled that this good man had advised me on that occasion to find his tent if I happened to get to Hamam. And now that advice had taken place with no design or premeditation but by Providence.

"Now that God has sent you to us," he said, "we don't want to lose you. Somehow I will take you to your mother in Aleppo, just to see her tears of wailing change into tears of happiness."

"Only," he added, "I warn you to be exceedingly careful not to be seen by any gendarme. There are strict searches made daily for runaways like you and men and women who do not have a permit to stay in Hamam. Whenever you get hungry, you must come here, but for the nights you must find shelter somewhere else. I wish I could keep you here with us, but that would jeopardize the security of my family and children. Losing my license and permit to stay alive would not benefit you at all, but would destroy all of us."

That would be the last thing to wish for such a noble couple, Boghos and Hripsimeh. I thanked them profusely and headed out.

I knew that God was with me.

As I walked around not knowing what to do, I met three young men I had known in Abu Harrar who had managed to escape from that hell. They told me the terrifying news that Haccu Bey, our archenemy, had returned from Ziyaret this noon, and had issued a strict order for a large-scale *sevkiyet* for tomorrow morning. The gendarmes were now busy combing all the tents to pick up the runaways and those who did not have identification papers.

It was evening now, and they took me with them to one of the caves in the cliffs rising from the western edge of Euphrates. In the pitch dark cave there were many other refugees like us — runaways who had no place to stay, nothing to eat, no right to life. And no cover to protect oneself against the damp and cold.

"Refugees?"

I don't know if it is proper to call us "refugees." A refugee flees to a refuge, flees from danger to a safer place. We were dispossessed, deported, displaced, driven out, but not to a city of refuge, not into the arms of a welcoming committee of charitable, sympathetic societies, but only to certain death in a hostile desert teeming with ravenous, murderous Chechens, Kurds, Enzehs, and the lowest Turkic tribes.

Yet in the absence of refuge, this dank cave was a refuge, and I thanked God for providing it for our use. I learned that there were a number of such caves all along the palisades.

The night was long and the misery longer.

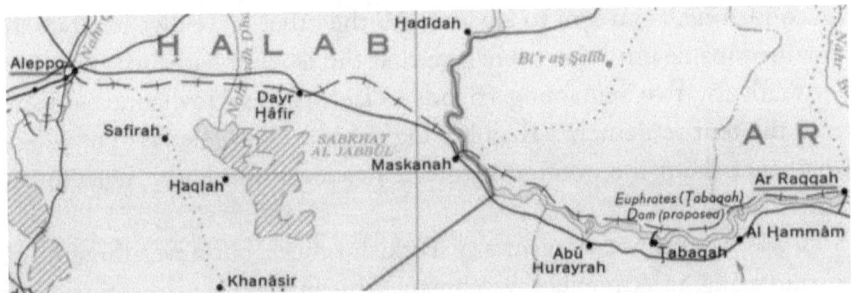

Approximate route of the deportation. Names are rendered in the text as Der Havr, Meskeneh, Abu Harrar, Hamam. This is from a modern map, but before the dam was built on the Euphrates that innundated the caves mentioned in the text. The distance of the march was approximately 100 miles. Der-Zor is another 100 miles farther down the river.

CHAPTER 31

THE CAVES

Sunday, October 22, 1916: Sixty-ninth day in the desert

Arshavir, one of my three new companions (what impelled him to do so I never learned) decided to leave the cave early, and was readily picked up by a hounding gendarme, added to the gang of the condemned, and sent to Ziyaret. All the other "cave dwellers" wisely remained inside until they were sure that the *sevkiyet* had already gone.

With my two remaining friends — Levon and Hovhannes — I entered the tent settlement. Then leaving them at their friend's tent where I had met them the evening before, I headed towards the Ouzounian tent.

I was careful not to meet any Turkish officer, but never thought of encountering an Armenian watchman. This unfeeling man stopped me somewhere among the tents to see my *vessica* (permit), which of course I could not produce. He ordered me to go with him to the gendarme headquarters. I told him I was on my way to see Boghos Effendi. He insisted that first I should go to the gendarmery and then to see my friend.

I happened to have at this time a hand stick (I don't know where I had picked it up) which I offered to him as a gift if he would let me go on my way. To my surprise and relief the rascal accepted the insignificant bribe and let me go.

Boghos Effendi and his good wife were glad to see me safe and asked me what I had been doing since the night before. I told them about the cave and the watchman's threat. Boghos Effendi told me not to fear that man anymore; he would see him. Then these wonderful people gave me something to eat and drink. After that they urged me to write a letter to my mother. They supplied the paper, envelope, and pen, and then Boghos took the letter to the post office of the settlement, paid for the stamp, and mailed it. This was the first letter I had sent from the desert.

The Caves

Monday, October 23, 1916: Seventieth day on the desert

Finding the shelter of the cave unbearably miserable my two companions and I decided to pay a tent owner to give us a space to sleep at night. We found an old man who agreed.

We "three musketeers" planned to seek a chance to escape from this death trap, but we found out to our dismay that such an attempt at this time would be inviting immediate death because of the tightest surveillance. The best thing for the present, we concluded, would be to hide. But attempts at hiding for us slaves were just like sticking our ostrich heads in the sand while keeping our bodies exposed to the view of the executioners.

Tuesday, October 24, 1916: Seventy-first day on the desert

The night in the old man's tent was a real torture for me. The "tribes" of lice he was "raising" in his tent were far fiercer than my "own cattle" that I had been carrying on my body all these months.

But I was not on a vacation or a picnic. To whom should I complain, and with what right?

Wednesday, October 25, 1916: Seventy-second day on the desert

While we three fugitives from death were fighting the unconquerable armies of lice in the middle of the night a child's voice warned:

"If there are any fugitives in these tents get out and run away. Gendarmes have started their search. There is *sevkiyet* in the morning."

In a hurry we left the old man's worthless shelter and made our way to the bank of the Euphrates. We kept moving to and fro on the solitary beach until morning to keep from freezing.

Early in the morning, while we were shivering, as if from hell itself an Arab gendarme made his terrifying appearance before us. Luckily, the villain was easily satisfied to leave us alone when I bribed him with half a mejid (about fifty cents). Levon gave his pocket watch, and Hovhannes his purse.

Thursday, October 26, 1916: Seventy-third day on the desert

We did not dare to leave the relative safety of the beach until we were sure the poor caravan of the *sevkiyet* had gone on its way to perish.

News of the bloodbath reached our ears daily from Der-Zor and elsewhere. My friends and I could not find an opportunity to escape to safety — to Meskeneh or Aleppo.

Both the days and nights were pregnant with dangers for us.

As the night approached we knew that the old man's tent was neither safe nor comfortable. So we three went back to one of the caves on the cliff. Beggars are not choosers. But we chose one of many equally dangerous evils — the cave.

Fortunately we lived through our misery in the cold, damp, and lice-ridden cave unmolested by any devil — a Turk gendarme.

Friday, October 27, 1916: Seventy-fourth day on the desert

My two friends left the cave for the tent settlement, but I chose to remain under the cliffs.

Hopelessness, depression, melancholy heavily struck me today.

I have no world, no country, no people, no family, no friend, no church, no ideal...

Why am I endeavoring to live? For whom? To realize what dream?

I am now in the bottom of a dark pit I can't climb out of.

Under the cliffs I lie gazing at the blue waters, listening to the roaring currents of the Euphrates, and thinking of the tens of thousands of victims of man's inhumanity to man the mighty river was carrying daily to the cavernous belly of the ocean. My thoughts rested on a number of those innocent victims washed over the river bank while I was in Abu Harrar, marked for death, as I was now.

The Caves

Instinctively my hand pulled out of my inner pocket the pencil and pad of diaries and started to compose a sad poem, the first and the last lines running with the same mournful note:

My poor heart cries tears of blood.

Suddenly a pang of hunger jabbed at my stomach and raised me to my feet.

It was late in the afternoon.

Hripsimeh, that gentle soul, scolded me for not showing up all day. She said her husband had been looking for me all day long, because he had an important thing to tell me.

As Boghos Effendi came in from outside, he, too, scolded me.

"I am glad to see you not arrested yet, because a great *sevkiyet* for Der-Zor is scheduled for tomorrow morning." And then he added:

"Listen to me carefully and do exactly what I am going to tell you."

He then told me that beside the caravan for Der-Zor there would be another caravan going in the opposite direction, to the west. This caravan of carriages would take twenty-five families to Jarabulus, all with permits signed by Haccu Bey. After a night at Meskeneh, the travelers would continue their way to the north, away from Aleppo.

"This is your only chance. In the morning I advise you to mingle with these travelers, being very careful not to be seen by any gendarme. Once in Meskeneh you will disappear from the caravan."

"May God be with you in every step you take, Brother Kevork," said Hripsimeh, "and give my love to Sarah Mairig and to your sister Mary."

I left the Ouzounian tent well-fed and comforted. I made my steps continuously to the usual cave with happy dreams, in spite of the day's melancholy and the night's obnoxious vermin and the cold's bitter bite.

Saturday, October 28, 1916: Seventy-fifth Day on the Desert

Early in the morning of this Saturday, my two companions and I left our "luxurious hotel rooms" in the cave and walked to the settlement. After they had gone to their customary haunts among the tents I entered the bazaar square and from there turned my direction to the west road.

The Web of Hope

There was a great activity going on. Carriages were being loaded and starting to roll. A crowd of about two hundred men, women, and children were on the road, some riding in the carriages, but most on foot.

Unnoticed I slipped into the crowd, as if I too was one of the privileged permit bearers. No one showed any interest in me. No one questioned me.

We left Hamam behind.

Nineteen hundred and some years before Christ an illustrious patriarch and his party traveled on this sun-baked desert road, as I, in a different circumstance, am doing the same journey about the same number of years on this side of Christ. It must have been at a point in the neighborhood of Hamam that Abraham of Ur of Chaldea and his family, slaves, and cattle crossed Euphrates to reach Haran, and after some years there recrossed it to continue towards the "Land of Promise."

And I wonder and wonder about how Abraham, with a party of hundreds of people, thousands of animals, and immense possessions could criss-cross this mighty "sea" of merciless currents with unfordable depth and invisible width. Did the Jehovah he worshiped open up a dry road for him between separated walls of water, as He did five hundred years later in the Red Sea for Abraham's hard-pressed fleeing descendants?

Surely the same Jehovah, who had been directing his footsteps on these sands at his 75, is directing mine at 21, as I put my steps on his four-thousand-year-old footprints.

As the desert sun rose higher towards its zenith, the heat climbed to the degree of Nebuchadnezzar's Furnace. Although hunger and thirst were not on unknown terms with me, on this stretch of road they acted as cruelly as a Turk. I offered all the cash coins I had for a drop of water to a fellow traveler, but he would not sell me a drop, lest he be left without it. I could not blame the man.

It was about noontime. The length of my steps began to shorten and I fell behind, lagging. Spotting me from his perch on a wagon, Boghos Effendi motioned to me. When I approached him, he handed me a piece of dried bread and a tin cup of water.

"Don't linger behind," he warned. "And don't let any one suspect that we two know each other. It may be dangerous for both of us. Meanwhile keep your hopes high. God will save you."

Invigorated and comforted, I opened my steps wider and resumed my position at the head of the caravan.

It was night when we arrived at the familiar grounds of the ill-famed Abu Harrar, the broad field of the bleached bones of tens of thousands of martyrs, where I had spent an eternity of misery.

Boghos Effendi fed me again. I rushed to hospitable Euphrates, drank sixteen cups of water, and, wrapping myself with a cover my benefactor loaned me, I went to sleep under his wagon.

Sunday, October 29, 1916: Seventy-sixth day on the desert

Early in the morning I left my shelter under the wagon. It was relatively a more comfortable night than the nights in the cave.

We began marching away from the haunting hollow stares of the thousand and one bleached skulls of my brothers and sisters.

The caravan was on the move.

Again the same hot sun, hunger and thirst, but no complaint.

At noon we were at Dibse, the notorious concentration camp the fiendish Turks turned into a slaughter center, where they systematically exterminated thousands upon thousands of deported, driven Armenians — men, women, children, babes — and set banquet tables for hordes of dogs they specially imported for that purpose only.

They massacred every caravan they drove here.

The whole surrounding became so foul that even the devils themselves would not endure the stench they had created, and left Dibse for Abu Harrar. They defiled that part of the desert, too, as they had done at Meskeneh and then Dibse.

As we approached the khan, the chief of the gendarmes escorting the caravan to Jarabulus ordered everybody in the party of assemble in the courtyard for a roll call of the travelers.

This was the same yard in which, several months ago, I was made to lie on a heap of human and animal dung; spent all the hours of the dark night in dread fear of the thrice damnable homosexual Ahmed Chavoush; heard him in the morning haranguing and terrorizing hundreds of us cowering "slaves" of his — "I am your Allah now. You are dogs, pigs, infidels. I can cut your throats, smash your heads, bury you alive or throw you in the river. I have the highest authority behind me to do all these…" This was the same courtyard he collected rent from all of us for resting in the dung-hills and donations for listening to his speech.

And now, on this Sunday noontime, another gendarme, under a different circumstance, is standing to call the roll of the travelers with permits.

"Lucky people," I envied them. "They are all in the roll but me. What shall I do now?"

"Those whose name I call, will leave the crowd and walk in front of me to stand on my right side," the gendarme said.

As he read the names several people crossed before him to stand on his right. After he read ten names, I notice that there were more than three people answering to one name.

"It is obvious to me that most of these people are fugitives like me," I thought. "I doubt if the officer has noticed the deception. I cannot be dishonest and unfaithful to my Christian principles of right and wrong. It is a lie and a sin to cross from the left to the right when someone else's name is called."

And I, like a "pillar of salt," stood alone, while two hundred or more answered to fifty names.

"Why are you standing there like a post?" the gendarme roared.

"Because my name was not in your list," I answered.

"Idiot," he said, "didn't you see so many cross over to the other side?"

Then turning around he ordered an aide,

"Tie this fool's hands, so that I can turn him over to the authorities at Meskeneh."

One of the wagon masters brought a piece of rope and tied my hands.

In my foolish, self-righteous reasoning it never occurred to me that even my Lord slipped away from evil people who were intent on pushing Him over a precipice.

Soon after the caravan started to roll on towards Meskeneh. The chief of gendarmes took hold of the end of my rope and forced me to keep up with his horse.

The Caves

Black thoughts began to crowd my mind: at Meskeneh the local Turk officials would torture me, and under special guard send me to Ziyaret or Der Zor, or finish me in Dibse, Abu Har…

"Lord," I said in agony, while running after the horse to ward off any lashing, "Lord, forgive my expensive thoughtlessness. You know I am not clever. Show me how to extricate myself from this situation."

Suddenly it dawned on me that I had a very small piece of gold money, one-quarter of a lira, about one dollar and twenty-five cents, wrapped around my knee, the only wealth I had.

Somehow I managed to get the gold out, and offered it to the gendarme as a gift. The man accepted it, threw the end of the rope he was holding back at me, and harshly told me to untie myself and run as fast as I could to Meskeneh.

"When my caravan arrives there, don't show your face to me," he added.

No eagle had swifter wings than I had legs. Hungry, thirsty, sweaty, tired, and poor I flew with borrowed vigor through dunes, rocky hills, sinking sand, unmindful of any obstacle, until Meskeneh took me in. The caravan reached Meskeneh exactly two hours later, but I never saw it.

(The rope that bound me on this memorable occasion has been carefully kept in a glass jar all these sixty years and is in my possession at this writing.)[40]

Long before the caravan arrived, I had already bought a large loaf of bread with the last coins the fellow traveler with water had refused, and on the advice of someone made my way to one of the many caves on the face of the mountain. In the safety of the cave, in the company of others like me, I ate, drank, and went to sleep.

CHAPTER 32

MESKENEH

Monday, October 30, 1916: Seventy-seventh day on the desert

This is my first day in Meskeneh, or rather in one of the many caves in Meskeneh.

The journey of the previous two days from Al Hamam through Abu Harrar and Dibse, and particularly the effort to keep pace with a horse while its unsympathetic rider held the rope tied around my wrists, and then the ordeal of running towards Meskene spurred by the remnants of dwindling strength, had given me blistered and painfully swollen feet.

Unable to stand on my feet I lay in the cave all day while everybody else had left in search of something to eat, or a chance to return to Aleppo.

I had plenty of time in the constant night of the cave for meditation, analysis, and evaluation of the events and experiences of the recent months on the desert. It was evident to me that the Lord's hand was keeping me and guiding my every step. But this conviction, I knew, did not give me the license to act foolishly as I had in Dibse. The Lord had dulled the chief gendarme's ruthlessness to the extent of accepting my trifling bribe to let me run to the safety of Meskeneh. I must be extremely careful, I concluded, not to undo what I had gained thus far by running away from certain death in the interior of the desert. The Lord is not responsible, I philosophized, for a second foolishness on my part. Then I thanked God for letting me leave behind Abu Harrar with its terrors and Hamam with its massacre.

When "the regular night boarders" of the cave began to come in, I knew that another night had come.

Meskeneh

Tuesday, October 31, 1916: Seventy-eighth day on the desert

The caves of Meskeneh, as those of Al Hamam and elsewhere along the Euphrates, must have served in centuries past as shelters for fugitives like ourselves. The refugees of this particular cave were about a dozen, all with shattered health, extinguished hope and crushed dreams, living each present moment in the fear of arrest and certain death. None of us was any better than the other. No position, no class, no worth. All were equal members of the same democracy — the democracy of the tortured, the condemned to death. We all were too conscious that death was following at our heels, as our shadows, more real than our shadows.

I wondered if anyone was able to sleep.

In an uncertain hour of the night, while every one was wrestling with his own thoughts, from the entrance of the cave a child's voice rent the silence with the warning that gendarmes were raiding the caves.

"God bless you, Aram," said those who knew the little hero from previous warnings.

In a minute everyone disappeared.

With a superhuman effort I, too, jumped on my swollen feet and scampered down the hill towards the Euphrates, thrust myself into a thicket of out-grown shrubs and reeds, and finding a pit I lay myself in it.

The thin layer of water at the bottom of my bed was cold.

And the heart of the world was very, very cold.

There was no one from whom I could expect warmth.

Yet the stars overhead blinked, as if playing a game of hide-and-seek with me. A shooting star or two streaked a blazing trail through the sky before it disappeared. But the hours dragged their feet to delay the departure of the night. And when, after week-long hours, the sun came to thaw out my numbed body I was too exhausted to leave my grave-sized bed of water. But the "glad" feeling that the caravan of death collected in the night must have left by this time lifted me up from my bed.

Slowly I limped my steps out of the thicket and found myself in the Bazaar. I had no special purpose in mind. Knew nobody, and had not a single penny to buy bread. I was reduced to the state of a beggar, but I had no courage to beg.

As I hobbled along on shaky legs, seeking for a spot to sit, to rest and to sun, someone called me by name.

"Varjabed, Varjabed," said a big young man with flowing black hair and beard. "What are you doing here, and in this condition?"

He was Baron[41] Onnig, an intellectual who, for a short time, had shared my room in the school of the Church of the Forty Martyred Children in Aleppo.

I told him briefly about the massacre in Hamam, my near-disastrous escape, and my dreams of returning to Aleppo.

Immediately this good man opened the bag hanging from his shoulder, took out a generous piece of bread, and handed it to me, meanwhile helping me to sit on a rock. Then he ran to bring me a drink of water in his tin cup.

While I was being refreshed and comforted by his kindness, he advised me to walk down a certain lane in the tent city until I found the largest black tent. Inside that tent, he said, "you will find a short, stocky old gentleman, Mardiros Agha Gertmenian, a man from Hadjin like you and an Evangelical as yourself. State your case to him. He might help you."

Baron Onnig restored my dwindling physical strength, my faith in the goodness of man, and my sagging spirit with hope.

The pain in my feet disappeared as I walked up the hill to the Gertmenian tent. The old man was alone and engaged in repairing a shoe.

"Mardiros Agha," I addressed him, "I am a native of Hadjin, and I remember very well that on your return from the United States you spoke to us in the Academy in 1909. I want to go to Aleppo. Can you help me?"

He scanned me from head to foot. He saw before him a dry skeleton with a matted head of hair inhabited with lice, dressed in rags, shod with footwear beggars would refuse, a ghost-like apparition.

"I have seen thousands like you come and go," he said. "I wish it was within my power to help you go to Aleppo, but it is not… But I will be glad to give you these two silver coins to buy some bread for yourself."

I was glad to receive his gift, and thanked him for it, although what I needed most was moral support.

I turned my steps towards the Bazaar where, with Mardiros Agha's generous gift, I bought enough bread and retired again into the cave for dinner, contemplation, and rest.

Wednesday, November 1, 1916: Seventy-ninth day on the desert

It was about noon when I met my friend Baron Onnig in the Market Place. He was looking for me, he said, to find out the result of my interview with Agha.

I told him of Agha's inability to assist me in getting to Aleppo, mentioning Agha's gift of two 8-penny silver coins to buy myself much-needed bread. He expressed his gladness to see me in better health and spirit today. I told him it was due to his moral support.

Then Baron Onnig offered me another piece of advice which proved to be an inspiration from God.

"Right now," he said, "go the same direction you went yesterday until you came to the last tent beyond which is the government house. At the last tent ask for Hampartzoum Effendi Kellejian and tell him your story. He is a man of God and an Evangelical. If there is a man who can help you, he is the one."

I had nothing to lose by trying this man too.

When I came to the tent I saw an old lady inside.

"Mairig" (mother), I said, "Is this where Hampartzoum Effendi stays?"

"Yes, my son," she answered sweetly. "It is time for him to be here any minute. Will you sit down and wait? By the way, my son, what is your name?"

"Kevork," I said, and before I could give the rest, she interrupted,

"Gejekooshian?" she asked.

"Yes," I answered in amazement.

"Thank you, Lord," she exclaimed, raising both hands heavenward. "We knew you would answer our daily prayer in his behalf."

Then she told me that her son Hampartzoum had met my mother in Hokedoon several times on his visits to Miss Rohner, the German missionary, and promised my mother to pray for my safe-appearing before him.

The lady immediately set before me a hot soup and a large quantity of bread and cheese, and continued her praises to the Lord for my miraculous appearing.

"Hampartzoum, can you guess who this boy is?" asked the old mother when her son entered the tent while I was still engaged in devouring cheese.

"How can I know one from the other among a million pitiable Armenians," he answered in a tone of futility.

"For whom do we pray daily mentioning his name before the Lord?"

"Kevork?" asked her son quizzically.

At her nod of affirmation this man of God raised his hands upward as his mother had done before him and offered the self-same prayer of thanksgiving,

"Thank you Lord, we knew you would answer our prayers for Kevork."

When the excitement caused by the miraculous answer to his prayers had somewhat subsided, he pulled out a letter from an inner pocket and handed it to me. The handwriting was that of my sister, and the warm words those of Mother's. At the reading of such love, longing, hoping, and praying a miniature Euphrates began to stream down my cheeks.

After my agitated emotions had quieted down this good man handed me a tiny bundle. It was my own purse, full of small coins, sent by Mother.

"Now," said Hampartzoum Effendi, to reinforce my famished spirit, "Now that the Lord has brought you to us, you will stay here until He provides the proper chance and means when I will take you to Aleppo and hand you personally to your mother."

I suddenly found myself in a delirium, a state of unreality, a dream that would vanish if I dared to open my eyes. Could such abundance of blessings fall on a person in such a short period of minutes? Dejection about half an hour ago in the Bazaar grounds, and now this "heaven on earth" to which the Holy Spirit directed me through Baron Onnig's mouth. Was this tent the holy Tabernacle of the Old Testament in which Jehovah dwelt and watched His people's steps? Beyond doubt, He was watching mine.

Meskeneh

It so happened that the Kellejian tent was pitched just a few paces away from the government building which housed the gendarmery. Every single officer staying there was vested by order of Talaat Pasha, the Minister of Internal Affairs, with the unquestioned authority and responsibility of destroying any Armenian he saw, more particularly, those who could not produce a permit to live.

One of these dreaded gendarmes, returning from the Bazaar where he had picked up several young men for forced labor, saw me in front of the tent and pressed me to join the gang. Then he led us inside the building to clean up the place.

"I have never seen you before," he began to question me. "Where did you come from?"

Terror forced me to lie.

"I have been here all the time. It may be that you haven't seen me."

"Where are you from?" he persisted.

"Marash," I continued to lie, remembering that I had suffered before for revealing that I was from Hadjin.

"Are you related to Hampartzoum Effendi of Marash?" he asked.

"Yes, Bey Effendi," I stammered. "I am his younger brother."

Even I was surprised at myself for daring to lie so boldly. And to compound the mess of lies, a young fellow pressed with me to this *angaria* — the forced labor — voluntarily jumped to my assistance.

"Yes, Bey Effendi, I know this boy. He has been here for several months, and is Hampartzoum Effendi's younger brother."

"I never knew that he had a brother," said the gendarme. "I am from Marash, too."

I felt crushed. I don't know how my unknown friend felt. But the gendarme kept an ominous silence

At the conclusion of the labor we were allowed to return each to his haunt. I came directly to Hampartzoum Effendi's tent, but said nothing about the unpleasant conversation. I was too ashamed of my lies.

He, instead, began to unfold before me a cheerful plan to accomplish my final restoration to safety. He said that God had provided a miraculous way for my deliverance, and it was this: In the last hour while I was being detained for *angaria*, he had been called by the governor and given a commission to take a young woman and her child to Aleppo.

"We will start tomorrow morning," he continued. "A horse carriage is provided, with a gendarme as our escort. I want you to get up early, and with extreme care walk the road in front of the government building, and when you find yourself behind the hill, throw yourself in the ditch alongside the road and wait for the rumble of our wagon. Then boldly walk over and climb into the carriage."

"The Lord is with you, Kevork. Don't be afraid," he added. Then he covered me with a heavy quilt near the entrance of the tent and bid me good night.

These optimistic assurances of the godly man were not able to quiet down my raging storms of doubts and distress. I had openly lied to the gendarme, and knew that he knew that I was lying. Black thoughts crowded my mind like a flock of buzzards descending on dead and not-so-dead bodies scattered on the Abu Harrar desert.

"If that blood-thirsty gendarme should decide to raid this tent this very minute," I began to worry, "and drag me out from under this comfortably warm cover to administer the customary pastime of flogging before sending me to my death in the darkest depths of the desert…"

All of a sudden the black thread of dark thoughts snapped. The throng of lice hitherto embedded in my body in an astronomical number became animated from their hibernation because of the unusual heat generated by the wind-, rain-, and cold-proof Circassian cape covering me, and with their fury drove me insane. The clothes lice began traveling in tribes to and fro on and in my rags. The biting, boring, and sucking lice mercilessly bit every inch of my body, bored their way through the meager flesh and reached the thin stream of blood to suck. Hair lice, crab lice, all schools and tribes, even the millions of eggs fastened in long lines on each hair of my miserable body having momentarily hatched, started a cosmic activity which even a dead body could not endure.

Immediately I threw the cover aside and tip-toed out of the tent towards the cave on the far end of the encampment, on the hill overlooking the Bazaar, where I had spent my previous nights. It did not occur to me at the moment what my God-directed trusting benefactor would feel when he discovered that I had disappeared from his custody when the prospects were so bright.

Once in the solitude of the cool cave the legions of lice went back to their hibernation, leaving me free to strip my thoughts of their blackness. The prospect of a successful escape under the protective custody of my God-sent guardian angel gradually became brighter, and a hopeful and invigorated young man emerged from the cave early in the morning.

Thursday, November 2, 1916: Eightieth day on the desert

Last day in Meskeneh

In accordance with a plan I had devised in the loneliness of the cave I untied the rope holding my ragged pants as a belt — the rope that had a few days earlier served to tie my wrists together in Dibse and drag me along behind a gendarme on his horse towards Meskeneh. Then I began to gather dry sticks of shrubs and reeds blown by the wind, and pile them on my rope as if I was to kindle a fire for cooking or warming purposes. Thus gradually I approached the open gate of the government house, stooped several times to pick up insignificant stalks of crushed plants and carefully placed them on my rope. In a casual and innocent gait I moved on, in front of the guard, still clutching my precious bundle of kindling, slowly away until the threatening figures of the guard and the hell he was guarding disappeared from my sight.

"*Park Kez, Der!*" (Glory to Thee, Lord!) I exclaimed as I threw myself into the trench along the road to wait for the melodious rumble of the wheels.

The pit was cold, but the desert sun by and by transformed the cold trench into a furnace. Hours followed one another, 8, 10, 12. Hunger and thirst in the desert are quite something else. There was nothing to do.

"O skeleton," I addressed my body, "how can you take all these punishments — death-marches and beatings, prolonged hunger and thirst, heat and cold, fatigue and sickness, lice, sores, filth and death around you, loneliness and dispiritedness, constant terror of life and death — and still stay sane and alive?"

"Youth, and a gleam of hope," answered the spirit that was holding my dried up skeleton straight.

I spent some time perspiring, time in prayer and thinking, and then pulled out my inseparable notebook and busied myself scribbling something.

At last, at 3 in the afternoon, the welcome sound of rolling carriage wheels made me jump out of the pit. The wagon was turning the corner of the hill into my view. Beside the driver, Hampartzoum Effendi was seated in the open carriage with his charges, the young woman and her child, at his side. There were two other Armenian men also in the small carriage, bound for Aleppo.

But the sinister sight of a gendarme comfortably seated in the carriage while fondly cradling his menacing rifle in his lap instinctively frightened me into hesitating from my enthusiastic rush. As I pretended to bend down to pick up another stick to add to my pile Hampartzoum Effendi admonished me to drop the bundle and hurry to the wagon.

Gladly I climbed in and sat by him.

Contrary to my expectation the man of God did not scold me for running away from the shelter of his tent the night before, but began to allay my fears one by one by relating that he had given a banknote to a gendarme who came to his tent last night looking for me; and also that he gave on my account two silver mejids to the gendarme sitting in the carriage. He told me that after my escape from his custody last night the Lord assured him that I would turn up today according to the plan.

Then he gave me some bread to eat.

The carriage rolled on the sandy road I had trudged on several months earlier. The thousands, of which I was one, men and women, boys and girls, were tortured, left to starve and dehydrate, massacred and permitted to be eaten up by packs of dogs and flocks of buzzards. Some were swept away by the currents of the Euphrates, and the rest were swallowed up by the vast desert. And now, through the grace of God, I, the least, was leaving the sands, the dunes, the caves, and the hills behind. "Lord, don't let me ever see them again," I repeated within my heart.

The carriage made its stop for the night at the khan in Der Havr. This was the station to which hundreds of unfortunate deportees had trudged with me for three terror-filled days. This was the place where Ahmed the sodomite dealt me a rifle-butt blow for resisting his evil intent and chained me to a cart-wheel for the night.

And now, Hampartzoum Effendi, the leader of the traveling party, made the necessary arrangements with the inn-keeper for the gendarme and the other two men, and rented another room for the young lady with the child, me, and himself. After a light lunch and evening prayer all retired to rest.

A loud and impatient pounding on our door woke us up at midnight.

"Who are you and what do you want?" asked Hampartzoum Effendi from behind the locked door.

"Hampartzoum Effendi, I am gendarma Ibrahim Effendi," answered the man from outside. "I have been riding all day from Hamam and my horse is too tired to travel. Will you make some room for me in your wagon?"

That familiar voice immediately sent cold shivers into my whole being. This man was one of those dreaded gendarmes who had marched us, the remnant of a decimated caravan of five hundred deportees, from Abu Harraf to Al Hamam a little more than a week ago and saw them massacred on the first night, from which massacre I was the only survivor through a miracle.

"Please, Hampartzoum Effendi," I beseeched. "Please tell him no, tell him you have no room for him. I know him. He took me from Abu Harrar to Hamam and massacred all my companions. Please…"

"Yes, Ibrahim Effendi," said my guardian angel to the ill-famed murderer, ignoring my entreaty altogether. "I will be honored by your presence in the wagon. You will be my special guest."

Then my guardian turning to me said,

"I don't want to see you lose your faith in the Lord. He took care of you all these months, and sent you to me in answer to my prayers. Do you think He will forsake you now? Besides, how could I refuse such an evil man the favor he is asking? By doing this small favor to him I may receive a larger favor from him, either for you, or for some other unfortunate."

Ashamed and wiser I buried my worries in prayer.

CHAPTER 33

LAST DAY ON THE DESERT

Friday, November 3, 1916

In the morning we all resumed our small spaces on the small carriage platform. Our escort-gendarme came along not only to tie his horse to the back of the vehicle and them climb in to occupy an ample room, but also to deposit a full-grow sheep beside us. Then came the dreaded black butcher of men, Ibrahim Effendi, to tie his tired horse on the other side and climb in expecting and getting room enough for two. The rest of us six travelers squeezed on each other to make the worthless bodies of these evil men hugging their rifles and blood-soaked bayonets, and also the smelly sheep, as comfortable as possible.

Rarely one talked to the other.

But the gendarmes were quiet, too.

I knew that the escort was already "silenced" by my guardian, but Ibrahim's silence was ominous. I knew that he recognized me. He was one of our camp gendarmes at Abu Harraf and had occasion to see me present my obituary reports to Superintendent Hussein Effendi.

After some travel of silent discomfort Hampartzoum Effendi suggested that he and I get off the overcrowded vehicle and march together for some time.

Walking, under the conditions, was a welcome relief.

"I sensed your turmoil," he said, "and that is why I asked you to walk with me."

Then this man, as stalwart as a Prophet of old, began to bolster up my faith in the ultimate triumph of goodness and justice, and the sure dawning of a brighter day for the remnant of our suffering race. He said that the Lord was leading me directly to my mother's arms, and I should have no doubt about it. He could understand full well, he continued, that the unprecedented experiences I had gone through all these months should have infected my whole being with the poison of fear and distrust, but total trust in the Lord can easily displace that pervading terror with faith, hope, and peace.

"Now," he exhorted me, "start making a habit of repeating to yourself as often as you can the powerful statement in the sixth verse of Psalm 117—

> The Lord is on my side. I will not fear. What can man do to me?

Armed with this spiritual weapon, you will be able to overcome every besetting situation in your life."

It was not hard to keep up with the wagon because it was rolling at a slow speed. After an hour or so one of the other travelers joined us, warning me that the new gendarme had asked him and his companion who I was and where I was from, and that he and his companion had told him that I had been a resident of Meskeneh for as long as they could remember.

The brotherhood of fellow-sufferers!

It was about noon when we climbed back on the carriage. After sizing me up for sometime, Ibrahim Effendi shot a direct question at me.

"Muallim, when did you leave Hamam?"

"Are you talking to me?" I asked, feigning ignorance. "I am not a muallim, and was never in Hamam."

"But I saw you in Abu Harrar, and escorted you and your party to Hamam where they were all slaughtered on the first night. How did you manage to escape it so sick as you were at the time?"

"I don't know what you are talking about," I answered with a bold lie.

Without making his duty to confirm or refute my statements, Hampartzoum Effendi assumed the authority of the Prophet and addressed my arch-foe:

"Ibrahim Effendi, this boy is in my charge. Allah has given him to me to take him to his mother in Aleppo."

"*Pek ala*" (very good), answered the fiend, and from then on shut his mouth.

Yet the fear of uncertainty about my foe's secret designs was growing within me like a batch of leaven despite my placid mentor's inspiring exhortation of minutes earlier.

The Web of Hope

The carriage kept on rolling over the road towards Aleppo, mixing up hope with fear and anticipation of joyful reunion with my dear ones with dread of capture and death-march once again. As the mysterious silhouette of the ancient metropolis of Syria came into view in the hazy distance, hope displaced fear for a while, until we approached the sector called Karluk, the infamous Center from which hundreds of condemned caravans were sent out to their death.

A little before we came to the outskirts of the city the gendarme with the sheep decided to take a short-cut to his home, so he left the carriage, untied his horse from the back and rode it, meanwhile struggling to keep the sheep in his lap. But both the animal and master were uncomfortable. Perceiving a rare opportunity to escape Ibrahim Effendi's evil schemes I offered to carry the sheep on my shoulders to which the gendarme readily agreed. My mentor raised no objection, knowing full well my state of nerves.

The carriage rolled away without me, or rather leaving me with another questionable companion.

The sheep seemed a light burden at first, but as at this time a heavy rain began to fall and soak the thick wool coat, the sheep grew heavier by the minute and the road rougher for my bare feet. My perspiration under the weight and heat of the fat animal was more abundant than the rain, and fatigue more than I could bear while trying to keep up with the horse.

At last we entered the city from the west, the Turkish and Arabic Sector, the streets unknown to me. Around a corner the gendarme asked me to let the sheep down from my back and hand him the end of the rope he gave me to tie around its neck. He told me to follow him to his home. But my inseparable suspicion made me immediately lose myself in the maze of narrow streets. I didn't know how I would find my way to Hokedoon. By this time it was night and the corner lamps were spreading their light.

A little Arab boy of about twelve standing under one of these lamps turned his head towards me when I approached. I offered to pay him one kurush (four pennies) if he would guide me to Bab-el-Faraj, the main square of the city. He consented at first, but after turning several corners he stopped to ask for the payment in advance. I did not have any coin available, so I promised to pay him double if he took me to Hokedoon, a couple of hundred yards from the Square. The boy led me through two more corners and then stopped again to ask for the two kurushes I had promised. In desperation I promised three kurushes if he continued until the foot of Sa'at Haneh (the Clock Tower), but he refused to take another step until I paid him three kurushes. I could, under no circumstances, stoop down before this little rascal to untie my small supply of coins bundled around my knee. Who knows what adverse event might have happened if I did that foolish thing.

He stood there unmoved.

And I, leaving him to stand there as long as he wished, walked away. It didn't take more than five minutes to find myself in sight of the familiar landmark of the Clock Tower in the center of Bab-el-Faraj. A sudden flood of hope, light, and joy made me cast off every vestige of fear that had been overwhelming me all these months, and I flew away on a beeline to nearby Hokedoon.

To my amazement, a welcoming committee — consisting of Mother, Sister, Brother, Aunt, cousins, and friends — was waiting for me at the gate which I had in sorrow and tears left to be chained to a gang of condemned men almost three months earlier. Hampartzoum Effendi had already given Mother the news of my walking in any minute. Mother's joy had no bounds. She fell on my neck, filthy, repulsive and vermin-infested as I was, comforting me with her kisses and tears and praises to God. Her "Prodigal Son" had returned to her.

Immediately she gave me a complete bath. She had already warmed plenty of water. She cast all my tattered and "inhabited" clothes into the fire after saving the priceless notebook that had served me for my desert diary.

The Lioness had at last found her lost cub, and she kept him all night at her angelic bosom, in her arms, as if to assure herself if it all was not a bubble, a dream, a fancy. Mother did not want to waste any precious minute in idle sleep; instead she spent every hour of the night in tearful, thankful, fervent prayer for God's compassion on His handmaiden's misery and answer to her supplications.

But the joys of reunion, bath and meal, sense of security and the warmth radiating from Mother's adorable personality were too much for this famished spirit and bruised, broken body to bear. There was no more reason to do so, but I did unwittingly resume the sickness begun in Abu Harrar and interrupted by the massacre in Al Hamam a fortnight before. Typhus again, with its fevers and nightmares of floggings, tortures, indignities, and then pursuit and escape from slaughter. It was through Mother's and Sister's loving nursing that in a short period of weeks I regained my health and sanity, as I had a year earlier in Bulgur Khan.

I was told that Hampartzoum Effendi had come to Mother to inquire about me before returning to Meskeneh. And to my deepest grief I also learned that this selfless man of God was robbed and killed in Der Zor where he had gone on a mission of mercy several days after bringing me to my mother.

"Oh Lord," I used to pray any time I fell into musing over those horrendous experiences, "Please, Lord, call to Thy holy presence the spirits of Hampartzoum Effendi and his mother; Boghos Effendi and his wife Hripsimeh; and Baron Onnig[42], and lay Thy hand on their heads with a special blessing."

As far as is known, no other person returned from this march.

Editor

Part III
To the Sun of My Hope

CHAPTER 34

I TURN A NEW PAGE

ALTHOUGH the perils of the "Valley of the Shadow of Death" were left behind when I managed to escape from the desert, yet the horrors of the recent months kept on visiting me, whether asleep or awake, and as a result I lay sick since my arrival. As soon as I was able to leave my sickbed in Mother's room in Hokedoon, I directed my cautious and feeble steps to the American Consulate. I had been there many times before in quest of official protection or financial aid, and each time had been turned away because I had no status whatsoever. My only claim on the American Consulate was the flimsy and worthless fact that from childhood to college age I had been brought up by American missionaries and spoke English.

I do not remember how long and how fervently I prayed on the way.

Once inside the Consulate, I handed an aide the letter I had composed earlier and addressed to the personal attention of "His Excellency, the Consul."

The aide returned from the Consul's inner sanctum and handed me a note. Miracle of miracles! The Consul was recommending me to the Director of the First *Imarat-hanée*, Work Center, permitted by and operated for the Ottoman War Department.

I don't think I walked to the Imarat-hane on my poor shaky legs. I am sure that my weary feet at once sprouted powerful wings to fly me.

When I presented the priceless note, the director immediately wrote and signed a temporary permit (promising a full permit as soon as possible) and assigned me to the most honorable position and office of dignity — collecting waste, cast-off cigarette butts, and paper from the grounds of the factory.

The Web of Hope

The Clock Tower in the Square at Aleppo, approximately 1900

THE NO-MAN BECOMES A RUBBISH COLLECTOR

This happy turn of page took place on November 23, 1916, exactly twenty days after my escape from the desert, on the first day I left my sick-bed, and after the n-th visit and application-petition to Mr. Jackson, the American Consul.

The permit, stating that I was an employee of the Imarat-hane, was for me a lease on life and insurance policy for freedom.

When at the day's end I came "home" from the noble work the Lord had provided for me, "home," a small, single, windowless and dark room at the farthest end of the caravanserai assigned to Mother and her children by Miss Rohner, in whose orphanage Mother was a cook. Mother and all the neighbors were happy at my good fortune.

The mere thought of wages for services rendered was altogether preposterous. The Turkish government never believed in, or practiced, paying an Armenian. An Armenian, as a second-class citizen — or no citizen at all, but an abject subject — should consider himself fortunate if he was permitted to serve his "lord and master," the Turk. Therefore hundreds and thousands of men and women who served the government as soldiers, as transportation men, as spinners of yarn, weavers of cloth, sewers or cutters, received nothing. My happiness was now based only on the fact that my life was safe. But the anxiety to feed, to clothe and to sustain this life was ever present and nagging. Employment with pay was nonexistent. Neither did Miss Rohner, the German philanthropist and missionary, pay her workers. The only recompense they received was food and shelter. Under such circumstances stealing was the most honored and accepted policy. Yet honesty and dignity were my mother's Christian principles from which she never wavered. Many professing Christians, ministers, and Bible-women were thieves and hypocrites.

Mother Pays My Penalty

Christmas came and went, and nobody noticed it. New Year came, 1917, that, too, went by unnoticed and uncelebrated. But it brought a new calamity to our family. Mother was stricken with a severe case of rheumatism with painful inflammation and stiffness of all the muscles and joints of her body. She lay in the dark and gloomy room where her three children would stand in torment because they could do nothing to comfort and soothe her — money, doctor, medicine, and hospital were all beyond them.

I learned at that time from my sister Mary that Mother deliberately imposed on herself the unreasonable penalty, the penance, of lying at nights on the bare cold dirt floor of her room, with no bed and no cover, because, during those months, her son — I — was forced to "lie on the cold sand of the Syrian Desert, with no bed, no cover, no shelter, no food."

My agony became unbearable. A stream of tears flowed down, when Sister concluded, "Mother is still paying your penalty."

In consequence of her inability to perform her services as a cook, she lost her position and the privileges connected with it.

Extreme Poverty

Our means to survive — the struggle to keep the skin on our bones — was worsening from day to day. February, March, and April brought no relief to our sorry plight, except the tiny loaf of bread I brought, distributed daily in the Imaret-hané.

On the 8th of March Miss Rohner closed the orphanage she was managing, evidently through German or Turkish pressure. Sister and brother, Aunt Gulenia and her children, and all the inmates and workers were turned out.

Now we were desperate. We had to look for help from somewhere.

It occurred to me to write a letter to Mr. Mardiros Sarkisian, who was in the employ of the Germans in Entilly as an engineer and interpreter on the Berlin–Istanbul–Baghdad Railway Project. He was one of Mother's "boys" in the Hadjin orphanage and my teacher at Evérék High School. He was the one who had spotted our family among the trekkers trudging through the mountains of Entilly in September of 1915, and had comforted us with food, water, and fresh fruit. If anyone could help us, he was the one, we thought.

Prospective Benefactor Needs Our Help

Two weeks later a note was handed to me by an acquaintance which dashed to pieces all our high hopes of a generous aid — Mardiros was in prison in Aleppo, and was asking help from us. Mother, sick as she was, advised me to rush to see and assure him that we would help him in any way we could. On my visit he told me that he had been arrested and sent to Aleppo prison accused of having helped Armenian refugees and fugitives. I brought home with me his soiled laundry, which my sister washed.

Mother sent word about the prisoner's needs — "direr than our own," she said — to some friends of hers and solicited food for him and his brother's widow who, too, was in prison in the women's section. On the next visiting day I took to Mardiros, and also to his sister-in-law, the specially prepared food and fresh laundry.

Mother — a solid rock — was as good as her promises of help to them. Our visits of service and comfort continued until the fall of Aleppo, when Arabs unlocked the prison doors the night before the British Army occupied the city.

After four months of service in the Imarat-hané as a "sanitation engineer" (that is, rubbish collector) — my position came to an end and I was put behind a spinning wheel to spin yarn for weavers of cloth. I was, luckily, not a novice at this new job, because for 18 months I had done the same work eight or nine years earlier in the weaving factory operated by the Hadjin orphanage.

From Rubbish Man to Teacher

One day in early May Miss Rohner sent for me. I had not seen her for over a year. Having heard from Mother (who was now able to move around) that the Lord had made it possible for me to escape the massacre in the desert, she expressed her wish to see me. At the interview, which was conducted in English, she wanted me to relate all the horrendous details of my experiences and my escape from the slaughter. At the conclusion of my story she offered me a job as one of the four teachers in a school she had just opened in the Hamidiyeh section of the city. I accepted the offer with deep gratitude and started my new duties on May 5th. The superintendent was Mr. Sisak Manookian, a highly respected and kindly educator, who later became a minister. My position was at once more comfortable and my rations better than ever before. Thus I became a member of the German lady's "official family." It was a coveted privilege to be under Miss Rohner's protection.

The superintendent assigned to me the teaching of *Güld'est'e*, a Turkish reader, a collection of noteworthy articles by famous authors. The language was at that time, as it always had been until a decade later, esthetically very rich, with extensive borrowings of words, idioms, and poetic expressions from Arabic and Persian. The students were, of course, Armenian refugee and orphan children.

Despite my new status and regularly-received loaf of bread, we, as a family, went through sickness and hunger. We were always hungry and never had a full stomach. It would happen occasionally, I confess with undying remorse, that acute hunger would tempt me to just taste a little bite from the bread, not intending to devour the whole of the small thing, but the "tasting" continued until there was nothing to take home for Mother to divide a portion for each of us. On my return empty-handed, ashamed, and bowed, Mother would "understand" with her inexhaustible understanding, with no word or look of reproach. It would happen occasionally, too, that Mother would give away her small portion of bread to someone in poorer, shabbier, and sicklier condition that we were. Oh, there really were tens of thousands worse off than we were. And none of us children could find a word of disapproval. We admired her self-denial

Mr. Manookian, the Superintendent, having been informed of our dire condition, gave my 15-year-old brother Setrak a younger class to teach, merely to entitle him to get a loaf of bread daily. Lean, feeble, starved, and and inexperienced, Setrak could not perform his duties satisfactorily, so he was sent home after two weeks.

At this time we were told that an Arab family in the Aziziyeh section of the city was looking for a servant. Setrak applied and got the job, but in three days he got fired, because he was too sick to be of any use to his masters.

Soon after, Mr. Manookian, as an act of Christian charity, invited Setrak again to teach the same class he had been teaching before.

Five days later, on September 3, 1917, Miss Rohner closed the school and terminated all of her missionary and charitable activities in behalf of the Armenian refugees. But instead of heartlessly abandoning her vulnerable adult male employees to their dark fate she sent about ten of us with a letter to Fayik Bey, the Captain of the Army Supply.

CHAPTER 35

THE PREACHER TRIES TO BETRAY ME

IN THIS GROUP now standing in front of the powerful Turkish officers endowed with absolute authority to condemn us to death camps or show mercy, there was a man, Mr. Roupen Markarian, the general manager of Miss Rohner's enterprises — orphanage, school, and other projects.

When I was a child in the American Orphanage, Roupen Effendi was a well-known and well-to-do shopkeeper. He was also my uncle Haroutune's bosom friend in their frequent drinking bouts. One day this cunning man became "converted" in a prayer-meeting conducted by Pastor Barker, the president of the American Mission in Hadjin, and easily gained the confidence of the good-hearted, trusting missionary. "Badveli" Barker, at once seeing in the tall and handsome "convert" a capable Christian worker, offered Roupen Effendi the position of minister in the Fénésséh Evangelical Church.

I used to attend his Sunday services and prayer-meeting in Fénésséh as a student in the orphanage high school.

When I became a tutor, he was one of my three traveling companions on a pilgrimage to St. Garabed Monastery a few days before the declaration of World War I (July 1914). On the return trip he and his companions were dinner guests at my Aunt Gulenia's in Kayseri.

Roupen Effendi was now in Aleppo, as the most affluent man and the heir of Miss Rohner's extensive interests.

In Hokedoon, where he had secured ample living quarters for his family of eight and his rich furniture, he conducted worship services and prayer-meetings which mother and we three children attended regularly, as did many others.

He knew that a few short months before I had escaped a general slaughter in the desert and with Providential guidance succeeded in fleeing to the bosom of my mother; and that it was only three months since

The Web of Hope

Miss Rohner had taken me under her protective wing by appointing me a teacher in her school.

As we, with conflicting emotions about our fate, lined up before Fayik Bey, Mr. Manookian, the headmaster of the school, handed him Miss Rohner's letter. After carefully reading the letter, the Captain raised his face towards us and and said with a smile:

"Siz hémshirémin évladlaru sunuz." (You are my Sister's sons.)

All of a sudden Roupen Effendi, the Armenian preacher of the gospel of love and compassion, interjected, pointing his finger at me:

"Bey Effendi, O bizden deyil" (He is not of us). And then continued: "A short time ago he escaped from a desert-camp and came to Haleb."

Terror, as I knew it, overwhelmed me over again. My poor, emaciated, precarious life was hanging by a hair, and this self-righteous man, the defender of truth, was dealing a blow to sever it.

In my altogether twenty-two years I never had an occasion to harm this man, always beyond my reach, that I should deserve his vicious attempt to imperil my life at such a crucial point.

Fayik Bey for a moment cast at me a penetrating look, during which, I thought, I was doomed beyond hope. In the universe of my consciousness there was no room for any other thought.

In that fateful look he must have read a volume of devastation within me.

At the end of the scrutiny he asked my name.

"Garabed Oghloo Kevork," I answered meekly.

After glancing over his "Sister's" letter on the desk in front of him, and finding my name there, he asked me again if I knew any trade except being a muallim (teacher).

"Tailor's trade," I ventured to answer, remembering the hours of high school tailoring courses in Fénésséh and childhood apprenticeship at my Uncle's.

"You will be my messenger boy in this office for the time being," he declared to the dismay of my traitor "friend."

The Preacher Tries to Betray Me

Betrayer Betrayed

Daniel had his lions in his den and St. Gregory his snakes in his slimy pit in centuries past. So we had in these murky days of our genocide a fiendish breed of degenerate informers, spies, betrayers, traitors, and extortionists, the product of planned and enforced deportation, slaughter, starvation, and ubiquitous human and moral breakdown. The sense of decency and mutual respect — the warp and woof of the sturdy national character — was, by now, almost entirely warped and frayed.

These pernicious dregs of the collapsed Armenian society could easily be spotted and shunned when they surfaced. When you saw yesterday's starving, much abused person all at once well-clad in a police uniform, a jaunty kid-skin "kalpak" on his head, a pair of brilliant knee-high boots around his legs, and a menacing leathern whip in his hand, then you were sure that he had sold his worthless Mephisophelean soul to the devil and was abroad with a mission of destruction.

One such fellow was Himayak, a young man of about 20, and a one-time inmate of Miss Rohner's orphanage. He developed a grudge against Roupen Effendi, who was "swimming in a sea of plenty," while all around was misery of sickness and hunger and terror. It may be that Roupen Effendi had somehow slighted, mistreated, or ignored him.

So Himayak made a habit of paying Roupen Effendi frequent visits in Hokedoon, cracking his silver-topped whip as a mark of authority and importance, and haughtily strutting across the long courtyard towards his victim's staircase.

One day, it seems, Roupen Effendi defaulted in the amount he usually paid for his "protection," so Himayak promptly brought a squad of gendarmes with him to drag the mighty and soulless Roupen Effendi to prison. The tears, wails, and entreaties of his wife and six children had no effect on the equally soulless extortionist.

His wife condescended to turn to me as the only one who could freely visit the prisoner (at the time I was in military uniform) and deliver him food, money, and a change of clean clothes.

During his several weeks in prison Roupen Effendi, the preacher, was the personification of humility, love, and compassion in voluble words. He was, in fact, more Christian that Christ himself. I continued my visits of comfort until three weeks later he was set free after complying with the enormous amount Himayak "Effendi" and his co-conspirator associates wished to extort.

The post-war years brought the wealthy ex-preacher and inheritor of Miss Rohner's enterprises to the United States, to his wife's two rug-dealer sons from a former marriage, who had been residents of this country for more than two decades.

Once in "the Land of the Free," Roupen Effendi promptly stripped himself from the pretense of religion and abstinence, and unashamedly gave himself to excessive drinking. In one of his drinking orgies he boasted publicly that he was never really converted. "It was all a sham to curry favor and respectable positions from the missionaries." He confessed, further, that all those years, each time he was to offer a prayer or preach a sermon, he pulled out of his hip-pocket his constant companion, the liquor flask, and took a generous drink.

His inspiration came from whiskey, not the Holy Spirit.

His wife Doodoo's nephew Charles (Chapar) Albarian, who often visited me in his elder years, told me about Roupen's shameful confession.

CHAPTER 36

IN MILITARY UNIFORM

It is still a deep mystery to me today, after almost sixty years since the fateful incident, that Fayik Bey, the highly-placed officer, did not succumb to preacher Roupen Effendi's treacherous betrayal of me. I would expect of Roupen Effendi succor, if anything, and not a plot to destroy me. Yet this high Turkish officer chose to ignore the evil intent of my "friend," and guided by the Holy Spirit (whom he did not know as a Moslem, neither did Nebuchadnezzar and Cyrus as pagans know Him) appointed me to be his office messenger. Fayik Bey was a good man. I wonder how Roupen Effendi felt at the gate of Heaven when Fayik Bey, the Turk, was let in and Roupen Effendi, the Armenian preacher of the Gospel, left out.

At once I was issued, at Fayik Bey's orders, a military uniform, with leggings and a cap. Thus I was transformed from an insecure refugee into a soldier, protected, safe, and free. (In the previous two or three years thousands of Armenian servicemen were disarmed and massacred, and other thousands in the labor battalions were shot and thrown into pits which they were forced to dig for themselves.) And now, here in Aleppo, Fayik Bey was placing Armenians into the tailors' battalion and other positions to clothe and feed the fighting army. It was in my new capacity as a soldier in uniform that I was entreated by Doodoo Baji to make several visits to her husband in prison with food, clothes, notes, money, and words of comfort. An official military *vessica*—identity paper—reinforced my freedom from the terror of ever-present death.

Hans

One night, in a dark covered-over street, I encountered a young German soldier who spoke to me in German. I asked him in French what he wanted. In fragmentary French he let me understand that he was lost and didn't know where he was. I told him that he was in the vicinity of the Armenian church and Bab-el-Faraj with the town clock tower. He thanked me heartily after I had led him to the bottom of the clock in the square, from where he could easily direct himself to his quarters. He was about my age. He begged me to accompany him to his room, which I did. This home-sick soldier boy showed me his family pictures. He said that he had spent some time in France, where he had picked up a little French. He opened a can of beer especially for me. I had never tasted beer in my whole twenty-two years. Out of courtesy I accepted the foaming mug and began to drink, thinking that it was some sort of tea. But the first gulp refused to go through my throat. Not only did it choke me, but it was also extremely bitter. The boy could not understand why a man of my age would choke on his national drink. I laid the mug down, and vowed never to touch a glass of beer again. Today, as I write these words, I am on the threshold of my fourscore years, and have kept that vow. My first and last taste of beer was at that friendly German soldier boy's room in Aleppo, on November 11, 1917.

This German boy, on another visit to his room, interested me in trying to learn German. Through his guidance, I secured a copy of a German-English reader from the German Headquarters. The first thing I learned was: "Das ist ein Auto."

About a month after our acquaintance and gradually growing friendship, I learned to my regret that Hans had been shipped out of Aleppo. For some time a strange feeling of loss annoyed me. And thus my study of German came to an abrupt end.

From Messenger-Boy to Tailor

After three months of serving as his messenger-boy, one day Fayik Bey sent me with a note to Osman Effendi, the commanding officer of the tailors' battalion. Osman Effendi was a short, plump, dignified, middle-aged soldier with a fierce and unfriendly look. But, as I later had opportunity to learn, he was a kindly man, quiet and non-violent. After glancing over his superior's note, he scanned me for a moment and then referred me to his lieutenant to place me under a master's supervision in the tailor-shop. This large and long shop housed a couple dozens of work tables, each occupied by four tailors, and each tailor busy with an over-sized pair

In Military Uniform

of scissors, cutting at one stroke army uniforms out of four to six layers of khaki material. There was another company of tailors, but not in the same compound with the cutters, whose duty was to sew these cut uniforms.

The cutters were considered masters. I could find no explanation why I should be sent to the company of master tailors. The simple fact was — although Fayik Bey did not know it — that my knowledge of tailoring hardly extended beyond rough basting, acquired at the high school trade course, a far cry from real tailoring.

My uncle Haroutune, a tailor's tailor, a veteran of twenty-five years at the trade, was here, presiding over a table, and directed towards me a wink of delight for having me in his company. Uncle Haroutune was not an officer, chief, or foreman. He had, in the spring of 1915 managed to escape from this same battalion to join his family in Hadjin, but unfortunately (future events proved it was *fortunately*) he was captured in Adana and thrown into prison, to wait for his turn to be hanged as a deserter, while hundreds were being hanged on trumped-up crimes. In the summer of the same year, when I joined my family in Adana, I had occasion to visit him in the prison while he was languishing in the shadow of the gallows. But, not too many days later, Uncle was providentially granted an Imperial pardon, hustled out of the prison back to his company in the tailors' battalion, and assigned to his former position as a master cutter. And it was in this capacity, again providentially, that he was able to snatch us, his two sisters and their children, from the the deadly clutches of the concentration camp in the fall of the same year.

With the cutters it didn't take me more than a few days to learn how to use the giant scissors to cut material several layers deep.

In this outfit there were two chief officers after Osman Effendi. The first one was Osman Effendi's lieutenant, or the foreman of the shop, whose name eludes me now after about sixty years. He was formerly an Armenian from Agn, but now a Turk, with a Turkish name. I could never understand why such a mild-tempered, tolerant, and good man, who never raised his voice, should turn into a Turk. Under his capable leadership the daily business of the cutters went on smoothly, with no scandal, no violence.

The second most important person was Vahram Effendi, an Armenian from Marash, who was the officer in charge of the supply room or the warehouse. By upbringing and religious faith he belonged to the Protestant church. He, too, was a good man.

In the cutters' unit there was Mustafa Bey, a tall, handsome Turk who had a special standing with Osman Effendi. Every one in the corps had a mixed sort of respect for this aloof soldier. He bothered no one. He was the only Turk among us.

All the rest of us were Armenians, some from Marash, Aintab, Hadjin, Agn, and elsewhere in Anatolia. Some spoke Arabic, and also Turkish. No one dared to speak Armenian. I was, by nature, shy and reserved, did not talk too much, did not poke my nose in others' personal affairs, and did not volunteer personal information. I was the youngest in the outfit.

Our daily ration continued to be the same small loaf of bread which was not enough to keep anybody well fed. It occurred to me to wonder how these servicemen managed to have money to spend on food, while I was compelled (by my conscience) to take the tiny loaf home to share with my family along with what any one of them could have gotten.

KARAVANAH

Occasionally, around the dismissal hour, as the whim moved the Army kitchen chief, a large kettle of soup or meal of a nondescript nature — *karavanah* — would find its way to our place. The soldiers, divided into groups of ten each, would surround their common pan of *karavanah* and fill their stomachs. Some men, like my uncle, would not condescend to stay for this "feast" but many others would. At first I did not stay either, partly because I was not armed with a spoon of my own, and partly because I wanted to be home as soon as dismissal was announced.

For the next *karavanah* I came prepared with a tablespoon, with the hope that the Army food might dull the sharpness of my constant hunger. When our group crouched around the vessel of food, I shyly sidled by a fellow twice as tall as I expecting him to make room for me. He did not budge. No one moved or took notice of me. When, at last, I succeeded in reaching the pan with my spoon the food had completely disappeared into the caverns of my dinner-companions, each one of whom had a cup-shaped ladle and dipped it into the food as fast as a prize-fighter's fist blows.

Not only disappointment, but disgust also, at such a show of bestiality in human conduct, made me put my still-clean spoon back into my pocket. I realized that my poor little civilized spoon in a hand, moving courteously and considerately, had no chance in a competition with ladles of giant size in the hands of gladiators.

Sentry Duty and Theft

Every one of us had the obligation to stand guard at the main gate of the ground housing the cutters' battalion and the richly stocked warehouse. One day a comrade offered to pay me if I stood guard in his stead at a certain period at night. I gladly grabbed at the welcome opportunity. This arrangement encouraged me to buy up other nocturnal sentry duties which began to provide much needed cash, meager though as it was.

One late night in January, while standing guard behind the locked street gate, with a rifle to the muzzle of which a bayonet was attached, I suddenly heard a loud knock.

"Who is there?" I asked, aiming the bayonet towards the door.

"Mustafa Bey," said a voice from the street. "Open the door, I have come with a carriage to haul some of Osman Effendi's belongings to his home."

Recognizing Mustafa Bey's voice, and knowing well his intimacy with our commanding officer, I opened the gate to let him drive in. Mustafa alighted from the wagon, inserted the key into the lock, lighted a lamp once inside the warehouse and began casually to load a great variety of "Osman Effendi's belongings." I continued standing my watch behind the gate, occasionally casting glances at what he was doing. When he had loaded the wagon as heavily as he could (I remember wondering at Osman Effendi's sudden need of his "personal belongings" at such an uncertain, dubious hour of darkness), Mustafa climbed to the driver's seat and drove the wagon out.

In the morning, Vahram Effendi, the supervising officer of the warehouse, was dumbfounded when he discovered the empty shelves that were heavily stocked the night before with goods and merchandise of all sorts and values as he himself had locked the door at closing time.

A rumor began to make its rounds among the fellows that a grand theft had taken place, and that the night guard—whoever he was—was implicated in it. A deadly terror seized me when the rumor reached me. Hitherto I was happy with the few paltry kurushes I earned through buying up others' unwanted sentry duties, and now I was being accused of grand larceny I was incapable of.

Immediately I walked up to the office in the warehouse where Osman Effendi and his two high officers—Vahram Effendi and the Lieutenant—seated were discussing the "theft." After saluting them I said I was the sentry when the event occurred. I told them exactly what had happened: Mustafa Bey came with a wagon at 3 o'clock in the night, and said that Osman Effendi had sent him with the wagon and the key to the warehouse, to take Osman Effendi's belongings to Osman Effendi's house. "And," I added, "I obeyed Osman Effendi's orders sent to me through Mustafa Bey."

"Throw this *kerata* (an abusive word) into the cell!" ordered Osman Effendi, and I found myself in a cell, a small, low-roofed cubicle in the compound. All day long, hungry, thirsty, and abandoned in the depressive semi-darkness of the cell I had plenty of time to plunge into the dark waters of the looming execution by hanging. Who has ever escaped punishment for crimes of this sort?

"Don't be afraid," said Vahram Effendi as he opened the cell door in the evening when everybody was gone. "Go home now. Have a good sleep, and come to your work in the morning. Osman Effendi will take care of Mustafa."

As I walked home that evening, absolved of complicity in the theft, I did vainly try not to conclude that Osman Effendi was really in collusion with Mustafa Bey.

My Turn to Steal

It did not take a trained detective to observe that almost all these fellow cutters were engaged in a devious practice. During the work hours, one would cut an ample piece of an expensive fabric, stealthily stuff it in his pants or shirt, then go to the toilet and wrap the trove tightly around his body. At dismissal time the chief tailor would stand at the entrance, beside the guard, and search with both hands over the body and legs of each soldier as he left. To my non-understanding amazement none of those looters would be exposed. Was the Lieutenant so stupid that he could not feel the unusual thickness of the plundered goods as he touched them? But I learned to admire his sympathetic understanding of these poor people's struggles for livelihood and leniency in letting them alone to convert their loot into direly needed cash in the black market. This former Armenian turned into a Turk — I know not on what compelling reason — was still a true Armenian in the inner recesses of his heart more than my "friend" Roupen Effendi, the preacher of the Gospel. Although I had no means of earning or somehow getting hold of some money to feed my family decently, and although on this account I had more reason to steal, yet I could not bring myself to follow my comrades' example. I took, as always, my puritanical upbringing by the saintly missionaries too seriously and withstood the temptation.

Still I kept on buying available night sentry duties with insignificant pay.

The courtyard was dominated only by the cutters' workshop and the stock room. The sentry's duty was the protection of this property only. But the courtyard at one corner, between the shop and the warehouse, continued as a narrow corridor to another complex, an *Imarat-hanée*, a work center for women who worked during the daytime at spinning, weaving, or sewing. These two separate departments had no connection with each other. Ours was military, run by and for the Army, and the other was civilian, run by a civilian director for the Army.

On one of my early sentry duties, hearing some muffled voices, I discovered to my surprise that an Armenian widow and her children had found refuge in a basement on the other end of the passageway. On several occasions I paid a short visit to this poor family and we gradually came to know each other. She had three children with her: a son, Ohannes, about my age; a daughter; and a younger son, Abraham, about 8. They were from Marash, and were Protestant. I felt a warm kinship towards them as fellow countrymen (Province of Cilicia) and fellow-believers.

Our conversations were usually about the general suffering of our race at the hand of a merciless government and the endless hunger that was reaping lives in wholesale. I told them on one occasion about Mustafa Bey's enormous theft, my imprisonment in the honorable thief's stead, and Vahram Effendi's releasing me. I mentioned also that most fellow-soldiers were stealing valuable goods and selling them to feed their families.

"Why don't you steal yourself?" Ohannes challenged me.

His blunt question caught me unprepared, but I answered,

"I can't... I am a Christian... 'Thou shalt not steal'."

"Look at yourself," he said. "Is this living? How can you survive with your sense of justness and goodness in a corrupt, wicked society where all from the top officer to the least chavoush live and thrive on robbery and bribery?"

I kept silent. He continued,

"Mustafa emptied the warehouse shelves in Osman Effendi's name, and you were cast in jail for their theft. What did you gain our of that rich robbery?"

"Nothing, except the terror of being hanged," I said meekly.

"These hideous Turks, they themselves steal from themselves and punish innocent men like you," he said heatedly. "Don't you know that this government planned and executed the policy to wipe us out by deporting, poisoning, under nourishing, and starving us?"

"Yes, I know," I agreed. "But what can you and I do to improve our situation," I ventured to ask.

"Listen to what I will propose to improve our situation," he said. "This is a time of war the like of which we never saw before. There is no law for us to obey. All moral and religious laws are trodden under foot by the government itself. The government has robbed us right and left, and we have the right to rob the government."

"How can we do that," I asked seeing a little justness in his logic.

"We can," he said, "and right now. Do you see my little brother Abraham? He can easily squeeze through the iron bars of the warehouse window, and once inside, he can hand us anything through the window. Then I will do the selling, and you will get your share."

You taught me how to steal, Mustafa Bey, I thought in my heart. May my sins fall on your neck, I said voicelessly. (I never saw Mustafa again after that fateful night when he drove away the heavily loaded wagon. Probably he became a Pasha.)

"Come on, let us go to the window," I said.

Abraham was a very smart child with a very small body kept frail by constant undernourishment. Ohannes raised his brother to the window and he easily jumped into the dark stockroom. With our directing the child fearlessly went from one shelf to another, from one barrel to another, from one drawer to another — meanwhile being strictly careful not to drop any tell-tale evidence on the floor — and handed all to us. The child's coming out the same way was no problem at all. Ohannes took the loot to his quarters.

Several days late Ohannes handed me two gold liras (worth at the time about ten dollars), an amount the like of which was beyond my means to earn legitimately. With this treasure — I did not disclose its source to my mother, or anybody — I bought a lot of good and hard to get food and other necessities.

The warehouse officials could find no evidence of theft. It was a perfect theft.

But when Ohannes suggested a second incursion into the storehouse my puritanical conscience rebelled against such common thievery. The one act had tarnished my soul enough, and I felt a second try abhorrent.

"No!" I said. "I wouldn't steal even from the Devil himself."

"You are a fool," Ohannes said, "but an honest fool."

Osman Effendi Promotes Me

One afternoon, while I was on sentry duty, Osman Effendi stopped in front of me and asked me a direct question. He had never lowered himself as to notice me before. If I gave him the right answer I would surely put then noose around my neck with my own hands, because it would be tantamount to confessing, in these war times, that I was a spy for the enemy.

"*Olan* (boy)," he asked, "I heard that among all these people only you speak English and French. Is that true?"

The Web of Hope

"I don't know that, Sir," I stammered in terror.

"Then tell me, do you speak those languages?"

I meant to deny, but the words came out differently, and I said, "Yes, Sir," and waited for the ax to fall.

"I am ordering you," he said in grave tones as if pronouncing my death sentence, "that beginning from tomorrow afternoon from 2 to 4 each day, to go to my home and tutor my two children in those languages. You don't have to report for work in the afternoons."

"*Évét effendim, bash ustunéh* (Yes, my effendi, [your order] on my head)," I answered, choking with emotions of sudden relief and gratitude.

At 2 o'clock next afternoon I found myself knocking at the door of my commanding officer's home. A lady in her early thirties opened the door. Two children, a girl of twelve and a boy of ten, standing by their mother, exclaimed in glee,

"*Anneh* (Mother), he must be the muallim."

"Come in, Muallim Effendi," said the genial gentlewoman. "We were expecting you." She led me to a table inside the room and introduced the children to me. Jennet (Paradise) was the girl's name (she seemed to me an angel from Paradise), and the boy's name was Izzet (Honor). I never learned the *Hanum*'s (lady's) name, neither did they know my name. I was Muallim.

The children accepted me with no hesitation, with no reserve. Of course, they had never heard a word of French or English in their short lives and had never seen the Latin alphabet. Their knowledge was only of Turkish with its Arabic and Persian words and idioms. We spent one hour with the rudiments of one language, and the next hour with the other language, with intervals of stories and discourses on many subjects that the children raised.

At the end of the two hours with these delightful youngsters I took my leave, bidding goodbye to the Hanum. Before turning the corner in the street towards my home, I heard Izzet calling to me to stop. As I stopped for him to reach me, he handed me two loaves of pure bread, telling me that his mother was sending them to my mother with her best wishes.

And this wonderful Turkish Hanum unfailingly sent with me to my mother the two large loaves every day of the months I tutored her children until the fall of Aleppo.

Meanwhile Osman Effendi never spoke to me, neither did I talk to him, until on another occasion he approached me at the gate and said,

"Muallim, I was told that you are a devout Protestant. From now on you are free on every Sunday to go to your church services. Sundays are all yours."

I learned later that my beneficent informer was Vahram Effendi, the chief of the warehouse, an Evangelical himself.

Concerning My Sister Mary

One day, in the latter part of March 1918, Mary received a message from Miss Rohner to report to her. At the interview the Fraulein disclosed that the administration of the Ottoman Military Hospital in Aleppo was looking for an Armenian girl who would read and write Turkish and, at the same time, talk in English to British, Senegalese, and Hindu captive patients.

"You can never expect to get a better opportunity than this," she said, and sent her to the hospital with a note.

She was immediately put in charge of the vast wardrobe department with a number of orderlies under her. She was responsible for keeping a record of incoming and outgoing patients and issuing uniforms to those who were discharged. At once she became a popular and highly respected officer. She could bring home some bread and other needed items. She remained there until the fall of Aleppo.

Concerning My Brother Setrak

In one of those days my younger brother Setrak, whose health was always delicate, fell critically ill. This time, somehow, we succeeded in having him admitted to the city hospital. The details of this miraculous admission escape me now, but we were happier to see him return from the hospital in improved health.

Shortly after his return from the hospital he was again at his teaching post in Miss Rohner's school. But unfortunately the Fraulein had the presidency of the school board turned over to a Turk, Nazim Bey, who immediately dismissed Setrak and the rest of the Armenians Miss Rohner had employed and replaced them with Turks.

Three days after he had been fired by Nazim Bey, Setrak found a job with the German officers as a servant. He remained at this safe job until the day Aleppo fell.

Osman Effendi Asks For My Help

All through the war years the government made a special effort not to leak to the outside world what inhumane atrocities it was perpetrating on the Armenian element in the country. Our only prayer was that the Allies very soon would win the war and put an end to the holocaust we were in.

We were deliberately being kept in the dark about the fortunes of the warring sides. According to the news spread around orally and the special war bulletins published by the government, the Central Powers (Germany, Austro-Hungary, and Turkey) had been winning every skirmish, every battle on every front, and the final victory was around the corner.

But the myth of the invincibility of the Turkish army had indeed blown up.

In September General Allenby's British army had broken through Jaffa in Palestine, in a few days occupied Jerusalem, routed the Ottoman defensives, and joining forces with the revolting Arabs, had advanced north capturing Damascus on October 1, then Beirut on October 10. And now this mighty wave was sweeping towards Aleppo. Every day countless express trains were speeding through the city, carrying the fleeing German and Turkish officers to safety in the interior of Anatolia, Konia, and Istanbul.

It was a matter of just a few days at the most for the victorious forces to invade, capture, and loot Aleppo.

On one of these nervous days, as I was standing on guard duty, Osman Effendi stopped in front of me and said in a low voice,

"Muallim, yours are coming very soon." He meant the British. "When they come, will you give my family and me a shelter and your protection?"

This was the first and only time I could and did talk to my commanding officer as an equal, or perhaps superior.

"With all my heart, Osman Effendi," I answered with a surge of compassion. "You and your Hanum have been good to me, and I love Izzet and Jennet, your children. I promise to protect you with my blood."

"Thank you," he said. "I knew you would."

View of Aleppo from the Citadel, approximately 1900

Kooshian Family, before the deportations. Mary, Mother Sarah, George, Setrak. This was taken in Hadjin by Murad Khodja in 1913, after George Kooshian's graduation from high school. He was then 17 years old.

CHAPTER 37

THE FALL OF ALEPPO

ALEPPO fell on the night of October 25–26, 1918. Secret agents of the fast-advancing liberators had already infiltrated the city and begun to stir up insurrection among the non-Turk elements. During the last few weeks, annoying small bombs had occasionally been dropped from the sky on scattered parts of the city, creating demoralization among the German and Turkish overlords

On the afternoon of October 24, my sister Mary came home unexpectedly and announced that she was not going back as the officer in charge of the wardrobe department of the great Ottoman Military Hospital. Because, she foretold, this night or next, the Anezeh tribes would swarm into the city before the British Army arrived, and sack the city indiscriminately, conducting orgies of rape and general massacre. They would spare no institution, no hospital. She heard this warning, she said, from the chief of the hospital.

Next morning, as usual, I went to the cutters' battalion as a Turkish soldier. Osman Effendi, for the first time, did not show up. Vahram Effendi, the superintendent of the warehouse, was there to receive us.

"We are free at last, my Armenian brothers," he said to us, the cutters' battalion, and then he proceeded to tell us that in the middle of the night Osman Effendi and his family had fled to Istanbul in company with the rest of the high officials of the city.

"The Turks are no more your masters, and you are no more Turkish soldiers," he said. "Go to your homes, get rid of these detestable uniforms, and keep yourselves behind locked doors to escape the unavoidable ravages that the savage forerunners will commit soon. Good luck to each one of you, and praise God for our deliverance."

We all ran out of the courtyard to the safety of our homes.

A succession of bombs continued to fall on Baghdad Station and the adjacent German headquarters, which had already been vacated.

At dusk a vast horde of desert tribes invaded and plundered the city as my sister had predicted the day before. One of their targets was the Ottoman Military Hospital, which they pillaged and wrecked. They molested all the female workers and nurses and dragged off and murdered all the patients who were too sick to escape. The officers of the ill-fated hospital had already abandoned their posts and sought safety in hiding or in the last express.

All night long shots pierced the air and our ears, but we kept vigil in prayer that the holocaust would soon end and peace break out with the morning.

And that is what exactly happened. A new and glorious day had dawned.

The Dawn of a New Era

The carnage of the fateful night having spent itself gave way with the rising sun to an unaccustomed calm.

And in the morning thousands over thousands of war-weary, repressed, and persecuted people streamed out of their dingy hiding places and stationed themselves on both sides of the road to welcome and cheer the endless British army wagons rolling into Aleppo.

I was, with my brother, in a dense crowd at the edge of the street not too far from Hokedoon. We both joined the multitude with our hearty shouts of joy each time a team of gigantic work horses pulled a huge lorry in front of us. On one occasion, with no special intent, I mingled English words of welcome with the foreign shouts of the mass.

"Welcome, welcome, our British liberators! God's blessings on you!"

A vehicle made an abrupt halt, and the driver asked in surprise,

"Who was that speaking English?"

"It was I," I shouted, jumping up and down.

"Come on up the lorry and sit by me," said he, motioning to me.

I tore the astonished crowd into two banks and walked in the middle towards the waiting wagon. The driver lent me a hand, pulling me to his side.

Thus I rode all day long with the victorious liberators on the very first day of our liberation.

My new friend took me to the restaurant of the city's foremost Hotel Baron. The next day he was sent back to Jerusalem and I never saw him again.

Two Ravaged Sisters

When I returned home in the evening of this glorious day of our liberation from the Turkish yoke, I found two young ladies with my mother and sister, all in tears. They, two sisters, had considered themselves fortunate when months earlier they were admitted to the Ottoman Military Hospital as nurses. They were happy as they performed their tasks faithfully. They had remained at their posts because they had no relatives left alive to turn to when the physicians, officers, caretakers, and most patients fled the swarming merciless attackers of the night of the rampage. As they witnessed the murder of patients too sick to move and the destruction going on right and left, they ran to their quarters and huddled in terror. The villains pursued the unfortunate girls, ravaged them, and plundered all their belongings, leaving them stark naked. They had to cover their devastated bodies with murdered patients' clothes and had come to my sister and mother seeking healing to their wounded spirits. It is beyond comprehension that these poor children of an abandoned and condemned race, after heroically enduring every indignity and calamity, should be victims of utter desolation on the eve of liberation.

Mother kept the girls with us for some days until they located some countrymen of theirs and moved on.

Prison Doors Broken Open

I did not know that in the night of the invasion the advance force had walked directly to the fort and government buildings, occupied them with no resistance at all, and broken the prison doors wide open to the thousands of prisoners, guilty or innocent, criminal or political, while the rabble accompanying it was bent on looting and killing. In the evening of the first day of liberation, as we were sitting with the two agonized sisters, we received the unexpected visit of two more persons — Mardiros

Sarkisian and Mariam, his brother's wife, both brought from Entilly and thrown into prison more than a month before. Our tears of sympathy for the two girls immediately gave way to tears of joy for seeing my beloved teacher and family friend of many years free.

Mardiros and Mariam talked about their hair-raising experiences, thus somewhat distracting the tormented girls' harrowing state of mind.

Late at night Mardiros and Mariam left our too-crowded one room apartment to seek shelter elsewhere.

Nemesis

I was in Bab-el-Faraj on the third morning after the inglorious end of the Turkish rule when I saw a large crowd of Arabs and others shouting invectives at someone in their midst, around whose neck they had a rope and were pulling like a beast, both hands tied behind his back. They were jostling him to and fro, spitting on his unprotected face repeatedly. His elegant clothes were in tatters, as he received fierce blows and kicks.

I drew nearer to see if I could recognize him

And I did. He was Nazim Bey, the high Turkish official, who had taken over the presidency of the missionary Fraulein Rohner's orphanage and schools, and out of which he had ousted all the Christian teachers and workers, replacing them with Turks. He, furthermore, had permitted the sale of orphans to Moslem homes.

Why this fool had not fled with all his co-criminals was a mystery to me as I watched his present abject condition, compared with his onetime arrogant and merciless demeanor.

Yet the unusual scene disgusted me with feelings of nausea and loathing, and I ran home to quiet down my perturbed nerves.

Nothing To Do But Loaf

The new-found freedom intoxicated all the repressed people. We could move around the city at will, unafraid, uncuffed, unwhipped. Everyone asked information of everyone he met about a lost parent, relative, or friend. The joys of reunion between family members and relations were invariably washed in streams of tears.

Everyone was now engrossed in one overwhelming anxiety, that of finding something to do to earn a livelihood for himself and for his family. But work with pay was nowhere to be found.

Fortunately the British Government of the Occupation immediately instituted centers for the distribution of soup and bread, and later on, of other necessities.

I often spent days in the railroad grounds in search of porter's jobs, but nobody ever hired me.

About two weeks later, on November 11, the war ended on all fronts, with the defeat and unconditional surrender of the Central Powers to the victorious Allied Powers, thus putting a light to the candle of hope eventually to return to our abandoned homes, tasks, and dreams in Cilicia, in Anatolia, in historic Armenia. Trains began to bring daily the remnants of a mercilessly decimated nation, ill of health, ill-clad, ill-fed.

Some of my old friends and schoolmates of Hadjin, Evérék, and Konia — those that had managed to survive — drifted in to the city. Apraham Ateshian, Toros Pushian, Yeran Sarkisian, Gilbert Topalian, Antranig Balian, Mikayel Vayejian and others, each looking for his own folks, but mostly in vain.

Letters to the U.S.A.

Early in November I wrote a letter to the only friend I could remember, the Reverend T. F. Barker, the pre-war president of the orphanages of Hadjin and Fénésséh, to inform him that my family had survived the holocaust, but that most of his "boys and girls" had perished. I gave him a brief outline of what had happened since the American missionaries had been forced to close their charitable and educational institutions at the outbreak of the war.

I wrote another letter to Krikor Alajajian (who was living in Binghamton, New York), the eldest son of my aunt Gulenia, to let him know that his mother, one brother, and two sisters were alive and waiting to hear from him. I undertook the writing of this letter on my aunt's urging, because none of her children, not even Krikor himself, could read or write in any language. They had never been permitted to go to school by the despotic father, because he would not spare them from the rug-looms. I also wrote about my mother and Uncle Haroutune, who were his aunt and uncle, and about us his cousins, all of whom he loved once when he was in Hadjin. I suggested that he should address his answer to my name in care of the American Consulate, for the sole reason that I was personally known there. This innocent and reasonable suggestion did not contain one iota of insincerity or fraud when I made it on this first occasion or on any other time I wrote letters. But Krikor's mind, having been twisted by his father's cruelty at home, upon receiving my letter began to interpret my suggestion with suspicious intent.

More on this sorry point later.

About the end of January 1919 news was relayed that a letter from Krikor, addressed to his mother's name, was waiting at the Consulate. Naturally I accompanied my aunt and cousin Stephen to pick up the letter. I was asked to sign the registration receipt. Then we were told that a draft for one hundred dollars had also been sent. I was asked again to verify with my own signature the cross (+) endorsement of my aunt on the back of the draft before the money could be paid out.

Niether at this time nor any other not the minutest thought occurred to me to draw benefit for myself for services rendered. But, unawares of me, the devil was working against me in far-away Krikor's mind.

Innocently we rejoiced that our dear ones here thus had received help from our dear one in the United States. Aunt Gulie did not volunteer to share her new acquisition with any one, and Mother, as pure-hearted as an angel, never expected any hand-out.

I wrote about the happiness Krikor had caused to his mother and to all of us by his letter and princely help, adding the same suggestion that to avoid delay in cashing the check all communications should be made in my name.

CHAPTER 38

THE BLACK LIST

As the weeks followed one another, flotsam and jetsam of the wrecked Armenian race began to wash ashore in Aleppo. The city with all its available space became overcrowded. Thousands over thousands of Turkish, Kurdish, Arabic, and various desert-dialect speaking, bizarrely dressed and tattered men and women and children poured in from corners unknown. The familiar quarters and grounds of the church and school where I had lived as a fugitive teacher in the summer months of 1916 were now thickly and freely covered with people and their lice.

On the wall of the Church of the Forty Martyred Children there was a large black board, on which news and messages of public interest began to appear. Those of us who could read were to explain them to the people.

I frequented the church every day.

In the course of time a new form of news made its appearance under the heading, *Sev Tzang* (Black List). A brave soul, with daring hand, began to list the infamous names and deeds of those who had, in the dark days, shamelessly and treacherously committed acts of false accusation, betrayal, extortion, collaboration with our national foe.

The "List" at once became a center of public interest, and a new wave of hatred against the growing number of traitors mounted. Names of respected men also made their appearance.

I was dumbfounded one morning to find the name of a well-known Protestant clergyman, the Reverend Haroutune Khachadoorian, on the list of evil-doers. The story under his name went on to say that this "man of God," as a highly-trusted Transportation Officer, had been receiving from the British Army Supply twelve wagons of food stuffs and delivering only eleven wagons to the Armenian Center for distribution. The missing wagon was detected as it stopped following the convoy and strayed towards a merchant's store, where quickly all the goods were unloaded and taken inside. Then the straying wagon joined the other returning eleven wagons.

Undoubtedly this shattering news reached the ears of the Chief Administrator of the Relief Agency.

Miss Ash and I

On January 7, an unexpected message came from Miss Ida Ash asking me to see her immediately. This English lady had been interned for the whole duration of the war in Dr. Altoonian's Hospital.

On one occasion she had ventured to come to Hokedoon to attend the evening prayer service, at the close of which I greeted her in English. She was pleased to have a little conversation with me. Then I gathered enough courage to offer to escort her to her residence. I said,

"Miss Ash, may I carry you to your home?"

She became greatly amused with my misuse of the verb "carry," and gently corrected me, explaining that in order to carry her I must take her on my back. "Boys don't carry on their backs girls of my age and size," she continued. "You should say, 'May I take you home, Miss Ash?'"

I thanked her for the correction, then "took" her home.

Having never seen her again, I had forgotten Miss Ash, but, evidently, she had not forgotten the funny Armenian boy in a Turkish soldier's uniform who was willing to "carry" her.

When I stood before her this time, she was an elegant lady, a very important person, the Chief Administrator of London's Lord Mayor's Relief Fund. She welcomed me with the question:

"Do you still want to carry me home?"

I tried to hide my rising blush under the thick cover of silence.

She told me that she was disappointed with Mr. Khachadoorian's behavior as relief transportation officer and had decided to put me in this responsible position. She defined to me in detail what she expected me to do: three times weekly I was to be at the British Army Supply Depot at 8 in the morning, take charge of the twelve lorries loaded with foodstuffs, and accompany them until they were safely delivered, without losing a single one on the road. I was to to sign a receipt at the Depot for twelve loaded wagons and secure a receipt for twelve wagon-loads of foodstuffs from the Center.

"As to your salary," she added, "You will receive two English pounds a month. You are not to touch anything that you are transporting, not even a loaf of bread."

I was exultant, elated, for such good fortune as I left Miss Ash's presence.

The next morning the officer in charge at the Depot had all twelve lorries ready as I came and introduced myself. He must have been surprised not to see his old friend, Haroutune Khachadoorian, but did not show any sign of disappointment at this time. The transaction went along smoothly. The Egyptian and Senegalese drivers climbed their perches and cracked their whips at the teams of the horses to start. I rode on the last lorry to keep a watchful eye on their movements.

That day all twelve wagons emptied their loads at the Center. Kevork Agha Kherlopian, the chief, thanked me as he handed me the receipt. We both understood each other.

This procedure continued for a time or two. I was not prepared for what was coming. On the third morning the Sergeant in charge of the Depot said to me while I was signing the receipt,

"Mister, I see that you are very young, honest, and inexperienced. You don't realize now that you are in a unique position to make yourself rich. An opportunity like this will never come to you again if you don't take advantage of it now. If you co-operate with me, there is a lot of money for you."

"How should I co-operate with you?" I asked.

"I had an unwritten agreement with your predecessor, a smart man and a minister of the Gospel. He would overlook it when one of these loaded lorries left the procession of the vehicles at a certain point and headed towards a different direction. I gave him a princely share for his co-operation. How about you and me coming to such an agreement?"

"Remember, you will be rich!" he added.

"Rich…!" What an enticing prospect for a man whose family was still malnourished, in spite of the relief given to the general public.

But vehemently I answered,

"No, Sergeant, I would never stoop to robbing my own poor people, and wouldn't think of betraying the confidence Miss Ash has placed in me."

"You bloody fool!" ejaculated he in anger and contempt.

He never bothered me again.

And when, some days later, friends were told of the British Sergeant's tempting offer and my refusal to comply, shook their heads in utter disbelief and said in chorus:

"I agree with the Sergeant that you are a great fool."

Another Lure to Temptation

Before the month was over, I was told one morning after I had delivered the caravan loads to the Center that Miss Ash wanted to see me at once. When I reported to her, she pointed to a large bag and asked me to deliver it to the Center and bring back Kevork Agha's receipt.

As soon as I lifted it I became convinced by the jingly sound of the contents that I was transporting a considerable amount of cash money. I shouldered it and trudged along the mile-long distance with uncluttered mind, sweating under the ever-pressing weight. In order to make a short cut, I entered Hokedoon from the front gate—my family apartment was upstairs—and laid the precious bag on a parapet, sitting close by it to catch my breath and cool off.

After a while I shouldered the weight again to resume the trek without stopping, until I entered the Center and handed it to Kevork Agha. He immediately poured the bag on the table in front of him and began counting. Oh, what a glittering, magnificent spectacle those pieces of silver, gold, and paper money presented to my starving—but far from avaricious—eyes.

Counting done, I ran to Miss Ash with the receipt. After a glance at the figures on the receipt Miss Ash told me, to my amazement, that she had me followed all along by two British soldiers to watch me. When I entered Hokedoon, instead of continuing my way, the spies became suspicious of my intention and watched more diligently.

"You are as clean as I thought you would be, and I am relieved. My detectives reported every step you took and every movement you made. The receipt you brought back proves that I can trust you whole-heartedly."

It never occurred to me, trudging under the inordinate weight and perspiring profusely, that I was being tested if I would succumb to temptation by dipping sticky fingers into the money bag.

On the first of February Miss Ash paid me the two pounds and transferred me behind a desk in the Distribution Center to interview refugees and recommend them to Kevork Agha for adequate food and clothing.

I remained at this responsible position, content only with the salary Miss Ash decided, until April 5, when, with the people of Cilicia, I went to Adana.

Another Massacre

Countless refugees, hearing that the war had come to its end, Turkey had laid down its guns in defeat, and finally, peace had come to reign again, were descending on Aleppo, hoping to find a way to return to their desolate home, rebuild, replant, re-plan a new life for themselves.

It was more that two months now since Armistice had been signed between the two warring giants — the Allied and the Central Powers — and Turkish rule over Syria and Lebanon had ended. The Turks, avowed murderers of Armenians, had fled the Arab country helter-skelter, leaving none of their number behind.

This was the assumption of the naive refugees, the misery-stricken remnant of the exterminated race.

But this assumption proved wrong. Tens of thousands of Turks had not fled at the fall of the city. They could not have, even if they had wanted to. They just changed their "color" like the chameleon. Being Moslem, they transformed overnight into Moslem Arabs. In the Mosque chanters of Koran are all Moslems, not Arabs or Turks. So they went underground as Turks, and surfaced as brother Moslems. These countless thousands of Turks stealthily contrived, devised, planned another general massacre of the Armenians, unbelievably returning from their graves and threatening to return to Turkey, the "Turkey for the Turks only," the Turkey from which they wanted the Armenians out once and for all.

The agitation they cultivated within the illiterate and baser Moslem elements during their undercover seclusion prepared the setting of a fast and unexpected massacre that took place on Tuesday, January 28, 1919. Thousands in the street and in the market-place were brutally slaughtered by the Turks in Arab attire, with the co-operation of Arab sympathizers of Turkey. The murderers again had a field day. In one single day perished all those that for five tortuous years had heroically endured the tortures of deprivation, starvation, and brutalities in the hope that return to their ruined homes was at last within grasp.

It was an outrage against morality and decency (which we Armenians were taught the British possessed), a phenomenon utterly incomprehensible, that the British soldiers present everywhere in the city did absolutely nothing to stop the blood-bath. Insensitively they witnessed the carnage, heard the moans and screams of the victims and fierce curses of the murderers, stepped across the fallen bodies and flowing streams of blood, and raised no voice of protest, not a finger of warning.

That hellish day, I know not the reason why, I stayed home in Hokedoon. Those that left Hokedoon that morning did not return anymore. Whatever the reason, it was Providential that none of my family left home. We had a couple of guests with us since the night before. Toros Pushian and Apraham Ateshian had just come to Aleppo, the central point, where all refugees gather. They were my chums from Hadjin – Evérék – Konia days, and had come now to see if they could find any of their relatives alive.

The news of a new massacre under the British nose shocked them both. In a day of two, when they could do it safely, they took the train and went to their "homes" — Toros to Tripoli and Abraham to Konia.

Search for Relatives

In February and March more and more numbers of refugees were processed by the Repatriation authorities and put on their way to former home-towns to resume their disrupted life style, if that was ever possible. Special committees and private individuals engaged themselves in search and liberation of captive women, girls, and boys in Moslem homes, villages, huts, hovels, and tents, all along Syria and its deserts, Lebanon,

Iraq, and Kurdistan. Most of the children found had lost their original identity, language, customs, and memory of parents, having been forcibly converted to Turk, Arab, Anzeh, Chechen, or Kurd. It was not unusual that some of these rescued children denied that they were formerly Armenians, and attempted to escape. In great number these circumcised boys and girls tattooed on the cheeks or foreheads were kept in supervised temporary shelters which, later, became orphanages kept and provided through American Near East Relief.

The daily new arrivals, after having their immediate needs provided, were sent "home" on trains.

At each arrival of the train we, too, searched for relatives, friends, and hometown people. Rejoiced when we met some, and cried for others slaughtered, drowned, left to starve to death in lice and typhus. From the wide-spread Malian and Kooshian families hardly a dozen returned alive.

Decimation, annihilation. The Turk had succeeded in his diabolical plan.

But, miraculously, my family was still intact at the end of the ordeal of death. We had started the uncharted road to exile with four members, and now, by the mercy of God, we were ready to return "home" to face an uncertain future. We were the same four, inseparably tied to each other. Aunt Gulie (Gulenia) had started from Kayseri with five, and now was returning with four, having lost a three-year-old albino child.

One day, in late December, Uncle Haroutune and two of his old colleagues — Mardiros Toorsarkissian and Mihran Munushian — asked me to accompany them to the British Occupation Office to request a permit to go to Adana. The officer in charge of transportation asked why these men wanted to travel so soon, and I answered that they were businessmen, and their families and businesses urgently needed their presence.

My interpreting, though odd in many respects, may have pleased the colonel, who at once wrote the order permitting the merchants' travel. Travel to the interior of Turkey had not yet officially begun.

Mother's Wings Spread Wide

In the month of March, Zaroohi Kirkyasharian, a young lady in her late 'teens, sprung up from an unknown quarter and, looking for living relatives, discovered us. Mother immediately spread her wing over the lone daughter of a cousin of hers.

And, Gulenia Mooshian surfaced one day. She was the only daughter of my paternal aunt Hnazant. We learned from her that her parents and five brothers had perished in the deserts, and only one brother, Panos, the eldest, was living in the U.S.A., where he had escaped in 1913, thus cheating the Turk-planned genocide. She, too, became a member of our family.

And then, at the beginning of April, another young lady of Hadjin, Makroohi Oghlookian, who had lost all her relatives, came to Mother for protection until some relative could be found. Mother compassionately spread her wings a little wider to protect another chick.

Mother, all through the calamitous years, had kept a protective watch over her only sister Gulie and her children as her co-workers and next-door neighbor. Aunt Gulie clung to Mother when orders for departure to hometown were being given, vowing that she would not go to Kayseri anymore, but go with her elder sister wherever she went.

So our family grew from its original four to seven, by the addition of the three young ladies, and to eleven by the addition of Aunt Gulie's family of four.

On the 4th day of April orders were issued for the people of the Province of Cilicia (Adana, Tarsus, Sis, Hadjin, …) to depart. In company with my cousin Stephen I went to the Transportation Office and secured eleven train tickets for Adana.

Each one of us eleven immediately packed into a bundle what little we had, and slept that night our last winks — if they ever came to our eyes.

Early in the morning we left for the station.

CHAPTER 39

GOODBYE ALEPPO

April 5, Saturday, 1919, was the turning point of my life, my family's life, and the lives of thousands like us. A dark era came to its end and a bright new day came along with promises of…unknown, indefinite future. But what does anybody care about at this point? We were bound for home. But what home? Yet we were free from the despotic Turkish yoke.

We eleven were already in one open freight wagon, over-crowded with many more refugees returning to uncertain freedom. Other open freight cars, ahead and behind ours, formed a long line of human islands. Every one was happy, with a sort of sad happiness, with the prickly pain for irretrievably lost dear ones and the joy of freedom at last.

At 7:30 the engines began to pull the long chain of cars cram full of human derelicts that the graves the demon-Turk dug for them did not receive.

About two hours later the train made its first stop at Katma. What a jumble of sad recollections this locale resurrected in me! Five years earlier, trudging on this tortuous road, it took us two days to reach Aleppo, while the train crossed it in less than two hours. We had arrived at Katma, on that September afternoon five years ago, with Mother on the verge of death on account of dysentery, and our hearts crushed. The band of Turkish gendarmes who, in fiendish orgies, relished molesting women, young and old, and massacring the innocent and defenseless men and children, were not around anymore, neither did I see the contemptible chavoush who would not let us fill our water cans from the nearby river without a tribute.

Did God create those devils with no conscience?

A sudden clank and jolt, and then huffs and puffs of the slowly moving train cut short my depressing recollections of Katma, this vast morgue of sun-bleached and powdered human bones.

We were now on the familiar road again, the road we were whipped, trampled, and cursed to march, leaving behind us much needed possessions, exhausted dear ones, cherished dreams and hopes, and our tears.

An hour later we passed through the first of 18 tunnels, dug and built by Armenian forced labor. After the engineering and constructing laborers were done, as a mark of gratitude to the authors of this enormous feat, the Turks massacred them. I felt the kindly spirits of the martyred laborers hovering over us, the returning remnant, in the darkness of each successive tunnel, over which, on the winding, tortuous mountain passes, we groaned and wept in agony.

God be praised. It was different five years later.

Yet painful memories crowd each other as the train spans wide distances.

Here is Kourt-Koulak (Wolf's Ear), with more grievous memories: Mother hopelessly sick; our feet, all three of us children, tired, sore, swollen; frightful villagers sneak-attacking from behind the tall trees, bordering part of the road, to rob, to abduct, to assist in killing.

And here is that slope, where sister, brother, and I continuously pushed the heavy cart (with Mother lying on it in delirium) to assist the ancient and scrawny horse to pull it up to the mountain top. It was in this night that the Turk, owner of the miserable cart, abandoned Mother and ran away with his cart.

The snow-crowned Amanus Mountains in the distance brought to my memory the snow-covered mountains of Hadjin and the famed Erjias of Fénésséh with their life-giving waters, while the waters of this region were polluted as we trudged on years earlier.

Were these waters still polluted now that the Turk had loosened his dirty grip?

At noontime the train made a stop at a station named Rajow. Painful memories flocked again into my mind: Mother burning with fever, hasn't taken nourishment for days, wasting away before our eyes, never whimpering, never complaining. "Madzoon," she whispers. Where can we get yoghurt at this desolate, enemy-populated, sparsely inhabited mountain country? Isn't this pleading tantamount to asking for water in Hell? My brother and I left at night for a nearby unfriendly village, and returned with water bought for a price, instead of madzoon.

Providence, mysteriously, must have transformed this purchased plain water into madzoon in Mother's body, because she smiled as we moistened her lips and forehead with it.

The train crossed over a small river, on the bank of which the brute gendarmes extorted "protection money" from us, the flock condemned for slaughter.

In the three-mile long Keller Tunnel the heat was so oppressive that the gentle Gulenia, my cousin, fainted away, filling our hearts with alarm, because she was precious to us as the only survivor from her family of numerous members.

Now the train climbed the slopes towards Entilly, the major railroad construction center, from where Mardiros Sarkisian (died October 21, 1975, at the age of 85) came to us with food and refreshments.

One after the other familiar names of places brought back sad memories: Airan (watered yoghurt), Bahche (garden), Sitma Punar (fountain of fever), Yar Bashi (summit), Mamooreh, Osmaniye.

When the train stopped at the station of Osmaniye (the first wilderness place my family was dumped out of the cattle-wagon bringing us from Adana five years ago), I came down to buy some delicious oranges and distributed them among my "family" of eleven. There was no trace of apprehension in my heart this time when I cast a glance over the vast camp-field of filth and lice and disease and wide-spread death of the bygone years. Yet I could not help but be troubled by the thought that the Turk, the eternal enemy of the Armenian, had withdrawn to his lair like a blood-thirsty beast whose fangs were extracted, and was vengefully waiting for them to grow anew so that he could tear the Armenian apart again. The beast's lair: the heartland of Turkey — Anatolia and Cilicia — where the survivors of the blackest genocide were headed as their historic rightful home.

The train left Osmaniye to resume the final leg of its journey to Adana. It was now sometime after 7 in the evening. Everybody was exuberantly happy with the prospect of seeing Adana once more. As the long train slowly crawled along over River Jihan (Jihun; Pyramus), a jubilant song — Dr. Nahabet Roussinian's "Cilicia" — swelled out from a thousand throats:

The Web of Hope

> When the gates of Hope swing wide open
> And winter from my country flees,
> When to their nests swallows return
> And trees dress in their garments green,
> My Cilicia I long to see,
> The land that gave sunlight to me.

And in the midst of uncontrolled excitement a Cilician April breeze mischievously grabbed my hat off my head and hurled it into the river below.

"Oh, Jihan," I exclaimed, "be content with my hat, and don't ask anymore for mutilated Armenian bodies."

At the Adana Station

The night wrapped itself up in a dark mantle while the hearts of all the repatriates were flooded with light and joy, when the wearied train slowed down to cross the steel bridge spanning the River Seyhan (Sarus). Then, all of a sudden, the twinkle of a myriad lights revealed Adana, sprawling over the plain on the opposite bank.

The hundreds of freight-train wheels came to a grinding halt at the sadly familiar station where five years earlier I had roamed in futile search of a living. Everybody was eager to get down in order to relax cramped limbs and hasten into the city. But a strict order was heralded not to leave our seats until morning, when officials would come to direct every one to proper quarters.

So our eleven-member "family" covered ourselves as best we could and went to "sleep," if ever sleep would come to us.

At last the beautiful Sunday morning of April 6 dawned on us and Adana. What a joy it was to see neat and courteous Armenian-speaking officers in French military uniform helping us get down from the train, cautioning affectionately, "Step down gently, son of Armen," "welcome to Cilicia, daughter of Haig."

Turning back I said to the train, "Good bye Aleppo, and all that you stood for," and then. "Good morning Adana, and to anything you hold in store for us."

CHAPTER 40

GOOD MORNING ADANA

DESCENDING from the train we were immediately led to the Gulbenkian factory building to rest until processing was done. The crowd was so big that we had to wait for our turn until late afternoon.

In the meantime relatives and friends came from the city in search of loved ones.

Aunt Anna showed up unexpectedly. Mother and Aunt Anna fell into each other's arms. She was Gulenia Mooshian's father's sister, and had witnessed the murder of her brother and his family in Der Zor. She knew that Gulenia was not among the massacred, and having come to Adana earlier, she was looking forward to her arrival.

Aunt Anna in tears of joy and gratitude took Gulenia, her niece, the only relative alive, and went into the city.

After cousin Gulenia's departure, cousin Zaroohi's two brothers were happy to take her home to their mother. This Kurkyasharian family of four had not suffered loss of life in the years of exile, we were glad to learn.

Makroohi, another young lady Mother had brought from Aleppo with us, luckily found a relative and left with her.

All this time Uncle Haroutune and Mardiros Sarkisian were with us waiting for our business to be over, so that they could take us to the city. But all of a sudden "Mamig" (Grandma) Malian showed up with her son Lazarus. She and her son and daughter had been left in Adana and were not deported as we had been. It was in "Mamig's" home that my father had passed away of pneumonia in 1902, and she had kept our orphaned family under her wings until arrangement was made for us to travel to Hadjin.

When "Mamig," this grand old angel with a heart as large as the earth and enough room in it for anyone in need, succeeded in quieting down her emotions and drying her tears, she insisted that we should go to her house.

Her house?

It was a one-room house. The room was a kitchen, dining room, bedroom, and sitting room. Occupants? Beside herself, there were her daughter Mariam and her husband with their two small children and Lazarus and his wife. And now, we four. Eleven in all.

Uncle Haroutune took his younger sister, my Aunt Gulie, and her three children, and left us with "Mamig."

The same night, a few hours after "Mamig" brought us to her home, a baby boy was born to Lazarus and his bride. The new mother must have been about sixteen years old. I was given the honor of naming the baby. I suggested "Zohrab," the venerated name of the illustrious Armenian author, professor of law, and member of Parliament, whose head was crushed by the "grateful" Turk at the beginning of the Genocide.

So the child was named Zohrab.

We Rent an Apartment

"Mamig" with her family of eight was dependent on what the two men (son and son-in-law) could earn as unskilled and unlettered laborers at a time when opportunities were scarce. They were really poor, yet they were kind and respectful, as if we were of royal blood.

After a week or so we found a vacant apartment across the street. "Mamig's" house and ours, both in the section known as Charchabook, squarely faced each other. "Mamig" was happy that we were still "under her motherly care."

We were fortunate, and the object of envy, for living in an upper story apartment. Our rent was twice as high as those on the street floor. It was strictly private, unlike those in the courtyard. We had an open but roofed-over veranda in front of the amply large one-room apartment, with wide glass windows, airy and sunny. The whole flat roof of the several one-room apartments in the courtyard complex also was ours to use as we pleased. We had a closet-sized shed on one side of the veranda or porch that served as kitchen. I can vividly and with deep commiseration remember how Mother or Sister struggled to ignite green twigs or yet-undried pieces of wood under the pot, blowing hard and long, choking and blinded, trying to induce flame. Eating was done on the porch or in the room. Sleeping was done either on the porch or the roof that served as our yard or in the room, depending on the season. Toilet facility was the poorest, one obnoxiously, thickly stinking open-mouthed hole of shallow depth, in a shed on the ground floor. It was to be shared by 30 or 40 residents of the complex. Water had to be hand-pumped from the well in the yard. We had a wooden stand on the porch near the top of the stairs to wash dishes, hands, and face. The flat board serving as "sink" had a hole in the middle, with no pipe. Pipes were unknown and not used at that time. The waste ran down to the front of the public toilet, drenching anyone who happened to be visiting it. Complaining on that ground was unthinkable. The inconvenience was an accepted way of life. Our apologies would have embarrassed them.

Below our flat in the first house lived Krikor Kurkyasharian with his family. He was the eldest brother of our cousin Zaroohi, whom we had brought with us from Aleppo. Zaroohi, who was now living with her mother and two single brothers, would come to see her brother and us, too. Krikor's occupation was making and selling ice-cream. On occasion we bought ice-cream from him for our guests, of whom Mother had many.

I Land a Job

A day or two after arriving at Adana I learned that Garabed Effendi Keshishian was the director of Lord Mayor's Relief Fund factory for women. Garabed Effendi had been the Sanitation Officer of Hadjin when I was a child. Later, when I was a student in Jenanian College, he was the dean of the boarding students. Somehow a friendship developed between us as both sons of Hadjin. When the war broke out and general persecution and exile were secretly being carried on and all the available men were being conscripted into the Turkish army, he disguised himself as a young student and traveled with me to Adana. There, after meeting his family, he enlisted in the army.

And now, after five years of national affliction, I went to see my old friend in the American Girls' College converted to the British Relief factory. He was both surprised and delighted to see me alive. He was glad to learn that Mother, whom he genuinely respected, and the children were well. Without a word from me he offered me the position of secretary in his office.

This was beyond my expectation. It was simply a miracle. On our fourth day in Adana I began to work in his office.

It was on the strength of this position that Mother and I dared to rent our prestigious flat in Charchabook.

Tarsus

As a trusted officer of the Lord Mayor's Relief Fund organization on occasion I had to travel to Tarsus with a sealed message and bring one back. As I strolled in the streets of the queen city of antiquity or on the banks of Cydnus, a train of past events brought memories to my mind.

It was only five years ago that I had greeted Tarsus for the first time. I was traveling from Konia to Adana. My companions were some of my schoolmates and Garabed Effendi, my present boss. As our four carriages rolled on towards Tarsus, in the dimness of the early fog we beheld an incredible scene. Thousands of human beings, Armenian men, women, and children, were trekking on the road, towards Tarsus. Moved by an extreme sense of compassion, I made the sacrifice of giving up my seat in the carriage to a young mother and her babe, a relation of Garabed Effendi's, so that she might ride with him to Tarsus. I did vividly recall my joining the tortured band of the marchers through the long corridor of the Cilician Gates, soaked by the pouring rain, trudging along the Cydnus.

Ashurbanipal the Assyrian had marched on these grounds. So had Cyrus the Mede, Alexander of Macedon, Caesar of Rome, waves over waves of barbarian hordes, Crusaders, Turkic cut-throats.

I was walking in the city proclaimed "free" by Mark Antony's edict, out of which city decades later, a "Roman citizen" would be born to be the foremost apostle of the Christian faith.

Below me continued to roll on the waters of Cydnus that 23 centuries earlier had almost cost Alexander his life. Cydnus, once navigable, was silted and shrunken, no more able to float Cleopatra's barge of purple sails, gilded stern, and silver oars.

On another occasion, I located a resident relative — a Gejekooshian of Hadjin had moved to Tarsus long before — who heartily welcomed and kept me for dinner.

Garabed Effendi created opportunities to push me forward. Once he asked me to prepare a speech and deliver it at a farewell party in honor of a departing American missionary at which he would be the master of ceremonies. I remember reading a humorous paper which I wrote in English for the occasion. It was about a certain village people in the Tarsus Mountains and their erratic habits, customs, and practices, which I had heard my mother tell. The guest of honor was so pleased with it that she begged to have it. I handed it over to her.

Brother Joins the Militia

On the 12th day after our arrival my younger brother, now 17, announced to us that he had joined the militia, a military force for civilians, initiated by the French caretaker government of the Province of Cilicia as the nucleus of the future army when the country would finally be turned over to the Armenians.

During the war the Entente Powers had agreed among themselves to reward the Armenians for their valiant and invaluable sacrifices by returning Cilicia to them.

First Easter in Freedom

On the 20th of April a sunny, cheery, hopeful Easter Sunday greeted us. The churches were packed with devout, thankful, tearful worshipers. These were the people whom the enemies of decency and justice had branded for slaughter. These were the people who had returned to life, as Isaac, the son of Abraham, had returned from Mount Moriah, after miraculously escaping the knife. The jubilation of these people on this first Easter, the day of Victory over Death, was far greater than that of Isaac's 4,000 years earlier. His "butcher" was his own father, overflowing with love and compassion for him, but the butchers of these men were their sworn enemies, seething with unending hatred, loveless, merciless, brutal, incorrigible.

And now, a general, universal requiem was being celebrated in the Apostolic church, and memorial services were being held by the Evangelicals.

After the church services, hundreds, thousands of families flocked to the cemetery to have priests read prayers over their dead, buried and unburied, bleached, drowned, devoured.

Mother made a search and succeeded in locating an old priest, who had been our family priest in early Hadjin days. She engaged him to perform a memorial service over her late husband's grave.

There was no one in the whole world who could point out where my father was buried. All graves were alike, unmarked, unrecorded, uncared for, flat, dirt-covered. No one had accompanied my father's pneumonia-claimed body, shrouded but uncoffined, on that by-gone Easter day in 1902, as it was taken away by grave-diggers to be buried God knows where.

Yet, as our trusty "Mamig," that pure-souled "prophetess" from whose house, 17 years earlier, father's body was borne away, pointed to a bare spot in the hallowed grounds of the cemetery, who were we to doubt her?

We surrounded the "grave," the venerable man of God at the head, flanking him "Mamig," her son Lazarus, her daughter Mariam, Mother, sister, brother, and myself. If father's ashes were not really under this ground, his spirit must have been hovering around us. We felt comforted as the good father read the prescribed Scriptural and liturgical passages and offered prayers in rapid and unintelligible mumbles, as rituals in classical language are conventionally pronounced.

Although I could not remember my father, if even I was the firstborn, I read a prepared tribute to my father. I cannot recall what I said, but Mother was pleased, and I am sure that father's spirit rejoiced.

CHAPTER 41

THE WEB OF HOPE IS SWEPT AWAY

WHILE every surviving native of Hadjin was craving to return to that dream city nestled in the highland fastness of the lofty Taurus Range to the north, we had the pleasure of receiving two visitors from Hadjin.

They were my two aunts.

The elder aunt, Mutébéreh, was the widow of my martyred uncle Melidon Malian. Melidon was one of the 78 unfortunate clergymen and church leaders on their way to the annual Church Union who were caught in the maelstrom of a Turkish orgy of massacre, and were one by one slaughtered as a butcher slaughters lambs. Aunt Mutébéreh had undertaken this arduous trip for the purpose of seeing Mother, her late husband's sister, to whom she was tied with a strong bond of affection and confidence. Besides this reason she also wished to escort her younger sister-in-law Turfanda as she was coming with her child to join her husband, Uncle Haroutune, who on his return from Aleppo had opened his tailor shop and made his residence in the metropolis of Adana.

During the difficult years of war, deportation, and genocide, these two women with tiny children were, somehow, allowed to remain in Hadjin and look after the aged parents of their husbands.

Mother had a small, low-roofed, windowless room adjoining her father's apartment, given to her long ago as the eldest daughter. In this room she kept neat small bundles and chests containing cash savings, purchased valuables and gifts received, heirloom objects and pieces of cloth and silk, all fruits of honest labor of almost three decades. There were mementos and books belonging to her husband. These fruits of her heroic self-sacrifice were laid aside for her orphaned children's future, especially as a dowry for her only daughter when she would be given away as a bride. Mother had carefully and prayerfully packed her dreams and tears in the chests and bundles, savings of a lifetime of wise, circumspect, and frugal living, and had locked the door of her cell for the last time eight years earlier, and then gone to Adana to be employed as head-cook in the Ottoman Orphanage and to be deported to unknown regions short years later.

And now Aunt Mutébéreh had come to see Mother.

Did she undertake the four-day-long journey over mountains and plains to cheer Mother's heart that her "vaulted treasures" were safe and intact? That she, Mother's close friend and confidante, had faithfully guarded the cell, next to the kitchen she daily used, against intrusion, forced entrance, robbery? Did she bring with her some money or goods to make our plight a little easier to bear in the time of our great need? Why should she leave her only darling child behind and come to a far-off city if not to bring hope and support to us?

Our assumptions were all wrong.

No, she had not come to bring us assurances and encouragement.

On the contrary, she had come to salve and appease her own troubled conscience by disclosing the unexpected steps she had been forced to take for the sake of the family. All seven of them — the aged couple and their daughter, and the two daughters-in-law with their children — had subsisted throughout the war years only on the use and sale of whatever Mother had saved and cached away, everything. Mother's "store" was completely vacated, in one single instant her dreams had vanished, "tears" evaporated, the planned security of her children's "future;" dissolved and the rich "dowry" of her daughter gone into thin air.

"What else could I do," she pleaded, "for five years in an isolated mountain town to feed them, in a town where no gainful work could be found by a willing hand of a condemned race? Besides, there was absolutely no hope for your return from the inferno you were sent to. Thank God for the fact that you returned."

Undisturbed, unruffled, unagitated, Mother listened to the agonizing, crushing account of her beloved brother's widow, and calmly answered:

"You did the only right thing by using anything you could find in my bundles and chests for the support and comfort of all you dear to my heart. Evidently, the Lord must have given me all those things in times past to save and store so that part of my family left behind might survive in those dark years."

Aunt Mutébéreh's sensitive and burdened spirit was relieved, and both kissed each other in tears of affection.

Before the week was over, having accomplished her mission, she left for Hadjin with a caravan of returnees, to the city that, no one could foretell, was doomed to be wiped out in a short time.

Gulenia Mooshian

About this time cousin Gulenia Mooshian (the only survivor from her family), was urged by her aunt Anna (the only relative left to her), to marry a young man of Hadjin (he too an only survivor), and left for Hadjin with them.

The future seemed bright and promising to them as they bade their last goodbye to us, not knowing that little more than a year later their city would be burned and they would be massacred.

Mother Becomes Ill Again

Mother had never completely recovered from the sickness she had contracted a couple of years earlier in Aleppo on account of my being brutally snatched from her and driven to death camps in the desert.

And now, in Adana, after the joyous emancipation from the tearing claws of the Terrible Turk, the same malady struck her again in the second month of our arrival.

Mother was seriously ill. Her illness was dragged on. Doctors were scarce, beyond our reach. Medicine scarcer, unavailable.

My sister Mary, and the old, trusty "Mamig" from across the street, attended on Mother constantly. Five months later double hernia set in on her. We succeeded, somehow, in having her admitted to the newly-established Red Cross Hospital and operated on. Shortly after, she developed pneumonia, while the sutures of the surgery became inflamed, and life became miserable again.

Mother left the hospital the day before the new year of 1920 to recuperate at home. How happy we were to have her with us again.

The Web of Hope

Setrak Leaves for College

Brother Setrak, after five months of service in the Militia, was discharged because of ill health, and now there was nothing for him to do. I went to see if our old friend Sisak Effendi could use his influence with Dr. Christie to have Setrak admitted to Tarsus College.

Sisak Effendi's strong recommendation must have had a favorable effect on Dr. Christie, for a few days later we were informed that he had consented to accept Setrak free of charge if he would work in the school to pay for his tuition. We had no objection to such an honorable arrangement. Mother gave her blessing from her sick bed, and Setrak left for Tarsus in September.

Mother Opens Her Arms Again

Because our apartment was one of the finest and had ample room to spare, Mother, after consulting with us children, invited her brother's family to move in with us. Uncle Haroutune, his wife Turfanda and their child Alexander were very glad to live with us. Asking Uncle to share the rent and other expenses was out of the question, improper, and contrary to the custom of the day. Wasn't our mother Uncle's "mother" long before we were born? When calamity struck his father's home in the 1880s sending his elder brother to dungeon in exile, then his father to prison and exile, and driving his step-mother from prison to prison and death, Mother rushed to take him to her husband's home and became "mother" to him for years. Besides, Mother reasoned with us, all four of us in the family, and Aunt Gulenia's family of four, too, owed our very survival to Uncle Haroutune's protection in Aleppo.

Motherhood, the nature, spirit, and all the exquisite qualities that go to make a woman a mother, were embedded in Mother. Not content with having her brother and family under the same roof, she invited her sister Gulenia and her three children to live with us, too.

This matriarchal arrangement of togetherness and protectiveness — a time-honored social practice — naturally created some disagreeable situations, but Mother was endowed with an immense capacity to overlook annoyances, such as lack of privacy, preferences, over-crowdedness, sensitivities, and so on, and would have us follow her example.

Aunt Gulie and especially her son Stephen, about my age, were, by acquired habit or by nature highly suspicious and sensitive. These adverse qualities had been most probably implanted and nurtured by their wicked and brutal husband and father. When one of us — sister, brother, or myself — happened unintentionally to push aside from their "marked" spot on the window sill or shelf or floor objects they had placed — be they a comb, a pin, a spoon, a pair of shoes — they would at once construe that we resented their presence, they got hurt, sulked for a long time, and then blurted out accusations.

Mother was sick, occasionally in the hospital, therefore totally unaware of what we were faced with. In our own home we were made to feel guilty and uncomfortable. To make the bad situation worse, Aunt Turfanda (she too a non-paying guest in our home) would take sides with Aunt Gulie and cousin Stephen, inflaming their senseless suspicions. It was unfortunate for us that our guests would never completely believe our explanations, denials, or apologies.

Letters to Krikor

On Aunt Gulie's request I resumed writing letters to her son Krikor in America, who at once sent a letter and a package of clothes and money to our address in Charchabook. The letter, naturally, was written to his mother and the package and money order sent in her name, but Krikor cautioned his mother and brother to be alert to see that I steal nothing from them.

I resented this unjust charge against my character and wrote to him in protest. His answer several months later was very harsh and insane. He stated that he did not believe there could be found one single honest man. For him everybody was a thief.

Consequently our relations became strained and I refused to correspond with him. Aunt Gulenia, supplied with enough money and necessities for her family, left our home six months later and rented an apartment not to far away. Meanwhile she found someone else to write her letters to her son.

I doubt if she ever tried to correct her son's false opinion of me. (She was a beautiful woman, young, tall, blonde, blue-eyed, pleasant, and shy. She was illiterate, as were all her children. Krikor only had learned to read and write after having gone to the United States and joining the armed forces.)

But she was my aunt, and I loved her and my cousins Stephen, Rachael, and Azniv. Our relations were never strained.

When Cousin Rachael, about 17 or 18 at the time, died of an unknown disease, unattended by a physician, several months after Aunt Gulenia moved away from our home to her private apartment, not only our hearts were broken, but the whole community of Charchabook Sector mourned the gentle and highly-beloved lamb's parting.

Titzouhi

After Aunt Gulie moved out, and Mother was still in the hospital with her long-drawn-out illness, a baby girl was born to Uncle Haroutune and Aunt Turfanda. "Mamig," our over-shadowing guardian angel, was the midwife, capable and neat. One week after this blessed event Mother returned home, and had the pleasure of holding her niece, a new addition to our family.

Uncle Haroutune accorded me the honor of naming the baby. I named my cousin Titzouhi (Goddess).

Titzouhi passed away in Beirut, about 1970. Two years earlier, Rosalie, Titzouhi's daughter, was our guest for three months until she got married. She now lives in Pasadena.

CHAPTER 42

MAKROOHI

O NE MORNING, while I was bent over my desk busily writing, a young woman stepped into the office and asked to see Garabed Effendi, the director. When I raised my head to answer the faintly familiar voice, we were both struck with a delightful surprise to find each other face to face.

"What are you doing here?" she asked with an agitated note.

"I am the new secretary to Garabed Effendi," I answered. And then in turn asked her the same question.

"And what are you doing here?"

"I am the director of the sewing department of Lord Mayor's Relief Fund factory," she answered with a captivating twinkle of the eye.

A tall, slender, neatly dressed, and extremely beautiful Makroohi, one of the three girls whom my mother "mothered" with us from Aleppo, was standing in front of me. She was excitingly, devastatingly beautiful, and there was nothing else I could do before this magnificent, statuesque Venus of Milo but instantaneously fall in love with her. She, too, caught the spark of excitement enveloping me, and comprehended that a powerful magnet was at work between us in a mysterious way.

From the day of this momentous meeting my mind and heart were totally occupied by Makroohi. Wherever I walked, whatever I did, I "saw" Makroohi. Foolishly I craved the impossible, that all day long she would be sitting in the office behind another desk, and in the evening walk out with me. But, on occasion, for trumped-up reasons, she would come to the office to stealthily take a letter or poem I had composed for her and go to her department.

But because of the prevailing conventions of the day we were both extremely circumspect, cautious, and formal in the presence of others. We were never alone together. We never saw each other outside the office, never exchanged a kiss but that of the eyes and heart. We gave no occasion for gossip, caused no scandal.

In the fall, one day, she stepped into the office. Her presence heightened the intensity of the conflagration consuming my whole being. But she was dismally sad. She said she had come to bid me farewell because the next morning she was leaving for Hadjin. Her eldest brother, Garabed Effendi Oghlookian, now in Hadjin and in possession of his parental home, wanted the only surviving member of his family — Makroohi — to be with him, in her own home.

"No body ever loved me before. I am grateful to you for your letters of love. I will remember you to my dying day."

She left in the morning, next day. She did not know she was going to her death a year later, when Hadjin was cannonaded, burned, massacred.

The Compatriotic Union of Hadjin

The small remnant of the once flourishing Hadjin, gathering from the dark corners of exile-lands, had, by this time, gone to their homeland to rebuild their ruined ancestral houses, repossess their abandoned properties, fields, vineyards, and garden-plots on the fertile banks and slopes of the twin rivers, to resume their pre-war occupations and businesses, or to collect long-overdue debts and livestock confiscated by the Turks. They all went with great hopes of beginning a new life. But this new life presented to them a thousand civic, economic, educational, cultural, and constructional problems which needed assistance from outside.

But where was such a friendly and sympathetic "outside"? Who would be willing to lend a hand to this people who, having lost everything, had returned to a place encircled by their age-old enemies, jealous, fanatic, belligerent? The outside had no interest in them. The Great Powers, after winning the war, fell into squabbling between themselves, concerning their share of the rich booty — lands, oil-wells, plunder. The French military care-taker government never showed sympathy to the Armenian survivors in any part of Cilicia under its care. France had her own secret aims to pursue, her policies, her political interests to look after.

The burden of assistance, it was obvious, fell on the shoulders of those sons of Hadjin who had chosen to remain in Adana and of those who had emigrated to the United States.

In the early months of the repatriation to Hadjin, appeals of help from the bishop of the Apostolic Church, from the head of the Evangelical community, and from individual relatives began to reach Adana. The newly-formed Armenian National Council of Adana referred the appeals to the leading figures of Hadjin residing in the city. These men decided to call a mass meeting on Sunday, July 4, 1919, on the grounds of the Abgarian School. Hundreds of people gathered out of curiosity to hear what the speakers had to say. The speakers called attention to the various urgent and unforeseen needs of the returnees to the ravaged, devastated birthplace and stressed the necessity of forming immediately a permanent union to provide all the needed assistance. It was suggested by one of the speakers to name the new association "Compatriotic Union of Hadjin." It was unanimously accepted. The Union was to have two branches: one, an Executive Committee; the other, a General Assembly; the first being accountable to the second.

Five prominent men were elected on the spot to form the Executive Committee, and four to the General Assembly.

To my utter disbelief and amazement, I, a totally unknown nonentity, was nominated and elected by acclamation for the office of First Secretary of the General Assembly, having as my assistant Michael Vayejian, my former classmate in college. Mardiros Agha Gertmenian, the venerable old gentleman who years before in Meskeneh had kindly given me two dimes in my direst need, was elected the chairman.

At the suggestion of my chairman later, on several occasions, I wrote to the Executive Committee for a report on their activities about the collection of funds and supplies and shipments. But each time this "august" body, the executives, chose to ignore and disregard the requests of the "lower body." We all knew for sure that these aghas collected enormous amounts of supplies and cash in the name of the impoverished town in the far-off mountains and appropriated them, dividing them between themselves.

The year ended. Nothing was sent. In vain insistent requests poured out of distressed Hadjin.

By the second month of 1920 Hadjin became besieged by tens of thousands of Kemalist Turkish forces, which put an end to it on October 16.

"Oknagank"

On one of these days Boghos Abrazian paid us a visit. He was an old mate of mine from Hadjin and Fénésséh orphanage days and a close friend. He had recently married a girl from Hadjin and wanted to introduce her to us. During the conversation we reminisced about the old days before the war, our running away from the orphanage in Evérék, and our return and forming of a student society under the name "Oknagank" (Helpers). The guiding spirit behind this society was the beloved Mother Barker, wife of the president of the orphanage. The chairman was Boghos himself, and I was the secretary. Boghos recalled that I had read a paper once in a meeting on the dangers of drinking from the same cup with others.

Thereupon Boghos suggested that we revive "Oknagank," inviting to membership all the boys and girls who had survived and returned to Adana. The purpose of the association would be to come together, renew the former bond, acquaint ourselves with each other's problems, and lend a hand where needed.

With Mother Barker's enthusiastic consent to resume her former position of "Mother" of us all we began sending invitations to those whom we knew. The response was immediate, and within a short time more than a score of our former "sisters" and "brothers," some with their spouses and children, came to their first meeting held at our house. The reunion was happy and tearful, with recollections and recountings of sad experiences.

These meetings were eagerly attended one Sunday afternoon a month on our veranda, and after some hours the members would reluctantly disperse after a treat of ice-cream and other refreshments.

The Society of Oknagank continued from July 4, 1919, to September 1920, when I left Adana for the United States. Two days before my departure several of these beloved ones came together at the studio of the city's foremost photographer to have our group picture taken.

My eyes fill with mist whenever I look at those kindly faces in the picture after 55 years.

I Become a Godfather

In due time Boghos's wife gave birth to a son, and I was given the honor to be the child's godfather and christen him. Thus I became for the first time in my life (for the last time, too) a godfather, and Mother became godmother.

In parenthesis, I may mention that I had the privilege of being a best man at a wedding in Hadjin, when the night watchman of the orphanage married a girl from the Girls' Orphanage. And I was a best man to my Hadjin classmate, the late Harry Izmirlian, on his first marriage in St. Louis, Missouri, in 1922 and on his second marriage seven years after the death of his first wife in Pasadena, in 1947.

Boghos and his wife are dead now, but my godson, Hampartzoum Abrazian, is living with his family in France.

I Become a School-Teacher

I continued my job as a secretary for Garabed Effendi at the Lord Mayor's Relief Fund factory all the months of that spring and summer, but seeing that the wages he was paying me could not adequately support my family, I regretfully resigned my position and applied for a teacher's position. At that time the Armenian Apostolic community was about to open its schools, and the Protestant community its own. I was accepted with three others to teach in the old Protestant High School building, where, in former years, my uncle Melidon (the martyred minister) and other eminent scholars had taught. Most of those scholars did not return from the Genocide.

The school opened on October 27, with four teachers and four classes. The courses were divided between us four. I was assigned to teach Algebra, Physiology, Armenian Language, and Music to the Senior and Junior Classes. Meanwhile, I was recommended by Garabed Effendi to the French president of Orozde Bac department store and Spain's Vice Consul, who had asked him for a teacher of English. This house-tutoring was done all through the school year after school hours.

The Web of Hope

Stephen, Haigag, and Setrak Go to School

Cousin Stephen, Aunt Gulenia's son, agreed to enroll as a student in the lowest class. Although I had no direct part in his education, he applied himself earnestly to his studies, and he learned to write letters to his brother in the United States.

Haigaz Kurkyasharian, Aunt Mariam's youngest son and Cousin Zaroohi's brother, also became a student. He was a member of the Senior Class, and a constant chum to me. He was a handsome, cheerful and sincere person and a devoted friend. Either he was in my home, or I was in his. In his free hours from school was an apprentice to his brother Minas in his dentist's profession. In his later years he became a well-known, well-beloved Doctor of Dentistry. He passed away in Yerevan in 1969. Aunt Mariam, his mother, was a perfect angel of goodness and purity of heart.

My brother Setrak, as mentioned before, had been sent to Tarsus College to get the academic education he needed so badly. But the poor chap, unbeknownst to me, had been cruelly abused there as a slave, forced to supply drinking and washing water for the vast compound by hauling it up from the river. Beside this time-consuming, energy-draining task, he was expected to do other menial work also, such as washing and drying hundreds of table dishes and setting tables. All this slavery, because he was admitted to this renowned temple of learning as a tuition-free student, an object of charity who, somehow, should pay for the privilege.

Setrak wrote home that he could find no time to attend his classes on account of his demanding services, nor had he time or inclination to study. He was sick and still was expected to furnish fresh water to the thirsty hundreds.

Immediately Mother and I ordered him to come home. He was a physical wreck when he came home for Christmas. At the opening of the school after Christmas I enrolled him in the Senior Class, and with my tutoring at home (and of Haigaz also), he became a good student, winning the prize in Armenian Studies at the Commencement Exercises.

It was an occasion of real joy and pride for me to see Setrak and Haigaz with a number of other graduates receive their high school diplomas at the end of the school year.

Zaroohi

Cousin Zaroohi, Haigaz's sister, one of the girls who accompanied us to Adana from Aleppo, married a young man of Aintab, a goldsmith by profession. She remained as a member of the Society of Oknagank as a former Hadjin orphanage girl. (Zaroohi and her husband now live in Montevideo, Uruguay.) Haigaz, too, was an active member.

CHAPTER 43

A BITTER MEMORY

I WAS BORN to remain an idealist all my life, one of those who envisions things, and expects actions, as they *should* be. No amount of ill-fortune and atrocious experiences of the Genocide years had been able to change and harden my simple and artless nature.

I believed that the teaching profession was my destiny, which I should embrace heartily. I set out to serve as a teacher with an earnest dignity, and naively expected to be treated with dignity. In my estimation the teacher's profession was no less honorable, dignified, and beneficent that those of the physician's or the minister's.

This Protestant High School (education was not in vogue at the time) in which I was called to serve, had a treasurer, an old physician, Dr. Salibian by name. When, at the end of the month, I went to his residence, introduced myself and asked humbly for my last month's wages, this heartless character from the medieval ages—His Excellency the Lord Treasurer—chased me out, as one chases away a bothersome stray dog. He ordered me not to bother him again until he could exchange his gold pounds into cheaper paper money

"When shall I come, then," I asked.

"Your soul is not leaving you, is it?" he scolded me angrily. "Come next week or the week after."

And he withdrew inside his palatial house, shutting the door in my face.

A week later when he saw me at his door, he ordered me to come the next week.

This humiliating state of affairs continued all through the school year, not only for me, but for my other colleagues. (Later I learned that this heartless man had treated in this manner all the teachers in the past.)

Disparaged and discouraged, I vowed not to teach in that school anymore as long as that wicked creature remained as treasurer.

The schools opened no more, because the following year political upheavals forced all Armenians to flee their historic homeland once and for all.

An Awkward Situation

The school year ended in June and my private teaching engagements with it. I found myself face to face with the grim specter of unemployment in a city now besieged by Mustafa Kemal's Milly (Revolutionary) forces that sporadically dropped bombs and sent bullets whizzing in order to create confusion and demoralization among the populace and the French Occupation Government. The political atmosphere grew blacker from day to day. Towns and villages in the Cilician Province were being captured and razed, and the Armenian population massacred or deported as in the years of Genocide just a few years earlier.

One morning in July 1920 I went out to the newly-opened office of the American Near East Organization to seek a job. I was pleasantly surprised to learn that the chief director of this organization was none other than Dr. W. S. Dodd, the well-known missionary, preacher, physician, and surgeon of the hospitals he founded first in Talas (1886–1911) and then in Konia (1911–1925). I had occasionally attended the prayer-meetings and Sunday worship services conducted in his hospital in Konia, in my student days. Although I had known him then, I did not expect him to remember me now after so many years.

(I learned later that this great friend of the Armenians contracted typhus and for recuperation had to leave Konia in 1916 and go to the United States. After the war he returned to his field of service as the Director of American Near East Relief for Mesopotamia, Armenia, Cilicia, Anatolia, and Konia. He died in 1928.)

With great eagerness I seized the occasion to introduce myself to him with my background and qualifications, and asked him for a position of service in any capacity he deemed proper.

"There is a need for you," he said, "in the orphanage we have just opened. I will send you now to Reverend Khachadoorian, the director, to make use of you."

Then he wrote a note, handed it to me, and put me on my way.

When I handed the note to the Reverend Director, whom should I see in front of me but the Reverend Haroutune Khachadoorian, the tarnished character of Aleppo days. In the first months of the Armistice he was put in charge of a tremendous trust and responsibility by the British Relief Service and because of gross misappropriations he was blacklisted as an embezzler and traitor to his trust and removed from his position. The British directress had appointed me to fill the post he was forced to vacate. (This incident is recorded in a previous page.)

It seems that after leaving Aleppo, he was called by the Evangelical community of Hadjin to be the pastor of their church, and when the city was besieged by the murderous Turks he had left behind his community, his wife, and numerous children to seek help for them. And in Adana he had secured for himself this highly lucrative position, now that his return was not possible.

After reading Dr. Dodd's note, Mr. Khachadoorian raised his eyes to me.

We had never met before in person, but instinctively we recognized in each other an antagonist, although there was no need for such an attitude. The nature of his stare conveyed to me the fact that this man would never be gracious to me.

"How does it happen that you know Dr. Dodd so well?" was his first unfriendly greeting.

Then he showed me to my quarters and my duty.

Thus I became one of his several teachers.

When the noon hour arrived, I noticed that, instead of sitting for meal with the whole body of the orphans, Mr. Khachadoorian and his teachers sat at a private table in another room, away and unseen. On this first occasion he introduced me to my colleagues.

As I remember, one of them was a Mr. Garabed Farajian, who, years later, served as a minister in Greece and then in California, where he died around 1953.

Another was Henry Gertmenian, who was one of my graduating students just a month earlier. A well-known Oriental rug merchant, residing in San Francisco until today, 1976.

Another young teacher was Souren Mozian, who, from the first moment, became attracted to me as a friend, and remained so until his untimely death in the United States a short time later.

Mr. Khachadoorian presided over the table, carefully rationing the food.

I left the table half-hungry, as, I presume, the others also did.

Next day, Souren, my new friend and colleague, drew me to a secluded corner and asked me to promise him not to reveal to anyone what he was going to tell me. When I promised what he asked, he told me that I should watch my steps in the institution, because the Director, the "man of God," the Reverend Haroutune Khachadoorian, had warned all the teachers and women workers to watch me carefully and report to him if anything was missing, as I was a notorious thief.

"I did not believe one word he said about you, but I cannot understand why he should make such an accusation. There must be something wrong, somewhere," he concluded.

"Thank you, my friend," I stammered with an obvious agitation. "Thank you for forewarning me about this slander. Reverend Khachadoorian's ungraceful attitude has a reason."

Then I told Souren the whole story.

"I see that this malicious lie is intended to defame you, as the result of jealousy," he said.

Haman, the Persian minister in the Book of Esther, was no more wicked than our Irreverend Haroutune Khachadoorian, the ordained minister of godly people, whose felonious deeds had been discovered and his name blacklisted and posted on the wall of the church in Aleppo a year and a half before by those who had caught him red-handed.

I displayed no signs of resentment towards the Director at meal time or on any encounter with him, guarding the secret within me.

A Good Riddance

A feeling of uneasiness took possession of me when, on the third day after my arrival, Mr. Khachadoorian called me to his office. This is it, I said to myself, he is going to discharge me on a trumped-up charge. At the same time, I reasoned, it would be utterly foolish of him to fire me, because he could hardly afford now to have Dr. Dodd, the General Director, and the public at large learn of the treacherous side of his character which, by all means, he would keep covered.

He invited me to sit down. Then he began to tell me in a soft and affable tone that a small branch of the orphanage had already been opened in Charchabook, with fifty orphan boys, a cook, and two woman helpers to do washing and general cleaning. "We need just one person to act as a teacher, supervisor, and companion to the boys. I have decided that you are that person. There will be no one else responsible for the Branch but you." Then he told me to go there at 12 o'clock noon, the same day, and begin my duties.

If Mr. Khachadoorian thought at that moment that he was thus getting rid of me from his immediate circle, he did not realize how much more I was glad to be rid of him and his glum and sullen and ill-tempered presence.

Immediately I packed my belongings and left for the Branch. The building, a two-story structure, with a large porch and an ample courtyard, belonged to Mrs. Armenouhi, one-time supervisor of the Ottoman Orphanage and a friend of Mother's. It was about five minutes' walking distance from my home. And, to top it all, a large open field was spread behind the building

The students and the ladies were eagerly waiting for their new teacher. Their enthusiastic welcome of me warmed my heart, unlike the resentful reception I was accorded by Mr. Khachadoorian.

During the couple months I was there, I never had to discipline any student, nor had any difficulty with the ladies. We experienced mutually friendly relations. I divided the children into different classes and taught them reading and writing. Occasionally I took them out to the field for an afternoon game, or on an outing, and told them stories from Armenian history before bedtime.

This smooth state of affairs continued for two months. My salary, never enough, went for rent and the upkeep of our home.

CHAPTER 44

MY SISTER MARY MARRIES, AND...

MARY knew nothing about it, although she was about twenty-two years old. Sarkis, through a go-between, my uncle Hampartzoum Malian, asked Mother for Mary's hand, and Mother gave her consent after consulting me. Then she relayed our decision first to Mary, and then to Sarkis, through Uncle Hampartzoum. Mary and Sarkis had never met each other.

Sarkis Soghomonian was a young man originally from Hadjin. His mother gave birth to him in 1886 during her second marriage, and after him other boys and girls. But her first husband was a member of the great Malian family, an uncle to my mother. From that first marriage a son was born, Mugurdich. My Mother and her cousin Mugurdich were intensely loyal and fond friends with each other all their lives. We Kooshian children loved our "Mugurdich Keri" (Uncle Mugurdich), his wife, and children.

Uncle Mugurdich Malian and his half-brother were business partners, producing and selling confections in their shop in Hadjin in the first decade of the 20th century. Whenever as a small child on my way to or from school I would stop in front of their shop, one or the other of these uncles would give me a piece of candy, a handful of broken leblebi (roasted chick peas), a small chunk of halvah, or a cube of lokhum.

Uncle Mugurdich perished in the Genocide along with his wife and children and his aged mother and sister. Sarkis alone survived, for in 1913, one year before World War I broke out, he had escaped Turkey and come to the United States. But when he heard what unprecedented atrocities the Turk was perpetrating on his innocent people in Turkey, he left the safety he had found in his adopted country, the "land of the free," and joined the Armenian Volunteer Corps sponsored by the French Army to fight the Turk on Middle Eastern Fronts in Palestine (Arara), Lebanon, and Cilicia.

The Web of Hope

During the months and the years following the Armistice he searched diligently for any one of his brother's or sister's families, but not a single child or adult had been left alive to return to him. He remained heartbroken about that fact.

When we Kooshians returned from the Genocide, we found Sarkis, a dashing Armenian soldier in a chic French uniform, always on horseback, going to and fro in Adana as a courier.

Gradually the course of international politics took on a dismal turn. The French, without the slightest knowledge of the Armenian National Council in Paris, signed a secret pact with the Turks in Ankara, by which they agreed to turn over Cilicia to Mustafa Kemal's insurgency. Consequently, in the summer of 1920 the French Occupation Government disarmed the Armenian Militia and the Armenian Volunteer Corps they themselves had organized during the war to liberate Cilicia for the Armenians. Thus "our friends" the French created a general state of demoralization among the Armenian population all over Cilicia.

Sarkis, demobilized and discharged from the Service, was now a civilian. There was nothing else for him to do but to return to the United States, but he thought it wise to marry an Armenian girl and take her away with him.

So, he expressed his intention to our Uncle Hampartzoum Malian, his martyred brother Mugurdich's cousin. Uncle Hampartzoum and his wife immediately recommended my sister Mary to him as an educated, English-speaking and charming young lady.

That is how it came to pass that Mary became Mrs. Sarkis Soghomonian.

Precious time was marching on irretrievably, and Sarkis had no logical reason to stay in Adana any longer. So, at 8 o'clock in the evening of Thursday, September 9, 1920, the engagement ceremony between the two of them — seeing each other for the first time in their lives — took place in our home, with the blessing of a priest, in the presence of some invited friends — Uncle and Aunt Hampartzoum Malian, Uncle and Aunt Haroutune Malian, Aunt Gulie and her son Stephen, "Mamig" Malian and her daughter Surpoohi, Haigaz and his mother, and others.

Two nights later, on Saturday, September 11, the wedding took place.

After two more days, Monday, the newlyweds left for the United States.

An unbearable emptiness was now created in the house by the sudden departure of the princess of our family. Mother was inconsolable. A greater part of her heart had been torn away. But the next minute she thanked the Lord that at least one member of our much tortured family had thus escaped the hell into which the cruel Turk was once more turning our historic homeland.

A Crucial Decision

After the departure of the newlyweds I returned to my duties in the orphanage, but no amount of involvement could dispel the dull, persistent sensation of gnawing and loneliness distressing my heart.

The next afternoon I took the boys to the field for a football game. As I ran to catch the flying ball, all of a sudden the sky fell on me, a million stars fell around me in fragments, my nose broke out in a stream of blood, and I became blinded instantaneously by the intense pain of a multi-fractured nose-bridge. This unexpected disaster was unwittingly unleashed by one of my older students when he rushed towards me to grab the ball himself, and crashed his shaven skull on my face.

Immediately I was led back to the "Home." The good ladies at once attempted to stop the bleeding and soothe my pain and shock. My poor eyes refused to open for a few days until the enormous swelling slightly decreased. (I sported this discolored, streaked and unsightly countenance for more than a month, and the crooked nose for more than half a century, patiently explaining the cause to inquisitive friends.)

It never occurred to me to see a doctor about this calamity. I took it in my stride and left the outcome to Nature. I couldn't afford a doctor at the time, anyway.

On the third day after the accident, able to see a little, I climbed the stairs of our apartment to see Mother and Brother. Uncle Haroutune and his wife and young son were still living with us, and Aunt Gulie, although she had moved into other lodgings, frequently came to see her sister and brother. When I walked upstairs I saw all of them sitting on the veranda and engaged in conversation. They were all shocked to see me in this unrecognizable condition. When I related to them what had happened, Mother exclaimed,

"You cannot stay here in this hell any longer. You must go to America as your sister has done."

"Mother," I said in anguished spirit, "you know very well that we never had enough money for our family's daily needs, and were never able to set a penny aside. How can I leave you now sick as you are, and my young brother, in such a turbulent country, and save my own skin? You both need me here, by your side."

"Yes, you must go," she repeated. Uncle reaffirmed his eldest sister's decision.

"I will give you one hundred dollars as part of your fare, if you take with you Stephen to his brother in the United States," said Aunt Gulenia.

Mother, elated at the favorable turn of the situation, announced:

"And I will sell anything of value to provide the rest of your fare."

The next day, with my half-shut eyes and swollen, black and purple face, I took Stephen to the government bureaus to get our passports, vaccination and other certificates (in Turkish and French), meanwhile satisfying the curiosity of officials and friends about the strange look of my countenance.

Then I went to see my staunch friend, student, and cousin Haigaz, told him about the steps I already had taken to leave Adana for the United States, and presented to him my financial predicament. At once he astonished me by offering fifty dollars he had saved by helping his brother in his dentist's office. The only term he set down was to give him a promissory note to pay the loan, with no interest, at the end of a year.

Then my brother and I sold some of our household goods, and, with the proceeds — 63 dollars — bought a rug, made in Adana, by local Armenian weavers. This rug had the word "Adana" woven on it, with the date 1920, also the Armenian national emblem.[43] Aunt Gulenia also bought a rug for her son, exactly the same as mine. These rugs were intended to serve us as bedding in our travels, and, in an emergency, to convert to cash.

On Sunday, September 19, I went to see Mr. Khachadoorian to inform him of my impending departure for America and immediate resignation from my position under him. He expressed his regrets (?) for my resignation, and good wishes (?) for my voyage.

But when I went back to the Branch in Charchabook to bid farewell to the three dear ladies, they began to cry, confessing in abashed terms that they had been watching me day and night, and especially whenever I left the grounds, to see if I should steal anything. They were glad, they said, that they could find no fault in me to report to Mr. Khachadoorian, who had given the order to them and was constantly questioning them on that account.

Parting with my students was more difficult. During the two months together in Charchabook Home, we had all become friends, comrades, brothers in a big family.

CHAPTER 45

FAREWELL TO ADANA

Tuesday, September 21, 1920

At 8 o'clock of that Tuesday morning, Cousin Stephen and I started to walk behind the hired motor truck as it slowly rolled away from our Charchabook home towards the historic stone bridge over the river Seyhan.

We were walking and talking with our dear ones, forever for the last time, who were accompanying us for a short distance as a bon voyage gesture, and with whom we had shared sweet times and bitter, of laughter and tears. In heavy heart were walking with us Stephen's mother and his sister Azniv, Uncle Haroutune, my wonderful friend and admirer Haigaz, my younger brother Setrak, and Mother, invalid and spent, heroically trying to keep pace with the rest of us.

Now, fifty-five years after that historic last walk with my mother, I am still astounded that I could be so foolish and insensible as not to conceive the enormity of the inner agony she was suffering. It did not occur to me that I would see her no more. While still within the limits of the city, Stephen and I bade farewell to our people and climbed aboard the truck. As the vehicle took on speed leaving the company behind, my backward glance caught sight of Mother trying to run after us with out-stretched arms and faltering legs, and certainly with tears, as if regretting that she let me go. Was she calling me to stop and go back to her? But the driver, foreign to such fine emotions, accelerated his speed in order to reach the sea at Karatash as soon as possible.

Surprisingly, the insurgent Kemalist forces were succeeding in their fight against the victorious Allied powers over the control of the occupied territories in Turkey. Their continual harassment drove the Italians out of Idalia, the British from Istanbul, the Greeks from Smyrna and its environs, and the French from Cilicia and all the cities within it.

The Turkish brigands, armed with abandoned Allied stockpiles of guns and weapons and fed on abandoned Allied food, now surrounded Adana. City after city was captured, burned, and the population either massacred or driven out into wintry death. All means of communication and transportation were at the mercy of the mortal enemy. The French Occupation forces were unwilling to protect the Armenian population against the Turks.

Railroads and highways leading out of Adana were in the hands of the enemy.

The truck was traveling so fast now on the parched expanse of the open country towards the south that the dust rose behind us in thick clouds and the distance we left behind became obliterated from our view. We were heading to Karatash (Blackstone), a secluded sea shore, the southernmost horn of Cilicia, the only access to the sea left to the French.

Ordinarily a train ride to the sea-port town of Mersin, directly to the southwest of Adana, would take about four hours at four dollars fare. But now we were traveling directly to the south, Karatash, in an uncomfortable truck, at fifteen dollars each, and from there — if and when a boat was available — pay an inflated boat fare to arrive at Mersin in four times more hours. The political circumstances thus forced us to travel over the two sides of a triangle to arrive at the angle that one side would easily take us.

Karatash

It was noon when we arrived at the sea. I had never seen a sea before. Its endlessness and dazzling azure fascinated me. The largest body of water I had seen before was the River Euphrates, at the banks of which, some years earlier, I oozed out an existence of death on my part, and witnessed death *en masse*. The blue of the sea and sky was so blended, interlaced, and baffling that I made the following entry in my diary:

> The sea is the daughter of heaven.
>
> The Supreme Power must have poured a bottle of bluing into to the sea, and then painted the sky with the liquid of the sea.

The meditation goes on:

> An infinite blanket of blue is concealing wonderful mysteries in the sky, and its fringes are hiding in the sea who knows what.

Yesterday, in Adana, a letter from my sister stunned us with the news that she and her groom were stranded at Karatash, unable to find a boat sailing to Mersin, before a week. Now, a week later, I looked for them in the village, but found no trace of them. They must have at last sailed, I comforted myself.

I noticed that the surface of the sea was dotted with numberless vessels of all sizes. One of them undoubtedly would sail, I hoped, and was overjoyed when informed that a boat was scheduled to depart that same evening at four. Immediately Stephen and I got busy processing our travel-papers and securing our passage.

Karatash was not a port city. If it ever was — no doubt it was — no evidence of it remained for us to see. Yet ruins of sorts were to be found.

We hired a couple of porters who first carried our belongings to the small boat, wading through the waters, and then returning to carry us on their backs. My carrier exhorted me not to be afraid, but hold tight on him while he splashed his watery way to the rowboat a hundred yards off the shore. I was scared stiff seeing a scrawny human "beast" under me, and a liquid grave all around. Earning his meager pay well, the worthy fellow gently deposited me in the tiny craft which, at once, rowed away to the motor-boat in the deeper distance. The sea, seemingly smooth, began to toss the frail craft up and down, raising the nose way up this moment, and then playing the same trick on the tail. It was an unusual and fearsome experience. Heroically the feather-weight boat weathered the mighty forces rocking it as a toy, and approached the sturdy motor-boat, named *Bodosaki*. Then we were helped to climb aboard.

We found this small motor-boat cram-full of passengers fleeing the sickened country. Not an inch of space could be spared in the boat to any newcomer. We, the two of us, tried to squeeze a spot for our scanty belongings on the deck, amid unfriendly frowns, among total strangers.

The boat started on schedule, tearing the field of waters into two walls on its sides, and gliding through the uncharted liquid highway it had dug. All at once I remembered seeing in a moving picture how a woman in a boat became sea-sick, and how helpless and dependent and miserable she was. And I recalled that I had laughed at her clumsiness and restlessness, finding her plight funny.

And now, on deck of *Bodosaki*, almost immediately, I became sea-sick, head dizzy, stomach churning, heart laboring, unable to stand or sit, helpless, clumsy, restless, and dependent. There was nothing funny or laughable about it, either. And to top it all off, the incessant tock-tock of the primitive motor was banging at my head. I spent the most miserable of my nights on the motor-boat *Bodosaki*, on the first leg of my flight to Freedom, Tuesday, September 21, 1920.

Amid the peacelessness of the night, my inner perception still kept itself engaged in some meditations on the reasons why I was so anxiously heading for the United States of America, leaving behind Mother, the dearest spirit on earth, and my brother, a young and inexperienced child. The thread of contemplations went like this:

Is there any one born and living in oppression and poverty that does not dream of going to America some day? The "dream" convinces the "dreamer" that America is the unique land of freedom, plenty, promise, and opportunity; America is the land where only angels dwell, where there is no evil, injustice, compulsion, oppression, and starvation; her streets are paved with gold and precious stones; money is scattered on the road, or dangling from trees to be picked up at will; her men and women have no worries of any sort; her mornings are always preceded with golden dawns and scatterings of perfumed rose-petals, and evenings close with magnificent sunsets; her skies reverberate with the songs of nightingales and canaries; her men do nothing but sit on the banks of gently flowing rivers and pull out luscious fishes with bare hand; America, Utopia, Garden of Eden, groves of orange and pomegranate, orchards of deliciousness, vineyards and vast wheat fields…

Upon arriving at Mersin we went to the Armenian church, where the pastor, the Reverend Hampartzoum Govkalayjian, kindly permitted us to camp in a corner of his churchyard until we could sail away.

I wrote a humorous letter to Mother, intending to cheer her out of the depression of "losing" two of her three children at the same time, her main support, aid, and comfort.

When I found Mary and Sarkis I learned that they had missed their military transport the night before and were waiting for the next vessel.

Stephen and I spent the next couple days visiting and strolling along the sea front, watching sunsets of far-off horizons and waiting for our ship.

Friday, September 24, 1920: Towards Smyrna

After having our passports validated, around 2 P.M. we were on board the giant Smyrna-bound sea-faring ship *Montaza* of the Khedive line. Uncle Hampartzoum and his delightful family — Aunt Naomi, daughter Nectar (not yet twelve), and son Vartan, younger — were our traveling companions.

The diary of the day records that there were a thousand or more people on board the "Leviathan" and hundreds of thousand-ton bales in her belly. The giant ship seemed to be a fortress of iron built in the sea, incapable of moving around.

All of a sudden, while we were still on the waters of the Cilician Sea, a sinister rumor went around the ship that the French authorities had disarmed the Armenian volunteer army stationed at Akarja, a suburb of Adana, before it had the opportunity to march to the aid of beleaguered Hadjin; that they had abolished the officially recognized Armenian National Council of Adana and environs; and also, that they had ordered the Armenian dailies to stop publication. Thus ill winds over Cilicia were gaining the velocity of destructive hurricanes. Events later proved these rumors true.

On boarding the ship we were ordered down to the huge dark, dank, and foul-smelling compartment below, where in previous days cattle had dropped their discharge. And now hundreds of us were crowded into it. Finding a tight spot, we spread out our rugs and went to sleep after some hours. I did not feel the start of the ship, nor did I hear the inescapable tock-tock of *Bodosaki*'s ancient motor. I enjoyed a long, sound, and invigorating slumber the kind of which I had missed since leaving home. When I went up to the deck in the morning, Mersin was nowhere to be seen, as if engulfed by the sea. "Cilicia the Desirable" had vanished too, save the hazy ghosts of a distant mountain range. The pang of a belated, unfulfillable and final longing began to torment me. My beloved homeland, my birthplace, the sod under which my ancestors lay, had irretrievably disappeared.

My inseparable companion, cousin Stephen, shared with me all our new experiences since leaving our families in Adana. During the day we sought the company of our uncle Hampartzoum, who entertained everybody within hearing distance with his inexhaustible store of stories, real or imaginary, always full of humor and optimism concerning the future.

I found among the passengers a former classmate of mine, Vahan Dumanian of Hadjin, bound now for Constantinople. He, too, joined our company, making it an enjoyable voyage.

I cannot resist the temptation, at this juncture, to transcribe a passage from the Diary:

> How bewitchingly red the sunset is on the sea.
>
> The Sun is hastening to his hiding place behind the round horizon,
>
> Scattering gold dust, and splattering liquid gold on his train,
>
> And spreading a royal scarlet carpet around his throne.
>
> Gradually, imperceptibly, all this glory is stored away, by unseen hands, to make room for the enthroning of the Nocturnal Queen.
>
> Then the Liquid Mirror, the sea, moved by intense excitations, embraces the queen's entire beauty to its heart.

It is most probable that on this second day of our voyage we were skirting along the last portion of the Cilician seashore. We had just left behind us Seleucia (Zilifke), built in 300 B.C. by Seleucus I; where my father had taken us from Hadjin to sojourn from 1898 to 1902, passing away in Adana on our return journey, and where my brother was born; in whose River Calycadnus Emperor Fredrick Barbarossa drowned in 1190 while leading his army on the Third Crusade.

We sailed on placid waters all along the Cilician Sea and the channel between Cyprus and the underbelly of Turkey. Leaving behind the Cyprian Channel, *Montaza* headed north into the Gulf of Adalia and anchored in the harbor of Antalya on Sunday morning.

Antalya

An extremely beautiful city, favored by nature. Yet my first reaction as *Montaza* cast her anchor was of fear, because this was the den of fierce and fanatic brigands, Armenian-hating partisans of Mustafa Kemal. The Turks all over Turkey had vowed not to permit surviving refugees to return to their former homes, which were given to Turkic refugees brought in from elsewhere. And now, since the Armistice, an Italian occupation force had established itself in the province, with the intent of skimming the cream off this highly lucrative sea port, but hardly able or willing to curb their political ambitions or savage appetites. (Not too many months later, the Italian force, a member of the victorious Allied Powers, with tail folded under, would slink away.)

It soon developed that *Montaza's* purpose in stopping here, which took two days, was to unload and receive cargo. The spectacle of the activities involved in loading and unloading was a spell-binding experience for me who had never seen the sea or a ship before except in moving pictures. The cargo our ship unloaded consisted of flour, rugs, and opium. The most amazing sight was the miracle-working machine, the winch, which winding and unwinding enormous lengths of wrist-thick rope or chain, grabs, moves around, hoists high up and hauls away bales weighing tons from the belly of the ship and deposits them in boats hovering around it in great numbers. The winch performed work in one hour that would take a hundred hands a month.

When the unloading ended, the marvel of loading began. This time the cargo was one thousand cattle and twenty thousand sheep and goats. The cattle were fastened two-by-two by the horns and lifted into the air about fifty yards from the surface of the sea and carefully deposited in the caverns of the ship. The smaller animals were lifted ten at a time, tied on a single leg, and brought down gently. Some of these poor creatures struggled and kicked as they traveled up and down in the air, and others were smart enough to refrain from useless rebellion.

On Sunday morning, as we entered the harbor, a twelve-year-old boy was found dead. The physician examined the body and declared it officially dead. A couple of the crew wrapped it in a shroud, fastened on some iron weights and, after the prayers offered by a French priest, cast it into the sea. The incident's gloom carried me back to my desert days, when thousands over thousands of Godforsaken Armenians perished unshrouded, unwept, unprayed, ungraved.

It was on this same Sunday morning again that the captain sent us an order to vacate the quarters we had settled into so that he could put the animals in our place, but there was no room on the already too-crowded ship for the hundreds of us. After we had settled in and around the life boats, another order drove us away to a barn in the rear. An hour later, still another order forced us to vacate this barn too for more cattle. This shameful treatment caused a small-scale rebellion, and we did not move from our new-found barn. Cattle were no better than we were, we reasoned, but we were proved wrong. The cattle crowded us out. The rebellion fizzled out.

Then in the deepest bottom of the ship a trap door opened, and we were herded into the pitch dark to spend the night. But on Monday morning we were ordered out again, and in order to make sure we moved the captain ordered our water supply shut off. Stephen and I found a distant spot on the deck among the machinery and settled there, roasting in the sun by day and freezing stiff by night. If we had died that night, we would have been buried at sea, wrapped in shrouds, weighted with iron and the French priest mumbling in Latin.

The deck, too, was overcrowded with mooing cattle, bleating sheep and goats, neighing horses, and bales and bales of hay and alfalfa.

Antalya was known as Attalia in the time of the Apostle Paul, from which port he sailed back to Antioch with Barnabas on his first missionary journey (Acts 14:25). Perga is at a few hours distance to the north. This famous sea-port town was built by king Attalus in 150 B.C. as the capital of the Roman province of Pamphylia. In the days of Levon the Great it became a part of the Roupinian Kingdom of Cilicia. Then successively it fell into the hands of the Greeks, the Venetians, the Seljuks, and the Ottoman Turks.

Its population of 25,000 consisted of Turks, Greeks, Armenians, Assyrians, Syrians, Jews, and others. At the beginning of 1915 the Armenians numbered more than a thousand, but fewer than a hundred returned from the Genocide. Most of the Turkish population now were refugees from Crete. I was told that the Turkish government here, and elsewhere in Anatolia, did not permit any Christian, particularly an Armenian, to travel to another province, and did not issue travel passports at all.

Standing at the head of the ladder to the ship, two local officers, one Italian and one Turkish, were carefully inspecting every new passenger. It was fortunate that no one on board was permitted to leave the ship to visit the city for sight-seeing. We were told that recently several Armenian passengers had not returned to continue their voyages after having disembarked to explore the town.

Several Turkish policemen searched the ship for three Turkish fugitives. The massive vessel could easily have hidden a hundred fugitives.

Having completed her loading and unloading, she sounded her whistle and slowly steamed off towards Smyrna on Monday at 4:00.

Tuesday, September 28, 1920: Rhodes

It was already dark as we steamed southward along the coastal waters of the Gulf of Adalia and approached the Cape of Gelidonya, where the western boundaries of the Cilician Sea meet the eastern frontiers of the Aegean. In these treacherous waters of the Horn in 1958 the oldest shipwreck ever found yielded Bronze Age relics after 33 centuries under the sea.

Poseidon, the god of the sea, had already plunged his mighty trident into the abyss and stirred up the sleeping ghosts of pirates and buccaneers of all ages past. Furious tempests rose up to torment the ship heavy with human beings, beasts, and material cargo, as if it were a ball to pass from one liquid crest to another. I shivered all night long with fear and cold huddled under the machinery on the deck, wrapped only in my small, flimsy rug.

In one of those hours of the night *Montaza* passed by Myra, the ancient port city of Lycia, where St. Nicholas (Santa Claus), famed for his generous gifts, was a bishop in the 4th century. Church histories tell that Emperor Diocletian persecuted him, but later Constantine set him free. According to tradition, Bishop Nicholas attended the Council of

Nicaea with one of our Armenian bishops, Catholicos Aristaces, the son and successor of St. Gregory the Illuminator.

At 9:00 in the morning our ship anchored in the harbor of the famous port of Rhodes, situated on the northern tip of the 545-square mile island of the same name. Rhodes is the largest of the Dodecanese Island group in the Aegean Sea, comprising a department of Greece. At this time the population of the city numbered about 24,000. This was the site of the sixth of the Seven Wonders of the ancient world. In 285 B.C. a gigantic bronze statue was built here, dedicated to the sun-god Helios, later identified with Apollo. According to tradition, the Colossus of Rhodes straddled the entrance to the harbor.

I was informed that Armenians were very few in Rhodes, probably fewer than fifty. The Island at this time was under Italian control. Having completed her loading, the ship weighed anchor and moved on at 3:30 P.M.

The Seven Wonders

Compiled by Antipater of Alexandria

The Great Pyramid of Giza.

The Hanging Gardens of Semiramis.

The Statue of Zeus at Olympia by Phidias.

The Temple of Artemis at Ephesus.

The Mausoleum of King Mausoleus at Halicarnassus.

The Colossus of Rhodes for Apollo.

The Pharos of Alexandria.

Some add to the list the "Fabled Walls of Babylon."

Not one of these man-made wonders remains today but the Great Pyramid.

The Web of Hope

Wednesday, September 29, 1920: Still at Sea

The tempest raged in full fury all through the night, and the ship wove her path through the Dodecanese Archipelago, leaving behind Halicarnassus, a sea-port city, where the tomb of King Mausoleus, one of the world's Seven Wonders, gave us the word "mausoleum;" and Pharmacusa, a sea-facing city, where pirates held Caesar 38 days for ransom. The Island of Patmos, where the Apostle John wrote the Revelation, was also left behind, to the west of our course.

The voyage was so rough that seasickness, with all its ugly consequences, was common all around. Most of those who settled on the open deck lost some of their belongings to the whim of the wind. It grabbed my pillow and deposited it in the sea, as if someone there needed it more than I. I was glad that the thief was content only with my pillow more than myself.

At 10:00 o'clock in the morning the ship anchored at Samos, an island that produces gum, I was told, as its Turkish name — Sakuz — signifies. This was the island that occasioned Pericles, the Athenian general (d. 429 B.C.) to deliver his defensive oration, when he was accused of starting the Samian War upon the entreaty of his *hetaera* (mistress). During the Balkan War it threw off the oppressive yoke of the Turk and joined Mother Greece. The city sprawls all along the sea shore. On the slopes of the mountain beautiful vineyards and olive trees greet the eye.

At 1:00 P.M. the ship left Samos, and by and by an enchanting parade of lovely islands came to view one after another. Were these the islands, I wondered, that Homer was writing about as the locales of the epic adventures of Odysseus?

As we sailed on northward in Kusadasi Kurfezi (gulf), we left, unnoticed, on our right, the ruins of ancient Ephesus, where in 365 B.C. an unknown fool named Erostrates, in order to achieve an immortal fame, burned down the Temple of Artemis, one of the world's Seven Wonders; where Paul challenged the idol-makers (Acts 19:23–41); and where the Council of Ephesus was held in A.D. 431.

It was 8:00 P.M. when *Montaza* cast anchor in the harbor of Smyrna.

CHAPTER 46

SMYRNA

Thursday, September 30, 1920

A FASCINATING PANORAMA greeted our eyes in the golden glow of the sunset as we gazed across the bay at the three-thousand year old Smyrna, the "Queen of the East." One would not be wrong for thinking that a supernatural being had torn a piece of the star-studded heaven and dropped it in his haste.

I recalled to memory the friendly rivalry between the Armenian Izmir and the Armenian Constantinople — a rivalry in the fields of education, literature, journalism, and diverse professions. I remembered with poignant nostalgia and grief the names of some greats who had vanished:

—Matteos Mamourian, editor, author of about 40 volumes, large and small.

—Krikor Chilingirian, editor, translator of Victor Hugo's *Les Misérables* and other French authors.

—Caloust Gostanian, translator of Auguste Compte's *Methode*.

—Mesrob Hubarian, lexicographer, translator of Victor Hugo, Racine, Chateaubriand, La Fontaine, and Moliere.

—And others.

Both of these centers of Armenian intellect — as all the other lesser centers — had been wiped out since 1915 by the diabolical design of the Turk.

This, then, was the famed Smyrna that lay in ruins for 300 years after Lydians destroyed it in 672 B.C., and Alexander the Great came along to plan its rebuilding.

This, then, was the storied Smyrna that joined the choir of the seven Greek cities that claimed that the immortal Homer was born and buried there.

This, then, was the ill-fated Smyrna that in 1624 fell into the hands of the Turks, who made streams of blood to flow in the streets.

So this was the city that in innocent ignorance was in its pursuit of happiness — ignorant that two years hence, on September 22, 1922, she would be sacked by the Turks again, set on fire, and her Christian inhabitants, Greeks and Armenians, butchered, burned alive, and driven into the sea.

And now, on this Thursday morning, September 30, 1920, my cousin Stephen and I left our ship *Montaza* and landed on the quay, the famous "Cordon," on which love-lorn couples and pleasure seekers loved to promenade every night. But now we could not afford to entertain such pleasant thoughts. Our passports were carefully scrutinized and processed by the local customs officials, and we were permitted to enter the city. We had no idea where to go but to the Armenian Church of St. Stephen.

We managed to occupy an open space among the graves in the churchyard, where other transients like us were settled. I found some old acquaintances among them, who had been waiting for weeks for a ship to take them to their destination.

Monday, October 1, 1920: Second day in Smyrna

We were comparatively safe now in the churchyard, with the gracious permission of the Bishop of St. Stephen, but the uncertain waiting of other travelers gave us reason to worry.

So, early in the morning Stephen and I went to the American Consulate to present our passports and secure visas. The doorkeeper sent us away for bothering him so early. At 9:00 o'clock we went there again.

This time an official ceremoniously stamped a date on our passports and handed them back to us, bidding us to come back in a week's time with a certificate from an oculist attesting to the good health of our eyes.

Stephen had no reason to worry. But I had misgivings about my very poor eyes. And the same afternoon, Dr. Enfiyejian, after examining them, shattered my hopes by declaring that I needed treatment for trachoma for at least two months, with a possible cure at the end.

The meager sum of 150 dollars with which I had undertaken this venture had already dwindled to 100 in the last ten days. What would become of me, I started to worry, if I was compelled to spend this precious sum for medicine, for food and clothes and eventual rent? I was in a

Greek city, with a language foreign to me, with no prospect of gainful employment, with no hope of obtaining assistance from any source.

Stephen's eyes were "bono," and mine were "no bono." He was adequately supplied with travel funds, and I was destitute. He could easily continue his journey to America, and I could not. Separation of the two cousins was inevitable. Fear and worry overwhelmed me.

News about the worsening political situation in Adana, where we had left our mothers and dear ones, came through newspaper reports to accelerate my worries and fears. My nights became nightmares of misery on the chilling and unsympathetic slabs of marble in St. Stephen's graveyard.

Tuesday, October 5, 1920: Sixth day in Smyrna

For days the local papers were reporting General Antranig's expected visit to the city on his way to Cilicia to liberate it from the impending bloodbath by the Turks and establish an independent Armenian state. The legendary hero of the Armenians arrived today at 11:00 A.M. on board the ship *Arcadia* in company with General Bonapartian and Lieutenant Jim Changalian. From the pulpit of St. Stephen Church General Antranig delivered a fiery speech promising victory over the Turks and delivery of the land of Roupinians back in to the hands of the rightful owners, the Armenians.

Last night the weather began to become very cold, and this morning a heavy rain started to drench us in the churchyard. It continued all day. A native of the city made the remark that when Smyrna sky gets sour, it forgets to smile for a long time.

Stephen wanted to go to the American Consulate. There a clerk copied a few notes out of our passports and, to my amazement, asked us to report again in five days.

Thursday, October 7, 1920: Eighth day in Smyrna

Autumn is only a name here, nonexistent. Winter has overtaken October altogether. The marble slabs on which we camp are seven-fold colder than the chill of the night. Many of the campers are afflicted with catarrh and jabbing pains.

Devout worshipers of the wealthy city flock into the church, but none has a word of greeting, of sympathy, of comfort. Not a kindly glance. These proud and haughty denizens of Smyrna were for some unknown reason spared the ordeal of the Genocide in 1915, and could not feel kindly towards the Armenians of the interior, the Armenians of Cilicia. We were considered a nuisance, unwelcome strangers, half-civilized barbarians, uneducated, low-class beggars.

Two of these vain pea-hens, while entering the church (presumably to pray), overheard a child in the churchyard call her mother "mama," and nudged each other, jeering,

"Where did this savage child learn the word 'mama'? Evidently from us."

(This remark is reproduced verbatim from the page of my diary of the day.)

Sunday, October 10, 1920: Eleventh day in Smyrna

To spare his "family" from exposure to rain and cold and sickness in the church courtyard, Uncle Hampartzoum Malian went to rent a room in a Greek khan. Yesterday he invited my cousin Stephen and me to share the "comforts" of his "hotel room" as part of his "family." We gladly accepted his kind offer and moved in at once.

The "room" was a dark windowless stuffy stable, where twelve of us, his "family," could spread our beddings side by side and "sleep." Sleep in this "hotel room" was quite different than in the open-air camp on the cold gravestones. Millions of fleas, flies, lice, and other nondescript bugs were in a tireless parade in this congested, foul, and dank room. Under the circumstances we had to tolerate the festive mood of the native denizens of the stable.

Uncle's "family," all bound for Pasadena, California, consisted of ten members, not counting Stephen and me. They were, beside himself, his wife Noemi, daughter Nectar, 10, son Vartan, 7, brother Aram, a servant girl Rebecca (who had to be left behind on account of no bono eyes),

Uncle's two cousins Haigaz and Levon Mehagian, Alice, 18 (later Alice Marsh) and her widowed aunt Rebecca (later Mrs. Gedigian).

Early in the morning, after bundling our belongings and leaving them in a designated spot, each one of us would go out on his own way and return at night to enjoy the "comforts" of sleep.

At 9:00 o'clock in the morning a rumor was afoot that the Armenian soldiers in Cilicia had been exiled and that a number of them had landed in Smyrna.

I rushed, with some others, to see if the rumor was true.

What a pitiful and disheartening sight it was.

I knew most of these exiles. They were young men who had, after their return from the Genocide, volunteered as recruits to be trained and sent to the rescue of the beleaguered Hadjin. Some others were American-Armenians, who had joined the French Armenian Legion to fight the Turks to avenge the Armenian Genocide.

I found among them a few close friends: Sarkis Bachejian, a classmate from Hadjin orphanage; Hampartzoum, another mate from Hadjin; Setrak, the younger brother of my godson's father, Boghos Abrazian; Setrak's cousin; and other acquaintances.

Sarkis told us an unbelievable story, and his fellow exiles corroborated it.

On the night of September 22, the camp of the Corps being trained for the rescue of Hadjin was suddenly surrounded by French tanks, cannons, and machine guns and with Algerian and Senegalese infantry and cavalry, who demanded surrender.

The Armenian officers and soldiers at once surrendered.

The Legionaries in the French Army also were in like manner demobilized and arrested.

The militia and the guards were all disarmed and put under arrest.

Four hundred of the Hadjin Rescue Corps were forced to march to Karatash, put in a small boat for an unknown destination, food and drink and natural relief denied. The French cruelty went as far as dousing the "prisoners" through a hose now with cold water, then with boiling water. In Mersin they were kept in prison for eight days, and then herded on board an old Italian boat, *Tyrol*. One hundred and fifty of them were dumped in Smyrna, and the rest bound for Istanbul.

There were on board *Tyrol* about 2,000 refugees from Moosh, Erzeroom, and Caucasia heading for the Caucasus.

Other informants added that the National Council members were "invited" to the presence of the High Commissioner and then dispatched to Karatash for exile. John Shishmanian, the commander of the Armenian Legion, was arrested and exiled to Beirut.

After the sudden wholesale arrests and the smashing of the Armenian dream of independence the French sent for the Turkish Kemalist brigands to come and take possession of Adana.

Terrified by these developments, at once I wrote a letter to my family to make an effort to join me in Smyrna.

What happened to General Antranig's plans for the liberation of Cilicia we learned later. Formidable diplomatic pressure and military threats from Paris forced the lion-hearted hero (at the mention of his name for decades before the Kurds and Turks used to tremble) to abandon all his hopes and plans and return to his home in Bulgaria.

About this time a secret pact of friendship was being signed in Ankara between France and Turkey, with the understanding that France would surrender the vilayet of Adana back to Turkey.

CHAPTER 47

LEAH

A COUPLE OF DAYS AGO, on Monday afternoon, I stopped at the churchyard to visit some friends camping there. Setrak Abrazian pointed at a lady who was engaged in conversation with a group of recently exiled soldiers. At my approach our eyes met, and we both were dumbfounded. Neither of us expected to encounter the other in this way.

She was Leah, Roupen Tateosian's wife. Roupen was my colleague, as the eldest of us four teachers in the Protestant High School last winter. I had occasionally been in their house, at their table, and enjoyed their high regard of me. After the commencement exercises they both had prepared to travel to Adana, but because of the strict ban against emigration from Adana exercised by the Armenian National Council, Roupen was forced to stay behind after sending Leah to Smyrna. She would wait for him there.

The night before my departure Roupen came to see me and deliver her some message from him in case I happened to stop at Smyrna. On my first day in Smyrna I made it my business to locate Leah Tateosian, so I went to the local YWCA office to inquire about her. A young lady kindly took me to the American Girls' College (from which Leah had graduated before her marriage). Miss McKalem, the president, informed me that Leah was employed as a governess to American Vice Consul Captain Hall's children. She further told me that Hall's home was in Boodjah[44], a town of an hour's distance by train.

Immediately I wrote a letter to Roupen, supplying him with all the information. But despite my wish to see her I had not dared to make the journey.

And now, miraculously, we were face to face. We shook hands warmly.

Before asking any questions about her husband she asked,
"Tell, me, Mr. Wit, what kind of world are we living in?"

"Round," I answered, and we both laughed.

Then our conversation turned on her husband.

I noticed a young man of about 18 standing by her and attentively gazing at me. I didn't pay much attention to him as my interest was in giving Leah all the information she was asking for.

The young man, unable to contain himself, at last ventured to ask me if I had been a student at Jenanian College. To my affirmative answer, he asked me if I could remember him.

Unfortunately not, I answered.

He then informed me that his name was Vahan Dakesian of Nazirli, and he was a twelve-year-old student in the Preparatory Department, Class C, and I used to talk to him comparing him to a favorite cousin of mine.

Then suddenly it dawned on me that this affable young man, standing in front of me on this unusual occasion, was the same child who, with his then extraordinarily alluring smile, used to remind me of my cousin Barkev, the only son of my martyred uncle the Reverend Melidon Malian. Barkev, now a boy of thirteen, was in Hadjin with his mother and all his paternal and maternal relations. I remembered with anguish that the city was under the siege and constant fire of the Turkish hordes, but it never occurred to me that they would all perish in three days.

And now this young gentleman, besides resurrecting in me pleasant recollections from the past, was also presently responsible, although inadvertently, for bringing two former friends face to face, thus relieving me from the difficult task of finding her. Leah stated that Vahan had been a source of comfort to her on his occasional visits to Captain Hall's house as one of the American Consulate's secretaries.

I consider and love him as the son I wished to have but was denied, she confided.

Having heard that some refugees from Adana had been brought to Smyrna, Leah asked and obtained her employer's permission to look them up and find information about her husband and conditions in Cilicia. Vahan had kindly accompanied her to the churchyard.

She profusely thanked him for acting as an agent of this miraculous meeting, and thanked me, too, for choosing the proper time of the day to meet her. Then turning towards him she asked if he would bring me to Boodja next evening to see her.

Last night Vahan came after me and together we took the train which took us in an hour to the village lost in the dense darkness, with hardly a score of lights blinking.

Vahan led me to the Captain's residence, where Leah was anxiously waiting for us. We spent a whole hour in reminiscing, in informing, in joking, in comforting. Her loneliness and longing were assuaged to a considerable degree.

"How good you are, Mr. Vahan, for bringing Mr. Barouyr to me," she said. (All through my college years and later I was known by that name until my arrival in the United States of America, when I relegated its use to signing poems and articles.) "Mr. Barouyr is a noble person, do you know that?" she continued.

"Of course I do," he answered. "I knew that before you did, in Jenanian College."

The last train to Smyrna whistled. Vahan and I jumped on our feet, and with a hurried goodbye ran into the dark to catch it.

Vahan Dakesian and I parted at the door of the khan where I was lodging.

Friday, October 22, 1920: Twenty-third day in Smyrna

I feel crushed today.

The eye doctor gave his verdict: my left eye seriously damaged with the dread trachoma will not permit me to travel to America.

Besides this, Stephen, my cousin with whom I set out from Adana, decided to join Uncle Hampartzoum's party as soon as a ship is available. Today Uncle received 700 dollars from his sponsoring cousin in Pasadena to replenish his travel funds. Mine, already inadequate, are dwindling fast.

Thursday, October 28, 1920: Twenty-ninth day in Smyrna

While strolling along the famous Cordon—the quay—with Stephen, we noticed a ship loaded with a multitude of refugees from Cilicia, which was not permitted to land. We were told that the Armenian Prelacy and the leaders of the community had petitioned the government to stop the influx of refugees, who were a burden on the public.

Among the passengers we recognized Roupen Tateosian, Stephen's teacher and my colleague, Leah's husband. Through the efforts of the American Consulate he was allowed to land and join his wife in Boodjah.

Sunday, October 31, 1920: Thirty-second day in Smyrna

Today, from the church pulpit, Mr. Ardzrooni, a political leader exiled from Adana, read the announcement of the tragic end of Hadjin's eight-month-old self defense that took place during the night of October 15 to 16. The heroic 550-year old city was set on fire by the invading Turks, the houses pillaged, and the population of 6,000 (the remnant of 30,000) massacred mercilessly. Only about 300 armed men and some women managed to escape the carnage, abandoning their dear ones, traveling over mountains, fighting attacks and sieges, and arriving at Adana after many days.

Monday, November 8, 1920: Fortieth day in Smyrna

Today the old ship *Montaza* brought from Adana Vahan Dumanian, a classmate of Hadjin years, who on his way to Constantinople made a stop at Smyrna and rented a room in the same khan where we were staying.

All of us natives of Hadjin now in the Smyrna khan gathered around Vahan and begged him to tell us about the fall of Hadjin and the plight of the handful of survivors who managed to escape.

He was in tears as he told us the gory details of the carnage of the last day,—children in vain seeking their parents, brother losing brother or sister, husband searching for wife and children, and the Turk mercilessly butchering old and young, meanwhile invoking the names of Allah and Mohammed.

There was not any one among us who had not lost an immediate relative. We all wept for vanished Hadjin and our perished dear ones—Vahan for his parents, sisters, brothers, and their families; Manuel Gertmenian for his father; Apraham Agha, Manuel's uncle, for his brother; Haigaz and Levon Mehagian for their parents, sisters, and their children; Uncle Hampartzoum for his old mother and brothers; and I for my aged grandparents, uncles, aunts, cousins, and all Kooshians and Malians and others.

Who were these valiant souls that braved through murderous orgy and escaped the holocaust? Vahan gave names for whom we thanked God, but grief shattered us.

The ten-page entry in my original diary of this day concludes with the following:

"Veneration and kisses to the blood-drenched heroes and martyrs of Hadjin. This final battle of Hadjin is a second Avarair, a second Arara, a second Thermopylae."

Friday, November 12, 1920: Forty-fourth day in Smyrna

Almost two months now, I have no direct news about Mother, brother, Uncle Haroutune, and Aunt Gulenia. My first letter from beleaguered Adana arrived today, making both Stephen and me happy with the news that both our mothers and the rest were well, and there was no reason for us to worry about them.

The letter further informed us that Stephen's mother and sister would join us in Smyrna in a few days to travel with us to America. All at once a bright light of hope began to spread all over me, despite the sad fact that I had poor eyes. So did Azniv have, I remembered, and somehow worry about my eyes vanished. Finances? That worry also miraculously left me.

Stephen had lately planned to join Uncle Hampartzoum's party, who were told by their agent to be ready to sail in a week or so. At the arrival of this happy letter he immediately canceled his plans and decided to stay with me until his mother arrived.

Tuesday, November 16, 1920: Forty-eighth day in Smyrna

Naxos, the ship to Marseilles, had anchored in the bay, and Uncle Hampartzoum with his "family" of ten and Apraham Agha Gertmenian with his family of seven today sailed away. Roupen Tateosian also sailed on board *Heffrom* to Patras, leaving his wife Leah for the vice-consul to bring to him in New York.

Thus Stephen and I were left somewhat dejected for parting from our travel-companions. As we were roaming around, we met a young man whom I knew from my desert days. This friend, Mugurdich Kademian, after learning about our predicament, kindly offered to let us sleep in his hotel room, which we gladly accepted.

Friday, November 19, 1920: Fifty-first day in Smyrna

An acquaintance informed us that Aunt Gulie was camping in the church yard and was eager to locate us. We both ran to embrace her and the little girl.

Stephen was happy to see his mother and sister, and I felt as if I had found my mother, too. The brooding sense of abandonment left me to a great degree.

Immediately Stephen left the hotel room and joined his mother in a rented apartment. I remained in the hotel with Kademian until a few days later I rented a separate room, and invited Sarkis Bachejian to share it with me. My poor chum, disarmed and exiled, could find no job in Smyrna, no matter how hard he looked for one.

In my student days I had heard his almost-legendary fame as the foremost surgeon of the land, and read his humorous articles and popular books. And learning that he now resided in Smyrna, I paid him a timid visit. Dr. Avedis Nakashian received me courteously as I introduced myself. After relating my circumstances I sought his advice concerning my eyes. He kindly referred me, with a note, to a Dr. A. Asche, an eminent specialist.

Dr. Asche, too, accepted me with respect as he read Dr. Nakashian's note. He, too, heard my story, and after an examination he assured me he would cure the inflammation caused by trachoma, so that the resultant cicatrix would by no means bar me from entering the United States. The man was so good that for his treatments of three times a week he charged me a minimal fee.

His friendship continued until the day I left Smyrna three months later. On the last visit to him, he wrote the following in my "Friendship Book":

> He who sows Courtesy,
> Reaps Friendship.
> And he who plants Kindness,
> Gathers Love.

Then he signed A. Asche, M.D.

I left Stephen with his mother and sister in the church yard, and retired to the room I was sharing with Kademian to write two very important letters: one to my mother, to let her know that Aunt Gulie had arrived, and another letter to Panos Mooshian in Chicago, informing of the final fall of Hadjin on October 15, and the tragic loss of his only sister whom my mother had brought back from the great Genocide. I also wrote to him that I had left my mother — his aunt — behind, and was on my way to America, and also that I was stranded in Smyrna with no funds.

All night long a nasty thought tossed me about in my scanty bedding with the fear that Aunt Gulenia would take her son Stephen with her to continue their voyage to America, leaving me behind.

Sunday, December 12, 1920: Seventy-fourth day in Smyrna

Ever since her arrival Auntie had been looking around in the city for a young lady suitable to be a wife to her eldest son, Krikor, to whom she was going in Binghamton, New York.

She finally found one, Alice Muradian, the daughter of a widow. Mother and daughter were living together in a room of their own, in an apartment where a married daughter lived with her husband and three young daughters.

This evening the engagement party took place, with a priest performing the ceremony between Alice and a photograph of the absent Krikor. Rings were exchanged between Alice and the silent picture in the presence of a number of relatives and friends.

Immediately the happy event was cabled to Krikor. In a letter that followed the cable, Aunt Gulie made me write to her son to send enough money to cover the boat-fares of five persons. "Because," she argued, "we cannot travel without your cousin Kevork, whose knowledge of the English language will be a great help to us. I cannot leave him behind."

My Aunt's magnanimity was like a soothing balm on a burning sore.

Saturday, January 1, 1921: Ninety-fourth day in Smyrna

It is New Year's Day today, but an ordinary day for me. Ninety-four days since I set foot on the soil of Smyrna, and the 104th day since I left Mother and dear ones behind. In a few days, on January 6, it will be the Armenian Christmas, and it will be as dreary a day as this day unless something is done to change it.

With Sarkis and Setrak, head to head, we plan to give an entertainment to Auntie and her newly-acquired in-laws — Alice, the bride-to-be, her mother, sister Anoosh [Manoogian], husband, and girls. To that end we prepared and rehearsed a skit, a short humorous play, based on our childhood experiences in Hadjin. We prevailed on Auntie to invite all her in-laws to her apartment for a Christmas party. Our presentation greatly amused the guests, and Auntie served them refreshments and candy to the children.

Anoosh and her three daughters grew intensely fond of me, and I, in turn, of them. They invited me often to eat with them in the evenings, and they would be fascinated with the stories I told them from the Arabian Nights, Monte Cristo, Tolstoi, and others. The time being too heavy on my hands I spent my days by reading books borrowed from the Armenian Library at a small fee, and relating the stories at night. Anoosh would invite me to the dress-maker's shop that she ran, where she would wash my shirt, repair the frayed collar, and press it.

One of those days Anoosh introduced me to a wealthy cousin of hers, Mannig, who lived in Boodjah with her husband and son Vahan. Roupen Effendi, Mannig's husband, was a dignified and well-educated gentleman, and Vahan, the son, was a student in the International College. They cordially welcomed me to their home whenever I commuted to Boodjah to see Mrs. Leah Tateosian, and then paid them a visit.

On one occasion when Mannig was serving me a demitasse of Turkish coffee, the customary entertainment for a guest, I insisted, out of respect, that she give the cup first to her mother who was sitting just in front of me, and then give me one. I have never forgotten all these years, and have often quoted her, when the old lady quipped, "The confused guest hosts the hostess."

On a beautiful January day, Sarkis and I decided to take a trip to Boodjah, to see Leah and cheer her up. After a pleasant time with her we decided to walk the road back to Smyrna, instead of taking the train that would take us home in an hour.

Leah packed us a small bundle of bread, cheese, and onion for lunch on the long and lonely road. As we plodded out of the resort of the affluent, our reminisces began to unwind as from an endless ball of string, so that in no time (in fact hours later) we found ourselves on the summit of a hill overlooking Paradiso, the famed center of the high educational institution, the pride of the region. Under the benign sun we sat down on a grassy plot, opened the lunch bundle and ate with prayer, laughter, and also with sadness for being removed far from our families.

The Web of Hope

That happy moment has lingered in my memory, intermingled with an unremitting sorrow, because in little more than a year Sarkis was killed in the massacre as the Turks burned Smyrna.

CHAPTER 48

PROFESSOR GULBENKIAN

EVERY SUNDAY of the more than four months I squandered in the streets of Smyrna, I found solace and pleasure in frequenting the Armenian Evangelical Church. Even I gave it a considerable donation for which I still (1976) hold a receipt, acknowledged by the treasurer. The preacher at the time I attended the church was Professor Av. Gulbenkian, a well-known poet and a long-time professor in the International College.

One day, on a visit to Leah, and then to Mannig, and some time spent spent in Vahan's pleasurable company, I foolishly missed the last train from Boodjah. And too proud to ask for overnight lodging, I took to the road.

The moonless night was lonely and dark and long as I walked through the uninhabited wide country. The noises of the nocturnal world would have been a symphony to my ears if only I had a companion with me, but in the absence of one everything around was fearsome.

In an undetermined hour of the night the welcome lights of Paradiso began to twinkle. The fitful thumps of my heart began to quiet down when I remembered that Professor Gulbenkian, the preacher of the church of Smyrna, lived on the campus of the college.

With no hesitation I knocked at his door after inquiries about the whereabouts of his house. He was surprised to find me in Paradiso on such an inconvenient, ungraceful hour, but when he heard of my stupidity in missing my train in Boodjah, he received me graciously, fed me, and showed a bedroom to sleep in. In the morning, at the breakfast table, he returned to me the "Friendship Book" I had given him on the previous Sunday, begging him to write something in it as a remembrance from him.

He had sacrificed valuable time to write on two whole pages — in an exquisite handwriting — a magnificent poem, consisting of eight stanzas, under the title of "To the Sun of my Hope," with the dedicatory line,

"From the pages of my heart, to my friend Kevork Barouyr," and then his signature.

Thursday, January 20, 1921: One hundred and fourteenth day in Smyrna

Sarkis left me today for a nearby town, Nif, where he had been promised a job at hard labor. He was happy for the opportunity to earn something, no matter how piddling it was. Setrak, too, decided to take advantage of the only available job and cheerfully accompanied him.

It was a standing joke between us to repeat what an Italian job master said some weeks earlier to Sarkis and Setrak when they appealed to him for a job:

> When the winter months pass,
> spring months come,
> jobs open up,
> and I need extra laborers,
> then I may hire you,
> should you apply to me then.
> Now go home and wait.

And after repeating this classic, Sarkis would add one of his own:

> Please, don't die,
> my little Donkey.
> Summer will come soon,
> and then you'll have
> plenty to eat.
> Don't give up hope.
> But that winter the little donkey died of hunger.

Mrs. Zaroohi Azazian, the lady from whom Aunt Gulie rented her apartment, invited me to leave the hotel room, now that Sarkis was no longer with me, and move into her house as a companion to her young son. No one in my financial predicament would be in his right mind if he did not take advantage of such a God-sent offer.

On the street level of the hotel where I was staying was a casino, and to reach my room on the second floor I had to pass through heavily alcohol-smelling drunkards and crowded tables around which, seated or standing, Greeks were noisily and passionately arguing about hot political subjects.

When the World War broke out, their pro-German king, Constantine, was forced to vacate his throne and go into exile, and in his stead his son Alexander was enthroned. But the young king suddenly died in December 1920. The Greek people became divided into two opposing parties, republican and royalist. The republicans wanted a republican form of government under the leadership of Prime Minister Elephterios Venezelos, and the royalists wanted the exiled King Constantine to resume his vacated throne.

In the ensuing election the Venezelos Party was defeated and Constantine was brought back to Athens with pomp and glory.

One of those nights I was passing through the crowded casino towards the stairs to my room when I was stopped by some Greeks to join them in celebrating Constantine's return to his throne. I told them politely that I was glad that their king had come back and wished him good health and divine protection. But the ruffians were not satisfied with mere words, they insisted that I drink a glass of raki (anise-flavored spirits) to his good health. When I refused, objecting that I had never drunk in my life and neither smoked, they interpreted my words as an insult to their worshipful king and became enraged and began to manhandle me.

Then and there the hotel manager rushed to my rescue and led me to my room. The curses of the enraged Constantinian royalists still echo in my ears: "Any one that would not drink or smoke to our king is not a man, but an ass."

Around the end of the month of January, one day, I took my "Friendship Book" to the office of Bishop Ghevont Tourian, the Primate of the Armenian Community, and begged him to write something for me to remember him by in the United States. This great churchman, author of a number of books and editor of more than one periodical, wrote a brief literary gem, under the title of "The Suffering People."

The following year, 1922, while I was in America, Smyrna the beautiful and proud fell into the hands of the invading Kemalist hordes on Saturday, September 9, after the war-worn Greek army had withdrawn. The blood-thirsty, sex-crazed and loot-hungry Turks simultaneously ransacked houses, set the city on fire, and put the entire Christian populace to the sword.

Bishop Tourian was miraculously spirited out of the inferno, first to Athens and thence to Manchester, England. In 1930 he was appointed Primate of the Armenian Diocese of America. While he was celebrating the Divine Liturgy on December 24, 1933 in the Holy Cross Church of New York City, heavily garbed in his ecclesiastical vestments, Archbishop Tourian was suddenly surrounded by a gang of political murderers and stabbed to his immediate death, a martyr like Saint Thomas à Becket, prelate and Archbishop of Canterbury (1118–1170).

Friday, January 28, 1921: One hundred and twenty-second day in Smyrna

Today Aunt Gulie received the anxiously awaited answer to her cable and letter, sent to her son Krikor to inform him that on the night of December 12 he had been officially engaged to Miss Alice Muradian. She had also enclosed with that letter a picture of his fiancée.

Krikor advised his mother to immediately set sail for Marseilles, France, where his agent, Michael Arslanian, would meet her and attend to all the legal details of our voyage to America.

With jubilant spirits Stephen and I ran to the ticket agency and secured passage for five persons to Marseilles aboard *Naxos*, a Greek vessel scheduled to sail on February 7.

Then I wrote a letter to my mother about the new developments, and another one to Sarkis and Setrak in Nif about the date of our departure.

On the Friday before our departure I took the day off to bid farewell to Leah in Boodjah, who was still serving as governess for the Vice Consul's children and was waiting for the day when he would take her to her husband in New York City. After leaving Leah I found time to visit Mannig Hanum and her husband Roupen Effendi and their scholarly son Vahan, who had made me feel welcome in their home ever since Anoosh had introduced us to each other.

When I told them that on Monday I would be off for America, and the purpose of this visit was to bid them goodbye, Mannig told me about an elder son who was in America too, and asked if I could take him a box of books.

I lugged the heavy wooden box to the train and home that evening.

When I arrived at Chicago after some months, and wishing to discharge the obligation I had willingly undertaken, I made some inquiries about where Cleveland, Ohio, was, and if Chicago and Cleveland were neighboring cities, as Smyrna and Boodjah were, as Mannig Hanum supposed and made me believe too.

Seeing that under the circumstances I could not attempt such a trip, I wrote a letter to Mannig's son, telling him about my acquaintance with his family and relating his mother's message. Then I asked him how to ship the box of books his mother had sent with me for him.

His answer was to keep the whole box to myself.

Now feeling free to open the box, I found in it neatly stacked Shakespeare's entire works, some works of Milton and Scott, Defoe's *Robinson Crusoe*, Stevenson's *Treasure Island*, and many others.

Monday, February 7, 1921: Last day in Smyrna

One hundred and thirty-two anxious days were spent in this city since I first set foot on its water front, the famed Cordon. My traveling companions—Uncle Malian with his numerous "family," Gertmenians, and others—had all left me behind and, by this time, already landed on American soil, free of any sort of worries. I was left behind with a fast-dwindling fund in a strange land, friendless, and with hopes dimming from day to day.

But God performs His miracles in a myriad mysterious ways, as the poet declared. Through the unexpected arrival of my Aunt Gulie and her new relationship with Alice and her people I gained protection and friends.

And now, thank God, I finally boarded *Naxos*, bound for Marseilles, with the last leg of voyage to America from there.

My traveling companions were, rather I was a companion to, Aunt Gulenia, her son Stephen, her little daughter Azniv, and Aunt's newly-acquired daughter-in-law-to-be Alice.

The group of friends that walked with us to the water front included Alice's old mother, her sister Anoosh Manoogian with her three daughters, and Mrs. Zaroohi Azazian, Aunt's landlady who had befriended me and given me shelter under her care. As we crossed over the plank onto the boat all the ladies and the children were in tears.

Sarkis, that unfortunate dear friend of mine from early childhood, also was in the group. He had taken the day off from his precious work at hard labor in Nif to bid me farewell for the last time. I had already, on a former occasion, introduced him to Anoosh, but this time I asked her to accept him in my place as my brother. (The following year Sarkis married Sirvart, Anoosh's daughter, but two or three months after his marriage he was killed along with his father-in-law at the hands of the Turks in the massacre at the fall of Smyrna.)

Naxos weighed anchor at 5:30 in the evening. From the deck we could distinguish Anoosh standing alone on the water front and waving a handkerchief as the ship started moving away from its moorings.

The wintry cold of the evening forced all but the crew to withdraw to their shelters.

CHAPTER 49

ON THE AEGEAN SEA

THE LITTLE passenger and cargo ship was like a child's toy in the hands of the mighty waves, listing this moment to the right and the next to the left. The ship acted all night like a drunken man who did not know where he was going. It is no wonder that Odysseus strayed for twenty years in these treacherous waters.

About noontime we were glad to sight Piraeus, the port city of Athens. The sight of thousands of sea-craft of all sizes bobbing up and down on the surface of the bay was a magnificent spectacle. As the ship glided towards its berth, we saw a great number of men crowding the wharves, scurrying to and fro, and thousands of vehicles traversing the streets.

We were told that the ship would linger in the port for three days to exchange travelers and cargo. Those travelers who were bound for America would usually disembark here to catch a ship to take them directly to their destination. The ship *King Alexander* was lying at anchor for the America-bound travelers.

Hundreds of mules were hoisted out of the belly of the ship and deposited on land. We, who had spent the night on the deck, were ordered to occupy the space vacated by the beasts. It occurred to me again that for some people by chance on a different level the common people were no different than the mute ass-horses.

Once settled in the "stable" I sat down to write letters to Mother, Anoosh, and Sarkis, the three persons very precious to me at the time.

WEDNESDAY, FEBRUARY 9, 1921: PIRAEUS AND ATHENS

Like sardines packed over each other, people were crowded in the filthy, foul-smelling and airless barn, where free and private movements were not possible. The chill of the deck with its healthy air was much preferable.

About 2:00 in the afternoon, with Aunt Gulie's permission, all four of us young people—Alice, Stephen, Azniv, and I—left the ship for a little excursion into nearby Athens, the Queen City of ancient philosophy, poetry, and oratory, just for the sake of boasting in future years that we once visited Athens the Glorious and saw some of its wondrous historic points. Alice using her Greek language enlisted the help of a young man to direct us to the train station.

"These are the sons and daughters of Socrates, Thales, Xenophon, Plato, and the other immortals," I thought, looking at the faces of those seated in the train. "This old man must be Socrates himself," I imagined when I saw him conversing with a group of younger men around him. The train was effortlessly climbing upwards through sloping verdant fields on each side, as if a massive carpet was spread in honor of those visiting Athens. I looked around intently hoping to catch a glimpse of Mount Parnassus with its nine beauteous Muses, or Mount Olympus of the romantic gods and goddesses, but they were not to be seen in these regions.

There were on each side of the rushing train stations, churches, houses, and a beach resort village, called Neo Phaleron. We took notice of a steel bridge on which autos were speeding as our train was crossing underneath. This was particularly astounding for eyes like ours which had never seen anything of the sort. There were stations at which a passenger leaving the train would climb high staircases to reach the nearby village.

After a journey of twenty minutes through interesting and pleasing scenery, the train stopped at the Upper Station of Athens. Alice with her Greek, and I with my English, found friends who volunteered to escort us upstairs towards the city.

Athens, "the Mother of Seven Philosophers," was the first European city I ever set foot in. And so it was, in fact, for each one of us in the party.

We had no definite plans to follow as we walked on. But all of a sudden I had a bright idea. Why not go to the royal palace, and, if possible, see His Majesty King Constantine V, the victorious hero of the post-war political revolution, in which he defeated the partisans of democracy and restored the royalist form of government in his favor. When I expressed this bold desire, the English-speaking fellow by my side, pointing to the palace, said:

"You can go to the palace court, but you cannot see the King. He is seen only on Sundays when he goes to the Cathedral."

Leaving our friend to go his way we pressed onward towards the palace hill. The city was beautiful in its neatness, tram tracks criss-crossing each other, autos rolling by, and orderliness of its traffic. Attractive high buildings, many-storeyed hotels, stores all around. On a square we noticed the statue of Kolokotronis on his fiery stallion, with one hand caressing the mane of the noble mount, and with the other pointing to the battlefield, inviting his fellow patriots to the defense of beloved Hellas.

At last we arrived at the top of the hill where the palace was situated. The broad street, lined on each side with casinos, cafés, and clubs, was paved. The palace was a large edifice, but externally unattractive, although, undoubtedly, magnificent inside. We entered the courtyard with no one to stop us. Once inside, our steps took an air of reverence. We walked the length and breadth of the place, looking around and up and down open-mouthed. An undefined awe forced us not to exchange a word with each other until we found ourselves out of the opposite door into a small wood. We we told here that the young King Alexander used to retire into this orchard to consult and converse with his Prime Minister Venezelos, and it was here that (as the rumor goes) he was poisoned by a monkey.

Mars Hill was just in front of us, where on a rock once stood Apostle Paul boldly to proclaim Jesus Christ and His resurrection to ears that would not listen. Above the Hill magnificently stood the Acropolis with its ruins of the Parthenon and the Temple of Jupiter Olympus, the first erected and the second reconstructed by Pericles, after its destruction in 480 B.C. by the Persians.

The mountainside was crowded by tourists and sight-seers, but we could not join them now. The time was slipping away and we were expected for the evening dinner by Aunt Gulie. If we had had enough sense, we could have started this excursion in the morning and found time to visit the historic points. We retraced our tracks back to the train, to Piraeus, to the boat, to Aunt, at 5:30.

While we were hungrily devouring our lunch, cruel orders were barked at us immediately to move out of our present barn quarters into which we had been herded just the night before, to a smaller barn this time where rest and sleep with fully stretched limbs was impossible for lack of space.

Thursday, February 10 – Monday, February 14, 1921.

Having its business completed in Piraeus, our ship weighed anchor late in the afternoon, and plied its course along the Saronic Gulf towards the Narrows of Corinth. In the banks near the Isthmus, children and others of the nearby houses were watching and waving greetings to us, the strange people of strange lands. This strip of watery passage, at the dusk of the evening, looked as if it was a giant ribbon of heavenly hue, slipped from the golden locks of a scurrying goddess.

The undulating plain extending from each bank, I imagined, was covered with a couple of immense gorgeously woven green carpets to accommodate the gods and goddesses of the region when they met for conference.

Every passenger is on the deck as we enter the Isthmus not to miss the experience of enjoying this historic strait's natural and structural marvels. The flanking mountains at once swallowed our 35,000-ton vessel with its hundreds of passengers. According to my notes taken at the time (although I cannot vouch for the accuracy of the numbers), "the height of the walls ranged from thirty to fifty meters, higher than the ship's main mast; the depth of the water was seven or eight meters; the width twenty meters; and the length four kilometers." On the walls, here and there, were electric lights to guide the traffic at night. Along the face of each wall there was a pedestrian walk, with a steel bridge connecting both lands which the isthmus had separated. The length of the gulf is about eighty miles, average width fifteen miles, with towns of Corinth, Lepanto, and others.

At the exit of the isthmus we sighted the land where Actaeon, an innocent hunter, for having surprised Artemis at bathing, was turned into a stag by her and torn to pieces by his own dogs.

On the Aegean Sea

Then we entered the Gulf of Corinth, also called the Gulf of Lepanto, an arm of the Ionian Sea, having on our left the island of Peloponnesus, the ancient land of Morea (Achaia, Arcadia, Laconia, etc.); and on the other the mainland. Half way in the gulf, from the land where Delphi is located, Helicon Mountain Range, the home of the Nine Muses, jutted out from the north.

To leave the waters of "Korinthiakós Kólpos" and enter the waters of the Gulf of Patras our boat had to round the northern tip of Peloponnesus, where Agamemnon assembled the chiefs of all the Greek states for war against Priam, the king of Troy.

Our boat made no stop at Patras, having no business there. It continued its way between the islands of Keffalinia and Zakinthos directly into the Ionian Sea. I had already been suffering with sea-sickness, but this time the turbulence of the open sea completely downed me. Thus I was condemned to spend all my time on my back in the quarters or on the deck. I would climb to the deck only when Aunt would suggest fresh air or sunshine. Appetite for any kind of nourishment left me, but I craved only for sour drinks and spiced stuff. Luckily, I was able to read lying down either in the barn or on the deck, so I was never bored by idleness.

There were several Armenian passengers on board. One of them, a man from Van, Bayatji by nickname, was an interesting character, a veritable store of stories. He told us that as a seller of cookies in Istanbul he attracted a large number of customers, merely by shouting: "*Bayat simitler*, I am selling ten days old, *stale* cookies." Hence his nickname, "Seller of Stale Things."

Another interesting person was Vahan, a teenager, who sang love songs in a sweet voice, combined with feeling and life.

Another one was Barouyr, a young man full of humor who considered himself "a native of Marseilles" because he had made a dozen trips to that city.

There was Legionnaire Haig who, with his folks, was bound for the United States. A fine, sociable, warm-hearted young man.

How can I omit mentioning Melpomene, the 16-year old Greek beauty with the sweetness, swiftness, and the grace of a doe, who would invite the longing looks of every one as she moved about. Her eyes had a thousand smiles whenever her glance fell on me.

And I continue to dream, day and night, about my mother in that ill-fated land of Cilicia, beleaguered Adana, the only city that had not fallen into the massacring hands of the Turks, because the French occupying force had not withdrawn yet. An irresistible sense of regret would seize me for leaving behind that noble spirit, my guardian angel, in ill health for several years and now with no means of livelihood or medical care. Left under the protective care of an inexperienced child of 18, my brother. The thought that she had suffered the stunning blows of "losing" to America two of her mainstays — my sister and me — and also "losing" her only sister Gulie with whom she had the closest relationship, losing all at the same time, would torment me.

And then, when these torturing dreams would leave me a spare moment, I would recall to mind Anoosh, her three lovely girls and Sarkis, all alone in an unfriendly country, with no relative left alive.

On Monday morning, the 14th of February, the ship entered the harbor of Marseilles. Every vestige of my seasickness suddenly vanished at the sight of land. In no time public health officials climbed aboard to examine the voyagers, and, imposing a 24-hour quarantine on the ship, they ordered the captain not to let the passengers disembark until the next day.

CHAPTER 50

MARSEILLES

Tuesday, February 15, 1921

While we were still on board *Naxos* our passports were checked and we were granted visas to land on French soil. Because we sailed from Smyrna by steerage, as we had done so from Mersin to Smyrna, we had not the slightest inkling that we had on board, in more respectable quarters, an illustrious figure in the person of General Sebooh. He was, short months ago, one of the valiant warriors engaged in repulsing the attacks of the Kemalist army under Kiazim Karabekir, who had sworn to Mustafa Kemal to smother the infant Republic of Armenia in its cradle, under the shadow of Mount Ararat. A group of dignitaries headed by the Armenian Consul, Mirzaian, came to the boat with bouquets of flowers and escorted him in pomp to his quarters in the city.

While our party of five was still in the customs house, Monsieur Michel, the agent engaged to attend to our affairs, walked in breathlessly, and spotting us he at once ordered a porter to load our luggage on a carriage he had brought. Then he drove us to Hôtel Richelieu in the heart of the city. After seeing us comfortably settled, he suggested that we immediately compose a cable, signed by Aunt, informing Krikor, her son, of our safe arrival into M. Michel's care. That done, he took care of the sending of it to the United States.

I had written to M. Michel from Smyrna several days before sailing that we would board *Naxos* on Monday, February 7, and would arrive at Marseilles on Monday the 14th, but, as Chance would have it, my letter did not reach M. Michel in time. It was delivered to him barely half an hour before he found us in the customs house. Surely God's hand was in our fortunes and misfortunes. If the passengers had been allowed to land the day before when *Naxos* moored at its berth, and if the city health officers had not imposed a day's delay for landing, he, unaware that we were on this particular ship, would not have come to meet us, and we would have fallen into the piratical hands of sharks, with which class all ports are infested.

During the five weeks circumstance forced me to spend in Marseilles before sailing for America, I, often alone and occasionally with company, made visits to public parks, amusement centers, fountains, caverns, museums, cathedrals, and historic landmarks. My notebook of that period contains page after page of detailed accounts, descriptions, historical facts, and personal reflections about places visited and objects studied. Under the title "Marseilles, The Capital of The Depart-Bouche du Rhône," the notes continue to record:

> Marseilles, the south-eastern seaport city of France, on the Gulf of the Lion, is one of the most flourishing ports in the world, possessing a very great number of manufactories and works. Marseilles owes its origin to the Phocaeans (600 B.C.), an ancient Ionian people.
> Principal monuments or attractions are:
> 1. Notre Dame de la Garde with its golden statue of the Virgin Mary, and its lift, leading to the large staircase that gives access to the chapel. Barouyr, the young man I had met on board *Naxos*, now residing in the same hotel, invited me to visit this wold-famous cathedral on February 18.
> 2. Porte d'Aix — the Triumphal Arch with its magnificent *bassi-rilievi* (low reliefs) and statues by David d'Anger and Ramey. Visited on February 19.
> 3. Fontaine Cantini, with its statue of the French Republic. On four faces of the fountain attractive bas-reliefs depict mythological stories. Visited on February 21.
> 4. Château Borély — The Borely Castle, with its museum of archeologic antiquities. *Magnifique domaine municipal de 47 hectares* — 10,000 square meters. Visited on February 23.
> 5. Le Tour de la Corniche — The Cornice Road. To go to Château Borély we rode this splendid walk, extending two miles (3,500 meters) along the seashore.

6. Fontaine des Danaïdes, near l'Eglise des Réformés, in the grounds of Borely Castle.

7. Palais Longchamps, zoological garden, Museum of Natural History and Fine Arts. A marvel of architecture. Visited on February 27.

8. On the way for a second visit to Longchamp Palace we stopped the next day to admire Fontaine Étranger. From the 12 mouths of sculptured lions water cascaded down into the basin. On top of the fountain is placed the Queen of The Republic with a cross in her hand, the symbol of freedom.

9. Caisse d'Éparque des Bouches du Rhône is just behind the Stranger's Fountain.

10. Square de la Bourse. In its marvelous garden is erected the statue of Pierre Puget (1620–1694), the beloved painter and sculptor of Marseilles. The beautiful building of the Money and Stock Exchange — La Bourse — was also artistically decorated with many mural sculptures. Commerce was represented by the figure of Pythias and Navigation with that of Euthymene. The facade of the Temple of Money was ornamented with the names of famous navigators: Tasman, Gama, Colomb, Durville, Cook, Magellan.

11. The Transfer Bridge, from which a magnificent panorama is gained. The floor of this bridge is 170 feet (52 meters) above the water.

12. The Cathedral. In Roman and Byzantine style.

13. Château d'If — The Castle of If at sea. A state prison, with which monument a number of historic events were connected. The hero, Edmund Dantes, of the famous pseudohistorical novel, *The Count of Monte Cristo*, by Alexandre Dumas (Père), was also imprisoned in the dungeon of If.

14. The Cannebrière — the famous artery that all the world knows.

15. The St. Jean Fort. Ancient fortress of the Knights of Malta.

16. The St. Pièrre Cemetery.

As the tram car, one afternoon, took us (all five of us in the "family") to the gate of the Cemetery, we noticed with amazed interest that on both sides of the street were lined next to each other a number of monument shops, all stocked with grave stones and statues of all sizes, where men were at work hewing, sculpting, and engraving, and small semi-circular florist shops where only women were engaged in preparing wreaths and bouquets for sale to the bereaved mourners.

We were strangers and only casual sight-seers, (and penniless, as far as I was concerned), and so could resist sellers' loud and insistent calls to buy a wreath or a statue and walk inside the "Silent City" without any gift to the dead. Yet, despite the crowd of visitors moving in all directions, the chill of the pervading loneliness of the Grim Kingdom engulfed us with melancholic thoughts.

The cemetery was divided into 26 quarters. It was naturally impossible for us in a few hours to stroll through these labyrinthine sections, and study all the inscriptions and architecture of the residences of the dead. So, with no special design, we followed the lane to our right.

Each tomb was a thing of special interest to a student like me who had never seen a cemetery like this one. Some tombs were miniature palaces or shrines. Most of these marble edifices were lavishly decorated and embellished, furnished with statuettes of the Virgin Mary, the Christ Child, angels, and saints. Through the glass windows it was easy to see in some of the tombs photographs of the deceased, or a crucifix between candles. Monuments with locked glass doors revealed candelabra standing on dainty needlework. Sacred pictures, beads of flowers, valuables, all sorts of gifts were offered the beloved dead by the surviving beloved.

Death had gathered into its chilled arms not only the famed and the humble, the old and the sick and the disaster victim, but the young and the child and the infant as well. At one spot a magnificent monument, erected in memory of an infant only two days old, arrested my astonished attention. Through the glass front a rich interior presented itself to my view. Evidently, this infant — a rose with promises of luxuriant scent and allurement, but cruelly nipped in the bud, or an angel with a life span far shorter than that of a butterfly — was so intensely loved and cherished that it was memorialized and immortalized. It was a soul precious far beyond any conceivable amount of wealth.

What a height of sensitivity and civilized spiritual attainment on the part of those who dedicated this temple to the memory of a lump of raw flesh! Yet I believe that the spirit of this child, an atom of God's immortal and infinite Spirit, is now hovering over those saintly parents and blessing them.

All of a sudden black thoughts, like a flock of ravens, swarmed into my mind and heart... I had in recent past come from another "cemetery," the Syrian Desert, on which a million and half innocent people — old and young, male and female, child and infant, born or ready to be born — had been ravaged and slaughtered by the Turks cruelly, inhumanely, systematically, in fiendish laughter and sadistic satisfaction. All unburied, unshrined, unprayed, unwept. Their flesh were picked from their bones by the jackals of the wild, vultures, rogues, the sun, the wind, the sand. Euphrates swept tens of thousands of them away into the mouths of the sharks of the sea.

Fortunate infant with the magnificent shrine in St. Pièrre Cemetery...and over a million unfortunate, graveless, forsaken Armenians whose dry bones are scattered all along the hostile expanse of sand in Syria.

A few days after our arrival at Marseilles M. Michel took Azniv and me (the two of us with bad eyes) to the eye-specialist who, after a thorough examination, announced "cicatrix," no trace of active trachoma. "Whoever has treated you has done a masterful job," he added, unknowingly giving credit to Dr. Asche of Smyrna.

A week later, on the 22nd of February, M. Michel came to the hotel to tell us that he had received from Aunt's son Krikor the amount needed for our ocean passage. Aunt's insistence to her son that she would in no way leave her sister's son — me — behind in a foreign land, evidently had its effect. He had sent my fare, too.

M. Michel promised to put us on the next ship, *Britannia*, which was due to sail on March 5.

March 4–20, 1921

As the day we hoped to board the great ocean-furrowing steamship approached, we were dismayed to learn that *Britannia* was under repair, and would not be in sailing condition for another two weeks, on March 21.

During my days in this great city I was never bored. To keep myself occupied I spent my days in reading, writing, and visiting mostly the Museum of Fine Arts, where I became fascinated by paintings, etchings, and sculptures of Spanish, Italian, Dutch, Flemish, and French masters.

Everything was new to me, and I was in another world. I had come from a backward country, Turkey, where civilization was at its lowest level. The ruling people, the Turks, stubbornly refused—because they were inadept—to adopt the higher cultures of the superior races they enslaved and ruled for centuries. The only civilization the Turkish government knew was tyrannizing, terrorizing, plundering, and massacring.

The contrast was so great that my amazement had no end.

The freedom women enjoyed here was inconceivable. Out in the street, in the market place, everywhere, women were selling and buying. Business was in their hands. Women here in the West were not "the long-haired but short-brained females" as the Turks regard the feminine sex, "inferior" to men. These women, unlike the women of Turkey, were emancipated, equal with men, and could do anything man could do. Whatever the Eastern woman regarded as degrading, the women of the West considered honorable, honest, and sacred.

CHAPTER 51

LAST DAY IN MARSEILLES

MONDAY, MARCH 21, 1921

My last day in Marseilles, and a very happy day indeed. Today we sail away to the dreamland Columbus discovered 427 years ago, and is now the "Land of the Free."

It is now exactly six months since I left Adana, the soil of Turkey, and my travel has been slower than that of Aesop's fabled tortoise. In fact, it could have been disastrous if Providence had not looked upon me with mercy and favor.

M. Michel, an upright gentleman among the pack of wolves that call themselves "travel agents," had decided and planned that we should sail to the United States as second class travelers, and not by steerage as we had done hitherto. His logic was to raise our status to the level of well-to-do, so that officials in the ship, and those at the receiving end, would treat us with deference. He and his good wife came over to the Hôtel Richelieu to speed up our packing and escort us to the ship. They both boarded the boat with us, and stayed until each one was comfortably settled in our cabins. They continually encouraged us not to worry when called for our final eye examination. The examiner was the same doctor — M. Michel's friend, who had some weeks earlier pronounced my eyes "cicatrix" and had commended the doctor that had treated my eyes in Smyrna. But fear overwhelmed us when Azniv underwent an intensive examination, and were relieved when she, too, was pronounced cicatrix. It was then that Monsieur and Madame Michel bade us bon voyage and left the boat to us.

The bell for dinner rang at 6 o'clock, and I rushed to eat a hearty meal before the dreaded sea-sickness laid its heavy hold on me as usual.

The night sleep in my bunk was a pleasant one, punctuated with dreams of blissful years waiting for me.

The cabin I was assigned to had three more occupants. One was an American gentleman who slept in the bunk below mine, and the other two were were young Armenian boys, Hayrabed and his cousin Kaloust, both from Tomarzah, a village on the plains of Evérék.

Tuesday, March 22, 1921.

All night long *Britannia* lay in anchor in the harbor and began to move early in the morning. As the vessel skirted Île d'If, we searched in vain for the dungeon where Monte Cristo was supposed to have been incarcerated for a dozen years.

We left the isle of Château D'If behind and ploughed on towards another small island in the waters of Marseilles, unaware of the unpleasant experience in store for us the next hour.

In front of our eyes all the passengers of the steerage class, each carrying a bundle, were loaded into rowboats and transported to the island to be forced into a barracks-like building.

It was a baffling situation

Then it happened to us, the passengers of the second class. We, too, were ordered to pack all our clothes and board the boats for the island. Like the others, we were herded into another barracks.

Inside the bare building we were lined up in single file, our backs to the walls, as condemned criminals. The place was as filthy and foul-smelling as any Turkish field or rubbish heap. The earthen floor was wet and sticky. It looked like an abandoned ruin with only the roof and walls remaining. Here and there on the floor there were heaps of soggy, moldy and stinking gunny sacks. In the middle of the hall there were two parallel rail-lines extending towards another chamber from which a sickening stench was pouring out towards us.

Unfriendly and rough officials bark at us orders to get a gunny-bag from the pile nearby and stuff in it all our clothes — both the clean ones in the bundles and the ones we take off from our bodies. We are all naked in the fashion of our first ancestor, only that we are not in the Garden of Eden, in company of angels. We write our names on the sacks, place them on the vehicles, and say goodbye to them as they roll away from our sight to be fumigated in the steam-house.

Last Day in Marseilles

Then, all of us, more than a hundred, get orders to march into an adjoining shower room, 100 by 30 feet, with a floor roughly, poorly, and sparsely paved with rocks, as cold as an ice box, as dirty as any open toilet, and as muddy as any street in Turkey. Each one stands under a nozzle to take a shower bath. Suddenly a stream of ice-cold water is sprayed on our already-chilled bodies. The next moment a shower of slightly lukewarm water falls on us, and as suddenly as it started it stops. We are dirtier and chillier than before. A hundred loud voices curse, protest, complain, all in vain. We all rush out of the bath house in search of our clothes, but they are to be found nowhere. The gunny sacks with our names on them are in large, highly heated tumblers, in the process of being "disinfected," "sterilized," "sanitized." No one can retrieve his bundle. Fuming with rage and exasperation the shivering crowd of naked people turn back to the shower house. But no more water, no heat, not even an attendant is in sight. People begin to perform their physical urges, adding dirt over dirt. Repulsive, disgusting, nauseating!

Now we are convinced that we have no other recourse but to wait, wait, with a nervous, impatient patience.

At long length a number of bundles roll back to us on a vehicle on the rail. Mine is not among them. I cannot understand why my clean clothes should need longer sterilization. I had left all the Turkish lice in the desert...

After two hours of intolerable wait — the miserable "bath" was over at 10 A.M. — my bundle also arrives, and I throw myself on it as a gift from heaven.

But what a "gift"...

It wasn't from heaven...

As I opened the "gift of heaven" an infernal stench blasted me. I could hardly recognize my new suit of jacket–vest–pants, top coat, hat, leather gloves, and woolens. They were badly shrunken and ruined beyond wear. The white shirts were covered with stains and the firmly starched collars limp and sick. I looked frantically for my shoes which were not to be found among the "slaughtered." Instinctively my eyes scanned the length and the width of the large hall. An abandoned object under the wall arrested my attention. To my great surprise and delight, it was my shoes which I had forgotten to place in the bag. My shoes had escaped the onslaught.

Maledictions and damnations in different languages continue to pour out from people now dressed in ruined clothes or from those who could not wear them at all.

It was about 2 P.M. when we had our mid-day meal.

Lisbon

Britannia, our ship, scraped through the historic Pillars of Hercules, the modern Rock of Gibraltar, and left the great inland sea behind to enter the waters of the Atlantic Ocean and make its call in the port of Lisbon. We arrived there in the afternoon of March 25 and anchored at the quay.

Lisbon, the enchanting queen city of Portugal, had spread her magnificent garment on the sides of green hills. This city was, in the 16th century, one of the intellectual centers of Europe and the home of poets, historians, and philosophers. In the past it was repeatedly tormented by earthquakes, but always healed its wounds and kept smiling.

The next morning I accompanied some Hungarian fellow-voyagers to help them exchange their money into U.S. dollars. The bourse with its surroundings was fascinating. Then following the main street we gazed at factories and public or private gardens. At the hilltop we stopped to marvel at the Museum of Arts, and at the fountain, an exquisite work of art, above which is effected an imposing statue, symbolizing the spirit of the Republic of Portugal. With amused interest we watched women come to the fountain to fill their pitchers and jars, and balancing them on their heads return home.

As the noon hour drew near we hurried back to the ship.

When I related all that I had seen in the town, Hayrabed and Kaloust, the two Armenian boys sharing my cabin, begged me to take them to see the town. So, after obtaining three passes, all three of us left the ship at 3 o'clock in the afternoon.

The weather was beautiful, the walk on the main boulevard was pleasurable, and things to see were so many. Leisurely we kept on going up the hill, open-mouthed, wide-eyed, simple-minded, naive and childlike, "innocents abroad."

All of a sudden, with no specific reason, I stopped on my heels and said, "Boys, it seems to me that we are walking towards an uncertain darkness. Let us turn back to the ship to ascertain the time it will sail. If time permits, then we can visit the cemetery."

The boys could say nothing but agree to turn back. We watched for a few minutes Portuguese peasant women nimbly, agilely carrying large and heavy baskets of coal on their heads, like the Arab women I had seen in the Syrian deserts carrying anything on their heads. It struck me at once that Portugal also was, as Spain was, once dominated by Moors, Saracens, and their Moslem culture.

As we approached the quay, from a distance of fifty meters we heard the whistle or horn of our ship signaling immediate departure. We ran panting and ranting and waving our passes towards the gang-plank which was at that moment being pulled away.

Our loved ones were in the grips of alarm and anxiety over us. Stephen also had been out and moments earlier had returned. Little Azniv had cried her already poor eyes red and raw, in fear that she would lose her brother Stephen and "brother" Kevork.

As we found ourselves in the circle of our dear ones many fellow-travelers came to express their joy in our last-minute escape from abandonment in a strange county. In five minutes *Britannia* started to sail away, leaving Lisbon to take care of its cemetery without our help.

Azores — Western Islands

Four days after leaving Lisbon, our ship wove its watery course through the Portugese Archipelago of the Azores in the mid-Atlantic, and made three short stops at different harbors. I was too fearful to venture out for sight-seeing, remembering my narrow bouts in Athens and Lisbon.

Stretching over a distance of 400 miles the nine islands of the Azores are divided into three distinct groups: Santa Maria and Saõ Miguel in the southeast; Terveria, Saõ Jorge, Pico, Grecioso, and Fayal in the middle; and Flores and Corvo in the northwest. In 1431–1453 Portugal took possession. They were at that time uninhabited. The Portuguese colonists called the whole group Azores, from *acor* or *azor*, a hawk.

The last call of *Britannia* was in the harbor of Fayal, the island of central Azores. From this place a great number of passengers boarded the ship in the middle of the night. I learned, subsequently, that two months earlier these passengers had been disembarked on this island by the disabled British steamship *Manoa*, and cared for all this time at the expense of the company while waiting for the next ship.

Social life on *Britannia* was not dreary at all, although sea sickness had me down on my back all the time.

The two young boys of my cabin, who were attached to me, were always amusing with their clever antics.

There was a group of a dozen Syrians who tirelessly entertained themselves and the rest of us on the deck with musical instruments, songs, and dances.

There was a Hungarian lady with her two very attractive and friendly daughters who were so solicitous concerning my health and comfort.

Armenians were very few in the Second Class compartment of the ship, while in the Third, to which we had no access, they were numerous. The few Armenians in our part of the deck were tied to each other with a special bond of deference.

I made the acquaintance of Mrs. Soghig Nighoghosian, a lady in her thirties, vivacious, charming, and witty. She was on her way to meet her husband in Providence, who had come to the United States fifteen years previously, right after their wedding. Mrs. Soghig, childless, had adopted a little waif, Maro, while she was on the Syrian deserts as one of those deported for genocide by the Turks.

Another charming lady, in her early twenties, was Miss Marie Kouyumjian, refined, tall, and buxom. She was going to Binghamton, where we were headed.

Miss Azniv Termonian, recently from Switzerland, educated in American schools, was a teacher in Marzovan, and was going now to her old friends in Philadelphia.

Then there was this lady, Helena, with her two sisters, Artemis and Stella. They boarded the ship in Fayal, having been among the passengers dumped there by *Manoa* two months earlier. All three were good company. Helena had a beautiful voice, and there was not a single Armenian folk song she did not know by heart. She preferred the clean air of the deck, she used to say, to the stuffiness of her cabin, and spent all her time on the deck resting in the lap of a longue-chaise. She was extremely beautiful, young, red-lipped, slender, and full of appeal. Just a month after her marriage in 1915, the Turks dragged her pharmacist husband from her bosom and slaughtered him in Sebastia in company of the intellectual leaders of the town. She was carrying within her heart the sorrow of her murdered love.

Thus, just a few of us — from the pitiful remnant of a nation whose roots went to the antiquity of 25 to 30 centuries; which had been endlessly subjected to the ignominies of exploitation, deportation, decimation and, as a final blow, to genocide; and which, to cap it all, had been denied any vestige of right to our native land — had at this time ventured out to seek shelter and comfort in the arms of the "Mother of Exiles."

This remnant on board *Britannia*, close to each other in bonds of the same suffering, the same dream, the same blood, and the same fate, would be scattered as soon as we set foot on the blessed soil of our dream land, our Paradise, probably never to meet again. As for me, this was true. I never met any one of these dear souls, not even any one of my family with whom I had begun traveling from Adana and Smyrna.

Yet, as we neared the end of our voyage, an intense anticipation to gaze at the welcoming countenance of the Statue of Liberty at the entrance of New York harbor and to stamp a fervent kiss to her each foot that was trampling over the broken shackles of tyranny was burning within my consciousness.

The Statue of Liberty! How I had loved it in my school days as I read about it in my English readers. It was to me the symbol of America's greatness in goodness, a monument to the truth that all men are created equal, and are endowed with the unalienable right to life, liberty, and the pursuit of happiness. And I was coming from a country — Turkey — where an Armenian was *not* an equal to the meanest Turk, and was, by

Turkish law — whether written or unwritten — denied the right to his own life, to his possessions, to liberty, to pursue happiness.

"The Mighty Woman with the Torch" was inviting me now to her bosom, because I was one of the "tired, poor, yearning to breathe free, a wretched refuse, homeless, and tempest-tost."

The New Colossus

Not like the brazen giant of Greek fame
With conquering limbs astride from land to land;
Here at our sea-washed, sunset gates shall stand
A mighty woman with a torch, whose flame
Is the imprisoned lightning, and her name
Mother of Exiles. From her beacon-hand
Glows world-wide welcome; her mild eyes command
The air-bridged harbor that twin cities frame,
"Keep, ancient lands, your storied pomp!" cries she
With silent lips. "Give me your tired, your poor,
Your huddled masses yearning to breathe free,
The wretched refuse of your teeming shore,
Send these, the homeless, tempest-tost to me,
I lift my lamp beside the golden door!"

by Emma Lazarus, New York City, 1883

Part IV
The Web of Hope

CHAPTER 52

IN THE LAND OF THE FREE

Tuesday, April 5, 1921: First Day

ON THE MORNING of the last day of our two-week-long voyage from Marseilles a rumor began to make its rounds that *Britannia* would steam directly to the harbor of Providence, Rhode Island and disembark her passengers there to avoid the inconveniences resulting from the quarantine imposed on New York harbor.

The rumor proved true.

Thus I was denied the privilege of laying the bouquet of my love, respect, and admiration at the feet of the famed Lady, the Statue of Liberty.

Britannia indeed entered the waters of Providence and docked at her own berth, after winding her course through the innumerable boats lost in dense fog hovering over the whole harbor as well as the city.

Excitement suddenly roused the dreamy passengers to action. Everybody was prepared to be the first to rush out of the giant vessel. An anxious crowd was waiting on the wharf for their dear ones. A jubilant Mrs. Soghig spotted her husband among the crowd after all these fifteen years of separation. There was no welcoming party waiting for us, and we did not expect one anyway. Yet it was heartwarming to see people embrace each other in cheer or tear. We lugged our bundles down the steps of the ship directly into the examination building. An eye doctor examined my eyes and was hesitant to pass me.

"What do you think is wrong with my eyes, Doctor?" I asked in a perturbed tone. "I had scrupulous treatments in Smyrna by a renowned ophthalmologist." Amazed to find among the "riff-raff" of immigrants someone who could be useful to him at this hour of rush, at once he stamped my certificate "bono," and asked me to linger a while and interpret for him till the line of the passengers came to its end. The remaining three adults of my party passed with no delay, but when little Azniv came before him the doctor became more fussy. Then, somewhat alarmed, I began to plead with him on behalf of my favorite cousin, appealing to his compassion, and recounting all the misery his rejection of her would cause us all. I do not presume that my earnestness softened his heart, but finally he decided to affix his approval to her certificate.

Meanness at its Worst

Happy over this good fortune, we then entered the customs house where a number of officers were busy searching through everybody's baggage. Stephen laid his family belongings before one of them who, after inspecting the bedding, bundles, and the rug, let him go with no trouble. But when it was my turn, he chose to overlook my scanty belongings except the 3 by 5 foot small rug.

"How much did you pay for this pretty rug in your country?" he asked in a friendly tone.

The official had already seen and handled Stephen's rug, the identical twin of mine, and had passed it free of duty.

Naively and truthfully I answered,

"Sixty-three Turkish liras."

It was far from my mind that this amiable official of the Spirit (Statue) of Liberty, Compassion, and Justice, had an ulterior motive in asking the price of the rug. He had no way of knowing that one Turkish lira would hardly be worth half a dollar at the time, and that the rug was bought with a widow's mite, at about 30 dollars in American money.

"Do you know," said the man raising his voice to harshness, "that you are smuggling into the United States an expensive merchandise? You have to pay 25 dollars duty."

Somewhat confused at the unexpected accusation of smuggling, I didn't know what to say. Then I stammered that I did not have that much money. In fact, I had only seven dollars, the amount given me in the ship in exchange for foreign currency.

"If you haven't got the money right now, it's all right," said this exception among the honest officials of America, the Home of the Just. "Then you can leave the rug with me. And when you have the money and send it to me, you can have it."

I walked over to Stephen, explained the difficulty, and begged him for 20 dollars. Reluctantly Stephen probed into his purse and pulled out a 20-dollar gold piece which he, evidently, was saving as a collector's item. Before he handed it to me, he cast a silent and regretful gaze on it.

Adding to the rare gold coin a 5 dollar paper bill of mine, I shoved $25.00 into the sinful hands of the extorter. He, in his turn, fixed a crook's admiring gaze on the dazzling face of the gold piece and ostentatiously buried it and the paper money in his purse of iniquity.

"You can take your lousy rug now," he said. "I have no use for it anymore. And, by the way, I hope that you will never see a $20.00 gold piece in your life, wherever you go."

The rascally thief's curse stuck with me with its ominous potency all these years, more than half a century, and I did never see or handle a 20-dollar gold coin again. Once I had just one 5-dollar gold coin, but as a loyal American citizen, moved by a surge of patriotism, I turned it in, when President Franklin D. Roosevelt issued an order that everybody must turn over their gold to the Federal Government.

MOMENT OF ELATION

As soon as I left the ugly creature's oppressive presence and breathed the all-pervading air of freedom, all of a sudden I felt an exceptional elation. I imagined myself to be the richest man on God's earth. In God's sight there is no pauper, I reasoned. God is still on His throne. "Praise God from whom all blessings flow…"

I was free now. Free to walk among free men. Free to be what I was, and free to be what I wanted to be. "What is more precious in life than freedom, freedom from…Turkey," I concluded. I did deliberately forget for this rarest moment of exhilaration the fact that I was heavily burdened with financial obligations to Cousin Haigaz, and to my Aunt, to her son Krikor, and now to Stephen, her second son. I felt rich, despite the fact that I had only two dollars to my name, and was facing an uncertain future.

I felt pride in the thought that with my entering into the United States of America its population of 106,000,000 grew to be 106,000,001. I was thankful also that deportation, exile, starvation, and genocide devised by the Turk had not put an end to my life, and God, in His mercy, had granted me a second lease, so that I could come to this blessed country.

(At this time the immigration quota system was not in effect yet, so our entrance was relatively with no difficulty. The restrictive quota law was to be enacted in 1924 on the basis of two percent of the 1890 resident foreign-born population. It was because of this law that I was unable to get my mother and brother to join me.)

First Shopping on United States Soil

When I joined my group it was time to rush to the train station. Miss Termonian, one of our friends in the ship, accompanied us to catch her train to Philadelphia. We learned from her that our friend Miss Marie had been detained by the immigration officials for her fiance to appear and claim her.

It was late afternoon by this time, and we hadn't eaten a bite since breakfast. Aunt Gulenia asked me to accompany Stephen to get some food for the starving family. We set out immediately in search of a grocery store, which we located after wasting quite some time. Stephen bought whatever he thought the family would enjoy. And when the storekeeper cited the amount of the charge, Stephen emptied the whole content of his purse on the counter, coins and paper money, for the man to take what he wanted. And the man did exactly what was expected of him: take what he wanted. The problem was that neither Stephen nor I knew the values of the coins and the notes at that time.

We two "innocents abroad," armed with loads of groceries, at last retraced our steps back to the station, after wasting more time in wrong streets. How great was our chagrin and Aunt's reproaches when she informed us that our 6 o'clock train had already left. Miss Termonian also had left for her destination, and we were left stranded in a totally strange town where we knew no one. We all were so dismayed, disheartened, depressed that we could hardly eat a bite. Stephen and I were responsible for this irritating situation, and we felt indeed guilty. So at once we both left our sad company and went around to seek information and advice. While engaged in conversation with an attendant, a pleasant lady providentially popped up in front of us and asked what our problem was. When I explained our sorry situation, she told us not to worry at all, she was a representative of the Travelers' Aid Society, and it would be her pleasure to help us. The first thing we had to do now, she said, was to quiet down the panic our family was in. She came with us to assure aunt Gulie that there was no reason for distress, and that in a few hours we would be on board the next train. That done, she suggested we send a telegram to Krikor that we would be in Binghamton train station at 1 o'clock the next afternoon. After that too was done, she left us, promising that she would come back to see us board our train at 10 o'clock.

The woman was just as good as her word. She settled us in our seats comfortably, and bade us God-speed after referring us to the care of the conductor of the train.

Like a Swarm of Flies

Aunt and her children went to sleep in their seats after a hectic day. But Slumber evaded me, exhausted though I was. Suddenly I felt myself all alone, in company of hundreds of people in the train. Dark thoughts began to crowd into my mind like a swarm of buzzing and whizzing flies.

"Where am I going?" I asked myself, and shuddered at the answer.

In the morrow I would meet Krikor face to face, my cousin, who had obstinately chosen to be hostile to me, since our — my family's and his mother's — return from exile. With no rhyme or reason in the world he preferred to suspect that I had appropriated money and packages he had sent to his mother. No matter how hard I had tried (in letters exchanged) to convince him that he was unjust in his suspicions and accusations, I had not succeeded in allaying his groundless distrust of me.

He wanted a "villain." He couldn't be himself, if he did not have somebody to blame for imagined wrong-doings. He was incapable of trusting others because of his upbringing by his tyrannical and rascally father (whose story was related in a former chapter.) He was persistently obsessive and unrealistic in this delusion, this negative feeling towards me, to the point of paranoia.

I realized that tomorrow I would be Krikor's most unwelcome, most uncomfortable house-guest, nowhere else to go, no friend or acquaintance to confide in, nobody to seek advice or solace from...

The Diamond Ring

In order to disperse these tormenting thoughts I left my seat in the dim light of the aging night and walked over to the rear of the compartment where the conductor was resting to have a chat with him.

"Why haven't you gone to sleep like all the others?" he asked as I sat by him.

"I have too much on my mind," I answered. "Crowds of worries will not let me have a wink."

"Where are you going?" the conductor asked.

"To Binghamton, with my aunt and her children," I answered.

"Where?" he repeated.

Puzzled at his question, I repeated the same answer:

"Bing-ham-ton," emphasizing each syllable to make him understand, but he said:

"I don't know if there is such a place. Are you sure?" he said, making me more puzzled.

Now I began to have doubts about my knowledge of English. Am I pronouncing the word wrong? Is there really such a town? Or, is it so unimportant that people don't know it? If a conductor of a train couldn't know the city we are going to, who else would know? My puzzlement grew by the bounds. And then I tried again:

"We are going to B-i-n-g-h-a-m-t-o-n. It is a city in the state of New York. My cousin lives there, and we are going to him."

"Oh, you mean *Bimton*," he corrected me.

"No, no," I insisted. "We are not going to *Bimton*, it is *Bing-ham-ton*."

"I see, my foreigner friend, that you pronounce the name of that city more correctly than I do. Some of you immigrants put us natives to shame with your better English," the conductor conceded.

"I liked you very much," he added in a friendly tone, "and I want to do you a big favor."

With a smile at my astonishment, he fumbled for a second or through his vest-pocket and pulled out a ring.

"This," he said, holding it toward the light to make it glisten, is a diamond ring mounted on gold, I found it in this wagon a few days ago. I can't find its owner, and I have no use for it. I will let you have it for fifty dollars. You can sell it anytime for hundreds of dollars."

"I do not have that much money," I moaned, grieving that I could not take advantage of such a rare offer which would enable me to wipe out all of my enormous debts.

"Alright, then give me twenty-five," he consented, magnanimously reducing the price to half.

"I do not have that much either," I answered plaintively, and gazing at nowhere I added, "All I have is only two dollars."

The next minute the conductor of the night train from Providence was the possessor of my two meager dollars, and I, the penniless immigrant encumbered with heavy debts, was the possessor of a costly diamond ring.

Thus my faith in the American milk of human kindness was restored by this philanthropic gesture of a total stranger to a total stranger, after the revolting experience I had earlier with the crooked customs official.

I thanked the man profusely, hid my new-found treasure in a secret pocket, and discreetly kept silence about my rare good fortune. Returning to my seat light-heartedly, I lured the elusive Slumber to come back home.

CHAPTER 53

COUSIN KRIKOR

After changing trains twice that night we arrived at Binghamton in the afternoon of Wednesday, April 6, 1921. To Aunt's, and specially to the betrothed Alice's, utter disappointment Krikor was nowhere in the station to welcome them. Stephen, bursting with frustration, hired a carriage to go to his brother's address and inform him of his mother's and fiancée's waiting.

In an hour or so the two brothers came and we all went to Krikor's home. A number of Armenians in the community had gathered in front of his residence to welcome us and congratulate their friend for his good fortune in having his family survive the greatest of massacres and join him.

Among the visitors there were several men of Hadjin who had come to America in 1912–1913 to escape conscription into the Turkish–Balkan War. To my delight, I found in this group two men who had my name Gejekooshian in its abbreviated form Kooshian. One of them was George V. Kooshian, a tailor from Hadjin, now married and with children. I remembered that I used to know his father as Vayting Emmig, Uncle Vartan. The younger man, a photographer by profession, was known as Sarkis Kooshian, a confirmed bachelor all his life. I remembered that I knew his mother as Auntie Teshghoon. The parents and all other relatives of both these cousins were lost in the Great Holocaust, the Genocide, and they had no dear one to look for. So both showed me warm interest and compassion, inviting me to visit them whenever I could.

Krikor was courteous with me, naturally having no time or thought to waste on me on this eventful, crowded first day.

And I was glad.

"I Will be Blunt with You"

On the afternoon of the second day Krikor, Stephen, and I walked to the railroad station to claim our baggage. After we had lugged it upstairs into the house, Krikor carefully inspected everything, more searchingly than the despicable customsman had the day before. The sight of my ill-fated rug with its identical twin belonging to Stephen immediately aroused the giant avarice sleeping in his heart. Turning to me, my dear cousin Krikor said in a stern tone,

"Kevork, I will be blunt with you. I was always against your coming to the United States, but when my mother wrote that she needed your services during her voyage I relented and borrowed money for you. Now you owe me three hundred dollars besides what you owe my mother. I expect you to pay me that amount in full before you leave for wherever you are headed. But I will let your stay in my house until my wedding day, only for the sake of the services you rendered my mother and fiancèe."

And he continued,

"I will credit against your debt twenty-five dollars if you turn your rug over to me. I would like to have both yours and Steve's."

Thus too soon his antagonism surfaced. I began to feel increasingly miserable for being under his roof, around his table eating poison and being compelled to accept his grudging hospitality. He did not know, and would not care to know, that at that moment I did not have one single penny to my name, nor did I have any prospect of raising such an amount as he demanded. And how could I part with a rug with which I had such warm intimacy?

Dreams and Ashes

In the midst of these thoughts my hand automatically pulled out of an inner pocket the diamond ring. I had wrapped it with a silken cloth of my dreams and hopes of independence and security. Now I cast an admiring and satisfied look at it as I presented it to my cousin.

"Here is a diamond ring that pays my debt to you to you twice as much and even more," I said with pride.

Surprised that I could be the possessor of such wealth, he took it, turned it this way and that, and, all of a sudden, burst into roaring laughter.

"Who sold this junk to you, and for how much?" he asked, interrupting his guffaws.

Puzzled, I told him that a conductor on the train had given it to me as a mark of philanthropy, swearing that it was a high-grade diamond worth hundreds of dollars, and he had asked fifty dollars for it, but consented to part with it for only two dollars because I had no more.

"You idiot!" he raged at me. "That scoundrel has cheated you out of your two dollars. This junk isn't worth a dime. With your two dollars you could buy two dozen of them in any five and ten cent store."

He handed it back to me, shaking his head at my stupidity.

And I wept over the sudden destruction of the castle of my magnificent dreams into a heap of ashes.

Evil Advice

The next morning Krikor took me to the local YMCA office to get me a job. On the way, referring to my "diamond ring worth hundreds of dollars," he instructed me in the subtleties of the American business and social life. In a patronizing and charitable mood, he advised me, for my own good, to be a *"khach-a-kogh,"* wily, cunning, crafty, tricky, deceptive.[45]

"Make *khach–a–kogh–ootune* your life-principle," he added, emphasizing every syllable of the obnoxious word, hoping that this unique advice would be stamped on my mind. "Without this principle you will never succeed in anything you do."

My abhorrence of Cousin Krikor's pernicious philosophy of life was at its highest intensity. I knew that my nature, my Christian upbringing and my mother's spirit (which was ever present with me) would never permit me to take advantage of such an infernal suggestion. I wanted to run away from him, but I knew I could not. I had nowhere to go.

"Father in heaven," I shouted wordlessly within my heart, "Deliver me from this Evil."

I managed to keep my revulsion bottled up.

Krikor introduced me to the manager of the YMCA, whom he greeted by his first name. He said that I was a highly educated man; a school-master, and master of a few languages; an immigrant fresh from Turkey; a guest in his house, and direly in need of a job to begin to pay off a heavy debt. The manager courteously expressed regrets that at present he had no opening for me, and promised to get in touch with him if he ever needed my services.

Cousin Sarkis Kooshian

Meanwhile I began to throw myself out of the suffocating atmosphere of Cousin Krikor's overcrowded house, and pay visits to my hitherto unknown cousins, Sarkis and George. Sarkis was a warm-hearted and sincere young man, hardly a few years older than I. Being a photographer by profession, he took my picture on my first visit to his studio and gave me several copies.

Sarkis Kooshian is long gone. I never saw him again after leaving Binghamton. But I have daily occasion to remember him — 56 years now — because that first only picture he took of me is hanging in my kitchen, enlarged and framed. God bless his soul.

"You don't have to tell me anything about your state of mind and miserable feelings for staying in Krikor's house," said he on this first occasion, "because *I* know him very well. Even an angel couldn't tolerate him." I was tempted, but refrained from disclosing my "state of mind and miserable feelings" yet. They had to wait for another occasion.

After some questions and information about the Armenian deportations and massacres, he gave me a handful of coins, explaining the value of each one, and advising me to buy some stationery and begin writing letters to my friends. "First thing for you to do is to write a letter to your sister in California. She and her husband Sarkis Soghomonian stopped here in December on their way to California. Your second letter should be to your cousin Panos in Chicago. Don't waste any time."

"And," he added, "don't write your letters in Krikor's house, or give his return address. He opens your letters. You can use my studio address."

Cousin Krikor Sends Me to Beg

Krikor never missed a chance to nag me for payment of my debts to him.

"I must have what you owe me before the wedding. Weddings cost a lot of money," he would repeat constantly.

One morning Krikor told me that Mr. Haroutune Philibosian, a wealthy Oriental rug merchant from Fresno, was in the town and was due to visit his niece and her husband in their ice-cream parlor on Main Street. He urged me to go there, meet the gentleman, explain my situation (debts), cultivate his compassion, ask for three hundred dollars, and then rush home to him with the booty.

Who was more crazy among us three, I thought to myself. Was it Krikor for suggesting such an asinine scheme? Was it Mr. Philibosian, the shrewd businessman, who would be naive enough to believe the story of a total stranger and part with such an enormous sum? Or would it be I, for daring to beg for an unreasonable amount of money with no offer of security, from a man I had never met before and was no relation of his?

Although totally ignorant of the techniques of swindling, I left to escape Krikor's oppressive presence. Not knowing what to do, I loitered in the street where Sokrat's ice-cream parlor was located. The morning wore out, the afternoon too, and I spied no one entering the store that looked rich enough to be defrauded.

Cousin Sarkis Advises Me

This foolish affair increasingly angered me. No more able to contain myself, I directed my steps toward Sarkis's studio, and being cordially ushered in, I poured all the stinking mess out before him. After listening to my bizarre story, he advised me to go directly to our cousin George V. Kooshian and tell him the whole story.

Rose, Cousin George's wife, welcomed me with open arms and warm heart. She was a graduate of Hadjin American Home School for Girls, which my sister also had attended. She was as compassionate and affectionate toward me as her husband was. When she invited me to stay for dinner I was happy, because I had eaten nothing all day having left Krikor's house before breakfast.

After dinner, when the two small children had been sent to bed, I told them all that was distressing me. Peter Rejebian, Rose's bachelor brother, who was boarding with them, was present too. They listened to my story with amused interest, but with no shock or indignation.

Then Cousin George related an experience of his relating to Krikor.

Some years ago, he began, he and another man of Hadjin formed a partnership and opened a plant for wholesale dry-cleaning and dying. Krikor, sensing an opportunity to benefit from it, succeeded in persuading the two partners to take him in as the third member of the firm. Before the year was over, Krikor had outwitted them by draining the cash, piling up unpaid bills, and resigning from the bankrupt company to face and satisfy a swarm of creditors.

"The first day I saw you in Krikor's house," said Cousin George, "I knew that some kind of trouble would be brewing for you. In conformity with his nature, I predict that a lot of trouble and anguish are in store for his mother, brother, sister, wife, and children to come. Krikor is in the clutches of an evil genius."

"Will you stay with us tonight?" suggested Rose after learning of my unenviable situation.

To which Cousin George added,

"Tomorrow you pick up your belongings from Krikor's house and come here to stay with us until something turns up."

Clouds Disappear

The bed, the night, the congenial spirit of the environment gave me comfort, and the buzz of worries gave way to peace. Instead of going directly to Krikor's house the next morning, I went straight to Cousin Sarkis's studio. When he heard me tell of Cousin George and Rose's invitation to stay in their home for the time being, Sarkis expressed his pleasure with encouragement.

"There is always a silver lining on the other side of the darkest cloud," he said. "Better days are waiting for you that will make you forget your distress."

While we were still engaged in conversation the postman delivered him a batch of mail. As he sorted them he handed me three letters, ever the first mail I received in America. And what letters they were! The beginning of the fulfillment of Cousin Sarkis's good-hearted prediction of a moment earlier of better days waiting to make me forget my present worries.

The first letter was from my friend and colleague Roupen Tateosian inviting me to stay with him and his wife Leah in New York. Leah had joined him a few weeks earlier from Smyrna, where I had visited her in February to wish her farewell.

The second letter was from my sister Mary in Pasadena, California. She was expressing her joy that I had at last succeeded in landing in America. A check for forty dollars was enclosed, advising me to go at once to Cousin Panos in Chicago.

The third one was the cause of my greatest happiness. It was from Panos himself in answer to my letter a week earlier.

Panos was my father's only sister's eldest son. He was the only living member of a family of six children, all of whom, with their parents, had perished in the Genocide.

Panos was telling me of his joy for hearing from me in the United States of America. When he had learned from my sister and her husband during their two hour train stop at Chicago on their way to California that I was stranded in Smyrna for lack of fare, he had cabled three hundred dollars to the American Consulate in my name, but the money was returned to him because I could not be located. All this time he was wondering about my whereabouts.

"And now I am sending you with this letter my check for two hundred dollars. Pay your Cousin Krikor 150 dollars for his 'hospitality,' and with the remaining fifty dollars buy your train ticket for Chicago. I am anxiously waiting for you."

Pay and Move Out

Cousin Sarkis was overjoyed at the turn of events, the miraculous change of my gloomy present to a brighter outlook Then he urged me to hurry to satisfy Krikor's claim on me, at least in part.

On the way to Krikor's I reasoned within myself:

It may be that Krikor will relax his oppression if I turn over the whole two hundred dollars to him, with the promise of sending the remainder from Chicago.

I reasoned also that Sister's forty dollars would be quite enough to take me to Panos.

With that decision made, in spry steps I walked the rest of the way, climbed Krikor's stairs two rungs at a time and knocked at his apartment door with a considerable air of independence. Aunt Gulenia, at the door, expressed a timid concern about my whereabouts.

I told Krikor and his family about all three letters, their contents, and the two checks. I told Krikor that I had come to pay and then move out. He was the happiest devil on hearing that he would be paid. Immediately he jumped up and led me to the bank to help me cash the checks. When I handed the two hundred dollars to him he was disappointed and asked for the forty dollars too, reminding me that I owed him one hundred more. I tried to reason with him that I needed a little cash for train fare and promised to send the balance as soon as I could, but he wouldn't listen.

"You can't leave Binghamton before you pay me one hundred dollars more," he threatened.

Dear Aunt Gulie, his mother, Stephen, his brother, and sweet eleven-year old Azniv, his sister, were all too cowed to raise a sound in my favor. Miss Alice, his fiancèe, too, deemed it convenient not to interfere with the affairs of the tyrant, her husband-to-be.

I refused to pay the Shylock the train fare so badly I needed, and began bundling my belongings.

"Will you leave the rug to me?" he asked again.

"No," I answered, "positively NO!"

"What have you got in that heavy box?" he was anxious to know.

"Books," I said to satisfy his curiosity. "Your fiancèe's aunt in Smyrna asked me to deliver them to her son in Ohio."

"Do you think that I did not open that box and find out what there was in it?" he smirked at me, and added, "You fool! Do you know how far Ohio is?"

My bundles on my back and in my hands I trudged down the steep staircase and arrived at Cousin George's. I related to them all the good things that had happened to me that day, and they were happy with me.

CHAPTER 54

COUSIN SARKIS SAVES ME FROM COUSIN KRIKOR

THE NEXT DAY was Saturday, and the wedding day of Cousin Krikor. Guests had arrived from the local community and outlying towns. Cousin Sarkis, Cousin George, his wife Rose, and I were among the guests. A priest from New York was specially invited to perform the ceremony.

As I followed the line of well-wishers to congratulate him and his bride, Krikor bent over to remind me in a rough whisper that I had better find the rest of my debt to him before leaving for Chicago.

I was probably the most miserable person among the guests. The spirit of well-wishing and feeling of enjoyment of the festive occasion had completely vanished. I could taste nothing at all for the fear that it could turn into poison, while everybody else was happy and gay with glasses of drink and full plates.

On my visit to his studio on Monday Sarkis wanted to know what Krikor's stern admonition to me was about at the wedding. I told him about Krikor's ultimatum.

On hearing this, Cousin Sarkis flew into a rage.

"Scoundrel!" he cursed. Then turning to me he said, "Go tell him right now that you owe him nothing. Tell him that you are going to pay the the one hundred dollars to Sarkis Kooshian when you are in Chicago, and when you are able to do so. Some months ago he borrowed a hundred dollars from me to send to his mother in Marseilles so that you could come with her. Then he borrowed a hundred more from George Rejebian for the same purpose. He borrowed one thousand dollars from Vahan Mardirosian for his mother and her party."

"Go now," he urged.

And I did exactly as he told me. Krikor was dumbfounded for a moment, then shook his head this way and that, crunching his teeth in impotent rage.

That same afternoon I went to see George Rejebian, Rose and Peter's elder brother, who ran a shoe-repair shop down on Main Street. He verified Sarkis's statement that Krikor had borrowed a hundred dollars from him towards my fare.

I had no more time to waste in Binghamton now that I was free of Cousin Krikor's clutches. So, next day, Tuesday, April 26, 1921, twenty days after arriving at Binghamton, I left for the train station. Peter Rejebian drove me in his Model T Ford, and waited to see the train leave.

An Angel, Panos

When I stepped off the train in Chicago Central Station, I saw an angel waiting for me, whose name was Panos. Panos was a popular name among the Armenians, used as the abbreviated form of Stephanos, the venerated name of the first Christian Martyr, and means crown.

I hadn't seen Panos for more than ten years. I had left Hadjin for Everek-Fenesseh in 1911, and he had left for America in 1913. We both were the grandsons of the same grandfather—Haji Kevork Agha Gejekooshian—his mother being the daughter and my father the son. Fate had not permitted us to grow and play together, although we were almost the same age. Before the turn of the century, in the tender years of childhood, my family was forced to leave our native town, and when after some years Father died, we returned to Hadjin and I entered the American Orphanage. Thus we had little or no occasion to know each other, because of different cultural environment.

After we had grown up enough in the first decade of the century, we came to know our relationship to each other. Through my mother's direction and suggestion I would occasionally visit my only aunt on the paternal side, and find myself in her soothing arms and under the shower of her tears and kisses. She would be at a loss about what dainty food to put before her beloved brother's orphaned son. Panos and the train of his younger brothers and only sister—Gulenia—would accept me with warm but silent affection because of their mother's lavish love and unrestrained tears.

Then, I used to see Panos almost daily when, in the fall of 1910, he came to the American Boys' Academy in my last year there. Now, both in our 'teens, we could understand and appreciate each other better. He came to know and esteem his only *kergin* (aunt), my mother.

He had come to the United States, and we were left behind, in the hands of the Turks. The holocaust of 1915–1920 had come to wipe out all that was dear to his heart. Panos was all alone in the world.

And now, when I came down the steps of the train, I found myself in the arms of an angel, Panos, the embodiment of the goodness, comfort, and security of all his and my lost ones. We both wept tears of joy and sorrow: Sorrow for our irretrievably lost, and joy for meeting each other. When our agitated emotions calmed down somewhat, he took me to the elevated train which brought us after an hour's ride to his establishment, Azad Ice-Cream and Confectionery Parlor, at 1401 Diversey Parkway.

As soon as we arrived, the ice-cream parlor became transformed into a banquet room, full of merriment, laughter, and conversation. Besides his partner Vartan Ouzunian, there were quite a number of other young men, all natives of Hadjin. Among them were Toros Pushian, my chum all through my school years, and Hampartzoum Keklikian, the future nationally-known surgeon, professor of medicine, literary critic, and author. These two had shared the miseries of the Genocide in previous years, and I was not aware of their being in America at this time.

On later occasions I met Mardiros Sarkisian (my teacher in Fenesseh, man of letters and editor in later years); Armand Gizirian (a lawyer later on, whose sister Yeranoohi became Panos's wife in 1924); Haigaz and Himayak Sexenian; Harry Izmirlian (my classmate in Hadjin, and whose best man I became twice—once in 1922, and then in 1947); Arshag and Haiganoosh Sexenian (Haiganoosh—Izmirlian's sister, who passed away a year later); the three Boyajian brothers, Hovagim, Setrak, and Armenag; Armenag and Haroutune Ouzounian; Hovagim and Sona Tatoulian, Mugitch and Nounia Sexenian; Vartivar Berberian; Garabed Cheldirian; Minas Terzian; Miss Haiganoosh Boyajian (the celebrated revolutionary of legendary fame, sister of reknowned Jirayr and Mourad).

After the party was dispersed, Panos took me to the house in which he had rented a bedroom, no farther than a couple blocks down a side street, and having proudly introduced me to his landlady he led me to his room upstairs. He opened up his closets and drawers to hand me pajamas, socks, shirts, underwear, towels, shaving stuff, and told me to use anything that belonged to him as my own. Then, pointing to a second cot loaned to him by the landlady, he said that it was my bed.

We talked and talked about my family, his family, especially about his sister Gulenia, the only survivor of the Genocide, whom my mother had brought with us from Aleppo to Adana and who finally perished with the population of Hadjin when it fell some time later. Before the night was spent—in sorrow and tears—sleep came to soothe our grieving hearts with her balm.

Thus Panos, gentle, sweet, and generous, dissolved all my fears and anxieties with the touch of an angel.

CHAPTER 55

PEACE CATCHES UP WITH ME

April 28, 1921–August 14, 1923: Chicago

My first night in Chicago proved to be the beginning of a happy relationship with my noble cousin Panos that would continue all through our lives.

When we woke up in the morning we hurried to the ice-cream parlor, where Vartan had already prepared breakfast for the three of us.

Vartan Ouzounian, the partner, was a friendly, decent, and cheerful man, about the age we two cousins were, but shorter in height. I had not known him in Hadjin. He, too, had escaped conscription into the Turkish war army, which was eminently notorious for its total disregard of the health, feeding, comfort, or wages of its Armenian soldiers. He had joined the exodus of the young Armenians who fled Turkey in 1913 to find political and economic asylum in the United States of America. He, too, was left all alone, having lost his parents, brothers, sisters, and relations in the Turk-devised barbaric Genocide.

The two partners, Panos and Vartan, worked in full accord with each other, respectful, considerate, and honest. Both were soft-spoken and clean of morals.

Vartan accepted me from the first moment as a brother, saved from fire, a fugitive from Turkish hell.

The two partners operated their business with no extra help. They had a mutually-agreed arrangement according to which one was to open the Parlor in the morning, and the other to close it at night. The roles were reversed the next week. They also had worked out a plan for each to take a day off at certain intervals.

The "Parlor" had several semi-private booths with marble-top tables, where patrons could enjoy their preparations of ice-cream and soft drinks. Besides these they sold cigars, cigarettes, pipes, loose and chewing tobacco, and cigarette paper. They sold confections of all sorts and ice-cream-on-a-stick dipped in chocolate, which Panos produced in the cellar of the store.

On the right side of the store, behind the service counter, there was a small office where Panos kept the records and where they could both retire for a short rest during slack hours. Their customers were mostly middle-class factory workers who at rush hours would crowd the Parlor for ham or roast-beef sandwiches richly spiced with mustard and pickles, pies, drinks, and desserts. Alcoholic beverages were never sold, because of the strictly-enforced Prohibition. This had become the law of the land with the ratification of the 18th Amendment on January 16, 1919, during the presidency of Woodrow Wilson, Democrat. (And this same amendment was destined to be repealed 15 years later by the 21st Amendment, which would be ratified on December 5, 1933, during the presidency of the next Democrat, Franklin Delano Roosevelt.)

For a period of two weeks Panos permitted his Hadjin friends to take me out to different note-worthy spots in the great metropolis — museums, public parks, the zoo, amusement centers, the stock yard, theaters, restaurants, the Loop, and Lake Michigan to swim.

One day three weeks later Haigaz and Mugitch Sexenian asked me if I would work as a tailor in their pressing shop. With the consent of my benefactor and protector I accepted the offer. Every morning except Sunday Chicago's famous elevated cars would take me to the Loop, where their shop was located on Wells Street. Human traffic was so great at all hours that both cousins, Haigaz and Mugitch, were always occupied with steam-pressing the crumpled suits of the passers-by. I was the ideal repair man to sew rips, buttons, and do quick alterations, which neither of the partners had the leisure to do.

But the daily travel from the the ice-cream parlor to the Loop and the return in the evening took a bite of two whole hours from my time, and this amounted to 12 precious hours wasted irretrievably in a week and to 48 hours in a month. So, on the second or third day of my employment on American soil, I went to a near-by bookstore and bought me a copy of *One Hundred and One Best Poems* and another, with the title *One Hundred and One Best-Known Songs*, to read and commit to memory as I commuted to and fro.

At once I became fascinated with each poem and its author. Thus, spurred by an innate craving after aesthetic thought, sublime imagery, and melodious phraseology, I diligently applied myself to the happy task of memorizing these gems of the great poets. By and by I committed to memory, and was able to declaim aloud or voiceless in their entirety, such works as Thomas Grey's "Elegy Written in a Country Church-Yard," Longfellow's "A Psalm of Life," Shelly's "Ode to the West Wind," J. R. Lowell's "To the Future," Bryant's "Thanatopsis," Shakespeare's "Hamlet Soliloquy," and passages from Byron, Keats, Burns, Tennyson, Browning, and others.

Although I did not continue for long the commuting to the tailor shop in the Loop, yet I kept on memorizing. This became a pleasurable habit with me.

Seeing that what I was paid by my good employers went for the travel fare and outside meals and nothing was left for other needs, Cousin Panos pulled me out of the tailor shop a month later and put me to work in his ice-cream parlor, at 15 dollars a week. I roomed with him and ate at the "Parlor" with Panos and Harry. My duties were to wait on customers, wash dishes, mop floors, and assist them in every way. Our relations remained warm and brotherly to the end.

My cousin's sole concern, it soon became evident to me, was for me to earn decent wages, so that I could begin to pay off all the debts I had incurred for the voyage to America. And, eternal thanks to his memory, I succeeded in doing exactly that in the months that followed.

The first thing he made me do in July, the second month after he employed me, was immediately to send my mother fifty dollars, my very first offering to her from the United States. He also gave me money from his own pocket to send to Mother, his unknown uncle's widow.

A ledger begun in 1921, still in my possession, shows that in the ensuing months I had not only regularly sent money home, but also paid Aunt Gulenia above and beyond what I owed her and her younger son Stephen. Full payments were made to Cousin Sarkis Kooshian, Cousin Haigaz Kurkyasharian, and my sister Mary Soghomonian. The ledger further shows that donations were made to friends and school mates still in the Old Country and in dire need.

—Uncle Haroutune Malian, $50.00, repeated several times.

—Yeran Sarkisian, classmate, $50.00.
—Mardiros Sarkisian, $10.00, repeated.
—Minas Kurkyasharian (Haigaz's elder brother), $10.00.
—Anoosh and children, $10.00, repeated.
—Michael Vayejian, classmate and chum, $20.00.
—Arsham Aijian, classmate, $40.00.
—Miss Annig Derghazarian, student in Constantinople, my future wife, gifts of money and packages.

A few months later, Panos introduced me to his Metropolitan Life Insurance agent, and advised me to listen carefully to his plan for me. If I was convinced by his arguments, Panos said, then I could agree to buy a life insurance policy. He further added that I would never regret it if I got insured, and that every wise and prudent American was insured, himself included. So, trusting in my cousin's judgment, I decided to buy a 20-year life insurance policy for $2,000.00, at the semi-annual premium payment of $27.34. Although the policy would mature in November 1941, yet the fund would remain with the said insurance company to defray the expenses of my funeral. (This wise move proved beneficial when I borrowed from it for travel to Cuba to get married, and, on another occasion, to pay a down payment for the purchase of the lot we built our residence and rental stores on.)

Another time a salesman came to the ice-cream parlor to sell a dictionary. Having in years past acquired the habit of consulting dictionaries and references in Turkish, Armenian, French, and English, at once I became fascinated with the encyclopedic content of the massive volume, and signed an order for it, paying for it with a part payment. Thus, in a few days, I became the happy owner, for $33.00, of *Webster's New International* Dictionary printed on India paper, and also of a complimentary copy of a world atlas. This dictionary served me satisfactorily as source of definitions, etymology, history, biography and geography, etc.[46]

Education

I was amazed and delighted to see that every morning and afternoon a couple of newspapers—the Tribune and the Daily News—were being

The Web of Hope

George Kooshian, soda jerk

delivered to the "Parlor." I had no conception that in the United States one day's newspapers could be so large in size and bulk, with pages as many as 100 or more, rich with informative and educational contents that were meant to be read. The papers that I knew in my former years in the Near Eastern countries consisted of only four pages.

Panos and Vartan usually glanced at the headlines, occasionally reading a little but mostly ignoring them. So I gathered all the cast away reading material and, after reading, clipped what appealed to me and filed them in envelopes — stories, poems, humor, editorials, literary pieces, biography, etc. I still have in my files a sheet from the Sunday Tribune of 1921, with the story of the historic trial and vindication of Solomon Tehlerian, who shot and killed in Berlin Talaat Pasha, the arch-murderer of a million and a half Armenians, the prototype of Adolph Hitler.

This made me get acquainted with the names of countless authors, so I began reading their works — the complete works of Rabindranath

Peace Catches Up With Me

Tagore, Fedor Dostoyevski, Leo Tolstoi, and French, Italian, German, and English authors.

The ice-cream parlor was kept open from 8:00 A.M. to 2 A.M. the next morning, 16 hours. One night after midnight, as I was all alone in the shop engaged in mopping the floor before closing, a woman hurriedly walked in and begged for a nickel to use the phone. After good-heartedly handing her a coin, I helped her over the sudsy floor to the nearest one of the telephone booths. Then I resumed the interrupted mopping. I could not believe my ears when I heard the woman, whom I had helped with my own coin, say into the mouth of the telephone,

"Police, I am calling from the Azad Confectionery on Diversy Parkway, to report that the attendant of the store robbed and raped me. I want you to come at once and arrest him."

As a leaf in the clutches of a fierce wind I began to shake in terror. The mop fell out of my hands, and what reservoir of fortitude I ever had suddenly ebbed away, leaving me void, unable to think, to reason, to decide on any action to protect myself from such an unexpected ruination.

"No, No!" I stammered within myself. "Such a dastardly, malicious, slanderous accusation cannot take place in the America. I must be dreaming…"

In a few minutes a burly policeman appeared at the open door. The man of the law, for a moment, surveyed the wet floor with the pail of soapy water in the middle; the orphaned mop lying the midst of a wet desert; myself in a work-apron, trembling with pale fear; and the gaudily attired vixenish prostitute menacingly facing me, and then said,

"Come on, sister, leave that poor boy to finish his mopping. Come along with me."

The strumpet followed the policeman sheepishly, unmurmuringly, leaving me to wind up mopping and run home, breathlessly.

A kindly policeman used to stop at the "Parlor" for a free cigar or ice-cream or sandwich and chat with us amiably. We used to call him, unceremoniously, Mike.

One night, after closing time, I was on my way to my room when all of a sudden a huge fellow sprang forward out of the pitch dark. He grabbed me by the shoulders and harshly ordered me to hand over "the bottle of bootleg booze" supposedly I was carrying in my hip pocket.

When I recognized him from his size, uniform, and voice to be Mike, I took courage and said,

"Officer Mike, I am George, the waiter at the ice-cream parlor. You know that I don't drink and don't carry flasks of booze. Please let me go home."

"I don't know who you are," he insisted. "But I know that there is no on one these Prohibition days that does not have moon-shine in his pocket. Come on, hand it over."

Having no flask to hand over, I pleaded again,

"Mike, don't you remember Moosh and Harry at the corner cigar and ice-cream store and me, George, who gave you a Robert Burns cigar this afternoon?"

"Why didn't you say so?" the drunken Mike sobered up to say at last. "Of course I know you. You are the new immigrant from Armenia working for Moosh. Go home now, and don't be on the street so late."

Leaving me to continue on my way, he went back into hiding behind a bush, in wait for another victim "with a flask of booze in his hip pocket."

The next day Mike denied the night's unpleasant encounter when I mentioned it to him.

"I wouldn't do that to *you*," he said.

One afternoon, when the busy hours were over and I was left alone to clean up cups and glasses, a poor blind man appeared at the threshold of the store. His dark glasses were protecting his sightless eyes and a cane in his hand was guiding him. Standing at the entrance, he turned his unshaven face towards the wall opposite where I was, and plaintively begged for a dole "in the name of God." Having not seen such a forlorn, destitute and handicapped person forced to beg in the United States since my arrival a few months before, I became so overwhelmed with a surge of compassion that I rushed toward him and escorted him to a table. I served him a generous portion of ice-cream, after depositing a dollar in the till. When he was through eating, I handed him another dollar, both dollars out of my 15 dollars a week salary, and led him out to the corner to find his direction with the aid of his unerring cane.

The broad and busy Diversey Parkway intersected another broad and busy boulevard, at the corner of which the wretched helpless blind man stood still, waited and blindly watched the traffic.

I had to return inside to my work, still following him with a compassionate concern, when all of a sudden the man took off his dark glasses, put the cane under his arm, and dashed like a straight arrow across the intersection, diagonally, from the southwest corner to the northeast.

"Oh, what a fool I am!" I said to nobody.

"Money on the Streets"

"The streets of America are paved with money, and the people have only to take the trouble to stoop down to pick it up," was an oft-repeated refrain among the peoples of the Eastern Hemisphere. I, too, believed this myth before my disillusionment the first hour of my arrival. I saw no money-tree anywhere, no money-covered street, no lake of liquid gold. Yet, in a saner day, later on, I became convinced that that myth was a fact, that dream was real in a different sense, in different ways.

Thanksgiving Day, my very first, was at hand. Cousin Panos, a couple days before the festival, handed me a crisp ten dollar bill and told me to go to the Stockyard[47] to buy the largest turkey I could find for Thanksgiving dinner. He had planned to entertain in the basement of his store all the single young men of Hadjin, about a dozen of us.

Chicago's famous Elevated Car soon took me to the world-renowned slaughterhouse, where, finding a long line of customers, I joined its tail end. When my turn came at last, I laid the ten-dollar fortune in front of the clerk, and, with an unfamiliar spirit of show-off, I said:

"The largest turkey, please."

As the clerk shoved toward me a package, he said,

"Eleven dollars, please."

Confounded, embarrassed, and crestfallen for being so cocky, I didn't know what to do. Panos had given me a ten dollar bill and told me to expect some small change. Now, as I looked down to the floor to open up and swallow me in front of the line of people behind me, I spied a one-dollar bill right between my feet. With no hesitation, I picked it up and casually handed it over to the man, as if I had taken it out of a secret pocket.

"Do you now believe," said Panos philosophically, when I related to him my perplexing predicament and its miraculous solution, "that the streets of the United States of America are covered with money, but you have only to bend the knee to pick it up?"

My First Turkey Dinner in the United States

Panos gave me the Sunday off, the Sunday following Thanksgiving, to go to church and then spend the rest of the day as I pleased, with the exhortation that I should not stay out late, as I was to open up the "Parlor" early the next morning.

After enjoying the spiritual fare provided by the church service, I decided to enjoy a cultural fare, too, by visiting the Museum of Natural History. But, I thought, it would be better first if I found a good restaurant and feasted on a turkey dinner. After all, I reasoned, this was a historic occasion — my first Thanksgiving in the United States, and, in fact, I had never eaten turkey meat in my life in the Old Country. Cousin Panos had paid me in the morning my princely wages, and I could well afford to spurge on a princely dinner at a gala restaurant.

I felt important for once in my life.

It didn't take too long to locate a respectable-looking restaurant. The waiter, recognizing what a "prince" I was, with a great show of respect led me to a marble-topped round table in the middle of the dining hall and lavished on me all of his meticulous service — clean white napkin, shining silverware, cups, glasses, saucers of this and that, and bottles of condiments. All this attention pleased my ego and served to enhance my appetite with the promise of fulfillment.

Some minutes later, a plate of turkey was placed before me. The waiter retired after laying the bill on one side of the plate in my view. But I paid no attention to the bill, as I was eager to begin to eat. After a short prayer of thanksgiving, I held the fork by my left hand and the knife with my right, and started to cut a mouth-sized morsel. The knife refused to cut the turkey, and the turkey resisted to submit to its destiny. I applied a little force on the fork and the knife, then a little more, and a little more, until the full plate suddenly jumped over the table, splattering all of its contents around the table, the floor, and myself.

My frustration turned into disgust, and, after a nervous attempt to wipe off some of the mess, I picked up the bill, paid sheepishly the "princely" charge of five dollars for my "princely" dinner, and made a hasty departure.

At some distance, I entered a dingy-looking, small and crowded eating place, and sitting on a round stool in front of the untidy counter, I ordered a plate of Hungarian goulash, ate, it, and left the premises after paying twenty-five cents.

Panos, my benefactor and employer, did not hear of my epic stupidity. The "secret" patiently waited for more than half a century to be recorded on these pages.

In the Barber Shop

Mention was already made of my initial employment as a tailor. One afternoon of that first month in Chicago, I went to a barber shop for a haircut, having been warned in advance that a haircut would cost no more than fifteen cents.

As I descended the few steps from the outer sidewalk in to the sub-basement barber shop, I was amazed to see a crowded hall with half a dozen white-uniformed barbers, each standing by a swivel chair, busily engaged in performing various forms of service, as shaving beards, clipping hair, washing heads, polishing shoes, etc.

When my turn came to occupy a chair, I asked the barber to give me a haircut. After the customary crew-cut was over in a few minutes, I would be allowed to pay his fifteen cent fee and leave.

But not so.

The amiable Italian suggested that I could have a shave, too. I had shaved myself all along. But I said to the man, it would be fine. That bit of service hardly over, he suggested that I could have a hair wash too. I was so overwhelmed by the goodness of the man that I didn't have the heart to deny him the pleasure of doing something more for me. After that was done, a boy came along and started polishing my shoes. The barber obviously was fond of me, because he presented me a bottle of this water and that.

When the catalogue of his services and gifts was over, he brushed me from top to bottom. Then I offered him fifteen cents. He looked at the the three nickles with amused contempt and said:

"Five dollars and a quarter."

I was flabbergasted. Then and there a suspicion sneaked into my mind that this man had taken advantage of my ignorance. Sheepishly I laid the "gifts" back on his shelf and dug in my several pockets in search of anything resembling money. All I could find amounted to one dollar and eighty-three cents. I offered this "fortune" to the equally flabbergasted barber, and with the embarrassed promise to bring the rest later, I ran out of the wretched place.

The truth of the matter is that during the 28 months I lived in Chicago, I could never muster up enough courage and create an opportunity to go back to this place and face that "good" and "generous" Italian barber.

Mangasarian

One day I read in the Chicago Tribune that a man named M. M. Mangasarian[48] was holding meetings on Sunday mornings in the grand Opera House and lecturing on literary and philosophical subjects. Because the lecturer was an Armenian, I became interested, and in company with Toros Pushian, my life-long chum, began attending his lectures.

From the first attendance I became fascinated. A typical program was as follows:

At 11 A.M. a trio sang a song by Cadman.[49] Then a solo was sung from Bach. Exactly ten minutes after the music the lecturer walked in from a side entrance and began to speak. His subject was "[William Jennings] Bryan's Objections to Evolution Considered," or "How to Breed an Intellectually Superior Humanity," or "A Religion for Americans," or "Voltaire in Hades." Then the meeting ended with a collection, announcements, and a song.

Mangasarian had been, as I was told, a Congregational minister for many years, and one day, having renounced his Christian faith, had turned to be a Rationalist. He had founded the "Independent Religious Society" in 1900, which was independent all right, but not religious at all, although he ran his meetings on the order of a church service.

Mangasarian was erudite and was blessed with charisma as a speaker. He traveled all over the world to deliver lectures on Rationalistic subjects. He was the author of numerous pamphlets and a few books, as: *A new Catechism* (1904), in opposition to Christian catechisms, and "What is Christian Science?" in which he contends that "Eddyism" is neither Christian nor scientific. Another one was: *The Truth about Jesus: Was He a Myth?* Some of his pamphlets were titled:

"The Gospel of Sport."
"Omar Khayyam's Philosophy of Happiness."
"Christian and Turk."
"The Gospel According to Bernard Shaw."
"Humanism, a Religion for America."
"Is the Morality of Jesus Sound?" etc.

Rationalism is a term employed both in philosophy and theology, and denotes a system in which the reason is supreme. Theologically Rationalism is the opposite of Supernaturalism, therefore a rationalist does not believe in God, in Christ, in the Holy Spirit or the Word of God. Furthermore he does not believe in any form of religion. He considers religion — as Karl Marx has done before — to be the opium of the mind. Rationalism, according to one of its historians, Kahnis,[50] "makes the educated reason of the time the standard of all religious truth."

In philosophy rationalism is opposed to sensationalism and empiricism.

Mangasarian's "Independent Religious Society" advocated "an intelligent religion as against mysticism — mysteries beyond comprehension and dogmas fixed for all time." "Our Bible is nature," it declares, "and our teacher is life. Our heaven is here and now. Labor, love, play are our three Sacraments." The printed program of the Society covetously invites the attendant to "come over into our camp, and let us count on your time, talents, and purse in the service of humanity." And this service to humanity is, as it points out, by (a) inviting friends to the Sunday lectures, (b) distributing programs and publications, and (c) setting an example of rational thinking and living.

Èmile Coué

The papers, one day, reported that Èmile Coué[51] had come to Chicago to give a series of lectures and demonstrate healings. This apothecary of Nancy, France, had become renowned for originating an unusual method of curing ailments. He had discovered the principle of self-mastery by auto-suggestion. It was mere curiosity that made us attend several of his lectures. Toros and I bought our tickets for the balcony, far in advance, because the man was so popular that—the papers said—the largest lecture halls were not large enough to hold all the people who wanted to see him in person, or be healed by him.

The bearded M. Coué was handsome, small in stature, dignified in manners and dynamic and convincing in speech. In his lectures he explained the psychology and power of suggestion and the dual—favorable and adverse—nature of auto-suggestion. He emphasized that auto-suggestion had enormous power to heal many illnesses. He gave a verbal formula for every one to repeat several times a day, three times in a row,

> "Every day, in every way,
> I am getting better and better."
> (Tous les jours, à tous les points de vue,
> je vais de mieux en mieux.)

After the lecture he demonstrated the efficacy of his method. Scores of patients were brought to him, several of them already on the platform, waiting and hoping to be cured. He would walk to them, ask the nature of their illness, and then move his hand over the sick part repeating audibly "Ça passe, ça passe, ça passe…" After some minutes of such suggestions he commanded the patient to rise from his sick-bed or drop his crutches and walk towards him at the other end of the platform. The audience became wild with excitement and amazement to see the bed-ridden rise and walk, and the lame leap and run with joy.

At each of the several lectures of M. Coue I attended I witnessed such miracles to happen before my eyes.

I never forgot his magic words and used them often:

> "Every day, in every way,
> I am getting better and better."

CHAPTER 56

THE FINAL BLOW TO ARMENIAN ASPIRATIONS TO INDEPENDENCE

ONE DAY in November 1921 the political situation in Adana took a sudden turn from its day to day ominous state to that of panic when Col. Edouard Brèmond, the Administrative Head of Cilicia, announced that the occupied country had been ceded by a treaty to Kemalist Turkey and in a month the French occupation army would withdraw from Cilicia.

The ancestral homeland of the Armenians, once ruled by Rubenid and Hetumid kings (1080–1375) and the just reward for sacrificial service in the Allied cause endlessly promised as an Armenian Independent State, was thus treacherously sold out to our butchers.

Aristide Briand, the French Prime Minister, had, with the consent of Great Britain, promised Boghos Nubar Pasha in 1916 that Armenian aspirations of liberation from Turkish tyranny and of independence would be realized, if the Pasha would organize an Armenian volunteer legion, equip it, and hand it over to the hard-pressed French Army.

In naive trust in the old fox's word the Pasha formed such a legion in due time and handed it over. But because the French forces were sorely needed for the defense of their homeland against the German juggernaut and could spare not a single private to fight the Turks, they transferred the Armenian Legion to General Edmund Allenby, the British Commander of the Palestine front.

Under General Allenby "Le Lègion des Armeniens" fought a decisive battle on the hills of Arara in Palestine and successfully repulsed the firmly entrenched Turkish Seventh Army under an obscure young commander named Mustafa Kemal. Kemal and his decimated army retreated to Aleppo, leaving the road to Syria, Lebanon, and Cilicia wide open to the Arab, British, and Armenian forces.

Because these prized slices of the northeastern and southeastern Mediterranean seacoast were apportioned to the French by the Sykes-

Picot agreement (London, 1916), the British occupation forces relinquished them soon after the Armistice and the French were free to "occupy" them. The British, through the heroic attack of the Armenian Legion, which suffered heavy casualties at the bloody combat, pulled the chestnut out of the fire and offered it to their war-ally, the French.

Soon after the French occupation forces had formed a government, the remnant of the Turkish Genocide of the Armenians began to return to its devastated homeland. The French officials repeatedly and openly reassured the population that the country would be turned over to them as an independent Armenian state as soon as the diplomatic and legal procedures were completed. Meanwhile they made meticulous efforts to keep the naive Armenians in the dark about the sinister underhanded perfidy they were engaged in with the enemy. They were negotiating a secret treaty with the Kemalists to surrender Cilicia in return for concessions in Turkey.

Rumors about high and low French officials receiving valuable bribes in money, rugs, and women were eventually substantiated by witnesses. French sympathies were definitely on the side of the butchers of the Armenians, while they persisted in deceiving and pacifying the fears and suspicions of the Armenians.

And now the final blow was being dealt to the Armenian dreams of liberation from the Turkish yoke, condemning a blood-drained people to the hell of slavery under Turkish rule from which it had all the reasons and rights to be freed once and for all.

The heads of the double-dealing French government now began to read the "gospel according to the wolves" to exhort the terrified Armenian population to have faith in Turkish mercy and sense of justice and remain under its rule. But no power on earth could convince the survivors just returned from tasting the "mercy" and "justice" of the devilish perpetrators of genocide and the habitual revelers in massacres, pillage, and plunder to make the mistake of trusting them. In utter panic the Armenians, betrayed by their "defender" and "big brother," left everything behind and scurried out of their fatherland before the French left.

The unfortunate fleers from the Turkish slaughter were refused admittance in to the United States and other countries, except into Cyprus, Greece, and neighboring Arab lands.

The Final Blow to Armenian Aspirations to Independence

My mother accompanied her brother Haroutune and family to Cyprus. But brother Setrak was detained by the French until later, and had to remain on board a ship for weeks, because no country would permit the ship at that time to dump its human cargo. After a month somehow he succeeded in landing at Beirut, from which it took him more than six months to join his mother.

Kemal Massacres Smyrna Christians

Eighteen months (May 15, 1919) before I came to Smyrna (October 1, 1920) on my way to America, the Greek forces descended by destroyers and transports to occupy the famed city and its outlying countryside. Smyrna was assigned to Greece as her share, as other parts of Turkey were apportioned to the Britain, France, and Italy.

The political and social atmosphere of the land was completely Greek when I was there, and the Turks seemed subdued outwardly, but were fuming inwardly.

The Armenians were completely free of the oppressive restrictions that had been imposed on them for centuries under Turkish rule.

The Greeks, now in control of the land that used to belong to them before the Ottoman occupation, were swaggeringly self-confident and lulled by illusions of invincibility. They failed to read the omens correctly when the French permitted Kemal's brigand forces to massacre Hadjin, Marash, and Zeitun, and handed Cilicia over to Kemal in exchange for the rights of exploitation of mineral resources and investment priorities.

And when rumors of Turkish Nationalist forces advancing toward Smyrna had reached them the Greek officials did not believe that the Turks could dislodge their hold on the city. It was too late for the Greeks to realize that their confidence in their erstwhile victorious allies was misplaced, when the Greek Prime Minister and Minister for Foreign Affairs were coldly told in the waiting room of the Paris Foreign Office: "Not a gun, not a shell, not a soldier, not a shilling was voted in support of the Greek enterprise."

Then and there the tragedy of Smyrna was sealed.

The Turks poured their uncontrolled fury upon the two unfortunate Christian communities — Greek and Armenian — in the presence of the so-called Christian Powers which had the sacrificial services of these unfortunate peoples to achieve victory over enemy Turkey. None of these eye-witness Powers — Britain, France, Italy, and the United States of America — raised a finger to stop the bloodbath, nor did they ever after raise a word of condemnation. They said they were neutral.

Thus Smyrna the Glorious was burned, murdered, and destroyed by the Turks, the blight of Civilization.

A few months later a surprise letter, dated from Athens, Greece, came to inform me that my chum Sarkis, Anoosh's two-month-long son-in-law, had perished in the massacre of Smyrna, along with his wife and son and countless others.

> General Noureddin, an officer well known for his strength of command and his contempt for foreigners, into whose hands Kemal had bestowed control of Smyrna, sent for the Greek Metropolitan. The two had met during the first month of the Greek occupation, and as he approached the General in the latter's conference room at the *konak* [the government building], Chrystostomos extended his hand in greeting. Noureddin spat, declaring he would not touch that filthy hand. He pointed to a dossier lying open on his desk. On the basis of these sworn accusations, he said, a revolutionary tribunal in Ankara had already condemned Chrystostomos to death. "There is nothing left but for the people to give their judgment," he shouted. "Now get out of my sight."
>
> The Patriarch was walking slowly down the steps to the Konak when the General appeared on the balcony and cried out to the waiting mob, "Treat him as he deserves!" The crowd fell upon Chrystostomos with guttural shrieks and dragged him down the street until they reached a barber shop where Ismael, the Jewish proprietor, was peering nervously from his doorway. Someone pushed the barber aside, grabbed a white sheet, and tied it around Chrystostomos's neck, shouting, "Give him a shave!"

The Final Blow to Armenian Aspirations to Independence

They tore out the Patriarch's beard, gouged out his eyes with knives, cut off his ears, his nose, and his hands. A dozen French marines who had accompanied Chrystostomos to the government house were standing by, beside themselves. Several of the men jumped instinctively forward to intervene, but the officer in charge forbade them to move. 'He had his hand on his gun, though he was trembling himself,' one of the men said later, "so we dared not lift ours. They finished Chrystostomos there before our eyes."

The Archbishop's murder was reported to Admiral Dumesnil aboard the flagship. He shrugged his shoulders: "He got what was coming to him," he said.[52]

CHAPTER 57

BOOK PEDDLER

ONE DAY in January 1923 an advertisement in the Chicago Daily News caught my attention. An educational firm, officially known as Educators' Association, was looking for ambitious young men to sell from door to door a one-volume book of cyclopedic content (*Volume Library*). The ad cunningly painted the picture of a happy businessman returning home with a briefcase in one hand and a thick sheaf of dollar bills in the other.

Who could resist the sudden surge of longing to be that man? The prospect of earning ten times more in less time enchanted me then and there. When I showed the ad to Cousin Panos, my boss, he perceived my excitement and readily permitted me to apply. At once I mailed a letter to the Post Office box number provided in the ad, not forgetting to present all the needed information about me with also the unneeded.

In due time an appointment was granted, and Panos suggested that I should honor it. I was deeply pleased when my interviewer accepted and assigned me to a class for new recruits. The tuition she charged for the several training courses did not seem too much in view on the future big gains, neither did I mind paying for a brief case, a prospectus (not the real Volume), and some forms and envelopes to mail to the office with the daily reports of interviews, sales, and other activities. The salesman's six days in the week belonged to the Association.

We were trained in the school to be fully familiar with the contents of the prospectus and conversant with statistics and other detailed knowledge. This impressive-looking handbook was prepared with the reproduction of random pages and maps and pictures from different sections of the Volume, and was of no value to any bibliophile.

We, man or woman recruits, were taught to memorize a prepared speech to pressure the client into buying our merchandise, but we were firmly cautioned not to disclose our main purpose at first. In order to be admitted inside the house we were to represent ourselves as members of the Educators' Association, who were concerned with the client's children and their education. Before entering a house we were to collect from neighbors all the necessary information about the family, number of children, names, ages, grades, and schools, and when inside, then gradually steer the conversation to selling our book.

It was only after gaining the confidence of the client that we should deliver our memorized speech and clinch the sale with his signature on the contract. After that was done, we should ask for and receive a down payment of three dollars, which we should keep as our commission from each sale.

Each new salesman would be living on his commissions for the first one hundred days, and only after that could he expect a salary of twenty-five dollars a week besides his commissions. He was also to pay for the postage on daily reports mailed to the office.

After paying the down payment the client would pay the balance of the sale price when he received the book C.O.D. The full price of Volume Library was fifteen dollars. After a sale was achieved the salesman would have nothing to do with the buyer; he was, in fact, not supposed to see him or her anymore.

When I finished the training course I resigned from my job at Azad Confectionery and Ice-Cream Parlor, where I had worked for the eighteen months since my arrival in Chicago. Saying good-bye to my benefactor Cousin Panos and his partner Vartan was difficult. I was embarking now on an unfamiliar course. A pasture was spreading before my inner eyes, so green, so lush.

One day, in the middle of February, I was assigned to accompany a Professor of the Association and watch and imitate the method he used in selling. When we were ushered into a house the Professor greeted the lady warmly by her name and began to inquire about her young son Bob. He represented himself as a teacher well-acquainted with the child's educational needs. The lady listened attentively to the Professor's memorized speech, and having been convinced that Bob would very soon become a better student for having the Volume Library, signed the form and paid him the down payment of three dollars he asked for.

The Professor then took me to another apartment in the same building and repeated the same procedure, first hiding the purpose of his visit, and gradually launching on his smooth talk about her school boy and his needs. This woman also, like the first, silently signed the contract, paid the down payment, and escorted us out.

Once out on the sidewalk, the Professor left me with an impassive dictum:

"From this minute on you are on your own."

Stunned, I stood there a long moment filled with a mixture of loneliness and fear. A wave of regret engulfed me for foolishly losing the comfort and security of the ice-cream parlor.

Then, in an instant, I found myself in the Elevated (train car), traveling a long distance, to see Mrs. Hovagim Boyajian. That lovely soul was a friend in whose home I had been welcome occasionally. Disregarding the instruction to disguise the fact I was a salesman, I told her in open candor that I had begun to sell a book very useful for school children, which would facilitate the school work of her son and daughter, and that she was my very first client. Sympathetically she listened to my very first sales spiel, and without a sign of hesitancy put her signature on the dotted line, paid my first commission of three dollars, served me a meal, and put me on my way with good wishes.

For months I traveled far and near, in the city, out of the city, out of the state. Knocked at doors, pushed buttons, encountered good will and ill will. Lodged in homes of strangers and newly acquired friends. A newly-married young lady with her husband, originally from Sis, Cilicia, who was a niece of an orphanage "brother" of mine in Hadjin, kept me in her home in Waukegan for a whole week, and wouldn't accept a dime for her hospitality.

Once I fell prey to the crooked scheme of a professional beggar, but miraculously I escaped the snare from snapping on me.

The fatigue at the close of the day, preparing and mailing of the daily reports about where and how I spent the day, and the insufficiency of the commissions to meet my expenses began to weigh heavily on my mind. The more I thought on the matter the more I realized that I owed no debt to the Association, I was not salaried and I had nothing in my possession that belonged to them for which I had not paid. I was merely being exploited, I concluded.

An incident provided the fabled "straw that broke the camel's back."

One day in a town in Indiana I managed to gather some information about a prospective customer. When I rang the doorbell the lady of the house appeared at the door. Careful not to reveal my real business, in a friendly tone I began to talk about her 12-year old daughter Rachel, and how to improve her school work.

"Get out of my sight!" she shrieked at me. And, pointing at my brief case, she added, "You are a sneaky, deceitful salesman. If you were a real official from her school you would know that we buried Rachael two weeks ago."

The grief-stricken mother's rage and contempt fell on me like a crushing landslide. The shame and remorse I felt at the moment tore my heart asunder for the deceptive method of selling taught by the instructor of the firm. I realized that I had compromised principles of honesty for "a bowl of lentil soup."[53] Then and there I vowed to quit door to door salesmanship. I mailed my resignation with the day's report.

Next day I came back to Chicago and boarded in Vartan and Noyemi Ouzounian's home, where I had left my belongings when I launched on the "lucrative" career of a short-lived salesmanship.

TABLE CLEANER — JANITOR — STOCK ROOM CLERK

In the classified ads section of the daily papers, I noticed that a restaurant in the Loop was looking for help at rush hours in exchange for a meal, and the famed Marshall Field Department Store needed janitors after work hours from 6 to 12 midnight. At once I applied for both jobs and was happy to get them. Suddenly the prospect of one square meal a day and sure pay at regular intervals restored my sickened sensibilities.

After a week or two at janitorship I decided that I was not prepared to stay as a janitor all my life, and that I should write a letter to the director to that effect. I thanked him in the letter for the opportunity he gave me as a janitor and called his attention to the fact that in my country I had been prepared to be an educator and would be indebted to him if he transfered me to a day job.

A few days later the director called me to his office, and after a few minutes of conversation sent me with a note to the manager of the vast china and glassware department on the 13th floor.

The manager, a soft-spoken middle-aged Norwegian, accepted me at once and, from day to day, taught me how to locate the particular wares and how to fill the orders that were pouring in. I can never forget this ordinary-looking genius. He was equipped with an amazingly sharp and high-speed mind which was the prototype of the electronic computer that was waiting to be invented dozens of years later. He had as complete control of the store-house of his mind with its many storage units as he had control of his glass and china warehouse. He was a wizard at mentally solving any algebraic problem you cared to present, and he would instantaneously give you the correct answer.

Farewell to Chicago

From the first day of my arrival in Chicago its inclement weather did not agree with me. All the 28 months I spent there could not acclimate me. The smoke-saturated air and the soot soiled my collar and whites daily, the cold penetrated into my bones, and the wind and dust irritated my already weak eyes. And I was stricken with serious eye trouble once and needed the care of an expert, but had no money to pay. The elderly lady and her husband with whom I was boarding at the time took care of my eyes like a real father and mother.

Casual mention of my discomforts in my letters evidently prompted my sister Mary to invite me to "California, whose weather was heavenly, devoid of smoke and soot, wind, dust, and cold."

"You never had a niece or nephew before," she argued logically. "But now you have them both. Why don't you come over to have them size you up?"

Overcome by that reasoning I decided to pay them a short visit. To that end I purchased a round-trip train ticket, with the intention of returning to my job at Marshall Field in case I could not land one there. (My 1923 records show that one-way ticket was at $140.00, and a return ticket at $86.00)

CHAPTER 58

PASADENA, CALIFORNIA

WHEN I landed in Pasadena on that beautiful morning, Saturday, August 16, 1923, I found in the station a couple waiting to take me to my sister's home. "Brother" Panos and his wife "Sister" Nunia Lazarian, originally from Zeitun, Cilicia, were next-door neighbors to the Soghomonians on Garfield Avenue, north of Villa Street, and whom in the years to come I wold have ample occasion to know better. This noble couple years later went to Syria and Lebanon as missionaries and died there in the service of the Lord they loved.

The Soghomonian family consisted of four members, and with me now it numbered five. The rented house was too small for five of us, with one bedroom and the only couch in the sitting room was to serve me at night. I was heartily welcomed by both my sister Mary and her husband Sarkis, and was profusely reassured that they would by no means let me return to Chicago.

Immediately I fell in love with the lovely climate of "sunny California," and especially with Annette (Anahid), my bewitching two-year old niece, and my 5-month old nephew, Sam, who would later become a well-known political science teacher and a popular speaker.

The first two weeks were spent in acquainting myself with the immediate neighbors:

— Rebecca and her new husband, Khatcher Agha Gedigian of Shar (a village north of Hadjin), who had emigrated in 1913. (This good-hearted couple would be very helpful to my wife a decade later.) They had a son, Harry, at that time, and Paul was waiting for his chance to be born later.

— Aghvor, Rebecca's eldest sister.

— Mariam, Aghvor's daughter, and her second husband. (The first, Yeremia, had died in the first month of their coming to the United States.)

— Alice, Mariam's younger sister.

—John and Siranoosh Vartanian, Russian Armenians, excellent friends with one child. He was in the rubbish-collecting business and had a huge truck. In those days having a car or a truck was a mark of distinction. John would pick up books with his collections and give them to me, because neither he nor his wife could read English.

And outside the neighborhood, on nearby streets, there were other friends:

—Uncle Hampartzoum Malian and his wife Noyemi, with their three children: My favorites, Nectar (Vicky), now 14, Vartan, 11, and Stephen, born on the first day the Malian family set foot on American soil.

—Uncle Aram, one of Hampartzoum's younger twin brothers.

—Stephen Avak Mehagian and his two younger brothers, Haigaz and Levon. (Stephen a few years later married Mary, the eldest daughter of martyred Dr. Armenag Haigazian, the president of Jenanian College at Konia, and in 1957 founded Haigazian College at Beirut in memory of his father-in-law.)

—Missak Manisajian.

All of these were Uncle Hampartzoum's cousins and were living under Aunt Noyemi's matriarchal rule.

—Samuel Zeligian Mardian and wife Acabi, with their four children, Aram, Sam, Daniel, and Florence. A baby, Robert, was born the second week of my arrival in Pasadena.

(Samuel Mardian was the sponsor of the Malian family and their gang. He became in later years a widely-known building contractor. At present, 1978, Aram, Sam and Bob have a multi-million-dollar construction company in Phoenix, Arizona, with Aram as president. Sam was the mayor of Phoenix for two terms. Robert Mardian was Assistant Attorney General under John Mitchell in President Nixon's cabinet.)

Finding the Lost

After a short period of rest and visitations, I made a few trips downtown to see if I could find a job. Luckily one was waiting for me. I could not afford to be very particular about the nature or the level of a job at this point, because I realized that I was master of no trade or profession, so should be content with whatever work was available.

Mr. Sommers, the tall, blond, affable young vice president of T. W. Mather Company—the well-known department store catering exclusively to the needs of women customers and employing only women as salespersons and managers, with no more than a dozen male employees—employed me as a janitor and part-time elevator operator. Mather's Department Store, an elegant structure of architecturally ornamented exterior, with its basement and four stories above ground, was for several decades located at the corner of Colorado Street and Marengo Avenue. It was finally torn down in 1970.

I worked there happily for two whole years, from September 1923 to September 1925.

It was with intense pride and joy that on that first Saturday evening I ran home to show my first pay to my sister and brother-in-law. But when I put my hand in my pocket to pull out the pay envelope it was not there. The search was in vain. The envelope with its precious contents had mysteriously vanished. Abashed at my clumsiness, and saddened for the loss, I left the house to retrace my steps straight to Mather's, examining every scrap of paper on the street. When I reached the main door on Marengo Avenue I found my envelope lying just in front of the door, stepped on but unpicked.

With my first pay I began paying my brother-in-law one dollar a day for my board and five dollars a month for lodging. This arrangement continued for some time until it had to be raised a little higher.

The Armenian Community in 1923

In my third year in the United States and the first in Pasadena, I found a mini-Armenia here, composed of a considerable number of families and singles, businessmen, tradesmen, laborers, builders, carpenters, tailors, students, and intellectuals. All of them (except those who were born in America) were immigrants from Turkey, escapees from massacres of 1894-6, 1909, 1913 (Balkan War), and 1915-22 holocaust, with very few Russian Armenian families. Quite a number of Armenians had been established for years in the Los Angeles area. Prominent among them were Oriental rug merchants: Pashgian Brothers, Stone Brothers, (Reverend) Haigag Khazoyan Co., Constantine Gertmenian Co., the latter's father-in-law the Reverend Sarkis Devirian and Sons, Mihran and Aram Salisian Brothers, Haroutune Philibosian and Sons, Mihran Constantian, Hagop Moomjian, and later on, Dr. Hagop Boghosian and others. They employed mostly Armenian help.

The Reverend Sanadroug Shamlian, a native of Zeitun and onetime minister in Hadjin and then in Fenesseh (when I was there), had in 1922 started religious services in private homes, and then in rented halls, to which most of the rapidly-growing Armenian community came for comfort and spiritual sustenance. All the older residents were members of local native churches. The American Congregational Board officially recognized the movement and adopted it as a Congregational Mission for the Armenians of Pasadena.

This mission, later, grew in number of attendants under the able ministry of well-known Armenian clergymen: Missak Aijian, Hampartzoum Ashjian, Haig Asadourian, Samuel Rejebian (in whose day the mission became independent under the name of Armenian Cilicia Congregational Church and by whose efforts a church building was built in 1937 on the northeast corner of Mountain Street and El Molino Avenue), Manasseh Papazian, Senekerim Sulahian, Siragan Aghbabian, Avedis Hassesian, Puzant Levonian, and Norayr Melidonian (in whose day in 1974 the church had to be sold).

When I arrived at Pasadena in August 1923, the mission services were being held on Sunday afternoons in the Y.M.C.A. under the ministry of the Reverend Missak Aijian, a native of Hadjin, who was ordained in the United States. I had known him in Hadjin as a one-time principal in the American Orphanage. His younger brother Kaloust was my favorite teacher in 1910–11 in Hadjin, and their sister Louise became a "sister" to me from the Genocide days in 1916 to this day in 1978. Again, a child, I had known their father Mikayel Agha Aijian, a legend for uprightness, one of Hadjin's earliest converts in the 1860s to the Evangelical faith by the first missionary preaching. This venerable deacon and his old wife were among the 78 butchered Armenian clergymen and churchmen in the 1909 massacre at Sai'-Getchit, near Adana.

As the janitor of Mather's Department Store I had occasion to know everyone. One day two young salesgirls, Edna and Alice, invited me to attend their Sunday School class at the First Baptist Church, which was located about a hundred feet to the north on Marengo Avenue. I began going there regularly to Sunday School Class for young people and attend both morning and evening services, and attend the Armenian church services on Sunday afternoons. I joined both the First Baptist Church choir and the Armenian church choir. I was elected to serve as secretary to the Armenian church board, as treasurer to the Armenian Missionary Society, and also as secretary to the local branch of the Armenian General Benevolent Union (1924–1931).

Varoujan Club

Early in 1924 a group of young people of both sexes, about 20 or 25, formed a club under the name of a beloved Armenian poet, Daniel Varoujan (1884–1915), one of the victims among the hundreds of intellectuals arrested at midnight of April 14, 1915 and brutally massacred at the outset of the Genocide. The purpose of the Varoujan Club was to keep the Armenian spirit alive among the new and old immigrants and thus fight against the danger of imminent assimilation in the Melting Pot.

The Club, throughout its duration of almost a decade, served the community socially and culturally as its membership and influence increased. It sponsored social gatherings, public cultural affairs where well-known professors, doctors, and ministers and musicians would gratuitously give lectures and musical renditions. The Club staged many theatrical performances (from the works of Moliere, Hagop Baronian, Shirvanzade, and others) for the benefit of Pasadena and Los Angeles churches and the AGBU. It also performed a unique service by donating to the Pasadena Public Library a considerable number of specially purchased books on Armenian art, literature, and history, written in English.

I was the Club's first representative among the speakers at the Vartanantz Commemoration (February 1925), held in the Armenian Holy Cross Church of Los Angeles. My subject on that occasion was "The Role of Armenian Women in the Battle of Avarair." I also did have an active part in the Club as permanent secretary, lecturer, librarian, and actor.

The Club came to its end when members were dispersed on account of the Depression of the 1930s.

Christian Endeavor

The Reverend Samuel Rejebian, the minister of Cilicia Congregational Church, became instrumental in creating a strong body known as Cilicia Christian Endeavor Society early in the second half of the 1920s. A great number of young Armenian adults from the community was attracted to it. The Society would hold Sunday meeting where besides Bible study and prayer cultural and educational programs would also be given. I was for a season of several months' duration the lecturer on Armenian history. For lectures of this sort the attendants were very hungry.

Mr. Rejebian, once my professor of English in Jenanian College (1913–1914), had narrowly escaped the Holocaust of the Armenians by emigrating with his young family to America in the summer of 1914. As a distant relative and my teacher, he was fond of me, and would go out of his way to push me in the direction of teaching Bible and preaching from his pulpits, from that of Cilicia Church in Pasadena, and that of Massis Church in Los Angeles, of which he was also the minister. He established the Massis Church, and built the building of the Cilicia Church. In gratitude to his good memory I must affirm that he emboldened me to serve as a lay preacher and Bible teacher. All these led me to public speaking and writing.

I am grateful for the opportunity of speaking at his burial in Pasadena in 1966, when his body was brought from his home in Dinuba, California. He lived 83 useful years.

The Armenian Translation of *Twice Born Men*

In 1928 I was unexpectedly accorded the privilege of translating into Armenian a religious book, British author Harold Bagby's *The Broken Earthenware*, whose American publication carried the more explicit title of *Twice Born Men*.

Pasadena, California

The Reverend Hovhannes Eskijian, a brilliant young minister who was the pastor of the Armenia Evangelical Church of Kessab, Turkey, had, in 1913, translated this book into Turkish (with Armenian characters), the language widely spoken and read by the Armenians of Turkey. At that time this translation became popular and was well received in every Christian community in the country.

When the First World War broke out and all the Armenians of Turkey were uprooted and deported to be eventually annihilated, this 30-year old pastor, too, was deported with his young wife, two tiny sons, and all his flock.

One Sunday morning in the spring of 1916, with extreme caution not to be picked up by the vigilant gendarme combing the streets, I made my way to the Evangelical Church in Aleppo, Syria. The preacher was the famed Reverend Hovhannes Eskijian, who delivered a heart-warming, comforting, and vivifying message to the congregation, which consisted of a very few daring souls. I had never met him before, and I never meet him again afterward. A short time later he fell victim to typhus, the grim reaper of the starved and emaciated masses of the forsaken Armenians. Thus he left his wife a widow, his children orphans, and the church-goers shepherdless.

Mrs. Gulenia Eskijian and her two small lambs became our neighbors in Hokedoon (literally, the House of Soul or Refuge of Mercy). Their one-room apartment faced our one-room apartment across a corridor five feet wide and twenty feet long, on the second story, in the farthest corner of the complex.

Mrs. Gulenia became a good friend to my mother and to us children. In the dearth of reading material in those dark days of persecution and death she used to supply me with books in English from the library of her lamented husband. I well remember that on one occasion she loaned me the first and second volumes of Victor Hugo's *Les Miserables*, and then she gathered together about a dozen women in our common corridor so that I could tell them in the evenings the sad story of the unjustly hounded and persecuted Jean Valjean, the courageous hero of the book.

The long years of genocide took their heavy toll, and those of us who survived the holocaust through the grace of God found ourselves scattered to the four corners of the globe.

It was a pleasant surprise for me several years later — after leaving our cramped apartments that faced each other in Hokedoon — to find Mrs. Gulenia and her two gracefully growing children in Pasadena, not too far from where I had my tailor shop. Our old friendship and mutual respect were rekindled.

One day, on the occasion of a visit I paid to her, Mrs. Gulenia asked me if I would be willing to render a service to the memory of her martyred husband. As the picture of the saintly Pastor Eskijian — as the picture of the dauntless Prophet Jeremiah — momentarily flashed before my inner eyes, I readily agreed to perform the service she was asking of me. Then she proposed that I should translate her husband's Turkish translation of *Twice Born Men* into Armenian, "because," she said, "the system of writing and reading in Turkish with Armenian letters will soon disappear after what the Turks did to the Armenian race. Armenians will scorn that language."

I agreed with her and disavowed any rights as a translator, allowing all of them to the name and picture of the Reverend Hovhannes Eskijian. Because I willingly acceded to her wishes, several months later she gave me a gift of fifty dollars when I handed her the thick sheaf of the handwritten manuscript of *Yergoo Angam Dzunadz Mardik*. Realizing that a gift of such magnitude was far beyond her means I refused to accept it, but her insistence prevailed.

In due time the book was published and she was pleased. On the flyleaf her husband's picture and name appeared as the translator, and she herself wrote the preface.

May her soul enjoy the sweetness and the glory of the presence of the Savior whose servants she and her husband were. She remained until her death in the late 1950s a true and faithful friend to me and my family. She, as an industrious and wise mother, devoted herself to the task of bringing up her two sons in the fear of God, instilling in them the spirit and willingness of being helpful to those in need. She gave them higher education, saw them married, enjoyed the birth of grandchildren, and closed her eyes praising the Lord in her cancerous condition. Her sweet soul continues to live on especially in her younger son Luther, who, after doing menial work as a teen-ager, became an officer in the United States Army in World War II, then an architect and builder, a pillar of goodness, a Christian leader, and an unobtrusive philanthropist bringing credit and honor to the memory of his parents.

Spite

Despite the sad fact that Armenians were, from ancient centuries onward, subjected to outrageous treatments at the hand of enemy neighbors and outsiders, and were most recently (1915–1922) almost obliterated, I came to this country with the unshakable conviction that Armenians were a people of enlightenment; a people of a glorious culture; a people most adaptable to any form of higher culture and capable of contributing to its growth.

But I discovered too soon, even in this famed Land of Freedom and Liberty, that formidable forces beyond our control and expectations made the general public "see" and "know" us — through their blind jealousy, prejudice, and racistic feeling of superiority — as "low-class Asiatics," "always starving," "an inferior race worth massacring."

Economic threat, cultural envy, social hatred as "foreigners" and historical malign depictions of us Armenians were prevalent in the 1920s, as they were in former years. There was no one to care and correct these wrongs, and make others see us as we really were, instead of seeing us "different" and worthy to be spurned.

There arose in 1924 a nationwide movement of hatred towards the Armenians which was aimed at stripping them of their citizenship and denying naturalization to future applicants. An unfortunate incident rekindled the dormant hatred to erupt. It was widely rumored that a rug dealer in Portland, Oregon named Thaddeus Kartozian, a native of Sebastia, Turkey, had sold a defective Oriental rug to a local judge, and a heated quarrel between the two ended in a suit. The charges against the rug merchant were, beside being a swindler, that he also was an Asiatic Armenian, a non-white, inferior race, slave to the Sultan of Turkey, therefore unworthy to be considered as an American citizen.

A reign of panic overtook the Armenian community. If the Supreme Court ruled against the Armenians, all of us would lose our citizenship, our social, financial, and moral standing, not only in the United States, but also in the whole world. The destiny and honor of our future generations would irreparably be ruined.

Mr. James J. Davis, the Secretary of Labor, through a correspondent of the *Christian Science Monitor*, advised the Armenian Committee (A. Karagozian, H. Gulbenkian, H. Telfeyan, G. H. Pushman, and M. H. Tiryakian) to spend at least $50,000.00 to insure the winning of the case. The Committee, in consultation with its attorneys, hired the services of two reknowned American anthropologists, Professors Roland Burrage Dixon and the German-born Franz Boas. These scientists proved to the satisfaction of the court that Armenians had racial relationship to the Europeans in that they belonged to the Albian branch of the Aryan race, and their language was a distinct branch of the Indo-European stock, just as the English, German, and other European languages. It was a long and painful process for us to gain our positive identity.

I am glad that I did personally contribute in 1924 my mite of five dollars to the ultimate winning of the case.

I have never had an occasion that would cause me to regret that I was born, raised, and remained Armenian. I was, I am, and I shall remain always proud of being an Armenian.

CHAPTER 59

FROM JANITOR TO TRADESMAN

HAVING RESIGNED from my position as janitor at T. W. Mather's Department Store for Women, I decided to become independent, and opened a shop for dry-cleaning, pressing, and dying. During the previous two years of employment, I had managed to save over five hundred dollars. a respectable sum at that time. With the expense of no more than two hundred dollars I rented a tiny shop for $15.00 a month, bought (and installed) a Hoffman steam-pressing machine, a singer sewing machine, of 1903 model, a heavy tailor's scissors, a counter, a couple of chairs, and other things such as a business needs.

The shop was a separate part of a grocery store at the north-east corner of Orange Grove and Summit Avenues. Because the shop's door faced Summit (No. 706 1/2), I named my business "Summit Avenue Cleaners and Dyers." In order to make the community know that I was ready to serve it, I put an ad in the Star News and also had 2,000 hand bills printed, which I personally distributed from house to house on several mornings. Thus, in a short time the venture began to function.

The Soghomonians — my sister's family with whom I was to board for seven years — were some months earlier compelled to move from their Garfield residence to a second floor apartment on Villa Street where Summit Avenue takes its opening. Uncle and Auntie Malian (with their numerous charge) were living on Summit, a stone's throw from our new home. The road to my shop was about three blocks to the north past the Malian home.

My first Automobile

One day in December an unknown customer walked into the shop to have a loose button fastened. In the course of conversation he happened to mention that yesterday morning he had driven from San Francisco and arrived at Pasadena the same evening. His story sounded like a miracle and, in amazement, I asked how he could accomplish such a feat.

"With my car," he said, pointing to a black car parked at the curb.

"Can you show me how it works?" I asked.

"With pleasure," he said.

We walked to the car. I watched him intently when he inserted a key into the ignition, pulled half-way out a knob to start the motor, and after lowering a hand brake he let the vehicle go a few yards forward. Then manipulating another lever he brought the car back to its original position at the curb.

"Do you see that it doesn't take too much to operate it," he assured me.

Fascination suddenly forced me to ask a silly question —

"Will you sell it to me?"

To my delight and surprise he agreed to sell.

"How much?" I asked, and he replied —

"One hundred and seventy-five dollars."

Immediately I gave him a check to that amount, fearing meanwhile that he might change his mind. Then he gave me the key to the car and a pink slip, advising me to mail it with a fee of one dollar to the Vehicle Department in Sacramento.

Transaction over, the man walked away never to be seen again, leaving me in possession of a black Model T Ford sedan with four doors (December 20, 1925).

I put the key in my pocket and soon, under the stress of shop work, forgot the momentous incident. At closing time suddenly the car loomed in front of me and silently reminded me of responsibilities I did not have before.

The thought of having a car of my own had never occurred to me. Only the well-to-do had them in 1925. And interest in learning the skill required to operate one was non-existent in me. Yet here I was, face-to-face with a vehicle which, like Alladin's jinni, was waiting for my bidding. The car's master, it is true, had given me — its master of the afternoon — a cursory demonstration but the lesson was lost on me as a seed fallen on barren soil.

With uncertain feelings I placed myself on the driver's seat. The first thing to do, I said to myself, is to insert the key into the ignition hole on the dashboard. Then instinctively I pulled a few knobs, one of which worked to start the engine. Now the problem was how to make the car go forward. A lever on the steering wheel made the car move. Holding tightly on the steering wheel, we — the Ford and I — left the curb in front of the store and traveled fifty or more yards north on Summit. When we arrived at the corner, where Painter Street intersects Summit Avenue, instead of heading west towards Fair Oaks Avenue I turned the car east on Painter, still tightly clutching the steering wheel. The car, like a faithful slave, traveled halfway on the street, and because I did not know that I should loosen my grip to let the car go straight on, it jumped over the curb, dashed through a wire fence, and ploughed through an orchard. I did not know how to stop it, but a walnut tree came in front of the rushing car and stalled it. Utterly confused, knowing nothing about what else to do, I got out, surveyed the extent of the damage we had incurred, and then climbed back into my seat, thanking my luck that there was no one around to spot us.

In some miraculous way I managed to back out of the orchard via the broken fence, and turn the head of the car, this time, towards Fair Oaks. At the corner common sense unconsciously made me loosen the tight grip sufficiently so that we could turn southward on Fair Oaks. The car was traveling very slow, and right in the middle of the street. Several cars honked and hollered, but I did not understand what they meant until a choking smoke from my car forced me to get out at the intersection of Fair Oaks and Orange Grove. Bewildered, I walked around it as if to discover the cause of the terrible heat and smoke. After waiting there long enough for the smoking to stop, I got in the car again and drove it through an anxious period of time until I succeeded in parking it in front of our house. (Later I learned that I had not released the emergency brake handle during the whole hour of travel a distance of a couple of blocks. This had caused the smoking.)

For several days the car remained parked, because I dared not drive it without some sort of instruction. Ten days later, on New Year's Day, Mr. Hagop Albarian payed us a visit after watching the Rose Parade. When he heard about my precarious situation as the new owner of a car, he sat behind the steering wheel of my car, carefully explained the role of each instrument, drove it for some distance, and then let me drive and reverse and park. This thorough lesson was enough to restore my courage to drive from that day on. He was the one who told me that the smoke rising from the wheels was caused because I had failed to release the emergency brake on my first drive.

With that lesson I drove cars for 45 years, until poor eyesight forced me to resign.

George Kooshian with his Model T Ford

On the morning after I crashed the car through the orchard on Painter Street the shop telephone rang. A female voice, after ascertaining that I was the proprietor of Summit Avenue Cleaners and Dyers, informed me that last night my helper drove my car through her orchard breaking the fence, and asked if I would be kind enough to send someone to fix it. While I was on the line, Norman Gertmenian walked in. Norman had been a pupil of mine six years before in Adana High School. Turning to the future physician, I explained the whole comical story and asked him to come with me to face the lady of the orchard. In a few minutes we were there.

The lady met us at the broken fence, and apologetically asked us to fasten the broken fence wires to the post. Norman, like a master fence mender, finished the job quickly and received the lady's thanks with a friendly warning to be careful not to have any more accidents. Good old days. Such a trivial mishap, if it occurred in 1978 (as I record these events) would end up in court, with a penalty of hundreds of dollars.

Mary, my sister, gave birth to her third and last child, Rosemary (at present—1978—a grandmother), on the 23rd day of December, 1925, just three days after I acquired my car. Owning an automobile in those early days was considered a mark of social standing and affluence whether one deserved it or not. Cars were few in number. Roads mostly rough, uncared-for, and unpaved. The network of present-day freeways was not thought of until after the Second World War of 1939–1945. So streets and country roads were free of traffic. Although having a driver's license was required by law, and policemen were stationed in the center of street intersections on platforms, yet drivers were seldom stopped for permit.

When Mary and her baby were discharged from Huntington Hospital after the customary two-weeks confinement, it was my privilege and pleasure to pack them in my car and bring them home. That I did as expertly as if I had been a veteran driver of many years, although it was on the fifth day of my only driving lesson by Hagop Albarian.

My car was dedicated to the service of my sister's family and friends. I made it a principle to pick up any Armenian, young or old, from sidewalks and street benches, and drive them to their destination.

In the spring of 1927 I moved my dry-cleaning business from the suffocatingly small shop to a newly-built store at 1765 East Washington Street which, at that time, was not annexed to Pasadena. Here I had to change the name of my business from Summit Avenue Cleaners to Ideal Cleaners and Dyers. In this location I had sufficiently larger space to operate, with better ventilation and wider area to serve.

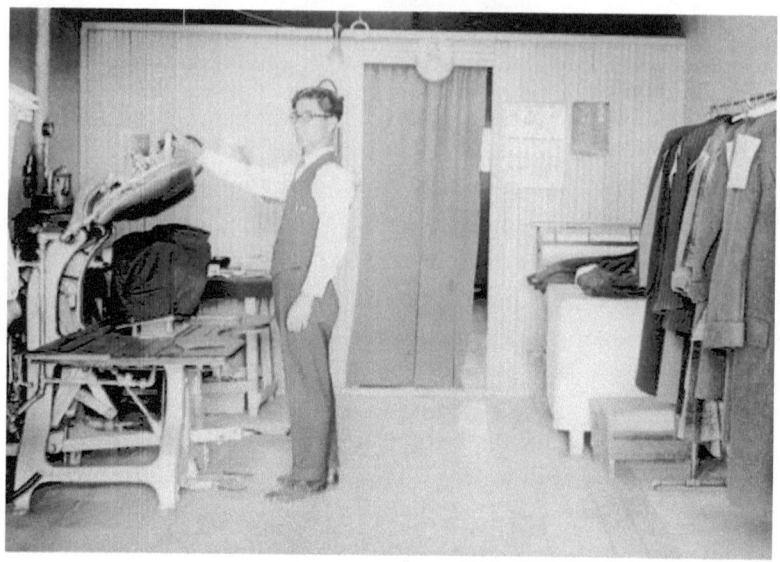

George Kooshian in his press shop, December, 1929

I Opened a School and Depression Closed It

Arthur Asadourian, a married young man who operated a small sweater factory, suggested one day that as an unattached Armenian it was my patriotic duty to start an evening class for children who had no chance in this country to learn to read and write their own mother tongue. If no one took a step in that direction, he argued, those precious children of the local community would soon lose their Armenian identity.

Though undeservedly maligned and discriminated against, a proud people we were, and sanguinely jealous to keep our ethnic identity alive despite the intensity of the fire burning under the mythical "Melting Pot."

The sincerity of Arthur's concern moved me to respond,

"But how can such an enormous venture be achieved without funds and dedication?"

"Dedication you have enough of, and as to money, you do not need it," he declared firmly. "The first thing you should do is to go personally from parent to parent and present this vital need. Declare your willingness to serve and you'll be surprised to find that they'll be enthusiastic and appreciative. You'll even find a free room for your classes."

Then he shoved into my hand a sheaf of twenty-five dollars to order text books.

I was stuck and could not lose time in indecision. The same day I ordered the needed "Readers" for three grades from Cilicia Book Store in New York, and began calling on parents of school-age boys and girls.

Arthur's vision and predictions proved right. I found every one of the friends I visited ardently embrace my plea. They were grateful that some one was interested enough in teaching their youngsters what deplorably they were missing. They even offered to pay ten cents a lesson per child. Mr. and Mrs. Manoog Evkhanian, the parents of two boys and two girls, offered the use of the front room in their Ashtabula Street house as a classroom.

Thus began the first Armenian school in Pasadena in September of 1929. As far as I could ascertain, mine was the first such attempt in Southern California.

The classes were held twice a week, from 6 to 8 in the evenings, for three grades. Fifteen children began to attend. To the credit of those fine boys and girls I must state that there was not even one single drop out during the whole five months I was conducting the classes. We were, both the students and the sole teacher, happy in the educational relationship we were forging.

On a certain day in January I had the great joy and pride of gaining United States citizenship, my fondest dream. This grand gift accorded me the privilege and freedom to travel to Havana, Cuba, meet my fiancée there, marry and bring her with me to Pasadena. But before leaving for Cuba I made arrangements for the continuation of the classes until my return with a young lady, Miss Nazeli Kalubjian, who claimed to have served as a teacher in Beirut a short time previously.

My mind at peace on this score, and having made satisfactory arrangements concerning my business, I left Pasadena at the end of February and returned in May, to be informed by Nazeli that because of the great crash of the American economy the school was disbanded.

To my chagrin, and to the detriment of my beloved students, I soon discovered that a pervasive panic had engulfed the whole country, sparing no one, and that a fresh attempt to revive the school would be futile.

CHAPTER 60

TO HAVANA

THE UNITED STATES DISTRICT COURT of Los Angeles bestowed on me, as on a hundred others, the most coveted honor of American citizenship, on January 26, 1930, after nine years residency in the country. Citizenship usually takes five years, but the delay in my case was caused by a strange quirk of fate: the application bearing the declaration of intention to become a citizen — known as "first papers" — was somewhere mislaid and could not be found for processing. Therefore I was compelled to renew it.

I take pride in noting here that the examiner on the history and Constitution of the United States complimented me as he said that he should step down from his examiner's position to let me take it over. Examination in those old days was strict and stiff.

The first thing I wanted to do after receiving my Citizenship Certificate was to travel to Havana, Cuba, meet my fiancée, Annig Derghazarian (who had been waiting there for me for the last two years), marry her and return together to Pasadena. It was obvious that such a momentous undertaking entailed a considerable sum of money, at least a thousand dollars. In all these nine years I had been scrupulous in meeting my obligations and paying my bills, but my small business had not grown enough to enable me to have a considerable savings account for a "rainy day," or, for that matter, for an eventual journey, wedding, hotel, gifts, honeymoon, and family life.

As I began to assess my financial status, I found that, after paying all the current bills for the next two months (which I did), I would have about $200.00 left. Immediately I began to borrow:

From my life insurance company, $262.00,

From Henry Gertmenian (Hampartzoum), a prominent Oriental rug dealer in San Francisco and a former student of mine, $100.00,

From James Giridlian of Pasadena, a close friend, $32.50,

From my sister Mary, $25.00.

I wrote also to Stephen Philibosian of Boston for a loan of one hundred dollars, promising to pay it back within a year with the interest. Mr. Philibosian, my brother-in-law's cousin, was in the wholesale Oriental rug business, with branches here and there. With his millions earned in the stock market and business, he was for years endeavoring to earn for himself the name and fame of philanthropist (in which he succeeded shortly before his death in the 1970s). Stephen was invariably warm towards me whenever we met. But he chose to refuse my request claiming that it was against his principles to lend money to individuals.

I trusted the operation of my cleaning business to a capable 18-year old friend, Setrak Ekmekjian (later Seth Baker, a psychologist and respected teacher of retarded students). According to our agreement, he was to hold all the income as his wages, and would not be responsible for any bill, expense, or rent until my return in two months.

Short of the desired one thousand dollars, but "rich" with a respectable sum of $620.00, I set on to act. I bought our travel tickets to Havana and back:
For my own train fare $95.00
For my boat fare $75.00
For wife's boat fare $45.00
For wife's train fare $47.00
Total $262.00.

On Thursday night, February 27, 1930, I boarded the Southern Pacific train in Pasadena and arrived at New Orleans, Louisiana, on Saturday morning, March 1. Crossing the Mississippi River was an exciting experience.

I spent the waiting hours in the passenger hall until 4 o'clock when I was, with 78 others, allowed to board the United Fruit Company's beautiful Caribbean Cruiser *Cartago*. The ship docked at her berth in Havana's wharf on Monday, March 3.

My First Day in Havana

As I was about to leave *Cartago* at noon I spied my fiancèe, fresh and desirable, waiting on the quay so expectantly, in company of a matronly lady. As soon as she spotted me after I left the Customs House, she rushed to throw herself into my arms. Soon the carriage she had hired for the felicitous occasion took us three and my luggage to the Greek hotel, Corteles 4, where she occupied a one-room apartment on the fifth floor.

After climbing the seemingly endless steps to the door of our room, Mannig Hanum discreetly left us to ourselves and retired to her apartment a few yards away from ours.

Once in the privacy of our room, my fiancée made me sit on one of her two chairs, knelt down before me, gently laid her arms over my knees and, with folded hands, offered a silent prayer. The solemnity of the gesture was so sacred to me that I did never dare to inquire about the content of that prayer. I surmised that it must have been laden with praise and thanksgiving. I never doubted that that sweet prayer with the swiftness of a dove flew to the presence of the Great Throne.

Prayer over, she brought from a corner of her room a large bouquet of roses and laid it in my lap.

Then she engaged herself to set the table for the two of us, and brought to the table a whole roast chicken, prepared and seasoned with her thousand and one dreams, desires, and prayers. A feast, indeed, for any honored guest, at any time, but I was so overcome by emotion, excitement, and bewilderment that I could not eat a single bite. Neither could she. The feast in front of us remained untouched. In that hour of excitement we were engaged in feasting with our eyes and hearts on each other.

Shortly after, a young lady walked in. She was unknown to me, as everybody else whom I would meet would be. But she, Parantzem Ouzounian, a friend of my fiancée, was the sister-in-law of my childhood chum, Apraham Ateshian of Elmira, New York.

A few minutes after Parantzem we had another visitor, Mr. Sahak Nicolian. He was, my fiancée said as she introduced him to me, the trusted agent she had hired to attend to our official affairs. He had come, Nicolian said, to take us both to the courthouse to have us registered. Mannig Hanum and Miss Parantzem also accompanied us. At the registration our witnesses were Nicolian and the carriage-man. The court clerk advised us to appear on the 19th of March for our marriage certificate.

Officially engaged now, and happy on that score, we came back home anxious to spend those eternally long 16 days as fast as we could.

The only electric light in the room — in any room — would be turned off at 11 P.M. by the hotel management. At that hour, or before, occupants of the hotel rooms had to go to bed. My fiancée had previously made arrangements with Mannig Hanum to let her stay with her at nights, so that I could stay and sleep alone in my fiancée's room. Mannig Hanum was my fiancée's guardian angel.

About my Fiancée

Her name was Annig DerGhazarian,[54] born in Adana, Turkey, on December 25, 1903. Her parents, Melkon Derghazarian and Hayganoosh Arakelian, were both natives of Harpoot who came to Adana to escape the massacres of 1896. But, after surviving those massacres, this ill-fated couple were both killed in the 1909 massacres in Adana. Annig, and her only brother, Manook, 5 and 3 respectively, were picked up from among the mutilated bodies and, later, placed in the Ottoman Orphanage that was specifically built and established by the government for the care of the orphans the Turkish Orgy had left behind.

I have already mentioned in a previous chapter how I met Annig in my mother's house in 1915, the first day I came to Adana. At that time she, with a hundred or more boys and girls, was discharged from the orphanage, to have them all join the innumerable caravans of deportees. Where and with whom she was staying at that time we never learned. Three months after my arrival, we were deported and she was left behind. My acquaintance with her, a child of 12 at the time, was casual and meaningless, therefore during our years of deportation we never had an occasion to remember her.

Many years later we had to learn that a childless couple, Mr. Yervant Kalpakian and his wife Hripsimeh, adopted Annig in Adana and took her with them in 1916 to Constantinople. She was cared for and put through a girls' school (Dubrotsasser Tignantz Varzharan), from which she graduated in 1922 as a registered nurse. Thus she escaped the fatal destiny of the Genocide.

The Web of Hope

Mr. Kalpak, an engineer and an artist, because of his fluency in the German language, was in the employ of the German Army's Engineering Corps. This powerful arm of the German Wehrmacht was eagerly engaged in completing the Berlin–Istanbul–Baghdad Railroad, spurred with the enormous greed of diverting the flow of the coveted Iraqi petroleum to German use.

Kalpaks, though married for 15 years, had their first child, a son, ten months after adopting Annig, and in due time, a daughter. Kalpaks, with the premonition of an imminent disaster, left Istanbul early in 1922 for the United States, barely before the victorious Allied Occupying Forces were forced to abandon the city and scamper to the safety of their respective countries. The advancing forces of Mustafa Kemal's Milli (Nationalist) Army soon stormed and occupied the Ottoman capital, from which erstwhile sultans had ruled an immense empire for 470 years, and thus the Kemalists put an end to both the vaunted sultanate and the venerated caliphate alike.

Annig, left behind to graduate, had to join thousands of orphans to be transported to Greece. There she found her long-lost brother and an uncle, Vartan Arakelian and family. For six years—1922–1928—she served as a nurse all over Greece in the employ of the Near East Relief Organization.

She came to Havana in compliance with my wishes and waited there for my arrival to marry her.

One day in 1919, months after we had returned to Adana as survivors of the Holocaust, Setrak, my brother, brought to Mother a letter written by Annig in Constantinople. It was addressed to a former colleague of Mother's, begging her to deliver it to "Sarah Mayrig" (Mother), if, by any chance, she had returned. In this first letter Annig was recounting, with nostalgic gratitude, all the loving care she had received from "Mayrig" as a child in the Ottoman Orphanage, and, further, she was expressing her joy for our family's return.

Hearing from someone of the pre-Genocide days, about whose living and whereabouts we knew nothing until then, was a great surprise, and a surprise that she should remember us.

As the eldest of the family it was my duty to acknowledge the receipt of the letter. Correspondence continued intermittently as long as I was in Adana. After my departure Setrak had to keep it up. When I was comfortably settled in Chicago I resumed the interrupted exchange of letters, first as a "brother." But gradually the formal mode of writing gave way to more serious and romantic nature. I began writing love poems and acrostics. Then exchange of gifts became frequent.

And one day, in the spring of 1922 when she was about to graduate as a nurse, I wrote to her if she would let me know what plans she had made for her future, and what she really thought of me. Further, I remember promising in that letter not to marry any girl until I heard that she had married someone else. I will never stop wondering what invisible force impelled me to write such a veiled but comprehensible proposal of fateful proportions to a girl whom I had seen as a child only a couple of times, and of whose physical and mental health I knew next to nothing. I have never stopped wondering why I dared to make such an advance when I knew I had no profession, no trade, no skill to earn a comfortable living for myself, and had not formulated a plan for economic security. Yet the die was cast, and the unmeditated inquiry about her plans for her life initiated a long, serious, and romantic correspondence for eight more years.

The political upheavals in Turkey prevented Annig from rejoining her foster parents in New York, but circumstances compelled her to find refuge and opportunity to serve as a nurse in Greece until 1928, whence she came to Cuba to wait for my arrival there.

THE DAYS OF COURTSHIP

During the following two weeks that the Court, after securing our signatures of intention to marry, allowed us to spend in courtship, Annig and I set to housekeeping in our hotel apartment, and went around in taxi or on foot for shopping, visiting, and sight-seeing. Mostly we would retire to secluded spots on the waterfront, sit on the edge of the quay, and dangle our legs over the wall toward the deep blue waters and engage in exchange of nonsense allowed only in the province of lovers. By the hours we would be reading love poems from masters of romance, and watch numerous schools of fish assemble down below to "listen" to the music of our love-laden words and gleeful laughter.

From our room in Old Havana a short walk took us to Main Street and to Parque Central. In the cool of the evenings we would, along with thousands of other couples arm in arm, take a leisurely and pleasurable walk over the half a mile length of the Paseo de Marti, Havana's most beautiful promenade, locally known as "El Prado." First built in 1772 as Paseo de Isabel II, its promenade is time-resisting mosaic marble, flanked on either side by evergreen laurel trees protecting a seemingly endless line of secluded marble benches, ideal spots for lovers.

Havana, the capital of the Republic of Cuba, rightfully called the "Queen of the Tropics," is a sight-seer's paradise. As you walk you cannot but admire the old Spanish architecture all around, especially that of the magnificent churches. You are fascinated by the Spanish-Arabian balconies and windows with wrought iron and wooden bars, public and private buildings, the Capitol, the Opera House, Marti Theater, Jesus Maria Street (the oldest), Peña Street (the narrowest), First of May Street (the broadest), Columbus and Main Memorials, Botanical and Tropical Gardens, Washington, Wilson, Theodore Roosevelt Avenues, famous Moro Castle, and so on and on.

Annig had made quite a few good friends, among whom I came to know:

— Mrs. Mannig Mikayelian, referred to as Mannig Hanum, and her two sons, Aram and Jirayr.

— Yeghia Agha and his wife Nevrig Hanum, an elderly couple from whose apartment a thin wall separated ours. They were living with a son, Yervant, who was a barber.

— Mr. Sarkis Medzmorookian[55] and his wife Bergroohi, a young couple with two daughters, Susan 8, Meline 5 years old.

— Mr. and Mrs. Karnigian. He spoke English, having once been a resident of the United States.

— Mrs. Makroohi, a warm and clean-hearted young lady of about 20.

— Mr. and Mrs. Seyissian, a young couple with a baby.

— Mrs. Takoohi Ouzounian, whom Annig knew in Greece as a colleague in hospitals. She was living in Havana with a son, Nourijohn, and a daughter, Parantzem (mentioned before). Three months earlier her eldest daughter had married my chum Apraham Ateshian of Elmira, New York.

— And other friends.

I found out that Annig was a popular figure in the cultural circle of the Armenian community as a speaker, and she had played in the operetta *Anoosh*. She could recite poems and prose pieces from Armenian authors. But she had not found or looked for a position of service at her profession for the sole reason that she was waiting for her fiance.

The night before the wedding day a sinister event suddenly came to almost tear down "the castle of dreams" we had built together for nearly ten years. While engaged in dreaming and planning for the future in the privacy of our room, a hearty laughter made her plunge into a prolonged fit of asthmatic cough. The shock of seeing before me a helpless and pitiful victim of that dread disease made me shudder. I recalled with sadness that, back home in Pasadena, my brother-in-law Sarkis had been suffering for the past several years with debilitating asthma attacks, causing my sister and me anxiety, agony, and fear. If Annig's coughs were the beginnings of that incurable disease, the thought struck me forcefully, is not the present moment the most opportune time to pack up my things and leave for home immediately? At the sight of her pitiful plight the debate within me did not last long. A voice from within persuaded me that it was my sacred duty to stick by her for better and for worse, because I had come this far just for her, and I had led her all these years to believe in my integrity. I had made her, rightfully or wrongfully, to leave her prestigious and well-paying position in Athens to come to this strange land, expecting that I would descend on her as a "prince" and "rescue" her from her "prison." How could I walk erect as a man hereafter if I forsook her now when she needed compassion and care the more?

After a while — it seemed to me an eternity — the spell spent itself and she left for the "last time" for Mannig Hanum's apartment. She never knew, I never told her, what nightmarish upheaval my sanity and emotions went through that fateful night.

CHAPTER 61

WEDDING DAY

Wednesday, March 19, 1930, Havana, Cuba

At last it dawned, the day of all days, pregnant with untold hopes, dreams, and aspirations.

Nicolian, our faithful agent, put his appearance promptly at 10:00 A.M. to escort us to the Courthouse. Miss Parantzem, Mannig Hanum, and the two little sisters, Susan and Meline, were on hand to ride with us.

At the court the Clerk, in the presence of our company and the two official witnesses — the agent and the cab driver — made us sign at the bottom of the legal documents after asking us a queer question, "For how long are you getting married?" and receiving our firm answer, "Until death do us part."

The Clerk then handed us our marriage certificate, a sheaf of awesome-looking papers, stamped with an embossed seal and tied with a red ribbon. Although the document was in Spanish, we accepted it and his felicitations in good faith. When the legal ceremony was over the Clerk took our pictures in the garden of the Courthouse with the camera I had brought from Pasadena.

The cab brought us back home, and the rest of the company dispersed to their homes to meet again for the affair in the evening.

We were man and wife now, no doubt, in the sight of the law and the world. Yet that fact was not sufficient to make us feel comfortable until a man of God also united us in Christian bond "in the name of the Father and of the Son and of the Holy Ghost." To that end we had previously made the necessary arrangements. Mannig Hanum had put her apartment and her services at our disposal. We had invited a select number of friends. I had also secured the services of Dr. M. N. McCall, the senior minister of the American Baptist Church of Havana, and his young assistant, the Reverend Herbert Caudill.

Wedding Day

In the evening the guests arrived, and a little later the ministers did. But at the moment the ceremony was to take place a slightly uncomfortable situation confronted us: the problem of language, a three-sided dilemma.

The ministers and I (the bridegroom) spoke English, and the rest didn't.

The ministers, the bride, and the guests — all residents of Havana — spoke Spanish, and I didn't.

The bride, the bridegroom, and the guests spoke Armenian, and the ministers didn't.

In order to solve the dilemma Dr. McCall suggested that the ministers perform the service in English and at the end of each sentence I translate it for the benefit of the guests, and then give my own vows and responses, and those of my bride's, in English. The service went on smoothly as I translated each word of the ministers' readings, charges, prayers, and exhortations in the midst of the guests' amused smiles for the humorousness of the unusual proceedings.

I wonder if ever such a wedding took place anywhere.

The bride was dressed in white silk specially tailored for her. Her friend Bergroohi was her matron of honor, her husband Sarkis our best man, and their two child-daughters were our flower girls.

After the ceremony several telegrams from Pasadena and Elmira were read, and Meline, 5, recited a nuptial poem I had written several months earlier and which had appeared in an Armenian weekly in Los Angeles.

The ministers left right after the wedding service, but the guests remained for candy and refreshments.

The Cost of the Wedding

> White silk, 4 yards $6.90
> Dressmaker, $4.00
> Stockings, 2 pairs $5.60
> White shoes, $4.50
> Necklace, $4.00
> Two wedding rings, $9.00
> Candy, refreshments, $4.35
> Taxi to and from Courthouse, $3.50
> Marriage license, $8.00
> For translation of license, $7.00
> To two witnesses, $10.00
> Dr. McCall, $5.00
> Rev. Caudill, $5.00
> Total, $76.85

At the Time of the Wedding

> My name George Barouyr Kooshian
> Hers Annig DerGhazarian
> Place Havana, Cuba
> Date Wednesday, March 19, 1930
> My age 35 (September 25, 1895)
> Hers 26 (December 25, 1903)
> My height 5 feet 6 inches
> Hers 4 feet 8 inches
> My weight 125 lbs. (in 1978 — 125 lbs.)
> Hers 110 lbs. (in 1978 — 145 lbs.)
> My race Pure Armenian stock
> Hers Pure Armenian stock
> Native land Hadjin, Cilicia, Turkey
> Hers Adana, Cilicia, Turkey
> Both penniless, homeless, without backers

Wedding Day

Susan, Bergroohi Medzmorookian, the Bride, the Bridegroom, Meline, Sarkis Medzmorookian

Honeymoon
(March 19–April 26, 1930)

Experience in the Old Country and in the New had taught me to expect bureaucratic red tape, foul-ups, and undue procrastination. For that reason on the morning following the wedding my bride and I rushed to the American Consulate to file an application for her visa. The official in charge carefully examined and retained our marriage certificate for translation, scrutinized and copied my citizenship paper and, after preparing all the necessary documents for the proper departments of the government in Washington, told us to wait about a month or so for the answer, not forgetting meanwhile to charge respectable sums for each transaction he made ($38.00).

Honeymoon, days of starry skies and azure seas! Cloudless, flowery days of golden dreams and fancy! Days, fashioned in heaven and lent to man for a fleeting period that never returns again! Period, in which all cares and worries sulk out of sight and mind! Washington's answer, too, could wait. Period of blindness and bliss!

The honeymooners at Moro Castle

One day we went with some friends to the famed Tropical Gardens where the brewery served free beer as much as one could drink. I was considered by everybody odd and unsociable because I refused to have it served at our table, stating that as a child I had made a solemn vow not to taste any alcoholic beverage. Because of this oddity I had been called an "ass" in Smyrna ten years earlier.

We had learned that Havana had an annual Carnival on Sundays during February and March. We attended one of these spectacular events, having little Susan and Meline as our guests. From our purchased seats we did fully enjoy watching the pageant of masquerading dancers and the music. The hilarity of the light-hearted and boisterous Latins was dazzling.

One of the unforgettable experiences of these days was a visit to the Maine Memorial Monument on the Malecon Boulevard (Seawall Drive), erected by the Cuban government in memory of the 266 American seamen who lost their lives in the battleship Maine disaster on the night of February 11, 1898. This event, I learned, was very intimately connected with Cuban history and that of the United States, since the blowing up of that battleship was instrumental in bringing on the Spanish-American War on April 25, 1898, which resulted in Cuba's liberation, her establishment as a free and independent country.

Incorporated in the Maine Monument are two cannons, anchor chains, and other relics of the Maine.

In this park we admired another monument, the one erected in memory of General Antonio Maceo, great hero of the Cuban War of Independence.

On the morning of April 15 we made a motor launch trip to Moro Castle. The fortress was built across the harbor on solid rock, starting in 1587, at a height of 95 to 125 feet above sea level. Waves of the sea continually break against its base without wearing and tearing it. We landed on real coral steps built by slaves, Indians, and Spanish civil prisoners, nearly four hundred years ago. Old guns and shells, once the pride of Spain, could be seen now on the grounds. The Maine had exploded in the harbor below. We were told that convicts and slaves were the laborers, who, under lash, quarried the coral rock of the Castle structure. The fortification with sea on two sides and 70-foot moats was intended to ward off pirates, and particularly the English captain Francis Drake. Through an aperture in the stone flooring, we were told, prisoners were thrown to the sharks below. We were shown the coral steps leading into dungeons at the bottom of which hungry sharks were waiting for the unlucky prisoner sent down.

On that memorable occasion we met many American tourists and sightseers and had our pictures taken together with some of them.

The time was light in our hands, and we squandered it light-heartedly, visiting cathedrals, churches, and parks.

One day after our wedding a stranger knocked at our door, introducing himself as Sarkis Mulkigian of Fresno, California, a vineyard farmer. He said that he had just got married and was compelled to leave for his farm, which had been left some weeks ago in the hands of friends. He begged in the name of Christ if we would take his bride with us to Pasadena and put her on the train there for Fresno. The distraught man assured us that he had supplied her with enough funds not to be a financial burden to anyone. She was illiterate in her own tongue and also ignorant of English. She was sorely in need of guidance. Our service in such a distressing circumstance, he pleaded, would be highly pleasing to God and would make him and his wife eternally grateful to us.

"We will be more than glad to help you in your need," I answered, calming his agitation. "Instead of taking one bride to California, I will be taking two," I added.

"What's her name?" asked my bride.

"Sanam," he replied.

"Oh, Sister Sanam!" exclaimed Annig excitedly. "I roomed with her sometime ago, and I love her. I am glad to hear you married her."

Mr. Mulkigian left us a happy man. In a few days he was in Fresno attending to his myriad chores in his vineyard.

Later we learned that Sarkis as a young man had fallen in love with the beautiful maiden in their village near Harpoot and asked her hand in marriage, but Sanam's father had rejected the poor suitor and married her to another. The heart-broken Sarkis thereupon (in 1913) had left his love and his village for the United States, thus unknowingly escaping the oncoming holocaust of war and genocide, and in the course of time becoming the owner of a prosperous sixty-acre vineyard on the outskirts of Fresno.

The Genocide devoured Sanam's husband, children, parents, and relatives, permitting her to survive and return to her desolated village to serve at menial jobs. Having heard that Sanam had survived the Annihilation, Sarkis in Fresno, made every effort to have her come to Havana so that he could go there and marry her, his sweetheart of twenty years before.

CHAPTER 62

TO PASADENA WITH A BRIDE (OR TWO)

IN DUE TIME the official papers having been processed and the visas of the two brides granted by Washington authorities, we took passage, on Saturday, April 26, 1930, on the cruiser *Cartago* of the United Fruit Steamship Company. We were assigned to a state room with ample sleeping berths for all three of us. On the morning of the second night on the sea we landed in New Orleans, Louisiana. The checking of our belongings in the customs house and later in the train station did not take too long, leaving an idle afternoon of long hours on our hands. Then I remembered that New Orleans had for decades past a renowned Oriental Rug merchant, Mampreh Dombourian[56] by name. In order to escape the boredom of the station's waiting hall I decided to take my two ladies to see him.

When we entered the trolley car from its rear entrance we took the nearest seats, happy for being on American soil and in an American conveyance, with no one to bother us. A particular instance came to my memory. A few weeks earlier in the Havana Park when I was engaged in the playground pushing little Meline on the swing, a native policeman came over and jabbered at me in a harsh tone. When I asked my bride what he was barking for, she translated that he was ordering me to pick up my coat from the lawn and put it on, if I didn't want to spend time in jail. I had to learn that it was a punishable offense to shed one's coat in a Cuban park, no matter how hot the weather was.

And now all three of us were comfortably seated side by side in an American streetcar, causing no harm to anybody, when the conductor came over with a harsh bark:

"Get out of those seats and go forward, you fools! Don't you know these back seats are for niggers?"

Stung and stunned we found seats among the white. I was from California, and knew nothing of such a degradation, such a discrimination.

At last we arrived at the factory. Mr. Dombourian met us at the door of his office. I introduced myself, my bride, and Sister Sanam. I told him that his name and fame was highly respected in California as a benefactor and that we had come to see him and present our respects.

He was very much pleased with what I said about him. He offered to take us on a tour of his premises first and then of the historic spots of his proud city. From the first floor to the fifth he showed us how the rugs were woven, designs and colors made, damaged rugs made as new and how they were cleaned and hung from ceiling-high beams to dry.

Then he filled us in his car and drove all over the town, stopping, explaining, describing, and reciting history.

Ignoring my apologies for taking up his valuable time away from his duties, he told us firmly that he knew the exact hour when the train left for California and drove his car home. Evidently Mr. Dombourian had called his wife beforehand, because she welcomed us as long lost friends. At dinner we were treated as royalty. Conversation was on church activities and Armenian affairs in general.

At the end of an interesting time with him and his family, he drove us personally to the station and bade bon voyage after seeing us comfortably seated.

On the morning of the third night the train made its stop in Pasadena.

Pasadena Becomes Our Home

As we stepped down from the train that first day of May, 1930, Pasadena—that had been my home town for the last seven years—welcomed us newlyweds with exceedingly cold and frowning weather. This chilly "greeting" made us shiver to our marrow until we heard the warm and cheerful outburst of welcome from the Reverend Samuel Rejebian—the pastor of Cilicia Armenian Congregational Church—who had braved the biting cold of the early morning to meet and transport us to my sister's house.

After seeing us safely at home this man of God left us with a prayer of blessing and best wishes. We found ourselves now surrounded with the wide-eyed scrutiny of the three children and their parents. The main object of their critical inspection was of course my bride, their new auntie and sister-in -law.

Sister Sanam, our travel-companion from Havana, did not escape their curious examination either.

To my pleasant surprise, I found my black Model T Ford sedan's tires adequately inflated and the battery still charged after sitting idly for more than two months. That same evening I drove Sanam to the train for Fresno, after wiring her husband the exact hour of her arrival there.

Our family relationship with this noble couple — Sarkis and Sanam Mulkigian — grew through the years into an intimate friendship. I had the rare privilege of being instrumental in her becoming a citizen of the United States in the fall of 1963. As I pen these words (July, 1983) they still live in Fresno, in extreme old age, in their own home, childless (having had only one child — stillborn). We have often driven there to visit them in their vineyard house, and in later years to their house in the city, and written or phoned.

Sanam, many years later. Sarkis Mulkigian on the left, George Kooshian on the right.

My sister Mary was, naturally, glad to see and welcome her brother's wife, whom she had known fifteen years earlier in the days before the Genocide of 1915, in the Ottoman Orphanage of Adana, Turkey. My intention now was to stay in her house as before, pay our share of rent and household expenses, and be mutually benefited in this way.

But on the advice of some old and experienced friends I decided to take my bride and move to the back of my tailor shop. Inexperience had kept me blind, but the sharper eyes of my advisers had detected that my wife was showing signs of pregnancy and privacy was the most essential need in such a situation.

My small, stuffy, rented shop was the least ideal home to bring a bride full of dreams, ideals, and aspirations; no floor coverings on the cement, no bathing facilities, no household furnishings a bride prides in...

I did not at that time quite appreciate the wisdom of the advice of these dear ladies, but subsequent circumstances proved the move prudent. We learned in no time my sister's husband had developed a growing dislike of my wife and myself, probably because of his frequent asthma seizures, which lasted to the end of his long life. (Mary passed on in June, 1974; he passed on four months later.)

An Attempt At Housekeeping

Heroism, either as a single act of a combination of acts, has never been premeditated, because reasoning and planning have no part in it.

It was merely grim necessity that forced us to leave my sister's house, after a stay of a couple weeks as her guests. It did never occur to me that this moving out would be somewhat like being shipwrecked and thrown on Robinson Crusoe's island.

As newlyweds we had nothing that a beginner needed to start the art of housekeeping. The tired Model T Ford made several trips to and fro to transport my library. Throughout our fifty-three years of our married life my long-suffering wife loved to tease me for having provided nothing for our marriage but books and books and books.

I brought from my sister's house, besides the loads of books and our clothes, the only mattress that I had bought some months earlier. But to our dismay, it was not in the new condition I had left it. In my absence in Cuba my sister had permitted the child of a friend to sleep in it with his mother, and the child had left some indelible marks all over it. My sister kept her sheets, pillows, and blanket. Fortunately we had a couple of woolen quilts.

My wife prudently had them made while in Havana, instinctively sensing the need of them later on. On several apple-boxes found in the neighboring vegetable market we spread our nuptial bed.

Some kitchen utensils and a two-burner cooking stove, generously given to us by a friend, set us on the course of an independent family. Gradually we acquired other cast-offs, second-hands, and also some honest gifts. Yet we were never unmindful of the then enormous financial debt I had incurred for our marriage, travels, and the necessary leisure spent in Havana.

Six months earlier a devastating storm of economic depression had swept all over the country, but I paid not much attention to it. I knew I was poor, had nothing to lose — no bank savings, no bonds or stocks, no mortgaged property to be foreclosed. Wasting no thought on financial losses I had the courage (?) even on borrowed money to go abroad to get married.

Now I began to sense that my favorite customers stopped patronizing me, the income dwindled to trickles, and bills were unpaid.

On October 24 of the previous year, 1929, the first year of Herbert Hoover's presidency, unexpectedly the stock prices plunged drastically and continued downward, dropping day after day. A panic seized the length and breadth of the country. The banks went bankrupt and were compelled to close their doors. Overnight the wealthy and the middle-class became poor, and the poor poorer. Money disappeared from circulation. As we walked down the street, it became common to hear someone ask us,

"Brother, can you spare a dime for a cup of coffee?"

Customers stopped coming to my shop, and my hands did not handle much earned money. Customers' own means of living had also received a severe blow. Most of my trusted customers, who owed me for services rendered on credit, could not pay. And some even became so belligerent that they chased me out of their premises when I dared to ask to be paid.

And now, this slim and small-statured bride of star-studded eyes, with a heart aflame with the fires of ambition and aspiration, with a soul equipped with soaring wings, was confined within the narrow, dank, and depressing walls of a tailor's pressing shop, in a deeply, darkly depressed country—the United States of America.

Sister Esther — An Angel of Mercy

Sister Esther Haigazian, a well-known nurse, educated and having served in Switzerland (she also was the superintendent of the Hadjin orphanage when I was admitted there in 1902), came one day to see Suzanne, the new bride. On learning that she too had been a nurse, serving in Near East Relief hospitals in Greece for the last eight years, she offered to help her as much as she could. True to her word, a few days later she came back with the gift of a nurse's uniform and a cap, and informed her that she had arranged with a doctor so that Suzanne could stay in his home to take care of his sick child.

On the appointed day I drove my wife to Dr. Robinson's home in Flintridge and left her there. After two weeks of care, the child having regained her health, Suzanne returned home happy with the riches of seventy-five dollars.

Some months later Sister Esther told her that a certain doctor in Pasadena was looking for a companion for his sickly wife during her month-long vacation at Surfside Beach. On a Friday evening Dr. Cunningham and his wife came to my shop and drove away with Suzanne to their beach cabin.

At the end of the week the good doctor picked me up and took me to the beach as his guest. My wife was glad to see me each Sunday. The vacation having ended, the vacationers returned home, and Suzanne's joy was great for having been amply paid.

Sister Esther was instrumental for Suzanne's finding a part-time job as a nurse-aid in Pasadena's Womens' Hospital.

Our pressing debts began to be paid.

Bundles of Blessing from Heaven

"A dream revealed to me," wrote my mother from Cyprus, "that your firstborn will be a son, and my intense wish is that you name him after your late father as he named you after his father. Furthermore, you will have the child baptized in your parents' church — the Armenian Apostolic Church. You are free then on to name your future children what you wish."

In due time God blessed us with a son in fulfillment of my prophetic mother's prediction, and we named him Garabed in my father's name and to honor mother's express wish. Then we had the child baptized in the Holy Cross Armenian Apostolic Church of Los Angeles.

Manuel Gertmenian — the future well-known and highly-respected grocery store proprietor in Pasadena and a former teen-aged student of mine in Adana — gladly consented to become baby Garabed's godfather, and remained a good godfather not only to his godson, but also to our other sons, employing each for many years in his markets in different positions preparing them for college and seminary.

Mother blessed us to her dying day for our compliance with her request.

The word Garabed is Armenian. As a common noun it means leader, and as a proper noun, forerunner, after John the Baptist, the "Forerunner" or "Preparer of the way for Christ" (John 1:15, 27). And because Garabed was born in the 11th day of January, 1931, and the same day in 1755 was the birthday of Alexander Hamilton, the first Secretary of the Treasury of the United States in President George Washington's first cabinet, I decided to add Hamilton to Garabed's name. But I had another and more important reason for this addition.

My mother's eldest brother was named Melidon, transliteration of Milton.

At 18, in 1886, for teaching and preaching on moral and religious matters in his home town of Hadjin, situated on the remote Taurus Mountains of Cilicia, young Melidon, accused as a dangerous revolutionary, was arrested by the ever-suspicious Turkish government. And, as it was an unalterable policy of the Turkish courts of justice for the Armenians, without a hearing or trial, he was sentenced to be exiled to the Arabic-speaking far-off seaport city of Acca (the ancient Acre) and cast onto a dungeon. After three years of torture in Stygian darkness, feet in sea water, he left the dungeon in ill-health. He taught in Armenian schools for some years, and with what money he saved he went to college in Tarsus. After his freshman year he was compelled to leave college, teach or preach for a year in a different city, and earn enough money to pay the next year's college tuition. Thus he graduated in eight years instead of four.

After his graduation from Saint Paul's College he entered the Theological Seminary in Marash, and on his completion of his studies he was invited to pastor the Evangelical Church of Sis, once the magnificent capital of the Armenian Kingdom of Cilicia (1080–1375).

In the third year of his ministry, on a beautiful day in April, he and a deacon from his church joined a group of delegates from all the Evangelical churches of the Cilician Mission on its way to Adana to attend the annual Church Conference.

The travel-worn caravan of pastors, deacons, and deaconesses stopped on the last leg of their journey to rest for the night in an inn of a Turkish village, called Saı' Getchit, a couple hours to Adana.

The Turks of the host village that night butchered every single one of those holy men and women, 78 of them, as sheep for slaughter. The Turks piled the bodies in heaps, after robbing them of their possessions and the clothes they were wearing. One of them was my uncle, the Reverend Melidon Malian, beloved pastor of the Church in Sis, who was, as his Lord, the spotless Lamb of God, slaughtered. (A martyred pastor's wife, Mrs. Yepros Topalian, with her throat half-cut but not dead yet, crawled out of one of the heaps, and stealthily, naked as she was, succeeded in making her way back to her home town several days later and made the barbaric massacre known to the world in a series of articles.)[57]

Uncle Melidon's indelible memory was the other and main reason that I added (Ha) Milton to my first son's name Garabed.

Bundles of Blessing (continued)

While my wife was still carrying her first child, Garabed Melidon, she expressed a unique desire that she would give birth to twins. After Garabed's birth we both earnestly prayed over and over again for the Lord to fulfill our desire for twin sons with the solemn promise that we would dedicate, educate, and prepare them to His service as ministers.

My wife woke me up one night to tell me that God had revealed to her in a dream she just had that He would honor our wish and bless our naked nest with twin sons. "Because," she continued, "I dreamed that a mother horse with two beautiful baby foals following her was climbing up our stairway to our own apartment." (We were living at that time in a rented upper-floor apartment.)

"Will you go back to sleep?" I pleaded. "Horses do not climb stairs."

"My horse and foals did. Unbeliever!" she said in reproof, and, turning her back to me, went to personally pursue her fond dream.

Month followed month, and one day her pediatrician confirmed that she was with child. But she would tell the doctor that she was sure that she would give birth to twin sons because she had been praying for that. The good doctor would greet her assertions with a laughter of amusement. But I did not dare to laugh because I was a partner of hers in prayer for twins. At last the doctor, in order to appease her, began to mark her chart with a question mark after the word twins.

Some months later she, as an experienced nurse, felt two different heart beats inside of her besides her own, and when she reported the fact to her doctor he examined her more carefully and, being convinced that she was right, he took x-ray pictures of her that proved without doubt that the twins were in fact there.

The babies were growing fast and heavy for her frail frame. The doctor, in fear of complications, ordered her to the hospital on her eighth month and coaxed two husky babies to step out into the light. The first of the twins weighed 5 pounds 6 ounces, the second 5 pounds 3 ounces.

[Ed.—The manuscript ends at this point. The twins, born on November 5, 1934, were named Percy Victor and Roy Malcolm. On May 15, 1941, a fourth son was born, George Barouyr Jr. Their mother Suzanne raised them with a determined will in spite of her chronic debilitating athsma. She died in her own home on October 28, 1982. George B. Kooshian, Sr., worked as a tailor to support his family. After the hardships of the Depression, and through the strenuous efforts of his wife, they were able to buy property across from the tailor's shop on Washington Street and build a two-story building with an apartment on the second floor and shops on the ground floor. The toll of living behind a dry cleaning establishment with its hot, steamy presses was heavy on Suzanne's health and she was relieved to move into a proper house. She made it, despite her frail condition, into a home where guests were welcomed and food was abundant.

The food was prepared according to elaborate old-country recipes, many of which were taught to her by her sister-in-law Mary. They were more often than not referred to by their Turkish names, reflecting the common language of Cilicia. They included *sarma*, stuffed vine leaves, and *dolma*, stuffed vegetables, and *kufteh* of two types, one a paste of finely ground lean lamb and *bulghur* (cracked wheat), served raw in the summertime, often with a madzoon-and-cucumber salad called *jajukh*, and the other a shell of a similar meat paste stuffed with seasoned ground meat, that could be served in a *madzoon* soup. Meals were accompanied by rice or bulghur *pilav*. Various stews were prepared of lamb with eggplants, squashes, or okra. *Lahmajoun*, a meat and bread pie, was the project of a whole day. The remains of a fowl or pieces of lamb could be cooked down with wheat or barley kernels into a tasty mush called *harisa* or in Turkish, *keshkek*, served with paprika and olive oil or butter.

Trips to the Armenian grocery store brought back Armenian bread, cheese, *bastegh* (dried sheets of fruit juice paste), *basturma* (beef tenderloin cured with fenugreek), halvah, and salty black olives, but the best baked goods were prepared at home. These included butter cookies called *khurebiyeh* and *cheoreg*, a stuffed roll, but most spectacularly, *pakhlava*. Suzanne learned this by acquiring the secret from baker Melekian's wife Anna Hanum, in payment of an obligation. Mistakes were eaten by the children. Suzanne loved cooking for her family and guests, and particularly gathering vine leaves and olives, which grew around Pasadena.[58]

Church attendance and Bible study were essential parts of family life, to the extent that Percy and Roy received the call to the ministry. Although the family's means remained modest, education was valued and all four sons graduated from Pasadena public schools and community college and later pursued advanced studies. All went to military service. Charles saw combat in Korea with the United States Air Force. Percy, Roy, and George served in the Army. After he returned from the war, Charles received his Master's degree in Engineering from San Jose State College. He lived in Hayward and Livermore, California, Las Vegas, Nevada, and Los Alamos, New Mexico. Percy and Roy both attended Westmont College and Fuller Theological Seminary and were ordained as Ministers of the Gospel. They became pastors of churches in Oregon, Wyoming, and Montana. It pleased God to receive Roy on May 18, 2001 in Billings, Montana, while he was still actively serving his congregation. George, the editor of this volume, is a teacher in Los Angeles and received his Ph.D. from UCLA in Armenian History. He lives in Altadena, California with his family. All four sons married and were fathers of families and raised children.]

EDITOR'S EPILOGUE

On Sunday, April 26, 2015, the Reverend Father Sarkis Archpriest Petoyan ascended the altar of Saint Gregory the Illuminator Armenian Apostolic Church in Pasadena, California, carrying on a platter a golden reliquary. Within this reliquary was the fragment of a human bone collected on one of the fields mentioned in this book. Seven days earlier in the same church there had been a service for the repose of souls. Remembered in this service were the million and a half Armenian Christians that had been sacrificed at the hand of the Turk in the early part of the twentieth century and in the one preceeding. The faithful in attendance laid flowers before a memorial stone, or khatchkar, in front of the entrance to the church.

But the service on this Sunday was entirely different. For three days before, on April 23, at Holy Etchmiadzin in Armenia, the Martyrs of the Armenian Genocide were enrolled in the Martyrology of the Armenian Church and April 24 was declared to be their feast day. From henceforth no longer, Father Petoyan explained, would there be any more requiem services for those faithful who had died, but they would be celebrated in hymns and invoked to interceed for us:

> O blessed and Holy Martyrs, rendered wise through the heavenly light; you have been like the grain of the wheat and have with a manifold crop of faith fructified our land of Armenia. Pray to God that He may keep our land in safety.
>
> You have been glorified with exceeding glory by the Father and have become more resplendent than the sun, becoming worthy to reign with Christ. Pray to God that He may preserve our homeland in magnificence.[59]

Then was fulfilled the word of the Lord that was spoken by the prophet Ezekiel:

> The hand of the Lord was upon me, and carried me out in the spirit of the Lord, and set me down in the midst of the valley which was full of bones, and caused me to pass by them round about: and, behold, there were very many in the open valley; and, lo, they were very dry. And he said unto me, Son of man, can these bones live? And I answered, O Lord God, thou knowest.
>
> Again he said unto me, Prophesy upon these bones, and say unto them, O ye dry bones, hear the word of the Lord. Thus saith the Lord God unto these bones; Behold, I will cause breath to enter into you, and ye shall live: and I will lay sinews upon you, and will bring up flesh upon you, and cover you with skin, and put breath in you, and ye shall live; and ye shall know that I am the Lord.
>
> So I prophesied as I was commanded: and as I prophesied, there was a noise, and behold a shaking, and the bones came together, bone to his bone. And when I beheld, lo, the sinews and the flesh came up upon them, and the skin covered them above: but there was no breath in them. Then said he unto me, Prophesy unto the wind, prophesy, son of man, and say to the wind, Thus saith the Lord God; Come from the four winds, O breath, and breathe upon these slain, that they may live. So I prophesied as he commanded me, and the breath came into them, and they lived, and stood up upon their feet, an exceeding great army.
>
> Ezekiel 37:1–10

APPENDIX I

ANECDOTES RELATING TO FATHER

One

One day my father brought me a kid with whom I fell in love at first sight. He was so lovely, irresistibly so. I carried him around in my tiny arms. As he grew heavier day-by-day, my strength failed to accommodate him with free transportation. So, holding the guide-rope around his neck, I led him hither and thither, at first in the neighborhood, then farther in the town, and, eventually, into the woods which skirted the town. He would graze contentedly as I ventured to explore the unknown.

One afternoon, after such a pleasant excursion into the forest of pines, the little devil decided in his goat's mind that he wouldn't come home with me. I talked to him in sweet tones, coaxingly, imploringly, but he wouldn't move. Then I tried to drag him by the rope; still he chose to stand his ground, refusing to give an inch of submission. My strength failed me, my patience got exhausted, and desperation mounted to an unbearable degree. During my lifetime of more than three-quarters of a century, I have encountered many an obdurate man and obstinate woman, but looking back now I deem that none could compare with that diabolos in the guise of a charming goat.

The day was already hurrying away, the darkness and strangeness were slowly tiptoeing towards us in the gradually chilling forest air, but the kid continued to be mean, driving me to streams of tears.

I grabbed a stick and fiercely beat the helpless animal, as cruelly as a child can.

A few days later, Father decided that the time had come to slaughter the little goat. As I watched the slaughter, the gush of the red stream from the slashed throat did not affect me so much as the telltale blue and purple stripes of the lashings I had administered upon his back. What senseless cruelty I had heaped upon him in secret was revealed in public to my father, mother, and all the onlookers when Father skinned the hapless animal.

The magnitude of the shame and remorse that overwhelmed me at that time crushed me to bitter tears over my crime.

Two

ANOTHER DAY, fastening the kid to a tree in a secluded spot, and leaving him to graze within the radius of his rope, I let my feet push me deeper into the forest in search of new worlds for a child of five or six to explore. In a clearing some distance away, I discovered a huge rock with an opening on one side. Crawling through it, I found myself on top of some steps going down.

As I descended the few steps, a new set of steps came to view, while the top ones left behind vanished. Fear at that time had not yeinfidelt shown its forbidding countenance to me. So I continued my descent on these subterranean magic steps into darkness. At the bottom, a shaft of light and a gush of fresh air invited me straight forward to a spacious open air circular space. It was filled with the debris of broken-down pillars, seats, and ruined walls. Finding nothing to amuse my childish interests, except a number of multicolored lizards basking on rocks and unmoved by my presence, I climbed back the same way I had come.

Knowing not that I had climbed down a helical (spiral) staircase into the arena of a ruined amphitheater of the Seleucidan Era, I related my adventure to my father that evening. His interest in my story took us both back there the next day. Dim echoes of the scanty information he gave me about the place limpingly lingered with me, until many years later, I learned to my horror that at that moment, I was gazing on an arena whose sand-covered floor had been soaked in human blood. Many a gladiator, his gladius (sword) in hand, stood on that ground, either to kill his adversary or be killed by him, on occasions by a beast. And the elite of the people, seated around the amphitheater, amused themselves with the sight of the gory spectacle. Gladiatorial combats were supposed to be derived from the custom of human sacrifice at funerals of heroes or of warriors fallen in battle, the victims being captives, slaves, criminals, or disgraced nobility.

THREE

A PONDEROUS TOME of a book had my father so fascinated that he spent hours reading it. So large it was, and heavy, that I was not permitted to hold it, nor to touch it. At that tender age, I was instilled with a wholesome awe towards it, although unable to comprehend the meanings of the words *Asd-va-dza-shoonch*, *Theopneustos*, The Breath of God, and *Soorp* (holy). I was made to understand the careful and diligent reading of it made the reader good, respectable, holy, and wise.

A swiftly fleeting view flashes before my inner eyes momentarily.

One hot summer day, sitting on his *chardak* (wooden porch, erected only for the summer months), Father was deeply engrossed with the reading of his precious Bible, oblivious of Mother's repeated calls to lunch or even of the evening's approach. Suddenly a fierce wind from unknown quarters brought down the whole structure of the chardak upon him and his Bible. Neighbors, just returning from their days' work, rushed to his rescue, and found him pinned down by a broken beam whose sharp point had stopped on a verse of the open Bible: "His Truth shall be thy shield and buckler."

The crowd that immediately gathered around the wreck wagged their heads in amazed awe at the unexpected miracle the Holy Book had wrought. But some skeptics continued to use Father's punishment as an example to warn each other from delving into the mysteries of nature and God's business.

FOUR

A CHERISHED MEMORY of Father before his tragic death is in connection with the incident of the little girl who fell into the tanner's pit.

A gentleman of the tanning trade had a pit dug near our house, in which he used to soak hides or skins in lime-saturated water. Without the slightest consideration for human or animal safety, this tanner had very conveniently left the rim of the infernal pit unfenced. In those days, the idea of a warning sign, boarding-off, or any kind of protection was unknown. The pungent stench arising from this miniature hell infiltrated every house and polluted the air of the paradise that Seleucia was, but no one thought of filing a protest that would have had no effect anyway.

The children of the neighborhood were naturally attracted by the bubbling of the noxious gasses in the pit; they would sit on the edge, dangle their unsteady legs downward, throw pebbles down on the hides and chatter with each other in utter fascination.

One afternoon, while my sister of four and another girl of her own age were sitting on the rim and babbling with each other, all of a sudden the girl fell into the "lake" of noxious sulphur and lime. My sister, instinctively grasping the fatality of the situation, ran towards our house, screaming for help. Fortunately Father was home at that particular time, and hearing the terror-stricken shrieks of his daughter, came out and jumped into the pit holding the lifeless child.

Jumping out, Father held the limp body upside down until someone from the gathering crowd brought a piece of rope. Father tied the victim's feet to a branch of a nearby tree, as he had hung my kid some short time earlier to skin him. A painful fear pervaded my whole body thinking that he would skin her too, but gradually I calmed down when I saw that he was patting the child's stomach and back until a stream of impure waters poured out of her mouth.

After a while, her parents arrived, and took the girl who at last showed a slight sign of life. She was immediately put to bed and nursed. Next morning we children were told that the girl had been revived and was expected to live.

Her parents and concerned neighbors from that day on began to praise my sister and father so much that I thought my sister was an angel come from heaven, and my father's medium and slim stature grew taller and taller in my sight until he became a giant. His countenance was bathed with the glory of the sun, and I imagined seeing an invisible hand placing a crown of gold on his head. No child ever walked prouder for having such a hero for his father and a tiny heroine for a sister.

What became of that girl, none of us knew, because before she could leave her sickbed, we left Seleucia never to return. On the way to our destination, Father died, many muddy waters flowed under the bridge, and at last Sister and I found ourselves in the United States of America.

Anecdotes Relating to Father

For a period of over six years it was my good fortune to live with my sister and her family.

One day, twenty-seven years after the tragic accident told above, my sister received a letter in Pasadena, California, from Aleppo, Syria. The sender's name as written on the envelope was totally strange to both of us. But as we read the letter, the stranger was expressing her gratitude to my sister for saving her life from the tanner's pit in Seleucia years before, and was begging her to accept as a small token of her appreciation a package of exquisite needlework pieces. She had obtained our address, she said, from our mother and brother who were visiting Syria at that time, and she had the unexpected pleasure of meeting them.

APPENDIX II

Anecdotes Relating to Mother

One

The offense I had committed that afternoon, at play, shouted out from within me so loudly that, I was very sure, mother had heard it. I never knew what real misery was until that moment. My conscience, it seemed to me, had been piercing my heart with the sharp-pointed awl my father was using in his trade.

When I walked inside the door, with downcast eyes, I began to search for a crack to hide myself from my all-knowing mother, but the dirt floor of the house refused to lend me one. But Mother, after sizing me up with a wise and penetrating gaze, quietly took down the gourd of ground red pepper from the nail on the wall, and serenely told me to open my mouth.

Sensing what was coming up, I opened my mouth, not specially to obey her, but to let out a bitter cry. At my scream she set the gourd aside, and began gently to explain to me that what I had done that afternoon was unbecoming to a child of hers. "Besides, it was a sin against God, who hates sin. No good boy ever does or says anything to displease those who love him — his mother and God. This sin you have committed today must be completely put out of you now for your eternal good."

"But Mother," I dared to ask in amazement and supplication, "how did you know what I did? Did you hear the shout that came from inside of me?"

"One of the neighbors," she said, "heard you curse one of your playmates in retaliation."

Then she continued to explain that the use of obscene words is a very bad habit, a low grade of speech, which brings no honor or value to those who use them.

After a few more words in her gentle way she repeated her command to open my mouth.

Anecdotes Relating to Mother

Sarah Malian Kooshian in Cyprus, 1941

I had vainly hoped that she had forgotten her first command to punishment after so much gentleness, but she was wise, kind, yet firm.

I had no other recourse but to comply.

"This," she infidelsaid, squeezing a generous pinch of red hot stuff between her thumb and index finger, "will sterilize your mouth from the germs of profanity making their nests in you. The burning memory of this experience will go with you all your life to immunize you. From now on you will find loathsome, distasteful, all vulgarity, dirty stories, swearing, unnecessary oaths, disrespect towards yourself and others."

More than three quarters of a century later I can testify to the efficacy of Mother's remedy administered in the tenderest days of my childhood.

Two

ANOTHER DAY, Mother needed some powdered red pepper. Until this day I do not know for what special purpose she was going to use it, but I am sure that it was not for the correction or seasoning of my speech. If it were so, I believe, the horrible thing that happened that moment would not have happened.

She walked straight to the nail on the wall in the half-dark niche, took the brown gourd down and thrust her combined fingers through its narrow neck to bring out a pinch, but instantaneously dropped the pumpkin shell with an agonized shriek.

What caused this woman of unusual composure and tranquility to lose her serenity so suddenly? Father instantaneously jumped up, and looking inside the gourd discovered the hideous form of a scorpion with an elongated body and segmented tail with which it stung Mother injecting its venom. What a scorpion was doing in a dark peppery bed was beyond human comprehension, but there it was comfortably nestled, who knows since when, and, probably, contemplating producing an army of equally repulsive baby scorpions.

Father didn't waste time to think what to do with the culprit. In no time he crushed it, and crushed all its dreams of producing an army of future scorpions.

Somebody covered Mother's poisoned hand with a thick coating of madzoon[60] (yoghurt), repeating the procedure rapidly. Thus the coolness and the curative property of madzoon served to retard the swelling and the excruciation of the pain.

"Why didn't you look before putting your hand inside the gourd," someone thoughtlessly reprimanded Mother, suffering as she was. Mother wisely ignored the reproach. But ever since I have been pondering that question whenever a human "scorpion" has stung my hand stretched to help.

THREE

GÖK SÜ, the famed Calycadnus of antiquity, had, at that tender age of five or six, an inexplicable fascination for me, that same river that had lured Seleucus Nicator tewnty-two centuries earlier to build on its banks a city in his name. It seinfidelemed to my subconscious an immensity of water that had issued from the bosom of future eternity. An endless land of enchantment began to extend from the other bank of the bridgeless river, that I imagined, must be the Garden of Eden, the dreamy story Twoof which my father had read to us from a book that he held in high esteem.

From that magic land across the river I could hear with my inward ears faint notes of heavenly melodies wafting towards me, but the covetous Gök Sü captured them in mid-air and carried them away wrapped in its mighty roar.

A foot-beaten trail would often take us to the river not too far for a tiny child to walk with his mother. In compliance with her admonishing I would play under the huge willow tree not too near the water's edge, while she busied herself with the family wash, a whole day's affair in those days. We carried the washables on our backs in bundles, a tiny bundle on my back, and the rest on Mother's sturdy back.

Once at the river, she would build a fire pit with proper stones and set the kettle on the fire, the kindling of which was brought also by Mother. She would add to the boiling water in the cauldron a handful or two of pure oak ashes for the purpose of softening the river water or sterilizing and whitening the boiling laundry. Taking the boiled clothes out of the pan, she would beat them on a huge rock, then soap them, rub them and soak them again. Then take time to feed us, her two children. It was of no consequence to her if she ate or not, the embodiment of self-sacrifice. Then she would resume the toilsome process with the remainder of the wash until the sun-dried pieces spread on rocks were gathered and folded into bundles.

Before the sunlight and warmth of the day were spent, she would give us children a good bath, scrubbing, rubbing, soaping head, limbs, and all, ridding us from the dirt we had collected, the dirt that only children know how to collect. It was her custom after such a thorough bath to hold firmly onto my hands and plunge me into the river. On one occasion, forgetting to keep my mouth shut under the water, I swallowed the whole river, at least it so seemed to me. And was astonished that Gök Sü still continued to roll on after I had drunk it all.

Another object of irresistible charm was a "house" floating on the river. This house was not like the one I or my playmates lived in. Yet women walked into it with bags and after a while came out with the same bags on their backs and went to their homes in the city. How intensely I dreamed of walking into that house of magic, gathering up some mysterinfidelious playthings and walking out to my home.

One day Mother threw a bag on her shoulder and walked with me the short distance to the "house of wonders." When we walked in, Mother handed her heavy sack to a man who seemed to be the only person living in this house. This man was like no man I had ever seen. He was altogether white from head to foot. He took Mother's bag and emptied its contents into a bin from the bottom opening of which brown-colored grains poured slowly through a hole in the middle of a huge round flat moving stone. Right under this stone there was another stone exactly like itself in size and shape, upon which the first stone rotated with a rattling, clattering noise. When I noticed that the brown stuff pouring down turned to a pure white stuff around the bottom rock, I became convinced that this man was the magician of the "house of magic," with the ability of mysteriously turning one substance into another, even turning himself into a white being.

Mother shouldered the sack of white powder, and together we walked home. On the way she explained to me that this house of magic on the river was a mill where wheat is ground into flour through the help of the man covered with flour. This flour we were taking home now, she explained, would be made into bread for us to eat. She continued to explain to me that the mill was operated through the river-water forcing some wheels that made the round stone turn over the other round stone and both together crushed the grain into flour.

The fascination of the mill and my admiration of the miller has never diminished to this day.

One day, many months later, a torrential rain of several days' duration forced the river to swell up in rage and overrun its banks, spreading itself over outlying fields and sweeping away the mill and miller, the favorite willow tree under which I had spent hours of play, gardens, animals, houses, children and men, and, worst of all, a playmate of mine.

I began grieving over the sorry conditions that took place, and Mother, seeing my morbid brooding, made a valiant attempt to straighten my unripe thinking and enlighten me with her wise interpretation.

"Change," she said, "is the dominant law of life. Everything you see around you now, will change sooner or later. Every day something you don't know about will happen to change the things you see and know. By the falling of the heavy rains changes took place. Change is not always bad. There are good changes, too. Don't worry, don't grieve for changes. God makes the Change. Trust God…"

The rage of Gök Sü shortly after quieted down, the mill and the miller came back to their accustomed spot, women resumed their washing on the river bank, and life returned to normal.

"Trust God," said Mother.

APPENDIX III

Letters From Uncle Haroutune
First Letter: About My Mother, sent from Amiantos, Cyprus, in 1928

When my eldest sister Sarah went to be Garabed Agha Gejekooshian's wife we could hardly realize to what a heroic life she was destined. Neither did she have any inkling of what multiform hardships were in store for her.

Calamity Strikes Again

A few years after she had left our home a second calamity struck my family. The first was our brother Melidon's exile. The second disaster was the arrest and banishment of our father and stepmother. Suddenly I, a child of five or six, found myself all alone, terrified, in tears. Having heard of the devastating blow, my beloved sister Sarah rushed to our house, dried my tear-washed cheeks and carried me in her ever-tender arms to her home.

It was in that house that I came to know what a God-sent angel she had become for her new family. At the time I came to live there, there were ten people living under one roof, all depending on her, expecting of her, commanding care and attention. Besides myself and herself, there were the patriarch and his spouse, their eldest son with wife and three very young daughters, their only daughter about the age of my sister. The house we ten were living in was one comparatively large room that served as sitting room, bedroom, sickroom, sewing room, dining room, and storage room, with an adjoining nook set aside for cooking.

"Sister, where is your husband?"

Having no one else in the whole world, now I was clinging to her as a sprig of ivy clings to the face of a cathedral. I was inseparable from her, dogged her constantly. The days added up to weeks and months, and, not seeing her husband in the house at all, I asked one day, "Sister, where is my *Kerayr* (brother-in-law)?"

Her eyes welled up with tears, and pressing me to her heart, she told me that a few weeks after their wedding her bride-groom had left the city with his younger Brother Bedros for *Séhél* to earn money and send home to support the large family.

"What is *Séhél*?" I asked, and she told me it was a far-off country where men go to find work. She said that these two men in the past six years could send home money hardly enough for one member of the family to be fed and clad one year. Very little money, partly because of the unfaithfulness of the messenger entrusted with the cash, and partly because of joblessness, sickness, temptations, personal support and inability to save in inhospitable surroundings.

"Just a few more stitches, darling!"

Missing the warmth and security of her arms around me, in the early months of my stay with her, I would wake up at nights, and, seeing her still sewing (no sewing machine in those days), sewing by the flickering dim light of a tired oiled wick or the deceptive flame of a pine stick, "Come to bed, Sister," I would beg, "I am cold and lonely." "Just a few more stitches, darling," she would invariably answer, "I will be with you shortly."

Second waking up. Second entreaty. The same answer from her to me. Same answer night after night, week after week. She was supplied with heaps of sewing, because she was a mistress in the art of sewing.

During the daytime she carried water to the houses of the rich, or to the public ovens where women needed water for the dough of their fortnightly bread baking. She had a narrow-throated copper jug on her back padded with a quilted saddle.

She was still in her 'teens, beautiful, tall, gracious, wise, and industrious, consequently very popular. She could always find something to do,e and with the wages she earned, meager though they were, she could feed and clothe her entire family.

"*Séhélji*s are coming!"

Every now and then a rumor would be afloat that the eagerly awaited beloved *Séhélji*s were coming home. Such hearsay immediately would heighten our hopes, thin our patience and accelerate our impatience. But our own *Séhélji* would not show up. In those blighted days of her disappointment I would often overhear my forlorn sister's heart-rending prayers hallowed with tears for the safe and early return of her groom whom grim Fate had separated from her even before she had a chance to know him. In those days hers was just one of the thousand similar crushing cases.

One day the rumor was verified by a *Séhélji* returning from the same parts, who told my sister that her husband with his brother would be home next Saturday. On that Saturday the whole town was on foot, and in festive mood went some miles outside the city to welcome the pilgrims of seven years absence, and escorted them to the city with music, dancing, merry-making, and fireworks.

The first stop for the *Séhélji* would be the church, where prayers of thanksgiving would be offered, a generous donation made and alms given to the poor. The conventions of the times demanded that the returnees should not go home directly, but should rent a separate room away from home to receive and entertain visitors and friends, and go home to their wives and children when visiting ends.

The "Bewitched Donkey"

In the first few days of his arrival I discovered that I was not half as happy over my brother-in-law's homecoming as I was over the fact that he had brought with him a donkey. It was a Cyprian donkey, much larger than the ordinary donkeys I had seen in the town. There was something noble about him, proud but with a veil of sorrow covering his face. Immediately I chose to imagine that this donkey was a prince once, but a witch turned him into a donkey. He seemed to me as big as a camel I had seen in the market place, and being seen with this prince of a donkey would, I was convinced, make me the object of envy among the boys of the town. To be an object of envy, to be admired as superior, is the dream of every boy.

My brother-in-law must have read in my eyes the greatest of my desires — he was the wisest man in the world — because he conferred on me the title of the official caretaker of the prized donkey. At once I built in my childish mind a magnificent castle of joy and happiness, with the prospect of spending my life in it in company of this "prince."

Without wasting another minute, I ran to the stable under the house, and loosing his rope I talked to him in the sweetest tone I could muster. I remember telling him that from now on he and I are brothers, and I will be happy to take care of all his needs as long as he stays in the form and guise of a donkey. "Because," I said to him nodding my head, "I know who you really are, an evil witch made you a donkey." Then I asked him point blank, if he would mind if I rode on his back when I teook him to the public trough for a drink. The graceful animal, moving his ears up and down, silently and in no uncertain way answered me that he wouldn't mind at all. And to my delight, he brayed a firm approval of me.

So, feeling encouraged by his reception of me, I pulled him outside and managed to climb on his back. Once on his back, surrounded by a crowd of children of the neighborhood, proudly exclaimed, "*Cho!*" (Let's go). But, to my utter shame and dismay, he moved not an inch. Thinking he failed to hear me in the turmoil of the spectators, I repeated my plea, but no response was coming. I prodded him with my feet, entreated him, but he wouldn't move. In exasperation, I dismounted and angrily pulled on his bridle. This time the stubborn animal gently followed me to the water-trough and drank his fill. At this point my irritation having subsided, I thought the noble animal had a change of heart, and would grant me the ride that would stir up the envy of my friends.

So I rode him again, but no! The brute had no change of heart or mind; he was simply a stubborn ass. He stood there as if nailed down. When I got down and pulled, the great Cheat followed me to the stable. Then and there I decided that he was not an enchanted prince, therefore, I renounced him as my "brother." We never became friends again, because he never let me ride him, although he willingly let his master ride him.

I was glad when my brother-in-law sold him a short time after and relieved me from the thankless job of caring for an ungrateful brute.

The Web of Hope

He Was Always on the Move

After the foregoing parenthetical rambling let me return to your mother's story.

She valiantly endured another period of loneliness when her husband left for *Séhél* after a few months. But this time his going-away lasted only two years, and in due time you were born. That year was a happy one for all of us; my sister had her husband, her first, and me.

At this time your father's partnership with his elder brother having been dissolved, he took his family out of his parental home which was still unoccupied, because none of my folks — father, mother, or brother — had returned from banishment. After seeing us settled, he left for Seleucia where, on a previous "*Séhél*-going," had seen his younger brother married and settled. My sister again began to earn our living, this time, fortunately, a smaller family. But, in justice to my sister, I must add that she never forgot to rush to the needs of the large family of her in-laws.

The Garden Yields Us a Living

At that time it occurred to us that our maternal grandmother, having moved to Sis (two days journey to the south of Hadjin), had left behind an orchard about five miles outside the city. This abandoned property had a number of fruit trees, a small tillable plot for planting seasonal vegetables, and a hut for shelter. Immediately we decided to take it over and make it yield us a living. Laborers were hired for digging and pruning. Sister and I planted seeds, irrigated the furrows, fertilized the soil, shooed the omnivorous unwelcome birds by fixing up couple of scarecrows and prayed away the destructive pests, thieves and natural elements, while you by our side were wrapped in your swaddling clothes.

When, at last, the warmer season arrived, and the early fruits began to smile at us, we moved to "our" orchard. My sister would climb the trees, or I would at times, and carefully pick the best fruits — mulberry, cherry, apricot, peach, plum, figs, apple. Soon my goods would be sold at good price, and I would return to my sister cash jingling in the pails and joy singing in my heart. This procedure kept us going happily on until the end of the fruit season, and with a good supply of winter vegetables.

Sudden Sickness

But suddenly I fell sick. With a tiny baby on her hands, and no doctor or medicine available for me, I became for my sister a source of bitter anguish. The worst part of the whole situation was that I was old enough now — thirteen years old — to realize that the weight of my sickness, combined with her "forced" widowhood, was pressing harsher on my only guardian, my dearest angel. Yet, night and day, she would spare nothing to make me comfortable, for she had, by sheer superhuman effort, snatched me from the clutches of "Death with the pale stare." And, whenever she found her skill and strength ebbing, she would fall on her knees to beg divine succor for us.

A Voice from the Banished

One day, in the fall, while I was recuperating in my bed having passed the crisis, a caravan-master entered the door and handed a letter to my sister, adding that our brother Melidon came to see him in Tarsus and begged him to deliver the letter to us. We could not believe our ears. As far as we knew, he was still in banishment, if not already dead. This man told us, furthermore, that Melidon Effendi requested him to bring me to him in Tarsus on the return of the caravan. When he saw me weak with sickness, instead of relenting, he became the more firm in his determination to keep his promise to take me to his highly esteemed friend in whose return from banishment he found boundless joy. Handing us, besides the letter, some cash that, he said, our brother had sent, he left us with a parting word that he would return for me in three days.

Our bewildered joy was great. We knew nothing about our brother's freedom from exile, and not a single word had reached us about our banished father and stepmother. The reading of the letter confirmed all that the caravan-master had told us. Furthermore, we learned that Melidon was a student in Jenanian College of Tarsus (later known as St. Paul's College), and wanted me enrolled in the Elementary Department of the Institute.

With laughter and tears, joy and sorrow, Sister busied to prepare food, clothing, and other necessities for my travel, and gifts to our "resurrected" brother. At times, during the three days of extraordinary activity, her lovely face would brighten up at the anticipation that under our beloved brother's watchful eyes I would become an educated man like him and make her feel proud of me.

On the specified day the caravan-master came, and pulling me gently out of my sister's embrace, the only real "mother" I had known, set me on the back of one of his pack beasts and moved on, leaving her with the stream of tears and the cries of her baby.

To Tarsus

Cambess Agha, the caravan-master, brought me to Tarsus after a journey of six days, a very miserable one for me. Neither the mountain air, nor the sunshine of the plains could give me healing and vigor. I could eat nothing, and could find no rest or enjoyment in anything. No one cared for me. My longing for the sister I left in Hadjin was pulling me backward, and the hope of being with my now "resurrected" brother in Tarsus was pulling me forward. But the villains in the caravan feasted on the abundant provisions my sister sacrificially had prepared for me and my brother, and the many gifts I was taking to him were cruelly stolen.

I cannot recall how we arrived at the inn in Tarsus. I was abandoned there in delirium until I opened my eyes in my brother's loving arms.

Finally, after some years here and there, my love for my sister made me return to Hadjin, where, to my pleasant surprise, I saw that my father had returned from his banishment and had married anew. He had lost his second wife right at the beginning of their arrest and imprisonment. I was pleased also to find my sister the mother of another baby, your sister. But your father was gone again, leaving her with two small children to shift for herself.

Sometime later Sister took her two children, left our home, left Hadjin, and traveled a long journey to Seleucia to be with her husband. She remained in Seleucia two years, during which time she gave birth to her third child, your brother Setrak. At the end of the two years, your father decided to return to Hadjin with his growing family, but, unfortunately, before bringing his family to Hadjin, he passed away in Adana, leaving you stranded and unprovided-for in a strange part of the country.

That year, 1902, by the design of Providence, our brother Melidon was in Hadjin engaged in school teaching and preaching. We all were grief-stricken at the news of the calamity visited on you, and immediately Brother went to see his friend the caravan-master, paid him in advance and sent him after you. Some months after your arrival at our home, Brother talked to Reverend Fidler for you, and to Miss Rose Lambert for your sister Mary, and you two older children were admitted to the American Orphanage in September of the same year.

Second Letter: About Himself, Sent from Amiantos, Cyprus, in 1930

I THINK you would like to know a little about myself.

I was born in Hadjin sometime in 1883. Two more children followed me, but didn't like the looks of things around them and hurried to leave the earth while in infancy. Mother, wearied of bearing a dozen children in about a dozen and a half years, bade her last farewell in 1888 to go after her eight departed offspring, leaving behind only four of us and our father.

Soon after Mother's death father married a Mohammedan girl lately converted to Christianity. But this situation soon came to a tragic end, bringing in a series of irreparable heartbreaks all around. Our home life was wrecked and the warm atmosphere of love, care, and security this wonderful new other had created vanished overnight, without the doing or knowing of anyone in the family. Suddenly Father and Mother were arrested by the Turkish officers, thrown into prison, and dragged to Adana to be condemned to be banished.

In another envelope I am sending you the tragic story of my father and your grandfather.

My eldest sister, Sarah, who would become your mother a few years later, was already married and had left our home; the only other sister, Gulie, was also married and gone to Marash; the eldest brother, Melidon, was already snatched from home and banished to Acre and incarcerated in a dungeon for another innocent "crime" two years earlier; and now this unforeseen calamity struck, leaving me all alone in the world.

The Web of Hope

As soon as the news of the catastrophe was relayed to my sister Sarah, she ran to our desolate home and took me to hers. Thus I became for more than half a dozen years one of the numerous mouths she was feeding.

I have already related, in the story of your mother, about the years I spent with her. In that account I wrote about how one day a caravan-master brought my sister a letter from our eldest brother, miraculously returned from his exile-dungeon, and now a student in Tarsus College, asking sister to send me to him.

I was seriously sick when the caravan left me lying in front of the outer gate of the Inn of Hides. During the six torturous days of travel I was not able to eat or drink anything. The company of the caravan, an unscrupulous band of rascals, with not the slightest sting of conscience, relieved me of everything I had, my food, my clothes, and all the gifts I was bringing from my sister to my brother "risen from the dead."

After a period of unconscious sprawl on the damp and cold pavement of hardened earth, I opened my wearied eyes to see a tall and kindly figure bending over me with a longing and compassionate smile. All of a sudden, that gentle and lovely face radiated faith and strength and security which roused in me a pleasurable consciousness, so that, despite the besetting pains and fatigue, I sat up, opened my eyes wider and clambering on my wobbly legs with a superhuman effort, I threw myself into his arms. Oh, those arms! I can never forget the comfort they gave me at that moment.

Strengthened by his presence, I walked with him the distance to the house of a distant uncle of ours who, long years ago, had made his home in Tarsus. They put me to bed, but I refused to stay in it, and quickly began to mend. In a month I was as healthy and lively as a kid.

But to my utter disappointment I was refused admission to the school as too young. So, I was given to a merchant as an apprentice, but ran away from him. Then I tried two or three other jobs, but nothing satisfied me. Young though I was, my only desire was to get education, to become like my brother, and make my sister as proud of me as she was of our brother.

And fortune smiled on me. A good man, Mr. Hagop Elmassian, an attorney from Constantinople, then a professor of Turkish in the college, paid two and a half pounds for my school tuition and I was admitted into the elementary school for the second semester.

That summer, 1896, an epidemic of cholera swept the city. Dr. Christie, the president, took all the students away from the stricken city to Lampron, a mountain resort of the Roupinian royalty of the Middle Ages, where the sick students quickly regained their health, and the rest continued their studies.

When we returned to Tarsus to prepare for the fall opening of the school year, Dr. Christie ordered my brother to go to Adana and teach in the Boys' High School for a year and earn the next year's college tuition. This is the same high school where you also taught in the school year of 1919–1920. Dr. Christie wouldn't let me stay in the school, but forced me to go with my brother.

We went to Adana, lived together in difficult circumstances, because Brother's pay was too meager. It was hardly enough to keep him modestly fed, not to mention his and my ever-growing expenses, and saving for next year's college tuition. Seeing that it would be a cruelty on my part to force myself on his scanty subsistence, I tried to find a job, but jobs of the kind I was offered did not appeal to me. If I could not afford education under such impossible circumstances, I could at least learn a trade and be independent. Because, I reasoned, it has been the exhortation of the wise that "a trade is a golden bracelet around one's wrist that can never be stolen."

After a year of disappointments in Adana, my longing for my sister drew me back to Hadjin. In her company I found the peace I had lost. Through her guidance I apprenticed at the tailor's trade, which at once appealed to me. At last I had found what "bracelet" I wanted on my wrist. For five years I worked at this trade accepting no pay.

During these years Father returned from his exile and remarried for the third time as his previous wife had been murdered by the Turks in the early days of their arrest. And as life became normal for us, I lived with my folks. In time, I finished my apprenticeship, became a master, and opened up my own tailor shop. Now it was my turn to teach aspiring apprentices, and in the course of long years many scores of master tailors graduated under me. You, too, were one of those student tailors on some summer vacation months of your orphanage days.

Adana - Street in Christian Quarter, June '09

Adana - Minaret from which Turks Fired on Christians

APPENDIX IV

How I Survived Sai'-Getchit

By Yepros Topalian

The widow of the Pastor of Feke Church

Detailed story of a horrendous massacre[61]

Translated by George B. Kooshian in November 1983, from the Turkish language with Armenian alphabet.[62]

Part I

The recollection of the following heinous event brings madness to my mind and terror to my whole being. What kind of heart can still remain calm after comparing the hellish look of those fiends and the noble countenances of the martyrs walking before them to be slaughtered like sheep.

The annual convention of the Union of the Evangelical Churches of Cilicia, scheduled to convene in Adana on April 15, 1909, was the occasion when we[63] started from Feke on April 13. After camping on the road the first night we arrived at Sis next morning where we joined a caravan of many friends on their way to the convention. Some of them were: the Reverend Levon Soghomonian, the pastor of the Second Evangelical Church of Hadjin; the Reverend Stilianos Arslanides, the pastor of the First Evangelical Church of Hadjin; the Reverend Milton Malian,[64] the pastor of the church of Sis (a native of Hadjin); Mr. Samuel Bedrosian; the Reverend Artashes Boyajian, the pastor of Kara Keuy (a native of Hadjin); Krikor Agha Seferian, of Yerebakan church; Mr. Armenag Kullebjian, from the church in Shar; Deacon Mikayel Agha Aijian and his wife, Madame Elsa,[65] delegates from the First Church of Hadjin; Mrs. Osanna Topjian[66], the principal of the American Boys' Orphanage of Hadjin; Sister Samin Tosjian from the church of Sis; and Uncle Kharajian.

All had with them their attendants fo the hired horses. And joining this big crowd we started merrily the journey towards Adana.

A short distance out of Sis a considerable number of merchants from Hadjin and Gurun also joined us. Before starting the journey, they told us, they had requested the governor of Sis to assign a security escort or two for their protection, but the governor had regretted that he cold not spare any armed escort, and had advised them to join the mail carrier on the morrow. But those merchants seeing our great caravan on the road had decided to join us.

As the travel party grew larger, our confidence also increased. With pleasant conversation we kept on going for about three hours, when we met a Turkish *zaptiyeh* [military officer] returning from Adana. Seeing such a large crowd, he stopped to warn us not to go to Adana, "because," he added, "it is not safe for you."

But our people began voicing different ideas. Reverend Astour [Topalian] said, "It is proper for an officer to say a thing like that. If a minor incident has occurred lately, by this time it must have quieted down. Whatever happens, it is the will of God."

Reverend Stilianos dismissed the warning, trustfully declaring, "God is able to protect His city."

Reverend Milton added, "Ahead of us on the road is the village called Sagh Getchit. Its *Mudir* [headman] will undoubtedly protect us once we are there."

Krikor Agha sealed these statements of confidence with one of his own, "Whatever God says, that will be done. Let us keep on walking in faith."

So the flock of sacrificial lambs kept on going to the den of wolves. About a couple hours later, on the outskirts of Saı'-Getchit, we met a young man of Kayseri named Garabed, who in an agitated voice said, "Why are you traveling at such a time? I was working in the fields, and when the Turks began to threaten to kill me I decided to flee the murderers."

No one paid attention to the man. "He is alone, that is why he is so easily scared. Talking like that happens at farms all the time." Then they continued going. It happened that in our caravan there were a number of blacksmiths transporting bags of charcoal for their forges in Saı'-Getchit. These men, impressed by the young man's warning, at once dumped their loads on the roadside and joined him back to Sis. But we kept going until we arrived at the lair of the murderers which was destined to be the slaughter-house of the unsuspecting martyrs.

Before we had time to begin unloading, the men of Hadjin working in this town came to scold us. "Why did you come here? The Turks of Adana have gone mad for Armenian blood, and we here are under siege with no hope of escape." It was only at that moment that we grasped the gravity of the situation. It was also at this time that a special courier, a man named Melkon Farajian, arrived to urge us to turn back with him to Sis. But it was too late, because ferocious gangs of fully armed bloodthirsty murderers appeared menacingly sauntering around.

Immediately the elders of our group—Reverends Stilianos of Hadjin, Milton of Sis, Astour of Feke, and Krikor Agha of Yerebakan—rushed to the Mudir to request him to give them an armed guard to lead them back to Sis, or to protect them against violence. "Because," they argued, "we all are in the employ of Americans, and should any danger happen to us you will be held responsible."

But the Mudir replied that at that moment he could not afford to assign any escort for their return, and that he would not advise them either to stay or to return.

The wily Mudir full well knew that it would be foolish of him to set free the prey already in the trap. Disappointed with the Mudir, they went to see Hadji Bey, the village chief, to beg him "in honor of the proclaimed democracy"[67] to take them safely back to Sis at any time he wished. Hadji Bey assured them, saying, "As long as I am here you have no cause to fear. No one will dare to touch a hair."

With their peace badly disturbed the elders went back to the Bey again to find out what plans he had for them. "My wife," he said, "is against sending you back. The Mudir is also against it."

Hopes smashed, they returned to the *khan* [inn] that was shortly to be their slaughterhouse. All earthly hopes vanished at the moment when the sun, intent not to witness the carnage that was to follow, sank his golden head behind the horizon.

The Web of Hope

Although a dim thought occurred of sending news of our plight to the government of Sis, we realized that breaking through the siege of the fierce fiends required the invincible might of a state.

There was only one recourse left and that was to pour our hearts out to God in earnest supplication which we did in a flood of tears. Hoping to find safety in numbers, some of the people of Hadjin residing or laboring in the town poured in tot he khan, augmenting the number of martyrs. Two of the merchants of Gurun left us, hoping to find protection in the house of a Muslim who had been a friend of theirs in the past.

A short time later, the armed criminals surrounded us, and some of them forcing their way into the khan barked at us to surrender all our guns, with the promise that they would spare us. And the men of God from behind barred doors entreated them, "In the name of Allah, please spare our lives. We carry no guns to surrender. We ask shelter from you as a harmless bird seeking safety on the branch of a tree."

But none of these heart-rending entreaties had any effect on their stony hearts. Meanwhile the Mudir and Hadji Bey, in company with a policeman, made an unexpected appearance and with a few kind words tried to sooth us before they went to their homes.

Fifteen minutes later rifle shots began to be heard from outside. Our people, now marked to be murdered, were, on one hand, imploring God for mercy, and on the other, beseeching the frenzied mass for pity, at the same time repeated our Lord's magnanimous prayer offered on the Cross for His enemies crucifying Him. But these maniacs were insensitive, impervious to reason. These tear-washed prayers were like the waves which after crashing on the shore rocks resume their former shape. While we were begging for mercy they were busy readying for the grand slaughter. When they bored a hole into the room where we were huddled in terror, we ran to another room, hoping it would be safer. In unabated horror, under the tumult of the uncontrolled rabble and constant crack of their firearms the night spent itself. We were delirious, knowing not what we were saying or doing, only waiting for the final hour. Suddenly we noticed that the deranged killers were attempting to set fire to the blacksmith shop adjacent to the khan, hoping to burn us all in this way. While the were engaged in arson, we were pouring water on their fire through a hole from our side. When they saw that they had failed to spread the fire to the khan, they gave up. But then they plundered the smithy completely.

Part II

No more able to stand the tumult round us, a thought of escape at any cost persistently nagged our minds. But the success of a break through the chain tightened about us needed weapons, agility, courage, and cunning, all of which we were woefully short. In search of a chance, we paid a fellow to call the Mudir back to us, and that master of deception came through the door of the devastated smithy, instead of openly walking through the khan's main door, and invited us to follow him to the safety of his house.

We followed him with revived hope, leaving our belongings behind. But what a fright was awaiting us. A turbaned, wizened old *hodja* [teacher of Islam], astride a donkey and followed by a hundred or more armed villains, addressed the Mudir in harsh tones. "Hurry up," he urged, "and do what you are supposed to do. I can control this mob no more."

The mob immediately dispersed at the Mudir's few words of rebuke. Then both he and Hadji Bey led us to the Mudir's stable on the ground floor. Already some of our belongings, also the weapons of the attendants, were confiscated. The rest of the luggage was brought to the Mudir's house for safe keeping. Soon these officials left for their quarters after throwing a few comforting words at us.

Before leaving Hadji Bey offered safe asylum in his house to the preacher Samuel of Karakeuy and his uncle Krikor Agha, which they gratefully accepted and followed him but soon after they returned, stating that the Bey had deemed the khan safer than his house. This Hadji Bey, they explained, was a frequent guest in Samuel's house in Yere Bakan and for that reason he wanted to protect them. Yet a suspicion crept into his evil mind that after their return home they would tell abroad all about the massacre and he would be implicated. That fear made him change his mind and decide to send them back.

Hadji Bey came again to us, and this time he engaged (my husband) Astour in conversation, from which it developed that long years earlier they were neighbors in Hadjin, and Astour's father was a dear friend of his. But at the end of this revelation, he rose up and declared that "The

The Web of Hope

Christians have attacked the Turkish village called Koyoon Evi [Sheep House], and I cannot control the villagers from retaliating."

Then the Mudir added, "If they attack you, tell them that you are working for the Americans, as you warned me, or say, you are Greeks and not Armenians." At the door, turning back, he added, "Don't be afraid, the rumor of the Armenian attack on Koyoon Evi is not true. As long as you are sheltered under my roof you are safe. Don't have any doubt about that."

Thus he applied salve to our burning hearts, and strength to our buckling knees. Relieved by these comforting words, we managed to take a little breakfast, and to quench our thirst we drank the pitcher of water brought in by Hadji Kara Mehmet Agha of Kayseri. The day was Friday, the holy day of Islam. The villagers suddenly stormed out in great uproar from their *namaz* [worship] in the mosque. It was apparent that they had received their instructions from their hodjas. Our ministers at once realized that the end was nigh. "Our lives are no more ours. We must be brave, stout-hearted, and steadfast in our faith." Thus exhorting each other they fell on their knees in tearful supplications.

At this moment Krikor Agha raised his loud voice and wailed, "Where are you, O Lord of Hosts and Savior who dwelt in the psalms and hymn of Israel? Look down now in mercy upon the mournful plight of your servants, and hear their entreaties."

From the upper floor the Mudir's wife leaned down toward us in the dark stable and said to reassure us, "Fear no more. The courier sent to Adana to find out the situation has just returned to report that the peace has been restored and enmity ended."

That welcome news caused Rev. Stilianos to shout, "Long live the Mudir Effendi. May Allah increase his years."

While he was voicing his and our gratitude by that cheer, rifle shots were sounding from outside. And, ominously, right at that moment, an orderly ran in to lead his master's horse out. The Mudir rode and galloped away, apparently not to witness the horrible onslaught that was to follow. His quick departure was a signal. For, the madding mob— armed with mailed clubs, daggers, swords, and flint and automatic army rifles— marched to the stable. Several of them bursting in began to bring their fatal blows on our heads, forcing us to run outside where the others were dealing death blows. The situation was beyond imagination. Some of us were falling down with the gasp, "Oh, mother!" and while others were imploring for mercy for the sake of their youngsters, the monsters were retorting with vile curses, "Shut up, *hunzer giavour* [pig and dog], how dare you speak in front of me!"

In order that I may not see the inhuman scene, I fell at that moment on the shoulder of my husband. One of the villains barked a fierce command, "Hurry up, get out of here." But I entreated him to spare our lives, "because," I wept, "we have seven children waiting for us." Yet the ruthless savage, with the foulest imprecations, brought down his nail-covered club on my head, blinding me with a torrent of blood.[68]

Stunned by this bloody sight my husband lamented, "Oh Mother, should I live to see such a thing happen to me?" and saying this, he collapsed. At this moment a heavier blow of the same club came down upon his prostrate head. "Oh, my children!" he exclaimed, and addressing me, he added, "Let me, Epros, let me go outside to die instantly rather than dying thus slowly."

I led him to the door. There, a shot hit me in the chest and I sank to the floor. (The shot that hit me were pellets.) He turned toward the door and there he received several bullets that ended his life. I never saw him again, who had been for thirty years the companion of my sorrows and of my joys. His going away took only a second.

While I was still writhing in pain, they robbed all the clothes I was wearing. They took the ten gold liras I was carrying in an inner belt next to my body. They tore my ear-lobes to snatch the rings. One *jani* [criminal] tried to cut my finger to get a ring, but his companion convinced him that the ring was copper and not worth soiling his hand with blood. They left me for dead.

Part III

Every one around, taking for granted that I was already dead, did not bother with me any more. In this melee Revs. Stilianos, Milton, and Mr. Armenag were hiding in an adjacent room behind a fortified door. But the despicable wolves, sensing that the hunted men were hiding there, attacked it with al their might. At that moment Mr. Armenag begged from behind the door, "Don't kill us, we'll become Moslem."

But the deceitful curs, promising not to harm them, made them open the reinforced door, and at once stormed in. First they snatched Rev. Milton's watch and chain and his money, and then they attempted to strip his clothes from his body. But he stopped them, saying coolly, "Wait, fellows, let me undress myself." Doing this, he handed them everything he possessed. Then the culprits robbed the other two in the same manner, and dragging them out killed them outright.

During this carnage Sister Samin Tosjian stealthily had made her way up to the Mudir's residence. The Turks, like hounds, pursued her there and barked orders to open the door. But she, seeing the futility of softening their granite hearts, implored, "Please spare me. I have with me 25 liras which I will hand to you now, and I promise to give you that much more." And seeing that her promises had no effect on the beasts devoid of conscience, promised as a last resort, "I will become a Moslem if you spare me."

"Good," answered the mean curs, "come out and we'll make you a Moslem." Believing them, she opened the door, but they, after receiving the bounty from her, with a single blow felled her dead. The Mudir's wife raised no sound from the next room.

All this time I was lying on the same spot where I had fallen when I was shot, and every passer-by was stepping over me. After having killed everyone, they dragged the dead out. And when they had accomplished their task they went away after the men of Hadjin residing in the town. By this time, seized with the fear of catching cold, coughing, and betraying myself, I walked out and lay down with the dead. Next to me was Sister Elsa (Aijian Mikayel Agha's wife). Hoping to find her alive, I shook her gently, but she had been dead for some time. To my surprise, Mrs. Osanna Topjian and Krikor Agha raised their heads. "Please lie down," I warned. "When they see you moving they'll kill you again."

The last person they had killed was the horsemaster of Rev. Stilianos. As they dragged him over me I felt that his blood had not congealed yet. After having finished all the resident men of Hadjin the murderers gathered nearby and began bragging to each other about their exploits. After a while Hadji Bey and the Mudir, the chief of the murderers, made their appearance and asked, did you clean up?" "Yes, Sir," they replied, "your order has been fulfilled." "Good," answered both arch-murderers, "but it isn't good for these corpses to remain here. Dump them in the ravine."

Before this, Mrs. Osanna begged in earnest, "In the name of Allah, give me a drink and them a bullet." No one heeded her. Next Krikor Agha raised his voice, "May I kiss the bottom of your feet, spare our lives."

But the enemy that knew not what crying for mercy means, mocked him, "Look at that old giavour, he hasn't croaked yet and is still talking." They fired a few bullets through them, Krikor and Osanna. Meanwhile some one brought a cart and threw in it as many bodies as it could hold. Because the cart had no ass to pull it the killers performed its duty. Arriving at the ravine they threw the dead one by one down the pit. Osanna could not control her burning thirst and cried again from her grave for water. But the heartless Turks aimed a bullet to her ear and quieted her forever.

Before throwing me into the cart they dragged me for some seconds, and a Turkish woman ran up to me and began to search into my scant underwear. After slipping the gold ring off my finger, she found in a hidden pocket two liras and a ghazi [an antique gold coin]. When they dumped me into the ravine one of them pointed me out to his companions. "That woman is not dead yet," he complained. "You have to finish her with a bullet."

The other replied, "Why should I waste a precious bullet on a worthless body which is croaking anyway?" They then went to cart off the rest of the dead.

Taking advantage of their absence I turned around and lay on my face, with my arm holding it high, with the thought of escaping from being choked when the other bodies were thrown down. When the dead of the second round were thrown down one fell on my head and another on my legs. The murderers left the scene when their task was done.

It was night by this time. I knelt down with some difficulty and whispered to the congregation of the dead, "Is any one alive?"

A young man of Guksun answered.

"Will you come with me?" I asked.

He said, "Yes," and holding my hands raised me.

"Where shall we go," I asked, "to the murderer Mudir, or shall we hide in a bush?"

"To Sis," the young man replied. Hand in hand we groped our way out of the ravine until after much difficulty we found ourselves on the road to Sis. On one hand, the misery caused by the wounds we were inflicted with, and on the other, the grief of the recent events flooding our hearts, increased the intensity of thirst. For that reason we indiscriminately drank all kinds of polluted water we chanced to see. Barefoot and half-naked we walked on and on. When we heard in the quiet of the night a footstep approaching, the terror that we knew so well compelled us to step aside and throw ourselves face down on the ground until the unsuspecting traveler's steps faded away.

After a tortuous walk of several hours we heard the footsteps fo another traveler. To avoid him, we again stepped off the road, but this one suspiciously stopped by us for a minute or two, but having not detected us decided to move on. And we, strengthened by fresh hope of soon entering Sis, resumed our halting walk. Thank God, we arrived at Sis at last with no further interruptions, but heavy with the grief of having left our dear ones in Saı'-Getchit. No semblance of humanity was left on us. Everyone gazing on our blood-drenched head, face, and body shrank away with shock and terror. We wended our way directly to my father's house. The meeting was indescribable for the pain and grief and lamentation. Now that all these abominable events are in the open, and everybody knows that Hadji Bey and the Mudir are the chief murderers with their obedient villagers actually massacring seventy-eight innocent men and women, what kind of justice is it that permits them to live free, as if they were innocent? I have the firm faith that the Almighty will act justly because His heart will be touched by the blood of the martyrs of Saı'-Getchit and the cries and tears, the prayers and entreaties, of the widows and orphans they left behind.

APPENDIX V

Kooshian Ancestry

I. Paternal Branch

A. Hadji Kevork Agha Gejekooshian (1820 Hadjin – 1898 Hadjin)

Had 3 sons, 1 daughter

1. Hampartzoum Gejekooshian

(1859 Hadjin – 1905 Hadjin)
  Had 3 daughters

a. Esther (1883–1915)

b. Haiganoush (1885–1909)

c. Rebecca (1887–1915) The Esther and Rebecca perished with their husbands and children in the Genocide of 1915. Haiganoush, with her husband and children and townspeople, was burned alive in a church by Turks in the massacre of 1909.

  No survivor exists from Hampartzoum's line.

2. Garabed Gejekooshian (1862 Hadjin – 1902 Adana)

Married to Sarah Malian (1869 Hadjin – 1944 Cyprus) in 1882
  Had 2 sons, 1 daughter

a. **Kevork Gejekooshian** In the United States George Barouyr Kooshian (September 25, 1895 Hadjin – March 15, 1984 Pasadena, California)

Exiled with mother, sister, and brother to Syria on September 6, 1915.

Returned to Adana on April 6, 1919.

Landed in Providence, Rhode Island on April 5, 1921.

Naturalized as an American Citizen on January 21, 1930, in Los Angeles.

Name legally changed to George Kooshian.

Married to Annig Derghazarian in Havana, Cuba on March 19, 1930.

She was born on December 25, 1903.

Naturalized in 1936 in Los Angeles.

Her parents were massacred in 1909.

Name legally changed to Suzanne (in Armenian, Shoushanig).

Died in Pasadena on October 28, 1982.

Had 4 sons.

(1). Charles Hamilton Kooshian (b. January 11, 1931 Pasadena)

Married to Virginia Wagner on November 23, 1955 Pasadena.

Had 3 sons (one deceased), 1 daughter

(a). Charles Hamilton Kooshian, Jr. (b. June 16, 1956 Pasadena)

(b). Sarah Louise Kooshian (b. November 26, 1958 Santa Ana, California)

(c). Theodore Arman Kooshian (b. October 8, 1961 San Jose, California)

(d). David Edward Kooshian (b. December 8, 1963 Santa Clara, California – d. March 12, 1979 Alameda, California)

(2). Rev. Percy Victor Kooshian (b. November 5, 1933 Pasadena)

Married to Carolyn Howie on December 28, 1962 in Pasadena.

Had 2 daughters, 1 son.

(a). Suzanne Elaine Kooshian (b. November 8, 1963 La Mesa, California)

(b). Catherine May Kooshian (b. July 22, 1966 The Dalles, Oregon)

(c). Mark Allen Kooshian (b. March 2, 1968 The Dalles)

(3). Rev. Roy Malcolm Kooshian (November 5, 1933 Pasadena – May 18, 2001 Billings, Montana)
Married 1964 to Lora Jean Peabody in Sunnyside, Washington.
Had 2 sons, 1 daughter.
(a). Brian Lee Kooshian (b. November 19, 1965 Eugene, Oregon)
(b). Bradley Scot Kooshian (b. April 30, 1968 Lebanon, Oregon)
(c). Bethany (adopted) (b. June 8, 1973 Portland, Oregon)
(4). Dr. George B. Kooshian, Jr. (b. May 15, 1941 Pasadena)
Married May 29, 1982 to Clary Elisa Vargas (b. December 27, 1948 San Juan del Sur, Nicaragua)
Had 3 sons
(a). George Barouyr Kooshian III (b. June 14, 1985 Hollywood, California)
(b). Stephen Alexander Kooshian (b. September 26, 1986 Hollywood)
(c). Christian Francis Kooshian (b. April 23, 1990 Hollywood)

b. Mary Gejekooshian (1897 Hadjin – 1972 Pasadena) Married in Adana on September 11, 1920 to
Sarkis Soghomonian (March 18, 1889(?) Hadjin – October, 1972 Pasadena)
After wedding left Adana for the United States of America.
Had 2 daughters, 1 son.
(1). Annette Soghomonian (July 8, 1921 Fresno, California – 1992 Cuyahoga, Ohio)
Married to Dick Moran in Honolulu, Territory of Hawaii.
Had 1 son, 2 daughters
(2). Sam Soghomonian (March 18, 1923, Pasadena – June 10, 2011 Tuscon, Arizona)
Married to Maria Figueroa.
Had 2 daughters.
(3). Rosemary Soghomonian (December 23, 1925 Pasadena)
Married to Don Vial.
Had daughters.

c. Setrak Gejekooshian (April 1902 Seleucia, Cilicia – 1979 London)
Married 1937 to Sirarpi Haroutunian (d. 1976 Cyprus) in Cyprus.
   Had 1 daughter
   (1). Sarah Kooshian (b. 1938 Cyprus)
   Married John Dobbs in London.

3. Bedros Gejekooshian (1865 Hadjin – 1915 in Genocide)

Resided in Seleucia, Cilicia.
   Had 1 daughter
   a. Zarouhi (1898 Seleucia – 1928 Cyprus)
   Was married.
   Survived Genocide
   Fell on her head and died.

4. Hnazant Gejekooshian (1867 Hadjin – 1915 in Genocide)

Married in Hadjin to Hovagim Mooshian.
   Both, with 5 of their 6 children, perished in the Genocide of 1915. One son, the eldest survived because he had been in the United States since 1913.
   a. Panos Mooshian (November 15, 1894 Hadjin – May 20, 1943 Los Angeles)
   Married 1925 in Havana, Cuba to Yeranouhi Gizirian (November 24, 1901 Hadjin–December 25, 1990 Los Angeles).
   Had 2 children.
   (1). Lorraine Mooshian (June 6, 1926 Chicago – January 1994 Los Angeles)
   Unmarried.
   (2). Charles Mooshian (October 23, 1930 Chicago – May 4, 1984 Los Angeles)
   Married.
   Had 1 son, 1 daughter.
   (a). Steven Armand Mooshian (b. 1957 Hollywood)
   (b). Gina Cristine Mooshian (b. 1960 Hollywood)

II. Maternal Branch

A. Krikor Agha Malian (1840 Hadjin – 1917 Hadjin)

Krikor Agha Malian had a brother and 2 sisters.
   He had 12 children from Mariam, his first wife (1850–1886)
   Second wife was a Kurdish girl also named Mariam, 1889. No children.
   Third wife, 1899. One daughter, Siroon.
   Out of the 13 children 8 died in infancy.

1. Rev. Melidon Malian (1867 Hadjin – 1909, butchered in Adana massacre).

Married to Mutébéreh Munushian of Hadjin (1887 Hadjin – 1920 Hadjin).
   Her head was cut off, and only son Barkev (1908 Sis – 1920 Hadjin) was massacred by the Kemalist Turks.

2. Sarah Malian Kooshian (1869 Hadjin – 1944 Cyprus)

Married to Garabed Gejekooshian (1862 Hadjin – 1902 Adana)
   Had 3 children
   Kevork (George), Mary, Setrak already mentioned.

3. Gulenia (Gulie) Malian Alajajian (1875 Hadjin–1966 Boston)

Married to Toros Alajajian of Marash (1865 Marash – 1913 Kayseri)
   Several children died in childhood. Lived only
   a. Krikor Alajajian, or George Elgin in the United States (1893–1967 Binghamton, New York)
   Married to Alice Manoogian of Smyrna
   Had 2 sons, 2 daughters.
   One son died.
   b. Stepan Alajajian (1896–1926 New York)
   c. Rachael Alajajian (1904–1919 Adana)
   d. Azniv Alajajian (1910 Kayseri–1966 Boston)

4. Haroutune Malian (1883 Hadjin–1944 Beirut)

Married Turfanda Hotzoorian of Hadjin.
  Among a dozen children lived only
  a. Alexander Malian (1912 Hadjin – 1926 Cyprus)
  b. Titzouhi Malian (1919 Adana – 1970 Beirut)
  Married to Vartkes Iskian
  Had 2 sons, 1 daughter Rosalind
  c. Gibrouhi Malian (1923 Cyprus, in 1976 was living in Beirut with husband and children)
  d. Isahak Malian (1928 Cyprus, in 1976 was living in Chicago)
  e. Siroon Malian (1900 Hadjin – 1920 Hadjin)
  Perished with husband and 2 children and relatives in Kemalist massacre.

B. Hovhannes Malian

Perished with wife, children, and relations in 1915 Genocide.
  Son Hampartzoum Malian (February 15, 1881 Hadjin – December 20, 1963 Los Angeles) [Ed.—Added by the Editor. In the text Hampartzoum Malian is called the cousin of Sarah Malian. Therefore he must be the son of Hovhannes Malian, Krikor Agha's only brother.
  "Uncle's 'family,' all bound for Pasadena, California, consisted of ten members They were, beside himself, his wife Noyemi, daughter Nectar, 10, son Vartan, 7, brother Aram, a servant girl Rebecca (who had to be left behind on account of no bono eyes), Uncle's two cousins Haigaz and Levon Mehagian, Alice, 18 (later Alice Marsh) and her widowed aunt Rebecca (later Mrs. Gedigian)."]

C. Sister married to Kulahjian of Hadjin. Perished with family in 1915 Genocide. Only one son survived.

1. Athanas Kuhlajian
    Died in Los Angeles in 1974.
    Left 2 sons, 1 daughter, and grandchildren.

D. Another sister, Neneh Malian

Married to Simon Agha Satchian of Hadjin
  Satchians had 2 sons and 2 daughters.
    1. Asadoor Satchian
    2. Hadji Bob Satchian
    3. Haiganoosh Satchian
    4. Zabel Satchian
  The whole family was deported.
  Neneh and son Hadji Bob and Asadoor's wife and children perished in 1915 Genocide.
  Simon Agha, Asadoor, and two girls returned to Hadjin where they all perished in 1920 massacre, but Asadoor escaped the slaughter and came to Adana. Married to Sarah.
  Lived in France, had several children, then in 1947 emigrated to Armenia.
  Asadoor died in Yerevan in 1967.
  His children
    a. Dr. Simon Satchian
    b. Haiganoosh Satchian
  (others)

III. Der Ghazarian Branch

1. Melkon Der Ghazarian (Harpoot – 1909 Adana)

Slaughtered in massacre with his wife, Haiganoosh, née Arakelian
  1 daughter, 1 son
    a. Annig Der Ghazarian (December 25, 1903 Adana – October 28, 1982 Pasadena)
      Educated in Constantinople.
      Nurse in Greece 1922–1928.
      Havana, Cuba 1928–1930.
      Married to George B. Kooshian in Havana, March 19, 1930.
      Came to Pasadena May 1, 1930.
      Mother of 4 sons above mentioned.
    b. Manoog Der Ghazarian (1907 Adana – died in Pasadena)

Married to Takoohi 1927 in Athens
3 children, 2 sons and 1 daughter
(1). Melkon Derghazarian (Athens)
Has children
(2). Haiganoosh Derghazarian
Married Hagop Kevirian (died in Pasadena)
1 son, 2 daughters
(a). James Jr.
Married
(b).
(c). Susan Kevirian
Married
(3). Aram Derghazarian (Athens – Pasadena)
Married to Shakeh Farajian
4 sons

BIBLICAL REFERENCES

By the Editor

All of the Biblical allusions made by the author that are not clearly indentified in the text have been gathered together here. All quotations are from the King James Version (1611) of the Bible unless otherwise noted. Very well-known passages are cited by reference only.

Chapter 1, p. 4. *Thus they hoped, and succeeded, in deceiving the world that they were vacating "the seat of the scornful" and abandoning "the way of the sinner" which history had assigned to them. Thus they managed to "sit" at the council table of the "just" and the "righteous."* Paraphrase of Psalm 1, verses 1, 5, 6.

Chapter 5, p. 14. *Alexander the coppersmith* is mentioned specifically in II Timothy 4:14–15: "Alexander the coppersmith did me much evil: the Lord reward him according to his works: of whom be thou ware also; for he hath greatly withstood our words." This may be the same Alexander mentioned in Acts 19:33 and I Timothy 1:20.

Chapter 8, p. 21. *"to the business of his heavenly Father."* Jesus as a twelve-year-old in the Temple at Jerusalem, Luke 2:49: "And he said unto them, How is it that ye sought me? wist ye not that I must be about my Father's business?"

Chapter 8, p. 23 *A mighty Power within himself sustained him all the time, as it was with this power that Daniel of old was sustained in the lions' den, and St. Gregory for thirteen years in the snake-infested pit.* The well-known story of Daniel in the lions' den is found in Daniel, Chapter 6. Gregory in the pit is the foundation-story of Armenian Christianity. Gregory was thrown into a pit (*Khor Virab*), from which he emerged to cure King Drtad of his dementia. The story of Gregory and Drtad echoes that of Daniel and Nebuchadnezzar.

Chapter 8, p. 23. *The writer of the article in Martyr's Book of Remembrance, referring to his dark interim, states that Melidon Effendi, in his seclusion in Zilifkeh, "wrestled with God as Jacob, and bargained with Him," and as Gideon "tested Him," until he discovered that God was calling him to His service.* "Wrestling with God" refers to the story of Jacob [Genesis 34:24-32] alone at the riverside afraid of his meeting the following day with his brother Esau, whose inheritance he had stolen. During the night a man appeared and wrestled with him for the whole night, leaving him lame in the hip. The man renamed Jacob Israel and blessed him, because he had seen God face to face and prevailed.

Gideon's test of God [Judges 6:36-37] came as he was about to lead an army of 300 Israelites against and overwhelming Midianite force: "And Gideon said unto God, If thou wilt save Israel by mine hand, as thou hast said, behold, I will put a fleece of wool in the floor; and if the dew be on the fleece only, and it be dry upon all the earth beside, then shall I know that thou wilt save Israel by mine hand, as thou hast said."

Chapter 13, p. 62 *Son of the Barren* refers to the birth of John the Baptist from the aged couple Zechariah and Elizabeth described in Luke 1:5-25; 57-80. *The "greatest prophet"* refers to the comment by Jesus about John in Matthew 11:11.

Chapter 14, p. 66. The quotation is John 9:1-3 (Revised Standard Version).

Chapter 18, p. 91. The miracle of the coin in the fish's mouth is found at Matthew 17:24-27.

Chapter 20, p. 111. The anointing of Jesus with nard (essential oil of spikenard, or *Nardostachys jatamansi*) is recorded in all four Gospels: Matthew 26:6-13; Mark 14:3-9; Luke 7:36-50; John 12:3-8. Some Bible scholars believe that these stories relate to two separate incidents. The Lucan account is as follows:

36 And one of the Pharisees desired him that he would eat with him. And he went into the Pharisee's house, and sat down to meat. 37 And, behold, a woman in the city, which was a sinner, when she knew that Jesus sat at meat in the Pharisee's house, brought an alabaster box of ointment, 38 and stood at his feet behind him weeping, and began to wash his feet with tears, and did wipe them with the hairs of her head, and kissed his feet, and anointed them with the ointment. 39 Now when the Pharisee which had bidden him saw it, he spake within himself, saying, This man, if he were a prophet, would have known who and what manner of woman this is that toucheth him: for she is a sinner. 40 And Jesus answering said unto him, Simon, I have somewhat to say unto thee. And he saith, Master, say on. 41 There was a certain creditor which had two debtors: the one owed five hundred pence, and the other fifty. 42 And when they had nothing to pay, he frankly forgave them both. Tell me therefore, which of them will love him most? 43 Simon answered and said, I suppose that he, to whom he forgave most. And he said unto him, Thou hast rightly judged. 44 And he turned to the woman, and said unto Simon, Seest thou this woman? I entered into thine house, thou gavest me no water for my feet: but she hath washed my feet with tears, and wiped them with the hairs of her head. 45 Thou gavest me no kiss: but this woman since the time I came in hath not ceased to kiss my feet. 46 My head with oil thou didst not anoint: but this woman hath anointed my feet with ointment. 47 Wherefore I say unto thee, Her sins, which are many, are forgiven; for she loved much: but to whom little is forgiven, the same loveth little. 48 And he said unto her, Thy sins are forgiven. 49 And they that sat at meat with him began to say within themselves, Who is this that forgiveth sins also? 50 And he said to the woman, Thy faith hath saved thee; go in peace.

Biblical References

John's account occurs after Jesus had raised Lazarus from the dead:

1 Then Jesus six days before the passover came to Bethany, where Lazarus was which had been dead, whom he raised from the dead. 2 There they made him a supper; and Martha served: but Lazarus was one of them that sat at the table with him. 3 Then took Mary a pound of ointment of spikenard, very costly, and anointed the feet of Jesus, and wiped his feet with her hair: and the house was filled with the odour of the ointment.

Chapter 24, p. 138. *"Shadow of Death"* [Psalm 23].

Chapter 26, p. 167. *Dreams also had no special significance for me, not being an Egyptian Pharaoh or a Babylonian monarch.* These refer to the well-known stories of the dreams of Pharaoh interpreted by Joseph, Genesis 41; and of Nebuchadnezzar interpreted by Daniel, Daniel 2.

Chapter 28, p. 177. *If the exile of Israel and Judah was for their idolatry, hypocrisy, and arrogance at the hands of Sennacherib of Assyria and Nebuchadnezzar of Babylon...*The account of the Assyrian and Babylonian captivity is found in the books of I and II Kings and I and II Chronicles.

Idem. *I began to read in the 12th chapter of Daniel* [Daniel 12:1–13]. The words that excited the hopes of the desperate refugees were "Blessed is he that waiteth, and cometh to the thousand three hundred and five and thirty days. But go thou thy way till the end be: for thou shalt rest, and stand in thy lot at the end of the days."

Chapter 31, p. 199. *It must have been at a point in the neighborhood of Hamam that Abraham of Ur of Chaldea and his family, slaves, and cattle crossed Euphrates to reach Haran, and after some years there recrossed it to continue towards the "Land of Promise."* Genesis 11:31: "And Terah took Abram his son, and Lot the son of Haran his son's son, and Sarai his daughter in law, his son Abram's wife; and they went forth with them from Ur of the Chaldees, to go into the land of Canaan; and they came unto Haran, and dwelt there."

Idem. *Did the Jehovah he worshiped open up a dry road for him between separated walls of water, as He did five hundred years later in the Red Sea for Abraham's hard-pressed fleeing descendants?* The story of the crossing of the Red Sea is found in Exodus 14.

Idem....*the heat climbed to the degree of Nebuchadnezzar's Furnace.* The well-known story of Shadrach, Meshach, and Abed-nego in the firey furnace is found in Daniel 3:19–25.

Chapter 32, p. 207. *Was this tent the holy Tabernacle of the Old Testament in which Jehovah dwelt and watched His people's steps?* Tabernaculum is the latin word for "tent", referring to the tent erected in the wilderness by Moses as the earthly abode of God before the Children of Israel. Exodus 33:7-10

Chapter 58, p. 400. *...a seed fallen on barren soil.* The Parable of the Sower, found at Matthew 13:1-23, Mark 4:1-20, and Luke 8:1-15.

Appendix I, p. 433. *"His Truth shall be thy shield and buckler."* Psalm 91.

Notes

[1][Ed.—All numbered notes are the author's unless indicated to be the editor's.]

[2]The Turkish government under this mad tyrant was extremely suspicious of any Armenian activity in the fields of business, culture, education, and religion, to the point of being ludicrous.

H_2O, the formula for water, was read and interpreted by an official censor to mean Hamid the Second is Zero. Immediately the author of the scientific article was seized and thrown into a dungeon with no chance to explain. Another censor stopped the publication of an Armenian daily, *Soorhandak* (Courier), because of its revolutionary name. According to this whimsical interpretation, soor—sword, han—raise, dak—strike, meant raise your sword and strike at the government.

It was a criminal offense for any one to use the words nose, star, Armenia, and certain other words, because, by using the word nose, one might allude to the Sultan's enormous nose, or by star, one might mean the imperial palace, the Yildiz Kiosk (*Yildiz* means star).

[3]Lewis Carrol, in explaining the words he used in his famous nonsense poem Jabberwocky, comments that the word "gyre" is a verb, derived from Gyaour, or Giaouar, a dog. He says, to "gyre" means to scratch like a dog (The Annotated Alice). All Christians and non-Moslems are invariably "*Kaffir*" in the eyes of all Mohammedans, because of the fact that Mohammed is Allah's only prophet and Koran is the only book dictated by Allah. *Kaffir* means one who hides the truth. The word is Arabic, the root being *Kaffir*, to blaspheme, to hide, to be skeptical of.

[4][Ed.—The Turkish language of this period was Ottoman, which was written in Arabic script. In 1929 Ottoman was abolished in favor of a radically reformed nationalistic Turkish vocabulary and syntax and a new Latin-derived writing system which uses some symbols to represent sounds differently from more familiar European languages. It would therefore be anachronistic to use modern Turkish spellings in this work, which might be misunderstood by English-speaking readers. Thus "Jemiyeti" and "Jemal", not "Cemiyeti" and "Cemal."]

[5]This Kaiser, on a state visit to Constantinople in 1898, embraced and kissed Sultan Hamid II as his own brother and proclaimed himself the defender of the Mohammedan world. In doing so he secured for Germany the monopoly to build a railroad from Berlin to Baghdad, the rich fields of black gold. Turkey, infatuated by Germany's vaunted military invincibility, sought and secured her alliance.

[6]According to classical mythology, Ciliz, accompanied by his brothers Phoenix and Cadmus, set out in search of his fair sister Europa, who, unknown to either of them, had been abducted by Jupiter in the guise of a bull.

Phoenix, weary of this hopeless quest, remained in a land that after his name was called Phoenicia.

Cadmus, at the oracle of Delphi, followed a cow to the land since called Boetia with its future capital Thebes. This same Cadmus is supposed to have invented the alphabet and introduced its use into Greece.

Cilix, too, got tired of the fruitless search and settled in a fertile country that in his name was called Cilicia.

[7] In an article in *Hadjin*, a bi-monthly magazine of which I was the editor (1936–1940), I wrote humorously that Abraham Lincoln was a native of *Hodgen*, having been born there. But, in order not to misinform the reader, I hastened to add that the name of his birthplace was Hodgenville, Ky., U.S.A., and not the Hadjin of Cilicia, my birthplace.

I conjectured the highly improbable guess that a native of Hadjin having come to America might have founded the Hodgenville of Kentucky and given the name of his hometown to it, adding the French word ville, meaning village.

Any standard gazetteer places the population of Hadjin, in its heyday, at 25–30,000, but to my utter amazement, I saw two recent copies of different atlases in both of which the now extinct Hadjin was recorded as one of the Great Cities of the World with a population of 125,000. Obviously the addition of the figure 1 in front of 25,000 was a typographical mistake.

But who am I to question the veracity of the statements of such learned geographers?

[8] This information is from an article I contributed on May 28, 1926 to the Pasadena Star-News, a daily newspaper published in Pasadena, California.

[9] [Ed.—The author here is referring to the court case United States vs Cartozian, 6F. 2d 919 (1925), in which Professors Frank Boas of Columbia University and Roland Burrage Dixon of Harvard University among others testified to that effect. This is referred to later in the text.]

[10] [Ed. — This was the dominant view of the origins of the Armenians at midcentury. Research continues in this field.]

[11] [Ed.—François Lenormant (1837–1883) was a French archaeologist and assyriologist; Charles-Victor Langlois (1863–1929), French historian and palaeographer. In the last fifty years the study of Armenian history has progressed with a new generation of scholars. An accessible introduction is George A. Bournoutian, *A Concise History of the Armenian People: From Ancient Times to the Present* (Costa Mesa, California: Mazda Publishers, 2002).]

[12] Adana was the capital of the vilayet (province) of the same name, created in 1875 by the Sultan of Turkey. It had a population of 100,000 of which the Armenians, up to World War I, numbered 70,000. Built of the right bank of the River Seyhan (or Sarus), it produced grains, timber, wool, cotton, sesame, tobacco, grapes, etc. Greek mythology says that Adana was built by Adana and Sarus, the two sons of Heaven and Earth, one giving his name to the city, the other to the river. Some say that Adan, in Phoenician, meant willow tree. In olden times the banks of the river Sarus were thick with forests of willow trees.

Adana is first mentioned in history in 50 B.C. The Armenian Kingdom of Cilicia was put to an end by the invasion of the Mohammedans in 1375. Thus forcibly having been stripped of her Armenian ownership and character, the whole of the province of Cilicia became a part of Turkey, and continued to be ruled by feudal chiefs. Adana Vilayet was divided into five districts: 1. Adana; 2. Mersin; 3. Jeveli Bereket; 4. Kozan (Sis), to which Hadjin and its surrounding towns and villages belonged.; and 5. Seleucia or Ichili (Ichei), with its surroundings of Armenag, Moot Gulnar, and Anamoor.

[13] *Garabed Geje-Kooshian* (a as in car, e as in bed).

Garabed, in Armenian, forerunner, after John the Baptist, Forerunner of Christ.

Geje-Kooshian (g as in get, j as in jet)

Geje is a Turkish word meaning night.

Koosh is a Turkish word meaning bird.

-ian is an Armenian suffix, also Latin, French, -ieu, meaning from the family of or belonging to. Descended from Indo-European.

The meaning of the whole word Geje-Kooshian is Bird of Night Family or from the Night-Bird Family.

It is most probable that way back in the forgotten past, one of my paternal forefathers used to work at his loom or any job he was engaged in, all night long. So his neighbors dubbed him with that appellation, forcing his former name into oblivion.

[14] *Séhél:* The economic pressure of the local conditions in most cities and villages compelled the laboring class, whether single or family man, to seek employment and living in other parts of the country. Such a man left his hometown, parents, wife and children, or a new bride, and went to such bigger outlying cities as Sis, Adana, Mersin, and Tarsus, and even beyond the confines of their province, as far as Caesarea, Smyrna, and Constantinople. A saying prevails until today that "a man of Hadjin and his lame donkey were seen in Hindustan." I do not vouch evidence that he will travel to far-off countries, for an opportunity to earn a living.

A man who goes to *Séhél*, works there, if he is lucky enough to find work, for years, at labor or trade, saves his earnings with the hope of returning home to his loved ones, and once home when his money gives out he goes away again.

Such going-away was called in the local dialect *Séhél ishdole*.

The dialect of Hadjin was a variation of the classical and modern Armenian, locally called *Hadjno Leezon*, the Tongue of Hadjin. It was a distinctive dialect, a favorite material for the study of linguistic scholars.

The word *Séhél* is the localized form of the Arabic word *sahil*, seashore. *Séhél ishdole* (going to *Séhél*) meant "going to more prosperous and promising cities near the seashore."

Séhélji meant "one who is gone to *Séhél*."

A person going to *Séhél* usually accompanies a caravan (of mules), himself traveling on foot, until after many days he reaches his destination. As soon as he arrives there, he looks around for other *Séhélji*s from his part of the country, preferably his hometown, to find lodging and a job.

Often these jobless *Séhélji*s languish and die in filthy khans, friendless, penniless.

Communication with home was almost non-existent. *Séhélji*s were completely cut off from home. Mail service was not trustworthy and was unavailable to these poor people.

The Web of Hope

The ones left behind never heard from their beloved in *Séhél*, and often they mourned for their *Séhéljis* as dead because of false rumor.

The *Séhélji* at his return was customarily met at the outskirts of the town by a number of friends and relatives, who escorted him directly to the church for his prayer and praise and an offering for his safe return. Alms to the poor could never be ignored. As he came to the door of his home, a sacrifice was offered according to the means of the family — a chicken, a dove, a kid, a goat, or a lamb, and the meat was distributed to the poor, of which class there were not a few.

Séhélji's returns were always occasion for festivity.

[15] This Seleucia in Cilicia should not be confused with several other ancient Hellenistic cities of the same name. According to the *Encyclopedia Brittanica*, it was known to the ancients as Seleucus Traccheotis or Trachea, modern Itchel, and lay a few miles from the mouth of the Calycadnus (modern Gök Sü or Blue River) at 36 degrees north latitude by 34 degrees east longitude. Doubtless it was built inland as a protection against attacks from the sea. There are considerable ruins, including the ruins of a castle on the acropolis. The city was built near an old site (Oldea) in 300 B.C., and at one time was a port with a large trade and the rival of Tarsus. During the Third Crusade, Frederick Barbarosa was drowned in crossing the river (A.D. 1190). The city was captured by the Turks in the thirteenth century. It still remains the capital of the district. It has been the birthplace of several famous men, among them the philosopher Xenarchus.

[16] [Ed.—This is "Mamig", who features prominently later in this work after the family returns to Adana from exile.]

[17] *Hadji*: From Arabic *Hadj* or *Hajj*, pilgrimage. *Hadji* is a Moslem who has made the pilgrimage to the *Kaaba* within the great mosque in Mecca, the holy city of Islam, the birthplace of Mohammed. No one can use this title, unless he has made at least one pilgrimage in his lifetime. The *Hadj* once performed, the pilgrim never omits to prefix this proud title of *Hadji* to his name.

The *Kaaba*, which in Arabic means a square building (from the root word *ka'b*, out of which our English word cube derives), is a small and nearly cubical stone building. It contains a spring which was sprung by the angel Gabriel, as the legend goes, to quench Ishmael's and his mother Hagar's thirst in the desert. It contains also the famous black stone, which Gabriel had brought down from *Jennet* (Paradise) as a pillow for the unfortunate wanderers (Hagar and Ishmael) to rest their heads on. This stone was snow-white at first, but the sins of men turned it black.

The *Kaaba* represents the direction (*Kiblah*) towards which Moslems kneel and bow in prayer. Before the time of Mohammed *Kaaba* was an idolatrous temple. It has since been the chief object of pilgrimage of the Islamic world.

A Christian *Hadji* is a man or woman in the Near East who has made a pilgrimage, at least once, to the Holy Sepulcher at Jerusalem.

The Armenians most probably borrowed this religious custom from the Moslems, beginning with the first Arab invasion of Armenia by Omar, Mohammed's successor, in A.D. 640, and during subsequent subjugations by other Mohammedan conquerors.

[18] *Agha* or *Aga*: A title used mostly in Turkey, which originally meant a commander or chief officer, but it was generally used among the civilians as a title of respect, whether

the person was a landowner or not. It was extensively used by the Armenians for older men.

[19] *Effendi:* A Turkish word used as a title of respect, added at the end of a man's first name, and means "sir" or "master." It is supposed to have come into Turkish from Greek *authentes*, "master."

[20] During World War I, Providence brought me back safely from one of the bloodiest massacres in the Syrian Desert in 1917 and placed me in a work center as one of a few sanitation inspectors. There were several similar centers (called *imarat-haneh*) in the teeming city of Aleppo, all run by Armenian conscripted labor. The morally corrupt Turkish government's cruel policy was to starve "the cow that gave milk." It had the "magnanimity" of distributing every other day only half a pound loaf of "bread," prepared with equal parts of flour, ashes, and charcoal.

On one of my rounds one morning I overheard an elderly lady talking to a younger one in the dialect of my own hometown. In tones of astonishment I asked the older lady, in the same tongue, if they were from Hadjin. In those dark days it was a rare miracle to find any person of Hadjin still living.

This time it was her turn to be astonished to hear the familiar dialect from the lips of a young man. She asked me whose son I was, and when she heard my mother's name she dropped the wooden spindle with which she was spinning yarn from her hands and fell upon my neck with sobs and kisses. She told me between her sobs that she was Sarah Kutufian, the spiritual sister of both my mother and uncle Melidon. She said that about thirty years earlier she had been arrested with Melidon Effendi, subjected to the same tortures, and was exiled to the same dungeon in Akka. Then she introduced me to her younger companion as her daughter born in the prison in those by-gone days.

At that moment this frail lady became transfigured into an unconquerable heroine, and one of those ancient saints who were martyred for their faith and ideals their abject torturers could never understand.

This hapless couple, having lost all their dear ones in the great Genocide, returned to Hadjin at the end of the war only to perish in 1920 when the Turk razed the city.

[21] *Acre:* The following information is from the Appendix to the *Oxford Bible for Teachers*, 1898 edition, p. 93:

> Accho (R.V. Acco), north of Mount Carmel, was occupied by Phoenicians, whom the tribes of Asher could not dislodge. It is only once mentioned in the Old Testament (Judges 1:31), and once in the New, under its later Greek name of Ptolemais (Acts 21:7). Under the Crusaders it became the seat of the Christian kingdom and the headquarters of the Knights Templars, from whom it derived its modern name, Saint Jean d'Acre. The plain of Accho is the most fertile in Palestine.

[22] [Ed.—This village is on the outskirts of the modern town of Imamoglu, 30 kilometers south of Sis, about a six-hour walk.]

[23] Quoted by Emily J. Robinson in her pamphlet, "The Armenians," p. 8. Printed by Frederick Printing Co., Ltd., 21 Garlick Hill, London E.C. 4.

[24] Rose Lambert, *Hadjin, and the Armenian Massacres* (New York, Chicago, Toronto, London and Edinburgh: Fleming H. Revell Company, 1911).

[25] [Ed.—Dr. Haigazian died on July 7, 1921 at the American Hospital in Mezreh, Mamuret-ul-Aziz [Kharpert]. He was already ill when he arrived at Mezreh, was placed in a quarantine area rife with typhus, and prevented by the Turks from entering the hospital until he had paid a large bribe, and died shortly thereafter. "Some Details of the Death of Dr. Armenag Harutune Haigazian, Intellectual and Educator in Mezreh, Kharpert in 1921 by Abraham D. Krikorian and Eugene L. Taylor, <http://www.groong.com/orig/ak-20140925.html>, accessed February 27, 2017.]

[26] [Ed.—Nora Lambert succeeded her sister Rose Lambert at the orphanage.]

[27] [Ed.—Dorwin Jonathan Storms (7 June 1883–19 November 1948) and Anna (Nancy) Good Storms (9 April 1880–22 December 1965). Their first son was Everek Richard Storms (19 October 1914–1983), who was born in Everek.]

[28] [Ed.—Vahagn Effendi was Vahagn Datevian (also spelled Vahakn), a prominent and high-ranking member of the Armenian Revolutionary Federation or *Hai Heghapokhagan Tashnaktsutiun*. He was a close associate and "bosom friend" of Jemal Pasha, who had him hanged. The orphanage was a project of Jemal for the Armenian orphans the Turks had made, who were thereafter instructed solely in the in Turkish language.]

[29] *Abuna*: Arabic, "our father," used as a title for a priest.

[30] *Baji:* Turkish, "sister"

[31] [Ed.—Bulgur Khan (Arabic, Khan al-Burghul) is located in the area of Souq al-Medina, the great covered market of Old Aleppo, mostly destroyed in the Battle of Aleppo (July 2012–December 2016). The southern portion was built in the 14th century and the northern portion in the 16th century. It was variously used as a private residence and in the early 20th century as the British Consulate. I was not able to locate a photograph to publish, but there are three at <https://dome.mit.edu/handle/1721.3/45936/discover>, accessed February 26, 2017.]

[32] [Ed.—Mr. Kroozian was ordained Khachig Kahana Kroozian. He served as a pastor in Reedley, California (November 1924–December 1927) and San Francisco twice (1927–1929; 1939–1941). For more details see George B. Kooshian, Jr., "The Armenian Immigrant Community of California, 1880–1935" (Ph.D. dissertation, University of California, Los Angeles, 2002), pp. 273, 276.]

[33] [Ed.—Included in this package were the notebook and pencil with which he recorded this account; see below.]

[34] *Chavoush*: Turkish, "sergeant."

[35] Ezekiel 37:1–6

[36] [Ed.—Hampartzoum Kradjian was never heard of again.]

[37] [Ed.—*Hafiz*, Arabic "guardian", used by Moslems for one who can recite the Koran by heart. Hafiz (Khajeh Shamseddin Mohammad Hafiz-s Shirazi) was a Persian poet who lived in the 14th century AD.]

[38] [Ed.—The Battle of Avarayr, AD 451, between the Christian Armenians and the Zoroastrian Sassanid Persians. Vartan Mamigonian led the resistance to the Persians. Vasag Suni defected to the Persians and is considered a traitor in Armenian tradition. The result of the battle was that the Armenians were defeated but Christianity was saved. Vartan and his followers are recognized as martyr saints by the Armenian Church.]

³⁹ *Kufteh:* Cracked wheat mixed with lean meat and then stuffed with seasoned ground meat and boiled.

Tahn: Diluted madzoon or yoghurt.

⁴⁰ [Ed.—Now in the possession of Charles H. Kooshian.]

⁴¹ *Baron*: From French, "Mister"; used as a title of respect for teachers. Accented on the second syllable.

⁴² [Ed—There is no information in the text about Baron Onnig's last name or his eventual fate.]

⁴³ [Ed.—Now in the possession of Charles H. Kooshian.]

⁴⁴ [Ed.—Modern spelling Buca, now a district of Izmir.]

⁴⁵ *Khachakogh:* Armenian, from *khach*, cross, and *kogh*, thief. Cross-stealer, hypocrite. This word was made popular by Raffi (1835–1898), the Sir Walter Scott of Armenia, through his famous novel, *Kachakoghi Hishadagaran* (Memoirs of a Cross-Stealer).

⁴⁶ [Ed.—In later years the dictionary served his children.]

⁴⁷ [Ed.—The Union Stockyards operated from 1865 until July 30, 1971.]

⁴⁸ [Ed.—Mangasar Magurditch Mangasarian (1859-1943).]

⁴⁹ [Ed.—Charles Wakefield Cadman (1881-1946), American composer.]

⁵⁰ [Ed.—Karl Friedrich August Kahnis (1814-1888), German theologian.]

⁵¹ [Ed.—Èmile Coué (1857-1926).]

⁵² *The Smyrna Affair*, p. 118.

⁵³ Genesis 25:34

⁵⁴ Annig is the diminutive form of Anna. *Der* means lord, master. Priests are known as *Der Hayr*, Lord Father. Ghazar is the transliteration of Lazarus. Hence, her name, Little Anna the daughter of Father Lazarus.

⁵⁵ [Ed—One may wonder at the apearance of Mr. "Big-moustache-ian".]

⁵⁶ [Ed.—Dombourian Oriental Rugs closed its doors in 2012 after 102 years in business. "Mampreh Dombourian was born in 1885 in Armenia, in what is present-day Turkey. He immigrated to Chicago during his teen years and began to work for Nahigian Bros., one of the largest oriental rug dealers at the time. The company eventually sent him to New Orleans to open a branch, which would be located across the street from the former DeSoto Hotel, now the Le Pavillon, on Poydras Street. The exact date of when he opened the store is unknown, but he became sole proprietor in 1910. He moved the shop to Royal Street in the French Quarter and renamed it Dombourian Oriental Rugs. Since then it has moved Uptown and has been at its current location in the 2800 block of Magazine Street since 1991.By the end of the month the store will be a part of the city's history. Greg Dombourian will vacate the building by mid-December." (<http://www.theadvocate.com/baton_rouge/article_96e910be-9cbe-51aa-a7dc-f912fbc92ef6.html>, accessed January 15, 2017.]

⁵⁷ [Ed.—These articles are included in translation at the end of this book.]

⁵⁸ [Ed.—These foods and some of the customs of the times are described in my doctoral dissertation "The Armenian Immigrant Community of California, 1880–1935", pp. 445–453.]

[59] [Ed.—A brief explanation of the Ceremony of Canonization and its meaning can be found at the website of the Armenian Prelacy, <http://armenianprelacy.org/press-releases/caninization>[sic], retreived June 22, 2015.]

[60] *Madzoon:* Known in the United States as yoghurt.

The word *madzoon* is Armenian and the root *madz* means "to thicken, to coagulate, to make sticky. This word *madzoon* has been applied, from time immemorial, to milk cultured into a delicious and highly nutritious food, rich in friendly bacteria and lactic acid, which are deadly enemies of putrefactive bacteria in human intestines. For countless centuries the Armenians have recognized its beneficial properties, and used it extensively in and out of their homeland.

No one can tell where and when madzoon came to being. It was known by the ancient peoples of Egypt, Syria, Asia Minor, and all that were in possession of animals. Father Abraham (Genesis 18:8) offered this dish to his three divine guests. The word Laban — the name of Laban the Syrian, Jacob's maternal uncle and father-in-law — literally means "madzoon" in Hebrew and Arabic. Xenophon (443–359 B.C.), the famous general of the Ten Thousand, ate madzoon in Armenia and praised it.

Richard Tille, writing on "Yoghurt and Culture" in *Health Culture Magazine*, says: "The Tartars of Genghis Khan brought yoghurt to Eastern Europe, and their descendants, the Khirghiz of the Russian Steppes, still prepare their 'kumys' (as they call it) from mare's milk. The Bulgarians, who came to Europe from Asia and settled in the Balkans in 675, brought their yoghurt with them."

Speaking of "kefir" of the Turkomans, Tille continues: "A skin-bag, filled with kefir, is hung on a nail on the main door of the house. The constant motion of opening and closing of the doors keeps the kefir milk in continuous motion — beating and churning. As some of the kefir is taken from the bag for consumption, fresh milk is poured in. Thus the fermenting process goes on continuously, the bag never goes empty, and a constant supply of kefir is maintained."

[61] [Ed.—Originally published in three installments in the *Weekly Avedaper*, American Bible House, Constantinople, Vol. 53, No. 9, February 26, 1910; No. 10, March 5, 1910; No. 11, March 12, 1910. I found this article in the UCLA library and brought it to my father to translate. It has been included here because it directly relates to the massacre of the Reverend Melidon Malian, the author's uncle. George B. Kooshian personally knew many of the individuals mentioned in the text. Footnotes in the translation are added by the translator. Editing has been limited to formatting and minor typographical corrections.]

[62] This subculture of writing Turkish with Armenian characters was invented and cultivated by the Armenians under Turkish rule, and it continued until Talaat and Mustafa Kemal Araturk, the most venerated "heroes" of modern Turkey, made it obsolete through the genocide they perpetrated between 1915 and 1923.

[63] "We"— Beside herself, there were: her husband, the Reverend Astour Topalian, the pastor of the Feke church, their attendant, and a number of delegates and guests from their church.

⁶⁴The Reverend Milton was the eldest brother of the mother of the translator of these lines. He wasted away his late 'teens and early twenties in a Turkish dungeon in Acre (Akka) in the late '80s and '90s of the 19th century.

⁶⁵Mikayel Agha and Lady Elsa [Ed.—*Hanum*, Turkish title of respect for a married lady, here translated "Madame"] were the parents of a large family of sons and daughters. One of their sons, the Reverend Missak Aijian, was the pastor and friend of the translator in Pasadena from 1923 until his dying day. Another son, Kaloust, was the translator's teacher in the Hadjin Boy's Adademy in the school year of 1910–1911. This student harbors to this day (1983) a debt of profound respect and gratitude for cultivating in him love of the Armenian language and literature. A daughter, Noyemi, was the teacher of this writer's younger brother, Setrak. Another daughter, Louise, the classmate of my sister Mary in Hadjin, became a "sister" to me in the days of the Genocide in 1916 and remained a "close sister" until she passed away in 1982. Mikayel Agha's grandsons, the Reverend Dr. Paul and Dr. Schyler Aijian, the sons of the Reverend Missak, continue to this day in the Christian principles set by the patriarch. Louise's daughters, Violet and Florence, and son Armen, are worthy to be the offspring of the saintly Mikayel Agha.

⁶⁶Osanna was the overseer of the American Orphanage in Hadjin when I was an inmate there. She was a widow at that time. Her only son, Diran, paid me a visit in Pasadena in the 1930s.

⁶⁷*Meshrutiyet* [constitutional government], the fake proclamation made all over the Ottoman Empire no more than a year earlier (July 1908) was intended to lull the Christian minority, especially the Armenians, with the intoxication of the belief in "freedom, justice, equality, and brotherhood" (*hurriet, adalet, mussavat, oukouvet*).

⁶⁸This heinous act jibes perfectly with the unalterable Turkish conviction that "a slave never deserves mercy, justice, and truth."

A WORD OF THANKS

I would never have been able to publish this book without the constant help and encouragement of my wife Clary throughout our entire married life. She is the one who always reminded me, never flagging in service, constancy, and love, to finish this project because I alone was able to do it, that it was my mission, and if I did not my father's witness would be lost. The great heart of this man is now presented to the whole world. My father left this book for his grandsons George, Stephen, and Christian, whom he never could know or see except in anticipation, and to their cousins the children of my brothers Charles, Percy, and Roy and their children's children.

The Editor

INDEX

Abdul Hamid II, 3, 26, 58
Abrazian, Boghos, 282, 311
Abrazian, Hampartzoum
    birth of, 283
Abrazian, Setrak
    in Smyrna, 311, 313, 320, 324, 326
Adana, 11, 31, 33, 34, 40, 43, 44, 56, 81, 270, 282, 292, 301, 334, 415, 422, 435, 458, 459, 461, 463–465, 468, 479
    arrival of refugees from Hadjin, 316
    ban on emigration from, 313
    cession to Kemalist Turkey, 385–386
    deportation from, 98–104
    exile camp, 104
    expulsion of Armenians, 91
    French disarm Armenians, 300
    history of, 486
    journey to by church delegates, 26
    locust infestation, 96
    massacre of 1909, 27, 39
    refugees from, 314
    return to, 266–268
    train station, 94
    worsening political situation in, 309
Agaean Islands
    description of, 301–306
Aghbabian, Siragan, 398
Ahmed Chavoush, 205
    abuses prisoners, 141
    boasts of murdering Armenians, 138
    demands bribe from prisoners, 135
    leaves caravan, 142
    rape of Hampartzoum Krajian, 134
    searches for victims, 137
Aijian, Kaloust, 398
Aijian, Mikayel Agha, 398
Aijian, Missak, 398
Airan, 265
Alajajian, Azniv, 59
    at Bulgur Khan, 113
    at US Customs, 353
    condition of eyes, 317, 339
    in Adana, 278
    in Athens, 330
Alajajian, Carnig
    at Bulgur Khan, 113
    death of, 112
    infancy of, 67
Alajajian, Gulenia, 57, 67–73
    at Bulgur Khan, 115
    in Aleppo, 262
    rescue from Sebill deportation camp, 113
    reunion in Smyrna, 318
Alajajian, Krikor, 60, 67
    antagonism of, 361–369
    correspondence with, 254, 277
Alajajian, Rachael, 59
    at Bulgur Khan, 113
    death of, 278
Alajajian, Stephen
    at Bulgur Khan, 113
    at Mersin, 300
    at U.S. Customs, 354
    begins school, 284

emigration of, 294, 296, 298
first day in America, 356
in Adana, 277, 278, 292
in Aleppo, 254, 262
in Athens, 330
in Binghamton, N.Y., 360, 361, 367
in Kayseri, 60–72
in Smyrna, 308–310, 315, 317–319
on *Montaza*, 303
Alajajian, Toros, 67–70
Alajajians
character of, 277–278
leave for America, 328
Albarian, Hagop, 407
Albarian, Louise Aijian, 398
Aleppo
Armenians of, 110
description of in 1915, 110
massacre of January 28, 1919, 259–260
American Baptist Church of Havana, 420
American institutions in Turkey closed, 81
American Mennonite Orphanage at Hadjin, 37
Arab
marauders, 135
offers to help George Kooshian escape, 189
Arabli Inn, 53
Arabs
as guards, 150, 153, 165, 190, 201
buy Christian children, 156, 158
fear of, 161
honor of, 175
in Aleppo, 110
join forces with General Allenby, 246
lynch Nazim Bey, 252
molest Armenians, 108, 152, 155, 162, 169

sell to refugees, 141, 154, 160, 161, 165, 167
villages of, 153, 161, 169
Arakelian, Hayganoosh
mother of Annig Derghazarian, 415
Armenian Cilicia Congregational Church, 398
Armenian collaborators, 188, 191, 233–234
Armenian General Benevolent Union, 399
Armenian language School
in Pasadena, 410–411
Armenian Missionary Society, 399
Armenians of Cilicia
betrayal by the French, 311–312
Armeno-Turkish, 20, 402, 463, 492
Asadourian, Arthur, 410
Asadourian, Haig, 398
Asche, Dr. A., 319, 339
Ash, Ida
in Aleppo, 256–257
tests George Kooshian, 258–259
Ashjian, Hampartzoum, 398
Ashot, Aram, *see* Minassian, Sarkis
Ateshian, Apraham
at Jenanian College, 80
in Aleppo, 253, 260
in-law of Ouzounians, 414, 419
Ateshian, Parantzem, 414, 419
Athens
visit to, 329–331
attorney from Everek, *see* Sarkis Effendi
Azad Ice-Cream and Confectionery Parlor, 370, 372, 377, 378
Azazian, Zaroohi, 324

Bachejian, Sarkis, 324, 326, 329, 334
in Smyrna, 311, 318, 320, 321
marriage of, 328
massacre of, 322, 328, 388
Bahadurian, Haig, 22

Index

Bahche, 265
Baker, Seth, 413
Balian, Antranig
    travel to Konia, 79
Balian. Antranig
    in Aleppo, 253
Barabian, Toros, 52
Barker, Ada, 79, 113
    pays George Kooshian's tuition, 81
Barker, Tomford, 42, 56, 113
    in Konia, 49, 50
bastinado, 130, 141
Bedrosian, Arshag, 52
Berberian, Vartivar, 370
Bodosaki, 298, 299
bones, 150
Boyajian, Armenag, 370
Boyajian, Haiganoosh, 370
Boyajian, Hovagim, 370
Boyajian, Setrak, 370
Boyajian. Mrs. Hovagim, 392
Britannia (vessel), 339, 340, 342, 344, 346–347, 353
Bulgur Khan, 111, 222
    conditions at, 113, 114
    conditions in, 118
    deportation of Armenians at, 116
    description of, 111
    Khachadoor Kroozian principal of, 111
    lice at, 114
    provisions at, 111
    vacation of, 118

Cartago, 413, 428
Catholic Varjabed, *see* Pasqual Effendi
Caudill, Herbert, 420
caves
    as hiding places for refugees, 127, 198–203, 207–209, 211, 214, 215
    raids upon, 209
Chakalian, Karekin, *see* Khazhag, Karekin

Cheldirian, Garabed, 370
Chilingirian, Krikor, 307
Church of the Forty Children, *see* Church of the Forty Martyrs
Church of the Forty Martyrs, 110, 118
    library, 119
Cilicia
    betrayal of by the French, 292
    Historical description of, 6
    historical description of, 7
    siege of, 287
Cilicia Congregational Church, 45
Circassians
    as guards, 159
citizenship examination, 412
closure of foreign institutions in Turkey, 83
Committee of Union and Progress" (*Ittihad ve Terakki Jemiyeti*), 4
confiscations, 77
Congregational Mission for the Armenians, 398
conscription, 75
Constantine Gertmenian Co. [rugs], 398
Corruption
    of American immigration official, 354–355
    of Haroutune Khachadoorian, 257
    of relief officers, 255
Coué, Èmile, 384

Dakesian, Vahan
    in Smyrna, 314, 315
Datevian, Vahagn
    arrest and execution of, 91
    director of Ottoman Orphanage, 86
    final visit to in prison, 104
    offers George Kooshian a job, 81
decision to emigrate, 293–295
deportations, 104–109

through Adana, 94
Der-Havr, 141
Derghazarian, Annig, 89–90
    adoption and education of, 415
    farewell in Adana, 102
    in Havana, 412–419
    letter to Sarah Gejekooshian, 416
    massacre of parents, 415
Derghazarian, Manook
    massacre of parents, 415
Derghazarian, Melkon
    father of Annig Derghazarian, 415
Dervishes, 48
Devirian, Sarkis, 31
Dibse, 148, 205, 207, 208, 215
Dirtadian, Aram
    in Adana, 87
    in exile, 104
Dirtadian, Dirouhi, 87
Dirtadian, Dirtad, 98
Dodd, Dr. W. S., 287
Dombourian Oriental Rugs, *see* Dombourian, Mampreh
Dombourian, Mampreh, 428–429, 491
dream of America, 299
Dubrotsasser Tignantz Varzharan, 415
Dumanian, Vahan
    in Smyrna, 316
    leaves Cilicia for Constantinople, 301
dysentery, 105, 106, 113, 148, 158, 179, 263

eclipse, 76
Efkereh, 63
Ekmekjian, Setrak, *see* Bker, Seth413
Elgin, George, *see also* Alajajian, Krikor
Enegeh, 175
Esayian, Roupen, 57
    conscription of, 76
escapees
    punishment of, 130, 141, 145
Eskijian, Gulenia, 401, 403

Eskijian, Hovhannes, 401, 402
Eskijian, Luther, 402
Euphrates
    arrival of deportees at, 144
    suicide of deportees in, 144
Evkhanian, Setrak, 57

Family life in the United States, 436–438
Farajian, Garabed
    teacher in Adana, 288
Fayik Bey, 236, 237
    goodness of, 235
    interview before, 230
Fenesse High School
    language policy, 45
Fenesseh
    excursion to, 51
Fenesseh High School
    graduation, 55
First Baptist Church of Pasadena, 399
forced conversions, 260
forced labor, 188, 213, 264

Gedigian, David, 41, 57
Gejekooshian survivors, 261
Gejekooshian, Garabed, 11
    Requiem for, 271–272
Gejekooshian, Hadji Kevork Agha, 14–15
Gejekooshian, Haroutune
    death of, 19
Gejekooshian, Mary, 80, *see also* Soghomonian, Mary
    at Bulgur Khan, 115
    betrothal and marriage to Sarkis Soghomonian, 292
    in Adana, 89
Gejekooshian, meaning of, 487
Gejekooshian, Sarah
    brings provisions to George Kooshian at Karluk concentration camp, 132
    cook at Bulgur Khan, 111
    cook at Hadjin orphanage, 39

Index

cook at Ottoman orphanage, 81
death of, 17
early life, 11
employed at Hadjin orphanages, 85
exile to Cyprus, 387
illness in Adana, 275
marriage of, 16
pennance of, 227
sends aid package to George Kooshian in the desert, 187
Gejekooshian, Setrak, 86, 230, 245, 246
   at Hokedoon, 126
   exile to Beirut, 387
   high school graduation, 284
   in Adana, 89, 101
   joins militia, 271
   leaves for Tarsus College, 276
   leaves Tarsus College, 284
Gertmenian, Apraham
   leaves Smyrna, 318
Gertmenian, Henry
   teacher in Adana, 288
Gertmenian, Manuel
   becomes godfather of Charles Kooshian, 434
   in Smyrna, 317
Gertmenian, Mardiros Agha
   chairman of the Compatriotic Union of Hadjin, 281
   in Meskeneh, 210
Gertmenian, Norman
   in Pasadena, 408
Gertmenians
   leave for America, 327
Giridlian, Levon, 58
Gizirian, Armand, 370
Gostanian, Caloust, 307
grave-diggers, 185
Greek Royalists, 325
guards
   corruption of, 191
Guerber, Maria, 37

Gulbenkian, Avedis, 323–324
Gurunlian, Giragos, 52

Haccu Bey, 192–194, 198, 203
Hadjin, 7
   dialect of, 487
   fall of, 27, 275, 316–317, 319
   last visit to, 43
   lost relatives in 1920, 317
Hadjin, Compatriotic Union of
   formation of, 280–281
Hafiz, 176–179
Hagop Boghosian [rugs], 398
Hagop Moomjian [rugs], 398
Haigag Khazoyan Co. [rugs], 398
Haigazian College, 396
Haigazian, Armenag, 45, 79, 396
   arrest and deportation of, 85
   death of, 46
Haji Hanefee Chavoush, 142
Hamam
   massacre at, 195–197
Hans, the German soldier, 235
Haroutune Philibosian and Sons [rugs], 398
Haroutunian, Mamas, 52
Hassesian, Avedis, 398
Havana, Cuba, 418, 424–426
High School
   graduation from, 40
Himfish
   brutality of, 150, 153
   scheme to deceive prisoners, 190
Hokedoon, 110
   location of, 126
Holy Spirit, 235
homosexuality, 143, 205
Hubarian, Mesrob, 307
Hussein Effendi, 153, 155, 172, 178, 191, 193, 195, 218
   allows George Kooshian to go to the Arab village, 174, 180
   appoints George Kooshian Obituary Recorder, 171

begins march of prisoners into Syrian Desert, 133
character of, 154, 186
commandant of Karluk concentration camp, 129
failure to exterminate enough Armenians is punished, 192
impotence of, 192
offers to take two prisoners to Aleppo in exchange for a bribe, 183

Ideal Cleaners and Dyers, 409
Izmirlian, Harry, 370

Jamentz, Samuel, *see* Jamgotchian, Samuel
Jamgotchian, Samuel, 49, 51
conscription of, 85
Jangulian, Haroutune
deportation through Adana train station, 94
Jenanian College, 269, 314, 315, 396, 400, 457
foundation of, 24
language policy, 45
opening in 1914, 83
seizure of, 85
students gather for 1914–1915 year, 79
teachers at, 45
Turkish spies at, 83
Jenanian, Haroutune
founder of Jenanian College, 46
founds colleges, 24

Kademian, Mugurdich
in Smyrna, 318
Kalfaian, Haroutune, 57
conscription of, 76
Kalpakian, Hripsimeh, 415
Kalpakian, Yervant, 415
Kalpakjian, Ripsimeh, 89
Kalpakjian, Yervant, 89
Karatash, 297

Karluk, 128
Karnigian, 418
Katma, 263
concentration camp, 107, 108, 263
Kayseri, 59
Keklikian, Hampartzoum, 370
Kellejian, Hampartzoum
death of, 222
escorts George Kooshian to Aleppo, 216
finds George Kooshian in his tent, 211
Kellejian, Sarkis, 40
Kemalist insurgency, 297
Keshishian, Garabed
in exile, 104
Keshishian, Garabed Effendi, 269–271
Khachadoorian, Haroutune
blacklisted for stealing relief supplies, 255–257
hostility of, 288–289
post-war career, 287–288
Khazhag, Karekin
deportation through Adana train station, 94
Konia
description of, 47
Kooshian, Annig, *see also* Kooshian, Suzanne; Derghazarian, Annig
Kooshian, Charles, 433–435, 438
Kooshian, George B. Jr., 436–438
Kooshian, George V., 360, 363–367
Kooshian, Mary, *see* Gejekooshian, Mary
Kooshian, Percy, 435–438
Kooshian, Rose Rejebian, 368
Kooshian, Roy, 435
Kooshian, Sarah, *see* Gejeooshian, Sarah
Kooshian, Sarkis, 360, 363
Kooshian, Setrak, *see* Gejekooshian, Setrak

Index

Kooshian, Suzanne, 420–437, *see also* Kooshian, Annig; Derghazarian, Annig
Kourt-Koulak, 264
Kouyumjian, Marie, 346
Koyoumjian, Haroutune, 52
Krajian, Hampartzoum, 133–162
Kroozian, Khachadoor
    as a priest, 490
    at Bulgur Khan, 111, 115
    background of, 111
    in Aleppo, 118
    shelters Alajajians at Bulgur Khan, 113
    warns George Kooshian to be careful, 126
Kulahjian, Athanas
    in California, 108
    in exile, 104
Kurkyasharian
    Haigaz, 284
Kurkyasharian family
    in Adana, 267
Kurkyasharian, Krikor
    in Adana, 269
Kutufian, Sarah
    arrest of, 489
Kyrban Bayrami, 182

Lambert, Nora, 56
Lambert, Rose, 37
Lazarian, Nunia, 395
Lazarian, Panos, 395
Levonian, Puzant, 398
lice, 54, 75, 84, 105, 113, 114, 128, 157, 163, 168, 169, 179, 201, 202, 210, 214, 215, 255, 261, 265, 310, 343
Lisbon
    visit to, 344–345
Loosinian, Arsham
    Ateshian, Apraham
    at Jenanian College, 79
Lord Mayor's Relief Fund, 269, 270, 279

Malian family
    in Pasadena, 405
Malian survivors, 261
Malian, Alexander
    in Adana, 276
Malian, Aram, 396
Malian, Hampartzoum, 396
    as child, 98
    party leaves Smyrna for America, 317
    takes George Kooshian to Turan Locantsi, 92
Malian, Haroutune, 17, 18, 80
    brings provisions to Karluk concentration camp, 130
    exile to Cyprus, 387
    in Adana, 276
    in Aleppo, 111
    in tailors' battalion, 237
    rescue of Gejekooshians from Jemiliyeh, 109
Malian, Krikor Agha, 29
Malian, Melidon, 20–28, 314
    arranges transfer of family to Hadjin, 37
    as child, 98
    imprisonment of, 23
    murder of, 27, 463–472
Malian, Mutebereh, 20
    last visit, 273–275
    murder of, 28
Malian, Naomi, 396
    in Adana, 91
Malian, Nectar, 396
Malian, Stephen, 396
Malian, Titzouhi
    birth of, 278
Malian, Turfanda
    in Adana, 276
Malian, Vartan, 396
Malian, "Mamig"
    at the graveyard, 272
    delivers baby, 278
    in Adana, 267–268

living quarters of, 268–269
Malians
    in Smyrna, 310–311
    leave for America, 327
    on *Montaza*, 300
Mamooreh, 265
Mamourian, Matteos, 307
Mangasarian, Mangasar Magurditch, 382–383
Manisajian, Missak, 396
Mannig (cousin of Alice Muradian), 321, 323, 327, 419, 420
Mannig Hanum (Havana), *see* Mikayelian, Mannig
Manoogian, Anoosh, 320, 321, 327, 328
Manookian, Sisak
    interview with Fayik Bey, 232
    kindness to Setrak Gejekooshian, 230
    superintendent of Fraulein Rohner's school, 229, 230
Mardian, Acabi, 396
Mardian, Aram, 396
Mardian, Daniel, 396
Mardian, Florence, 396
Mardian, Robert, 396
Mardian, Samuel, 396
Mardian, Samuel Jr., 396
Markarian, Doodoo, 235
Markarian, Hmayag, 52
Markarian, Roupen, 57, 231–235, 241
Marseilles, 334–341
Martin, John S., 35
Martyrs of the Armenian Genocide
    canonization of, 439–440
massacre of January 28, 1919, 260
massacres of 1895, 58
Mather's Department Store, 397, 399, 405
McCall, M. N., 420
Medzmorookian, Bergroohi, 418
Medzmorookian, Meline, 418
Medzmorookian, Sarkis, 418

Medzmorookian, Susan, 418
Mehagian, Avak
    at Jenanian College, 80
Mehagian, Haigaz, 396
Mehagian, Levon, 396
Mehagian, Mary, 396
Mehagian, Stephen Avak, 396
Mehmed Tahir Effendi, 92–98, 100
    childhood of, 98
Melidonian, Norayr, 398
Meskeneh, 161, 164, 188, 191, 192, 202, 203, 205–208
Mesrob Vartabed
    at Bulgur Khan, 119
Michel, M., 335, 339, 341
Mihran and Aram Salisian Brothers [rugs], 398
Mihran Constantian [rugs], 398
Mikayelian, Mannig, 414–415, 418
Minassian, Sarkis
    deportation through Adana train station, 94
Montaza, 300, 302, 304, 306, 316
Mooshian, Gulenia, 275, 371
    in Adana, 267
    in Aleppo, 262
Mooshian, Panos, 262, 319, 363, 366–367, 369–381, 390, 391
Mooshian, Yeranoohi, 370
Mosque of the Mevlavies, *see* Whirling Dervishes
Mozian, Souren
    teacher in Adana, 289
Mulkigian, Sanam, 426–430
Mulkigian, Sarkis, 426–427, 430
Muncherian, Mibar, 59
Munushian, Mihran, 261
Munushian, Mutebereh
    marriage of, 25
Muradian, Alice, 326
    betrothal to Krikor Alajajian, 320
Mustafa Bey, 238–240, 242, 243
Mustafa Kemal, 5, 287

Nakashian, Avedis, 318

Index

Nardip Khan, 137
Narinian, Michael
    travel to Konia, 79
Naxos (vessel), 326, 328–335
Nicolian, Setrak, 414, 420
Nighoghosian, Soghig, 346

Oghlookian, Makroohi, 262, 267, 279, 280
Oknagank, 282
Omar Agha, 73
Onnig, 210, 212, 222
    directs George Kooshian to Kellejian tent, 211
Orphanage for Boys
    moves to Everek-Fenesseh, 39
Osman Effendi, 236–240, 242
    appoints George Kooshian to teach his children English and French, 243
    asks George Kooshian for protection, 246
    flight to Istanbul, 249
    gives George Kooshian Sundays off to attend church services, 245
Osmaniye, 265
    massacre of 1909, 103
Ottoman Orphanage, Adana, 81, 86–91
Ouzounian, Armenag, 370
Ouzounian, Boghos
    appearance in the desert, 154
    arranges escape of George Kooshian, 203
    in Hamam, 198, 200
    rescues George Kooshian from the desert, 204
Ouzounian, Haroutune, 370
Ouzounian, Hripsimeh
    in Hamam, 203
    rescues George Kooshian, 197
Ouzounian, Nourijohn, 418
Ouzounian, Noyemi, 393

Ouzounian, Parantzem, *see* Ateshian, Parantzem
Ouzounian, Takoohi, 418
Ouzounian, Vartan, 372, 376, 393
Ouzunian, Vartan, 370

Papazian, Manasseh, 398
Parseghian, Haigazoon, 52
Pasadena, 23, 37, 486
    Armenians in, 20, 22, 31, 45, 49, 58, 90, 278, 395–400
Pashgian Brothers [rugs], 398
Pasqual Effendi, 177–179
prejudice
    by Turks, 95–96
    in America, 403–404
    in Smyrna, 310
Protestant High School (Adana), 283, 286, 287
Pushian, Toros, 41, 57, 382
    in Aleppo, 253, 260
    in Chicago, 370
    in exile, 104
    travel to Konia, 79

Rejebian, Peter
    in Binghamton, N.Y, 365
Rejebian, Samuel, 45, 398, 400, 429
remittances, 374–375
Rohner, Beatrice
    as head of Bulgur Khan, 111, 113
    as head of German Orphanage, 118, 227
    ceases charitable activites, 230
    closes German Orphanage, 228
    friendship with governor, 116
    gives George Kooshian a job as a teacher, 229
    secures permits for some, 126
    visit of, 118
rug merchants, 398
rug-making, 67–68

Sahag II Catholicos Khabaian

great uncle of Suzanne Kooshian, 26
Sai'-Getchit
  massacre at, 26, 27, 435, 463–472
  massacre of Mikayel Agha Aijian at, 398
Saint Daniel Monastery
  excursion to, 64
Saint Garabed Monastery
  excursion to, 56–66
Sarkis Devirian and Sons [rugs], 398
Sarkis Effendi, 163, 177–179
Sarkisian, Mardiros, 40, 228
  at Entilly, 106
  death of, 265
  in Adana, 267
  in Chicago, 370
  in prison, 228
  in the United States, 106
Sarkisian, Yeran
  in Aleppo, 253
Sarunj, Valley of, 43
Sarvoni, Yeran
  Ateshian, Apraham
    at Jenanian College, 79
Satchian family, murder of, 65
Satchian family, survivors, 65
Satchian, Asadoor, 62
  escapes Genocide, 65
Satchian, Haiganoush, 62
Satchian, Haji Bob, 62
Satchian, Mariam, 62
Satchian, Neneh Malian, 43, 62
Satchian, Peprooni, 62
Satchian, Zabel, 62
Sebooh (General), 335
Sehel, 12, 487
Seleucia, 13, 301
Serengulian, Vartkes
  deportation through Adana train station, 94
Sermayehsizian, Manoog, 56
Sev Tzang, 255
sevkiyet
  meaning of, 192
Sevkiyet Memouri
  meaning of, 134
Sevkiyet Merkezi
  meaning of, 128
Sexenian, Arshag, 370
Sexenian, Haiganoosh, 370
Sexenian, Haigaz, 370
Sexenian, Himayak, 370
Sexenian, Mugitch, 370
Sexenian, Nounia, 370
Seyhan
  stone bridge across, 94
Seyissian, 418
Shamlian, Sanadroug, 398
Sharian, Bedros, 39
Shishmanian, John
  arrest and exile of by the French, 312
Shukru, 93, 95, 98, 100
Sima Baji, 109
  hides George Kooshian, 118
Sitma Punar, 265
Smyrna, 307
  fall of, 5, 326
  massacre of Christians, 328, 387–389
  refugees from Cilicia, 316
Smyrna and Constantinople
  murdered Armenian intellectuals of, 307
sodomy, 134, 143
Soghomonian family, 405
Soghomonian, Annette, 395
Soghomonian, Mary, *see also* Gejekooshian, Mary, 363, 394, 430
Soghomonian, Rosemary, 395
Soghomonian, Samuel, 395
Soghomonian, Sarkis, 363, 395
  background of, 291–292
  betrothal and marriage to Mary Gejekooshian, 292
  in Adana, 292

Index

Somoonjian, Levon and Mariam, 171–179, 181
Stone Brothers [rugs], 398
Storms, Anna Good, 56, 77
Storms, Dorwin Jonathan, 56, 77
Storms, Everek Richard, 77, 490
Sulahian, Senekerim, 398
Summit Avenue Cleaners and Dyers, 405

Talas, 57
Tateosian, Leah, 321, 323, 326
   in New York, 366
   in Smyrna, 313–315
Tateosian, LeahLeah, 318
Tateosian, Roupen, 313
   arrives in Smyrna, 316
   in New York, 366
   leaves for America, 318
Tatoulian, Hovagim, 370
Tatoulian, Sona, 370
Termonian, Azniv, 346
Terzian, Minas, 370
To the Sun of my Hope, 323
Toorsarkissian, Mardiros, 261
Topalian, Gilbert, 52
   in Aleppo, 253
Tourian, Ghevont, 325–326
Tourian, Levon, 40
   in the United States, 106
Toursarkisian, Samuel
   in the desert, 151
Transfiguration, Feast of the, 56
   description in 1914, 61
Travelers' Aid Society, 357
Turan Locantasi, 92
   hatred expressed toward Armenians, 95
Turkified Armenians, 237, *see also* Tarhir Effendi, 241
Turkish with Armenian letters, *see* Armeno-Turkish

typhus, 82, 113, 114, 118, 222, 261, 287, 401
typhus, recovery from, 115

Vahram Effendi, 237, 239, 240, 242, 245, 249
Varoujan Club, 399–400
Vartanian, John, 396
Vartanian, Siranoosh, 396
Vartavar, *see* Transfiguration, Feast of the
Vayejian, Michael, 281
Vayejian, Mikayel
   in Aleppo, 253
Vazejian, Michael
   travel to Konia, 79

Whirling Dervishes, 48
Wingate, Jane Smith, 58
Wingate, William, 58
   defense of Kayseri Armenians, 58
women, status of, 340

Yapoojian, Vartivar
   death in the desert, 151
Yar Bashi, 265

Zartarian, Roupen
   deportation through Adana train station, 94
Zeitoon
   fate of resisters at, 84–85
Zeki Bey
   and deportation of Armenians from Aleppo, 116
zikr, *see* Whirling Dervishes
Ziyaret, 192, 193, 195, 198, 200, 207
Zohrab, Krikor
   deportation through Adana train station, 94
   murder of, 94

ILLUSTRATION CREDITS

All illustrations are scanned from photographs from the Author's collection except as noted. All are believed to be out of copyright and public domain except as noted.

The following were evidently copied from old books: United Armenia, Reverend Doctor Jenanian, Reverend Doctor Haigazian, view of Caesaraea, Jenanian College Dormitory.

The illustration of the Ajemi Cafe in Adana is from *Life in Asiatic Turkey. A journal of travel in Cilicia-Pedias and Trachœa-Isauria, and parts of Lycaonia and Cappadocia ... Map and illustrations, from original drawings by the author and Mr. Ancketill*, uploaded to Flickr by the British Library. I have rendered it in monochrome for publication.

The map of southwest Asia minor is heavily modified by the Editor from "Generalkarte des Turkischen Kriegsschauplatzes: auf Grund der Carte Generale des Provinces Europeennes et Asiatiques de L'Empire Ottoman" [Berlin: Heinrich Kiepert, 1916], retrieved from the Library of Congress, https://www.loc.gov/item/2013593013/. (Accessed March 08, 2017).

The two maps of deportation routes are modified from "United States Central Intelligence Agency. Syria. [Washington, D.C.: Central Intelligence Agency, 1967] Map. Retrieved from the Library of Congress, https://www.loc.gov/item/2014587893/. (Accessed March 05, 2017)".

The view of Hokedoon Alley is an image uploaded to English Wikipedia by user Kevorkmail, the copyright owner, and is licensed under the Creative Commons Attribution-Share Alike 3.0 Unported license.

The following images were retreived from the Library of Congress: *Aleppo Haleb and environs. Public square* [Aleppo Clock Tower], https://www.loc.gov/item/mpc2004004486/PP/; *Aleppo from Castle*, https://www.loc.gov/item/mpc2004007518/PP/; Bain News Service, Publisher. *Adana - Street in Christian Quarter, June '09* [1909], https://www.loc.gov/item/ggb2005016639/; Bain News Service, Publisher. *Adana - Minaret from which Turks Fired on Christians* [1909], https://www.loc.gov/item/ggb2005016640/.

Captions are by the Editor unless supplied with the illustration.

ABOUT THE AUTHOR

George B. Kooshian was well known throughout his life as an author of many articles and of poetry in Armenian and English that were published in *Nor Or, Hayastani Gotchnag,* and other publications. He served as the Secretary of the Compatriotic Union of Hadjin from its inception in Adana on July 4, 1919 until his death in 1984, and was for a time the editor of the journal *Nor Hadjin.* He preached, taught the Bible, and lectured frequently. He served as the Secretary of the Board of Deacons of Immanuel Baptist Church in Pasadena for many years. He was the respected friend and advisor to many clergymen, Armenian and American, Catholic, Apostolic, and Evangelical.

George B. Kooshian, Jr. is a teacher in Los Angeles, California. He received his M.A. and Teaching Credential from UCLA, then his Ph.D. in Armenian History in 2002. His dissertation was "The Armenian Immigrant Community of California, 1880–1935."

www.ingramcontent.com/pod-product-compliance
Lightning Source LLC
Chambersburg PA
CBHW021112300426
44113CB00006B/127